The End of Iberian Rule on the American Continent, 1770–1830

In this new work, Brian R. Hamnett offers a comprehensive assessment of the independence era in both Spanish America and Brazil by examining the interplay between events in Iberia and in the overseas empires of Spain and Portugal. Most colonists had wanted some form of unity within the Spanish and Portuguese monarchies but European intransigence continually frustrated this aim. Hamnett argues that independence finally came as a result of widespread internal conflict in the two American empires, rather than as a result of a clear separatist ideology or a growing national sentiment. With the collapse of empire, each component territory faced a struggle to survive. *The End of Iberian Rule on the American Continent, 1770–1830* is the first book of its kind to give equal consideration to the Spanish and Portuguese dimensions of South America, examining these territories in terms of their divergent component elements.

Brian R. Hamnett is Emeritus Professor, Department of History, University of Essex.

The End of Iberian Rule on the American Continent, 1770–1830

BRIAN R. HAMNETT

University of Essex

CAMBRIDGE
UNIVERSITY PRESS

CAMBRIDGE
UNIVERSITY PRESS

University Printing House, Cambridge CB2 8BS, United Kingdom

One Liberty Plaza, 20th Floor, New York, NY 10006, USA

477 Williamstown Road, Port Melbourne, VIC 3207, Australia

314-321, 3rd Floor, Plot 3, Splendor Forum, Jasola District Centre, New Delhi - 110025, India

79 Anson Road, #06-04/06, Singapore 079906

Cambridge University Press is part of the University of Cambridge.

It furthers the University's mission by disseminating knowledge in the pursuit of education, learning and research at the highest international levels of excellence.

www.cambridge.org
Information on this title: www.cambridge.org/9781316626634
DOI: 10.1017/9781316795996

First published 2017

A catalogue record for this publication is available from the British Library

ISBN 978-1-107-17464-1 Hardback
ISBN 978-1-316-62663-4 Paperback

Contents

Abbreviations

Acknowledgments

This book has been a long time in gestation. It owes many intellectual debts to archivists and librarians and their staff in a range of countries. Arguments were tested in conferences, seminars, and presentations. I should like to single out in this respect the Colegio de México in 2008–10 and the Pontífica Universidad Católica del Perú (with the Instituto Francés de Estudios Andinos) in 2011 and 2014. The British Academy and the Nuffield Foundation supported research in Mexico and Brazil. The Universities of Strathclyde and Essex, respectively, enabled work in Quito and Bogotá, and Brazil and Chile.

Conversations with Mexican colleagues, Josefina Vázquez and Andrés Lira, Juan Ortiz Escamilla, José Antonio Serrano Ortega, Guillermina del Valle, and Brian Connaughton, Manuel Chust, Christon Archer, Jaime Rodríguez, and Gabriel Paquette greatly facilitated refinement of the argument. Similarly, this work has been enriched by on-going contact with Peruvian scholars, Scarlett O'Phelan and Luis Miguel Glave. Daniel Gutiérrez Ardila (Universidad Externado, Bogotá), Juan Luis Ossa (Universidad Adolfo Ibáñez, Santiago de Chile), and Natalia Sobrevilla (University of Kent) commented on sections of the manuscript. I am grateful to Carmen Forsyth for excellent instruction in Brazilian Portuguese at the University of Essex.

Colchester, July 2016.

Introduction

The empires of Spain and Portugal have already generated a rich historical literature. Yet, the process and consequences of disaggregation still require elucidation. This is the theme of the present book rather than the origins of Independence movements or national sentiment.[1] My overall concern is to explain why the empires lasted so long, why there was such strong identification with them, and how Spain and Portugal finally lost their continental-American territories.

Few attempts have been made to view the Hispanic and Lusitanian Monarchies together in comparative form. This has always seemed to me the outstanding omission in our historical studies.[2] When I taught at the University of Strathclyde, my first attempts to do this were in Latin

---

[1] See Brian R. Hamnett, "Process and Pattern: A Re-examination of the Ibero-American Independence Movements, 1808–1826," *Journal of Latin American Studies*, 29, ii (May 1997), 279–328, and "Spain and Portugal and the Loss of Their Continental American Territories in the 1820s: An Examination of the Issues," *European Historical Quarterly*, 41, no. 3, (2011), 397–412.

[2] Notable exceptions are: James Lockhart and Stuart B. Schwartz, *Early Latin America. A History of Colonial Spanish America and Brazil* (Cambridge 1983); Lyle N. McAlister, *Spain and Portugal in the New World, 1492–1700* (Minneapolis 1984) and Jeremy Adelman, *Sovereignty and Revolution in the Iberian Atlantic* (Princeton 2006). James D. Tracy (ed.), *The Rise of Merchant Empires: Long-Distance Trade in the Early Modern World, 1350–1750* (Cambridge 1990) and *State Power and World Trade, 1350–1750* (Cambridge 1991). Jack P. Greene and Philip D. Morgan, (eds.), *Atlantic History. A Critical Appraisal* (Oxford 2009), in which see Kenneth J. Andrien, "The Spanish Atlantic System" and A. J. R. Russell-Wood, "The Portuguese Atlantic, 1415–1808," 55–109. Sanjay Subrahmanyam, "Holding the World in Balance: The Connected Histories of the Iberian Overseas Empires, 1500–1640," *AHR*, 5, (2007), 1359–85.

American history courses from 1800 to the present. At the University of Essex, I brought Spain and Portugal into the picture in "Comparative Spanish and Portuguese Empires, 1500–1750." Later, I taught "Comparative Nationalism in Latin America," a real minefield of problems, from Independence movements to the present day.

Just as Brazil's growing importance from the time of the gold boom of the 1690s to 1760s rescued Portugal from obscurity as a lesser European Power, New Spain as a source of revenue and credit bailed out Old Spain as it tumbled toward its military, financial, and political collapse in the later 1790s and early 1800s. For these reasons, the Lisbon and Madrid governments intended to preserve what they could of their commercial monopolies with the empires. The Lusitanian and Hispanic Monarchies were strikingly different, however, in their historical contexts and evolution. Portugal, in contrast to Spain, remained largely isolated from the rest of Europe, as a virtual non-participant in the continuous power struggles between the eighteenth-century dynasties. From the 1670s, Portugal's primary focus as an imperial power lay in Luso-America, the territory broadly known as "Brazil." Portuguese Western Africa remained subordinate to Brazilian interests as part of the South-Atlantic network of slavery and commerce, extending at times to Spanish American ports like Montevideo and Buenos Aires. This system exercised a persistent hold on the political and economic life of Brazil well into the nineteenth century.[3]

Dominic Lieven's identification of the core problem of empires certainly has a bearing on the Iberian case.

Perhaps the biggest single problem was that the best responses to the internal and external challenges to empire *pushed in opposite directions*. Internally, maximum decentralization, cultural autonomy, mutual vetoes, and agreed power-sharing between communities were not only much the most human and civilized policies but also the ones in the long run best to limit inter-ethnic conflict. Such policies were, however, hardly the ones best designed to maximize the state's military and fiscal resources, in the face of external challenge to its existence.[4]

---

[3] Kenneth Maxwell, "The Generation of the 1790s and the Idea of the Luso-Brazilian Empire," in Dauril Alden (ed.), *Colonial Roots of Modern Brazil, Papers of the Newberry Library Conference* (Berkeley 1973), 107–44; "Portuguese America," *IHR*, VI, no. 4 (November 1984), 529–50; "The Atlantic in the Eighteenth Century: A Southern Perspective on the Need to Return to the Big Picture," *TRHS*, 6th series, 3 (1993), 209–36. Gabriel B. Paquette, *Imperial Portugal and the Age of Atlantic Revolutions. The Luso-Brazilian World, c. 1770–1850* (Cambridge 2013), 133, compares and contrasts the Spanish and Portuguese Constitutions of 1812 and 1822.

[4] Dominic Lieven, "Dilemmas of Empire, 1850–1918. Power, Territory, Identity," *JCH*, 34, no. 2 (April 1999), 163–200: pp. 196–97.

Tensions such as these provided the long-term explanations for the breakdown of the transatlantic Monarchies. One of the central theses of
C. J. Bayly's *Birth of the Modern World*, is the following:

During the years, 1756–63, warfare in the Americas and Asia between Europeans,
or between Europeans and indigenous people, hastened the crisis of the old régime
in Europe. It helped to crack the financial systems of the old régime and throw
doubts on the capacity and legitimacy of its rulers.

Bayly points to the connection between war and government-finance as
the key to the crisis of the Great Powers during the later eighteenth
century. Such pressures accounted for the urgency of reform of the old
structures and the emergence of the phenomenon described in the historiography as "Enlightened Absolutism." The Seven Years' War
(1756–63) revealed the increasing cost of war.[5] Transatlantic warfare
after 1795 further pushed up the cost of navies and weaponry, with
paralytic effects on government finance and, in particular, Spanish commerce. The Lusitanian Monarchy, a historic ally of Great Britain,
became unavoidably caught up in the general struggle during the
1800s, especially after Napoleon's establishment of the Continental
System in 1805.

The period 1770–1830 was dominated by the three great revolutions
of the western world. It began with the rebellion of the British North
American Thirteen Colonies (1776–83), the collapse of Bourbon France
and the Revolution of 1789–99, which was then followed by the
Napoleonic Consulate and Empire to 1814–15. In the final phase were
the collapse of Bourbon Spain in 1808, the Wars of Independence on the
Spanish American continent (1810–25), the division of the Portuguese
Empire into the European sector, with its African and Asiatic dependencies, and the development of a separate Brazilian Empire still under the
Braganza dynasty from 1822–89. Metropolitan Spain's inability to
resolve the disputes with the American territories helped to explain
why the momentous events after 1808 took the course that they did.
The view that Brazil took a different course to Spanish America, with the
minimum of violence, has rightly been contested.

The habitual separation of the Hispanic and the Lusitanian
Monarchies into different compartments has had a distorting effect.
Furthermore, their European metropoles should not be separated from

---

[5] C. A. Bayly, *The Birth of the Modern World, 1780–1914* (Blackwell, Oxford 2004), 86,
91–96.

the overseas dominions as distinct case studies. Spatial networks operating through patronage, personal relationships, common beliefs and notions, and the exchange of ideas contributed to the enrichment of the connection between Portugal and Brazil, as also between Spain and Spanish America.

Viewed in totality, Spain and Portugal were just as much *parts* of their Monarchies as their American territories. In the period examined in this book, we are witnessing crisis on both sides of the Atlantic. The separation of Brazil and Spanish American Emancipation, to use the term current in the 1820s, should be seen in relation to the structural determinants of imperial collapse at the metropolitan centers.

Spain and Portugal lay at the core of the crisis that beset their continental American Empires in the last decades of the eighteenth century. I have long held the view that we should look for the essential explanation of the disaggregation of the two Monarchies on the American continent in the irresolvable problems of their two metropoles.[6] Traditional history has largely seen the period in terms of the opposition between American patriots and metropolitan rule. Often the conflicts more resembled civil wars within the American territories than straightforward struggles between colony and imperial center. Many fought to resist the break-up of the Monarchy and to defend its unity, whether as an absolute or a constitutional monarchy.

Imperial identities and loyalties remained the strongest in Mexico and Peru. In fact, this latter aspect of the question has been largely superseded in the historical literature by explorations of the origins of Independence, even though hardly anyone thought in terms of separatism at the time.[7] Simon Bolivar recognized that fact, in 1813, by his policy of "War to the Death" against anyone opposing the idea of outright separation from the Monarchy.[8]

Despite the variety of jurisdictions within them, several centripetal factors held the Ibero-American Monarchies together. These included dynastic loyalties, the Catholic Church under Royal Patronage, the senior bureaucracy and judicial agencies, the crucially important mercantile

---

[6] See also Adelman, *Sovereignty and Revolution*, 395: "The revolutions that made the world anew were the consequence, not the cause, of the end of imperial sovereignty."

[7] See Marcela Echeverri, "Popular Royalists, Empire, and Politics in North-Western New Granada, 1809–1819," *HAHR*, 91, no. 2, (May 2011), 237–69.

[8] See Part II, Chapter 5.

élite, the mining sector (where appropriate), and the shared political and religious cultures within both Monarchies.[9]

Only in the later decades of Spanish rule on the American continent did the metropolitan government significantly strengthen its armed forces. Colonial militias of varying degrees of impotence existed before the military reforms enacted in response to the British seizure of Havana and Manila in the Seven Years' War. Madrid henceforth perceived external defense rather than internal order as the priority, despite the impact of the rebellions of 1780–81 in New Granada and the Perus. New Spain's Bourbon Army proved able to hold back insurrection after 1810. The Army of Upper Peru, created by Viceroy José Fernando Abascal of Peru in 1810, opposed the Buenos Aires' revolutionary junta's attempt to control Upper Peru. The former Army, although weakened, survived Independence; the latter continued in the field until 1824, sustaining the Spanish cause until final defeat by Bolívar and Sucre.[10]

Personal and professional linkages, which often cut across royal institutions and specific territories, acted as long-term elements in binding metropoles and overseas dependencies together. In colonial Brazil, the interrelation between formal institutions and the personal relationships of those who manned them explained how the system subsisted.[11] Arrigo Amadori's examination of the interconnection of the two Spanish American viceroyalties and the metropolitan government during the period of the Conde-Duque de Olivares' supremacy (1621–43) points to a "system

---

[9] António Manuel Hespanha, *As vésperas do Leviathan. Instituicões e poder político. Portugal – século XVII*, 2 vols. (Lisbon 1994), has developed these points in the Portuguese context.

[10] See Lyle McAlister, *The "Fuero Militar" in New Spain, 1764–1800* (Gainesville 1957) and "The Reorganization of the Army in New Spain, 1763–1765," *HAHR*, 33 (1953), 1–32. Christon I. Archer, *The Army in Bourbon Mexico, 1760–1810* (Albuquerque 1977). Leon Campbell, *The Military and Society in Colonial Peru, 1750–1820* (Philadelphia 1978). Allan J. Kuethe, *Military Reform and Society in New Granada, 1773–1808* (Gainesville 1978) and *Cuba, 1753–1815: Crown, Military, and Society* (Knoxville 1986). Juan Marchena Fernández, *Oficiales y soldados en el ejército de América* (Seville 1983). Clément Thibaud, *Repúblicas en armas. Los ejércitos bolivarianos en la guerra de Independencia en Colombia y Venezuela* (Bogotá 2003). Juan Ortiz Escamilla (coordinador), *Fuerzas militares en Iberoamérica, siglos XVIII y XIX* (Mexico City, Zamora, Xalapa 2005). Anthony McFarlane, *War and Independence in Spanish America* (New York 2014). Kenneth J. Andrien and Allan Kuethe, *The Spanish Atlantic World in the Eighteenth Century* (Cambridge 2014).

[11] See Stuart B. Schwartz, *Sovereignty and Society. The High Court of Bahía and Its Judges, 1610–1757* (Berkeley 1973).

of multiple interrelationships."[12] Eric Myrup argues that Portugal managed to keep its disparate empire together for so long by virtue of the fact that

social networks not only played crucial roles in the interactions between the Portuguese and other peoples, but they also were a central feature in the activities of the colonial state ... the Portuguese empire was brought together by an evolving web of human relationships that lay beneath the surface of formal colonial government.[13]

This is also an approach I adopt here. My intention is to throw the spotlight on élites resident in the Americas, local interest-groups and the provincial milieux.

The interrelation between institutions and informal relationships explained how the empires lasted so long. In the late-colonial Hispanic world, however, official attempts to break up older networks contribute to the explanation of why the Hispanic Monarchy broke apart in a way completely different to the process of separation between Brazil and Portugal. Ministers strove to save their Monarchies by reform but often met with obstruction. A sense that time was running out prevailed among ministers by the 1790s, if Spain and Portugal were to salvage their positions as international powers. At first, entrenched élites in Spanish America were unsure of the new direction of policy and hardly knew how to respond or on what legitimate basis to challenge metropolitan goals. Within several decades, legitimacy became a political issue.

In Spain, the call for reform had been nothing new:. It did not come into being with the change of dynasty from Habsburg to Bourbon in 1700. The *arbitristas* of the first decades of the seventeenth century had already been asking why, when it possessed such a great empire, Spain had not become a prosperous country.[14] Discrete reforms of the administrative structures at the center of imperial government had already begun in the last two decades of Charles II's reign, in the 1680s and 1690s.[15] Much, however, hinged on the sense of the term "reform" and on the objectives of government policy. Even before the end of the War of Succession in the

---

[12] Arrigo Amadori, *Negociando la obediencia. Gestión y reforma de los virreinatos americanos en tiempos del conde-duque de Olivares (1621–1643)* (Madrid 2013).

[13] Erik Lars Myrup, *Power and Corruption in the Early Modern Portuguese World* (Baton Rouge 2015), 2–3, 5.

[14] J. H. Elliot, *The Count-Duke of Olivares. The Statesman in an Age of Decline* (New Haven and London 1986), 69–70, 89–101.

[15] See Henry Kamen, *Spain in the Later Seventeenth Century, 1665–1700* (London 1980) and Christopher Storrs, *The Resilience of the Spanish Monarchy, 1665–1700* (Oxford 2006).

peninsula (1701–15), the new Bourbon king and his ministers were interpreting reform in terms of centralizing government agencies and strengthening royal power. Imperial Spain saw itself increasingly pressed between France and Great Britain, both of which also had powerful interests in the Caribbean and on the American continent. Commercial rationalization and tighter fiscal management were the responses.[16]

The idea that the entire Monarchy constituted the "Nation" took shape in the course of the eighteenth century. Constitutionalists, as much as absolutists, accepted the idea of Hispanic or Lusitanian Nations consisting of the Monarchies as a whole. The difference between them was that the absolutists saw the dynasty as the apex of union, while Liberal constitutionalists regarded the Constitution as the unifying agency. Both, however, were monarchists and defenders of continued union. The Portuguese Cortes of 1821–23 reaffirmed the unity of the Monarchy but sought to reassert Lisbon's pivotal position as the commercial and political center, a view regarded as a threat to their interests by the Brazilian élites, which had benefited so much from the presence of king, court, and government in Rio de Janeiro from 1808 to 1821.[17]

This present book falls into a historiographical context. We should turn now to examine its position in relation to those of other authors. José María Portillo highlights the problem faced by absolutist ministers and their constitutionalist successors in laying solid foundations for a transoceanic political structure during the period from the 1760s into the 1820s. Portillo's concept of "Atlantic careers" demonstrates the institutional linkages across continents through the developing careers of the educated individuals who staffed senior levels of magistracy and administration.[18] There will be many examples of these "imperial careers" (as I should prefer) in the forthcoming pages. Abascal, for example, spent his mature years in the Indies, gaining knowledge of how the Monarchy really functioned.

Jorge Domínguez places the focus on élite–State relationships in his exploration of the disintegration of the Hispanic Monarchy: "the critical factor was the political bargaining relationship between local elites and

[16] Henry Kamen, *The War of Succession in Spain, 1700–15* (Bloomington and London 1969), 42–56, 114–17, 199–241. Geoffrey J. Walker, *Spanish Politics and Imperial Trade, 1700–1789* (Bloomington and London 1979).

[17] Paquette, *Imperial Portugal*, 19–25, 95–103, 140–47, 324.

[18] J. M. Portillo, *Crisis atlántica. Autonomía e independencia en la crisis de la monarquía hispana* (Madrid 2006), 16–21, and the same author's *La vida atlántica de Victorián de Villava* (Madrid 2009), 23, 28–29.

the government of the empire and of each colony." Domínguez shows how Mexico, Venezuela, Chile, and Cuba all responded in different ways to the crisis of 1808–10. Despite stirrings in Cuba from the 1790s, conditions on the island made for the survival of Spanish rule during the nineteenth century. His argument is that political institutions in the first three territories proved unable to adapt (at varying stages) to the crisis in the Monarchy. Domínguez, nevertheless, portrays the Spanish state as "a centralized bureaucratic empire," which rather overstates the position.[19]

Three volumes by Barbara and Stanley Stein focus on the relationships between Spain and the Empire, showing clearly how New Spain shored up the metropolis. Rather than Spain acting as the dynamic center of the Monarchy, by the 1790s it became the principal burden. The parallel studies by John TePaske, Jacques Barbier, and Carlos Marichal have also penetrated metropolitan Spain's fiscal tergiversations, most especially in relation to Mexican resources. The urgent need to tighten the relationship with New Spain is the focus of the Steins' latter two volumes. Spain, however, became ground down in the process. Accordingly, they argue that the crisis in Spain antedated the Napoleonic intervention in the peninsula in 1808, a position I have consistently adopted myself. Yet, the Steins do not examine in depth the perceptions and objectives of the American elites, particularly provincial and local power-groupings. We have no discussion of what the situation might have been in Peru, for instance. There is no attempt at any comparison or contrast with the Lusitanian Monarchy.[20]

Jeremy Adelman's study integrates comparatively Brazilian developments with those of Spanish America. The book advances considerably our understanding of the crises of the two Monarchies. Above all, it rejects nationalist stories of emerging or embryonic nations trapped within

---

[19] Jorge Dominguez, *Insurrection or Loyalty. The Breakdown of the Spanish American Empire* (Cambridge, MA, 1980), 241, 249, 255.

[20] I am referring to *Silver, Trade, and War. Spain and America in the Making of Early Modern Europe* (Baltimore and London 2000), *Apogee of Empire: Spain and New Spain in the Age of Charles III, 1759–1788* (Baltimore and London 2003), and *Edge of Crisis. War and Trade in the Spanish Atlantic, 1789–1808* (Baltimore 2009). Jacques Barbier, "Peninsular Finance and Colonial Trade. The Dilemma of Charles IV's Spain," *JLAS*, 12, i (1980), 21–37. John J. TePaske, "The Financial Disintegration of the Royal Government in Mexico during the Epoch of Independence," in Jaime E. Rodriguez O. (ed.), *The Independence of Mexico and the Creation of the New Nation* (Los Angeles 1989), 63–83. Carlos Marichal, *Bankruptcy of Empire. Mexican Silver and the Wars between Spain, Britain and France, 1760–1810* (Cambridge 2007) and by the same author, "Beneficios y costes fiscales del colonialismo: las remesas americanas a España, 1760–1814," *Revista de Historia Económica*, 15, no. 3 (1997), 475–505.

empires, in favor of a view of the two Monarchies as spatial and cultural unities. They are broken apart because of the collapse of their metropoles, a thesis also developed here. As a result, the continental-American territories were plunged into a crisis of legitimacy, which they had not anticipated. The end result was a conglomeration of divided, confused, and largely unstable successor states, saddled with the task of constructing nations out of their sometimes disputed territories. New Spain, however, is virtually unmentioned.[21]

François-Xavier Guerra's perspective of the Independence period moves the focus away from socio-economic causality toward intellectual and cultural shifts. François Furet's revisionist approach to the French Revolution may be perceived in Guerra's work. This relies heavily on the notion of the expansion of the "public sphere." Applied to the Hispanic world, the idea includes private meetings, the press, clubs, masonic lodges, and reforming-societies. However, Guerra puts the metropolis at the epicenter of the crisis of the Hispanic Monarchy, a position with which I concur.[22] Guerra describes a phenomenon, which he calls "las revoluciones hispánicas," and interprets them as the "transition to Modernity as much as the negotiation of independence."[23] He defines "modernity" as "the nation envisaged as a voluntary association of equal individuals." I should prefer to omit reference to "modernity," and draw attention less to a common revolutionary process throughout the Monarchy than to many different ones, often conflicting. On the other hand, I agree with Guerra's argument that unitarism represented the crux of the problem between metropolitan government and the aspiration of the American élites toward some form of home rule within the Monarchy.[24]

The issue of representation, a central theme of my book, was openly discussed after 1808, though in different forms throughout the European and American territories. As Roberto Breña argues, the American élites and the deputies sent to the Cádiz Cortes of 1810–13 came up against the Spanish peninsula deputies' determination not to comply in practice with the declared principle of equality of status between the American and European sectors of the Monarchy. Both Breña and Guerra argue, as I do in this book, that constitutionalist ministers after 1810 and 1820 opposed

---

[21] Adelman, *Sovereignty and Revolution.*

[22] François-Xavier Guerra, *Modernidad e Independencia. Ensayos sobre las revoluciones hispanas* (Madrid 1992), 85–113.

[23] Guerra, *Modernidad e Independencia*, 21, 115.

[24] Guerra, *Modernidad e Independencia*, 115–48.

the transformation of the unitary Monarchy into "una monarquía plural."[25]

The term "colonialism" is rarely far from any discussion of empire. Jaime Rodríguez' two major studies of Hispanic-American Independence reject the idea of anticolonial struggle, putting emphasis on the Cádiz Constitution of 1812 as the culminating point in the debate concerning the transformation of the Monarchy. The Cádiz Liberal tradition of 1810–14 and 1820–23, however, tolerated no substantial devolution of power to the American territories or division of sovereignty. This was unacceptable to many Americans. Several Hispanic American territories' developed their own constitutional forms, moving toward republicanism and federalism.[26] Furthermore, in both Guerra and Rodriguez, we lose sight of the bitterly contested armed struggles across Spanish America. We have no sense of why men and women took the decision to risk their lives and livelihoods by resorting to arms. There is little appreciation of how warfare and insurrection in Spanish America shaped the character of the states that followed Independence.[27]

Works by Germán Carrera Damas, Juan Ortiz Escamilla, Marixa Lasso, Alfonso Múnera, Núria Sala i Vila, Cecilia Méndez, and others argue cogently in the opposite direction. I would also place my own work on this scale of the argument. Ortiz, followed later by Eric Van Young, places the issues of loyalty, insurgency, neutrality, or indifference, within the village context. Lasso and Múnera attach prime importance to the active participation of blacks and mulattos in the struggle for racial equality on the New Granada Caribbean coast, while Carrera Damas opened discussion of non-white action on behalf of the Royalist cause in Venezuela in 1812–15. Andean peasant involvement on one side or another, as armed bands, or suppliers of victuals or information, in the conflict between the rival Royalist and Patriot armies in the early 1820s

---

[25] Roberto Breña, *El primer liberalismo español y los procesos de emancipación de América, 1808–1824. Una revisión historiográfica del liberalismo hispánico* (Mexico City 2006), 109–110, 130–35, 142–48, 155. There were some sixty American deputies in the Extraordinary Cortes of 1810–13.

[26] Jaime E. Rodríguez O., *The Independence of Spanish America* (Cambridge 2008) and *Nosotros somos ahora los verdaderos españoles*, 2 vols. (Zamora and Mexico City 2009).

[27] Rodriguez, *Nosotros somos*, p. 633, "The Independence of New Spain was not the result of an anticolonial armed struggle. Above all, it resulted from a *political revolution* [author's italics] which culminated in the *dissolution* [same] of an international political system." There is a sharp contrast with Anthony McFarlane, *War and Independence in Spanish America* (New York 2014) and Juan Luis Ossa Santa Cruz, *Armies, Politics and Revolution. Chile, 1808–1826* (Liverpool 2014).

was already evident from the studies by Raúl Rivera Serna in 1958 and Gustavo Vergara Arias in 1973. To my mind the action of non-élite socio-ethnic groups cannot and should not be ignored.[28]

One last point here: I have not adopted an "Atlantic history" perspective. My emphasis on the Andean dimension, the internal linkages within the territories of Meso-America, the Caribbean or Brazil and the Pacific-coastal trade focused on Lima should help to explain why. In this sense, I believe it to be misleading to position the totality of Ibero-American experience within a narrower "Atlantic" framework. These other dimensions require parallel elucidation rather than subordination to a model that may well have outlived its original usefulness.

---

[28] Raúl Rivera Serna, *Los guerrilleros del Centro en la emancipación peruana* (Lima 1958); Germán Carrera Damas, *Aspectos socioeconómicos de la Guerra de Independencia* (third edition, Caracas 1972); Gustavo Vergara Arias, *Montoneros y guerrillas en la etapa de la emancipación del Perú (1820–1825)* (Lima 1973); Núria Sala i Vila, "La participación indígena en la rebelión de Angulo y Pumacahua, 1814–1816," in Pilar García Jordán and Miguel Izard (coordinators), *Conquista y resistencia en la historia de América* (Barcelona 1992), 273–88; Juan Ortiz Escamilla, *Guerra y Gobierno. Los pueblos en la Independencia de México* (Mexico City and Seville 1997); Alfonso Múnera, *El fracaso de la nación: región, clase y raza en el caribe colombiano (1717–1810)* (Bogotá 1998); Eric Van Young, *The Other Rebellion. Violence, Ideology, and the Mexican Struggle for Independence (1810–1821)* (Stanford 2001); Marixa Lasso, "Los grupos afro-descendientes y la independencia: ¿un nuevo paradigma historiográfico?" and "Cecilia Méndez, "La guerra que no cesa: Guerras civiles, imaginario nacional y la formación del estado en el Perú," both in Clément Thibaud, Gabriel Entin, Alejandro Gómez and Federica Morelli (coordinators), *L'Atlantique révolutionnaire. Une perspective ibéro-américaine* (Paris 2013), 359–78 and 379–420.

PART I

ONE SOLE MONARCHY, "ONE SOLE NATION" – ADVOCATES, CRITICS, AND CHALLENGERS

I

Negotiation, Networks, Linkages

Like all other European and Asiatic dynastic empires, the Iberian empires functioned according to a combination of internal dynamics and external pressures. The relation between core and peripheries operated in a complex fashion. In political terms, the core – the centers of power in Madrid and Lisbon – exercised dominion over all the components of the Monarchy, but this did not always signify effective control. Distance, time, and a type of self-attributed leeway on the part of enforcing agencies on the spot considerably modified the efficacy of royal policy. Added to these factors was the political necessity of reconciling through informal negotiation metropolitan interests with the power groups formed within the American territories.

COMPOSITE MONARCHIES

These were not unusual in the sixteenth and seventeenth centuries when Spain and Portugal largely began their experience as colonial powers.[1] At first sight, the Kingdom of Portugal's territorial unity made it appear

---

[1] The Austrian Habsburgs secured the crowns of Bohemia and Hungary in 1526, after gaining the Burgundian inheritance in 1477. After 1516, the grandson of Mary of Burgundy and son of Philip I of Austria and Juana of Castile succeeded to both the Spanish kingdoms in 1516, and in 1519 was elected Holy Roman Emperor. From 1520, the Kingdom of Castile acquired large swathes of territory in continental America. The three Basque Provinces and the Kingdom of Navarra, all associated with the Crown of Castile, retained their traditional privileges. When the Spanish Habsburg king acquired the Crown of Portugal (from 1580 to 1640), institutions of the two (hitherto rival) Monarchies remained distinct. See Richard Herr and John H. R. Poll (eds.), *Iberian Identity: Essays in the Nature of Identity in Spain and Portugal* (Berkeley 1989); Jocelyn N. Hillgarth, "Spanish Historiography and

15

otherwise. Certainly, Portugal was not a composite monarchy in the same sense as Spain, which consisted of several kingdoms, principalities, and territories until the first Bourbon monarch forcibly united the Crowns of Castile and Aragon. On the other hand, the kingdom of Portugal shared with Spain a complexity of jurisdictions and sovereignties, such as those exercised by the secular nobility, the episcopate, the Military-Religious Orders and the towns, parallel to those of the crown. Both the Hispanic and Lusitanian Monarchies were *ancien régime* societies in which corporate loyalties and identities predominated, and in which the monarch acted as arbiter of this complex network. Continual negotiation subsisted between the unity represented by the Crown and the autonomy of the parts. For Spain, the overriding problem never ceased to be jurisdictional and monetary fragmentation. We might describe each of the two Monarchies as a unity of pluralities.[2]

Even though the Crown shared jurisdiction with a wide range of estates and corporations, it could not be entirely ignored. Colonial and metropolitan administrations had somehow to find equilibrium in order that the overseas territories should continue their business as peacefully as possible. The "state" in colonial Brazil, for instance, sought sporadically to assert its authority amongst a labyrinth of competing interests. As Schwartz points out, it allowed dominant social groups to control resources in so far as this remained compatible with the interests of those in power in the metropolis.[3] An example of such a criss-cross of interests would be the tactical alliance of Brazilian planters with Portuguese merchants anxious to limit the influence of the nobility in the circles of power in Lisbon.

In practice, effective authority depended on the capabilities of each monarch, viceroy, and captain general. These latter worked closely with the municipalities, which regulated local trades and, as best they could,

---

Iberian Reality," *History and Theory,* 24, no. 1 (1985), 23–43; J. H. Elliott, "A Europe of Composite Monarchies," *Past and Present,* 137 (1992), 48–71.

[2] Nuno G. F. Monteiro, Pedro Cardim, Mafalda Soares da Cunha, *Optima Pars. Élites Ibero-Americanas do Antigo Regime* (Lisbon 2005), 193. Regina Grafe, *Distant Tyrannies. Markets, Power, and Backwardness in Spain, 1650–1800* (Princeton 2012), 36, 117–19, 132–37. Bradley Benedict, "El Estado en México en la época de los Habsburgo," *HM,* XVIII (julio 1973–julio 1974), 551–610. Hespanha, *As vésperas do Leviathan,* vol. 1, 739–61.

[3] Stuart B. Schwartz, "Colonial Brazil: The Role of the State in Slave Social Formation," in Karen Spalding (ed.), *Essays in the Political, Economic, and Social History of Latin America* (Newark, DEL, 1982), pp. 1–23: see pp. 10–12.

the food supply.[4] Amadori draws attention to the perennial problem of enforcing or persuading obedience to the royal executive in Madrid. Olivares met resistance at every level in his attempts to rationalize the administrative structure of the Monarchy and speed-up the processes of enforcement, in response to Spain's urgent European commitments after 1621. Negotiation frequently characterized the way power was exercised. In effect, social interests permeated royal administration, making it distinctly porous. Little possibility existed of isolating the Council of the Indies and the American *audiencias* from their social context.[5]

Eighteenth-century governments faced similar problems. Although commercial and administrative reforms set a course for tighter political control and increased revenues, American interest groups were even stronger and more entrenched than they had been in the Habsburg era. Nevertheless, the royal government was able to introduce a range of reforms, though it encountered opposition, subversion, delaying tactics, and indifference. Metropolitan ministers ultimately took the decision to confront the most powerful corporations, the Consulados of Cádiz, Mexico City, and Lima, purge the *audiencias* of local interests, bring financial administration under closer supervision, and control the municipalities. Such policies had mixed results. Although government, on the whole, was neither stultifying nor oppressive, its policies were frequently contradictory and unsystematic. Much depended on the competition for power within the courts and ministries of Madrid or Lisbon. Even so, many ministers and colonial administrators proved to be of the highest standard in terms of education and capabilities.

In Spain and Portugal, relations between government and nobility took different directions. In Spain, the Bourbons still employed senior noblemen, as individuals, in the highest positions of state, including the officer corps and the diplomatic service, but they promoted lesser and provincial notables alongside them. Charles III's government did this strikingly by attacking the career base for the higher nobility in the university higher colleges. Leading ministers from the 1770s onward came more from the professional classes, many of them lesser nobles, rather than grandees. American viceroys and Intendants, furthermore,

[4] Benedict, "El Estado," 585–93.
[5] Amadori, *Negociando la obediencia*, 19–20, 82–84, 89–101.

usually came from military backgrounds under the Bourbons.[6] In Portugal, by contrast, hierarchy within the nobiliar estate crystalized upward, and the polarity between Court and provincial nobilities increased. High civil, military, and ecclesiastical offices, at least until the time of Pombal from 1750 to 1777, tended to be concentrated in the senior nobility, which held most positions on the governing Councils. Noblemen, including the middle-ranking *fidalgos*, also staffed the governorships and captaincies of the overseas territories, including the office of Governor-General of Portuguese America. Yet, the same tendency toward the selection of military officers apparent in the Hispanic Monarchy could also be seen in the Lusitanian Monarchy during the eighteenth century. In fact, service in Brazil, Angola, or India, unpopular as it generally was, often contributed to promotion within the ascending scales of government.[7]

HOW ABSOLUTE WAS ABSOLUTISM?

Responses from governments to the political and religious turmoil across most of Western and Central Europe from the 1520s to the 1640s led to the construction of a juridical basis for absolute monarchy, in which the basic text was Bodin (1529–96), *Six livres de la République*. Absolutism in the historical sense signified the king's release from constraints imposed upon him by the corporations of the realm – nobility, clergy, provinces or realms, and towns – and, in the Iberian context, from the corporately structured *Cortes*, the representative body inherited from the Middle Ages. In Habsburg Spain, the Cortes met at royal summons until the accession of Charles II in 1665 and sporadically under the Bourbons after 1700, though only to ratify hereditary succession, as in 1760 and 1789, when the Cortes last met under the *ancien régime*.[8]

The monarch in both Spain and Portugal remained, however, subject to divine law and the "fundamental laws of the realm," swearing to respect them at accession. These latter were the codified laws and charters of privilege ("*fueros*" in Spanish; *foros* in Portuguese), which established the

---

[6] Francisco A. Eissa-Barroso, "'Of Experience, Zeal, and Selflessness': Military Officers as Viceroys in Early Eighteenth-Century Spanish America," *The Americas*, 68, no. 3 (January 2012), 317–45.

[7] Da Cunha and Monteiro, *Optima Pars*, 191, 196, 214–15, 222–23, 231–32.

[8] See the valuable discussion in Roland Mousnier, "Les concepts d' 'ordres,' d' 'états,' de fidélité' et de 'monarchie absolue' en France de la fin du XVe siècle à la fin du XVIIIe," *Revue Historique*, 502 (abril-juin 1972), 289–312.

juridical relationship of the constituted bodies of each kingdom or principality, with the nobility and Church at the head, to the king and to one another. The doctrine originated, in part, in the belief that royal power was delegated by God to the monarch. This entailed mutual obligations by the monarch and the religious authorities to sustain one another. The king's principal function was still to see that justice was dispensed.[9]

Repeated obstruction by local or privileged interest groups generally led to modification of government policy or outright frustration of the desired goals. Tenacious adherence to "the fundamental laws of the realm" provided the principal means of curbing royal power. Portillo, however, points out that none of the Spanish political thinkers discussing the future constitutional form of the Spanish dominions – Gaspar Melchor Jovellanos, Antoni Capmany, Álvaro Flórez Estrada, Francisco Martínez Marina – ever explained how the proposed revival of the "traditional constitution" of rights and privileges deriving from the medieval Hispanic kingdoms might be applied to the Americas, that is, to the *whole* Monarchy, rather than just the peninsula.[10]

The principal difference between absolute monarchies and parliamentary systems was that in the latter the representative body exercised a determining control over the raising of taxation. The gradual – and often interrupted – growth of royal power at certain points in the Castilian Middle Ages had already occasioned the imposition of the sales-tax, the *alcabala*, from 1342. Despite this, monarchs and ministers regularly ran into financial difficulties, most notably during the 1640s and 1650s, and were unable to implement the policies they wished in part or in full.[11]

In the Spanish peninsula, the component kingdoms of the Crown of Aragon, including the Principality of Catalonia, retained their distinct institutions and practices throughout the Habsburg era. Philip V's *Nueva Planta* decrees of 1707–16, however, submerged their representation into the Castilian Cortes as punishment for opposition to the new Bourbon dynasty during the War of Succession. The Kingdom of Navarra

---

[9] John G. Gagliardo, *Enlightened Despotism* (London 1971), 90–93. Grafe, *Distant Tyrannies*, 120–22.

[10] Portillo, *Crisis atlántica*, 22–26, 82. For the Americas, note the argument in John H. Coatsworth, "The Limits of Colonial Absolutism: the State in Eighteenth Century Mexico," in Karen Spalding (ed.), *Essays in the Political, Economic and Social History of Colonial Latin America* (Newark, DE: University of Delaware Press 1982), 25–51.

[11] Charles Jago, "Habsburg Absolutism and the Cortes of Castile," *AHR*, no. 86 (1981), 307–26.

and the three other Basque Provinces kept their institutions and privileges, since they had not been compromised.[12]

Absolutism in practice was more precarious than the term would suggest. Real power often proved to be tenuous, since the business of government required a range of ministers and subordinate officials to administer the state and assuage the array of interests that pressed their cases at court. This may be described in the following way:

> The theoretical concentration of authority in the person of the monarch masked the influence of individuals, corporate groups, and the various councils. It implied a unity of interests that did not exist, Decrees, backed by the full majesty of the head of state, supposedly ended discussion. Behind this façade of unanimity, the structure in reality encouraged fluid manoeuvring.[13]

Considerable leeway was left to the administrative agencies in the Americas. The viceregal courts in Mexico City and Lima exercised broad powers of patronage. This enabled the viceroys to co-opt a wide range of interests into their networks of power.[14] Local élites implicitly played a significant role in the political processes as they did at the apex of the social structure:

> [B]ecause government itself was defined to include the participation of extragovernmental groups, local notables had a legitimate voice in rule … Formal government was a partner in the unacknowledged contract between the state and the upper levels of society, but it was an indisputable and unique partner, because it originated outside colonial society, had a greater degree of continuity than the shifting local alliances, and had the symbolic authority of the king behind it.[15]

The American viceroys were, as Cañeque states, the king's living image, rather than the head of a centralized colonial bureaucracy emanating from a political center. American government, then, did not take the form of an unbroken chain of command: on the contrary, political power was dispersed throughout the system, while the king's authority remained "absolute." This "dispersion" of power meant that metropolitan and royal

---

[12] Manuel Dánvila y Collado, *El poder civil en España*, 6 vols. (Madrid 1885–86), vol. III, 410–29, 568; vol. IV, 9, 27, 44–46, 215, 241–48. Grafe, *Distant Tyrannies*, 127–37, 150, on the monetary and fiscal implications.

[13] MacLachlan, *Spain's Empire in the New World*, 45.

[14] Cañeque, *King's Living Image*, 157–83.

[15] Louisa Schell Hoberman, *Mexico's Merchant Elite, 1590–1660* (Durham and London 1991), 180–81.

authority in the localities and at the level of the Indian *pueblos* remained in practice relatively weak.[16]

While it is true that the viceroys presided over "courts," their powers were never clearly defined. Competing authorities and hierarchies in the Church, the Inquisition, the *audiencias*, and *cabildos* counterbalanced, though rarely countermanded, viceregal authority. In New Spain, outright conflict within this ruling élite in 1624, 1647, and 1692 did gravely compromise viceregal power. Cañeque convincingly argues that this competition for power had nothing to do with formal or informal checks and balances but derived from a combination of the Hispanic political inheritance and American realities. The *audiencia* was a Castilian institution, which right from the first decades stood at the core of administration in the Indies. However, its constitutional relationship with the viceroy, who did not appoint its magistrates, and with the city councils, which arose originally from among American residents, remained largely undefined.[17]

Bourbon monarchs were wedded to the idea of reinforcing the absolute power of the Crown and its governing organs, stressing the divine origin of royal sovereignty. This policy affected the Indies as much as peninsular Spain. Evident in the reigns of Philip V and Ferdinand VI (1746–59), this tendency became considerably more pronounced under Charles III (1759–88). The objective was to tighten metropolitan control and reinforce peninsular supremacy. We can speculate concerning what might have happened had the metropolitan government decided upon the opposite course of action, namely the institutionalizing of American penetration of governing agencies through some form of limited home government within the framework of the Monarchy and in accordance with its juridical structure. In such a way, men educated in the Indies or shaped by the experience of everyday life would have constituted the effective governing cadres, regardless of whether they were of Spanish peninsular or creole origin. Instead, Charles III's ministries controversially opted to do the opposite.[18]

By the nature of the Iberian monarchies, neither the Braganza nor the Bourbon dynasty intended to eliminate the corporate juridical structures of society, but, where they could, to subordinate them, including the

---

[16] Cañeque, *King's Living Image*, 76.
[17] Cañeque, *King's Living Image*, 52–54, 75–76, 111–12, 162–63.
[18] Francisco Sánchez-Blanco, *El absolutismo y las Luces en el reinado de Carlos III* (Madrid 2002), 51–52, 186.

Church, to royal and ministerial objectives.[19] Religious symbolism and ritual gave legitimacy to the dynasties in Spain and Portugal, and instilled a sentiment of loyalty in their subjects. Since this divine infusion also guaranteed existing networks of respect and obedience beyond the structures of the state, little force was necessary in maintaining imperial rule. Most rebellions, even recognized the authority of King and Church.

Once the Holy Office of the Inquisition began to function in both Monarchies, it quickly acquired a bureaucracy of its own, plus a circle of lay officers, instilled an atmosphere of distrust, opened the way for calumny, and stifled the exchange of opinions through fear of anonymous denunciation, confiscation of property, and imprisonment.[20] No such formal institution, however, was ever established in Portuguese America. For that reason, the Brazils acquired a reputation of greater safety for the spread of ideas and the clandestine practice of variant religions. Pombal went some way to clip the public significance of the Inquisition by abolishing the open-air drama of the acts of penitence (*autos da fé*) in 1773–74.[21] Bourbon monarchs and their ministers, for their part, would have liked to exercise tighter state control over the Inquisition but they did not dare risk a direct assault.[22] The constitutional position of the Holy Office never ceased to be a troublesome matter for viceroys and bishops, who frequently complained that it did not seem to be controlled by anyone. The Inquisition could hardly be regarded as an expression of state control, since it often seemed to be a rival power to the viceregal administration, opening dangerous divisions at the top level of political life.[23]

[19] See, for instance, Coatsworth, "Limits of Colonial Absolutism," 25–51.
[20] Henry Kamen, *Spain, 1469–1714. A Society in Conflict* (London 1991 [1969]), 38–44, and by the same author, *The Spanish Inquisition. A Historical Revision* (New Haven and London 1998).
[21] Dauril Alden, *The Making of an Enterprise. The Society of Jesus in Portugal, Its Empire, and beyond, 1540–1750* (Stanford 1996), 111–13. Anita Novinsky, *Cristãos Novos na Bahia* (São Paulom 1972), 108–15. James E. Wadsworth, "In the Name of the Inquisition: The Portuguese Inquisition and Delegated Authority in Colonial Pernambuco, Brazil," *The Americas*, 61, i (July 2004), 19–54.
[22] Francisco Martí Gilabert, *Carlos III y la política religiosa* (Madrid 2004), 39–43.
[23] Teodoro Hampe-Martínez, "Recent Works on the Inquisition in Peruvian Colonial Society, 1570–1820," *LARR*, 33, ii (1996), 43–69: see pp. 61–62. The principal tasks were "moral control and ideological repression." See also, Irene Silverblatt, *Modern Inquisitions. Peru and the Colonial Origins of the Civilized World* (Durham and London 2004), 57–97. Cañeque, *King's Living Image*, 106–17.

The Council of Castile remained the superior authority in the Spanish administration, its powers reinforced whenever it met together with other Councils in the form of an Extraordinary Council. Such a body could issue orders of restraint, requiring "silence and obedience," whenever the government wished to obviate public discussion of a controversial policy. This it did in 1767, when the Crown took the decision to expel the Society of Jesus from all its realms. It showed the capacity of absolutist government to act decisively on occasions, especially when civil and ecclesiastical authorities were united in a common purpose.[24]

During the 1770s and 1780s, a relative slackening of censorship enabled freer discussion of issues and the circulation of printed matter, some of it even imported. This period corresponded to the ministry's adoption of certain principles associated with the European Enlightenment and their extension to the overseas territories. Several bishops, royal appointees, were themselves proponents of the new ideas and methods. The American Inquisitions began to appear less formidable, although customary practices of censorship and investigations of moral conduct continued. This situation lasted until the metropolitan government started to panic in 1789–90 at the reception of news from France. Revolutionary ideas emanating from Paris were seen as threats to the alliance of Throne and Altar, which was being dismantled in France.[25]

THE LIMITS OF COLONIALISM

As historical interest in the imperial experience of the Iberian powers deepened during the 1960s and 1970s, J. H. Parry identified three main characteristics of empire: first was the capacity of the metropolis to maintain control over its outlying or overseas territories, the second in terms of the economic and strategic benefits accruing to the metropolis from its colonies, and the third in the responsibility assumed by the metropolis for the defense and security of those territories.[26] This present book draws attention to the difficulties Spain and Portugal faced as imperial metropoles. Kenneth Andrien, for instance, has argued that "the overall decline

---

[24] Gabriel Torres Puga, *Opinión pública y censura en Nueva España. Indicios de un silencio imposible, 1767–1794* (Mexico City 2010), 71–72. Víctor Peralta Ruiz, "Las razones de la fe. La Iglesia y la Ilustración en el Perú, 1750–1800," in Scarlett O'Phelan Godoy (compiler), *El Perú en el siglo XVIII: la era borbónica* (Lima 1999), 177–204.

[25] Torres Puga, *Opinión pública*, 350–51, 545, 547.

[26] J. H. Parry, *Trade and Dominion. The European Overseas Empires in the Eighteenth Century* (London 1971), 3–4.

of Spain in Europe during the seventeenth century was due largely to the crown's inability to increase its control over the economic resources of the Monarchy."[27]

Despite the mercantilist tendencies of the two metropolitan governments, neither Spain nor Portugal was able to mobilize sufficient resources either to become the effective metropole of its empire or to prevent rival states from engaging in commerce, legal or otherwise, with these overseas possessions. Accordingly, "manufactures" arose in practically all of their American continental dependencies. These responded to growing market demand in the *internal* trade, which has still not been given sufficient attention in the historical literature. We might describe this process as proto-industrialization, and it sprang up within the colonial system, complementary to rather than in opposition to whichever of the external trades predominated in any particular territory.[28]

From time to time, metropolitan governments instructed their overseas representatives to suppress these industries. Philip II (1556–98) had instructed Viceroy Francisco de Toledo of Peru in 1569 to put an end to them. After apprising himself of American needs, Toledo put the order to one side and, accepting realities, drew up his own regulations for the workshops in 1577, while seeking to improve working conditions. The king persisted but without success. In 1596, he instructed Viceroy Luis de Velasco to prohibit the establishment of new workshops but authorized those already in existence.[29] Whether these decrees were intended to be serious attempts or simply repeated statements of principles, which could rarely, if ever, be put into effect, is difficult to assess. The reality was that production continued, whether in workshops (*obrajes*) producing woolens or in artisan domestic form, usually producing cottons, or in other commodities such as ironware, foodstuffs, alcoholic beverages, furniture, stocking or hat-making, or ancillary to sugar-production as basic refineries. The woolen textile industry of Quito competed with southern Andean cities for the Peruvian and Chilean markets. The Upper Peruvian mining city of Potosí took its

---

[27] Kenneth J. Andrien, *Crisis and Decline. The Viceroyalty of Peru in the Seventeenth Century* (Albuquerque 1985), 204–5.

[28] Carlos Sempat Assadourian, *El sistema de la economía colonial. Mercado interno, regiones y espacio económico* (Lima 1982); Richard J. Salvucci, *Textiles and Capitalism in Mexico. An Economic History of the Obrajes, 1539–1840* (Princeton 1987); Juan Carlos Garavaglia, *Mercado interno y economía colonial* (Mexico City 1992).

[29] Fernando Silva Santisteban, *Los obrajes en el virreinato del Perú* (Lima 1964).

textiles mainly from not-too-distant Cochabamba. In New Spain, woolen manufacture in Querétaro, in response to the expansion of markets in the center-north and north after c. 1740 encouraged Puebla to transfer primarily to cottons, the raw material taken from the Gulf and Pacific coasts. City merchants financed raw-material production, putting-out to artisan producers, and the final distribution.[30]

Many of the predominant groups in the Americas, irrespective of origin, came to hold, as we shall see, significant commercial and financial interests in such industries and in the distribution of their products, regardless of whether they also had interests in the external trades, mining or agriculture. Among leading producers in Querétaro, supplying the mining zones, were Tomás de Ecala and Pedro de Septiém, Subdelegate of nearby Celaya-Salvatierra in the Intendancy of Guanajuato from 1796 to 1810. Production doubled or trebled during the transatlantic war years in the 1790s and 1800s. In the Guanajuato towns of San Miguel el Grande and Acámbaro, the owners of *obrajes* were mainly merchants and among the wealthiest residents.[31]

Portuguese America was no exception. It may come as a surprise, in view of the historiographical attention given to the plantation economy and the slavery tied to it, to discover that Brazil also experienced this phenomenon of protoindustrialization, despite the predominance of the export trade.[32] A range of activities, sometimes ancillary to the export trade, sprang up in coastal cities and through the interior. Sugar had to be refined before export and around 1800 refineries, often on plantations, existed by the end of the eighteenth century; gold had to be smelted into bars; slaves and free workers needed clothing and housing; furniture, carpentry, and vehicles were all needed; iron-making was vital in many spheres. Shipbuilding developed from the mid-seventeenth century,

---

[30] John C. Super, "Querétaro Obrajes: Industry and Society in Provincial Mexico, 1600–1800," *HAHR*, 56, ii (May 1976), 197–216; Javier Ortiz de la Tabla, "El obraje colonial ecuatoriano. Aproximación a su estudio," *RI*, nos. 149–150 (1977), 471–541.

[31] AGI México 1812, testimonio del expediente instruido sobre precaver robos en Querétaro, ff. 1–5, 12 obv-19, City Council to Viceroy Branciforte, Querétaro 27 October 1794 and 16 April 1795. AGI México 1809, Corregidor Miguel Domínguez to Viceroy Berenguer de Marquina, Querétaro 17 November 1801.

[32] A. V. Martins Filho and R. B. Martins, "Slavery in a Non-Export Economy: Nineteenth-Century Minas Gerais Revisited," *HAHR*, 63, iii (August 1983), 537–68; Douglas Cole Libby, "Proto-industrialisation in a Slave Society: The Case of Minas Gerais," *JLAS*, 23, i (1991), 1–35; John Dickenson and Roberta Delson, *Enterprise under Colonialism: A Study of Pioneer Industrialization in Brazil, 1700–1830* (Working Paper 12, Liverpool 1991).

principally in Salvador but also in Pernambuco, Alagoas, and Pará during the following century. Caulking, cordage, and sail-making accompanied this. Cottons were produced in land-locked Minas Gerais even before the gold boom of the 1690s–1760s. The royal policy of exploring the river systems and founding townships along the river banks facilitated settlement, transportation, and commerce, assisted by knowledge of the timing and levels of flooding. Southern Bahia, the Amazonian river network with its focus on Belém do Pará, and the Paraguay River and Pantanal area became of primary importance in this respect. That brought the interior, such as Goiás and Cuiabá, and even the far west into the commercial orbit.[33]

Minas Gerais, which dropped out of the export trade across the Atlantic after the disintegration of the gold boom, became the major center of textile and iron-working. Initially, gold stimulated the deployment of capital and labor into industries for the local and interregional markets. Pombal's projects for stimulating manufacture in the Portuguese homeland and his creation of three monopoly companies to develop Grão Pará-Maranhão in the Brazilian north, Pernambuco-Paraíba in the north-east, and whaling on the coast, did not lead to any metropolitan attempt to restrict or suppress colonial manufacturing. Within Minas Gerais, the large slave population, previously employed in gold-panning, was distributed among provincial industries. This province of around 320,000 inhabitants at the end of the eighteenth century accounted for one-fifth of Brazil's total population, estimated at between 2.3 to 4 million inhabitants. It also had the largest concentration of slaves, which from the 1770s were employed in neither mining nor plantations, and this continued to be so after Independence under the post-1822 Brazilian Empire. An explanation for that lay in the abundance of available land, which attracted the free population away from hiring their labor.[34]

Into this situation of local proto-industrialization and interregional trade came the Royal Decree of January 5, 1785, prohibiting the manufacture of cottons, woolens, lines, silks, and embroidery, as well as iron-working. It arrived at a time when 30,000 spinners were at work in Minas Gerais alone. How the Crown proposed to enforce such a decree was entirely unclear and what effects it had, if any, still need to be explained.

[33] Dickenson and Delson, *Enterprise*, 11–12, 15–16, 21–22, 25, 33–36, 47–48.
[34] Martins and Martins, "Slavery," 537–38, 541–43, 556–60. Libby, "Proto-Industrialisation," 4, 23–24; Dickenson and Delson, *Enterprise*, 23.

Although its issue pointed to an existing reality in Brazil, the Crown soon found that it needed to repeat the decree in 1788 and 1802, which suggests the difficulty of enforcement. We also need to know whether there was any connection between its arrival and the attempted rebellion in Minas Gerais in 1789. Whatever the case, the ministry, dominated by Rodrigo de Souza Coutinho during the 1790s, lifted the prohibition of iron-working in 1795. When in 1808 the royal family and government transferred to Brazil, the 1785 prohibition was lifted altogether and industry officially encouraged in the colony.[35]

In many respects, Portuguese home industry was hardly more advanced than Brazil's, although it did benefit from a high tariff, which shielded it from more technically advanced British producers. Even so, market capacity in Brazil remained restricted, even after the freeing of external trade in 1808 and 1810. British textiles still had to pay tariffs. Accordingly, Brazilian industrial production survived the transition from colony to Independence well into the nineteenth century.

MAGISTRATES IN GOVERNMENT

The principal judicial and administrative organ of Spanish royal authority was the *audiencia*, a high court that acted as administrative and legislative organ as well. As the Castilian Crown extended its authority in the Indies, this organ became the crucial unit of government. The audiencia was meant to be the instrument of Castilian absolutism in the Americas. Appreciation of the importance of the *audiencia*, first established in Santo Domingo in 1511, is fundamental to any understanding of how the Hispanic Monarchy functioned overseas. As in Spain, the *audiencia* combined both administrative and judicial functions, but in the Americas it acted as the viceroy's consultative committee (*Real Acuerdo*) and governed in the absence of a viceroy (the *audiencia gobernadora*). It also coordinated the fiscal bureaucracy through the position of its financial attorney (*fiscal de Real Hacienda*). The jurist, Juan de Solórzano Pereira (1575–1655), who from 1609 to 1627 acted as one of the magistrates (*oidores*) of the Audiencia of Lima, listed fourteen specific faculties of the Spanish American *audiencias*, all indicative of the court's decisive political role.[36]

---

[35] Dickenson and Delson, *Enterprise*, 13, 28, 30, 41–43.
[36] Solórzano Pereira's celebrated *Política indiana* appeared in 1647 in a compact Spanish version of the longer *De Indiarum Iure*, developing the Roman Law tradition in a Spanish imperial context.

Colonial laws, finally codified in 1682 as the Laws of the Indies, specified that *audiencia* magistrates were not to marry into local families within the territory of their jurisdiction. In practice, however, several did, with the result that local legislation in 1627, 1634, and 1688 repeated the proviso, though evidently without much success.[37] The result was heavy magisterial involvement in local society and its affairs. The discrepancy between theory and practice, law and reality, in Spanish America was outstanding. The whole system functioned for so long in the Americas because of the discrepancy. What happened in practice from day to day, receiving *de facto* sanction, enabled Spanish colonial America to sustain a delicate balance between despotism and anarchy. Should that tenuous equilibrium be removed, those latter tendencies could unpleasantly confront one another.

Solórzano argued that American *audiencias* had become more powerful than their peninsular progenitors. They acted as the principal administrative body and were the ultimate court of appeal before recourse to the Council of the Indies in Madrid. They supplied the senior members of the fiscal bureaucracy, were attached to the military command as judge advocates, exercised the *Patronato real* over ecclesiastical appointments, and one of their number performed the duty of judicial Protector of the Indians. Finally, they performed the judicial examination of district administrators at the end of their terms of office. Given this range of major functions, the Crown required regular scrutiny of their conduct in office.[38]

In Portuguese America, the situation was different. The *Relação* or High Court, modeled on the High Court of Oporto for northern Portugal and the *Casa de Suplicação* of Lisbon for the center, south, and Atlantic islands, was never as powerful as its Spanish American counterpart. In fact, only one existed in Portuguese America, the *Relação* of Bahia, belatedly established in 1606 under Habsburg rule, though not functioning between 1626 and 1652, when the north-east region was contested with the Dutch. Officially, ten magistrates dealt with civil cases, while an *ouvidor geral* (from 1696) heard criminal cases. The question remains why this should be so. The explanation may lie in the relative proximity of the enclave economy of coastal Brazil to the metropolis, in contrast to the inland locations of the Spanish American mainland. The relationship between the Governor-General of Brazil and

[37] Enrique Ruiz Guiñazú, *La magistratura indiana* (Buenos Aires 1916), 292–99.
[38] Juan de Solórzano y Pereira, *Política Indiana* (Antwerp 1647), 763–74.

the High Court was never satisfactorily resolved, despite the fact that both offices represented the Crown's desire to increase its control over the American dependencies.[39]

The High Court of Bahia did not assume a governmental role in the absence of a Governor-general or exercise political powers comparable to the *audiencias*. A second American *Relação* began operations in 1752 in Rio de Janeiro in response to the volume of judicial business resulting from the gold discoveries in the interior. The crown, however, had first legislated for this in 1734, but it took eighteen further years for it to become a reality, largely because of the shortage of funds in Lisbon. When in 1763 the crown transferred the capital to the south-eastern city, the Viceroy (the title preferred for the Governor-General after 1720) presided over the High Court. Along with the *Relação* of Goa, established in 1544 as the first overseas Court, these three *Relações* remained the only ones in the empire until the establishment of a further two in Maranhão in 1812 and Pernambuco in 1821. These latter foundations reflected the presence of the Royal government in Rio de Janeiro between 1808 and 1821. With the abandonment of Lisbon to the Napoleonic Army, the Crown raised the Rio *Relação* to the status of the *Casa de Suplicação*, which in Lisbon had exercised supreme judicial power over all the High Courts.[40]

The struggle with the Dutch after 1624 for control of Brazilian sugar and the Portuguese rebellion against Habsburg rule in 1640 formed the background to the decision to establish an Overseas Council in Lisbon in 1642. Although modeled on the Spanish Council of the Indies, it reflected governmental intention to keep foreign competitors out of Brazil and salvage what was left of the Asiatic territories after Dutch spoliation. The Overseas Council, however, had to compete with existing councils, notably the Councils of State and Finance, and jurisdictions to determine the extent of its authority. The *Relações* fell under the jurisdiction of the *Casa de Suplicação*; ecclesiastical affairs were supervised by the *Mesa da Consciência e Ordens*, established in 1532; while the highest court in the Monarchy continued to be the *Desembargo do Paço*, appointing to all judicial offices.[41]

---

[39] Stuart B. Schwartz, *Sovereignty and Society in Colonial Brazil. The High Court of Bahia and its Judges, 1609–1751* (Berkeley 1973), 102–3, 12–21, 245–46, 269.

[40] Myrup, *Power and Corruption*, 22–23.

[41] Myrup, *Power and Corruption*, 7–8, 20–29, 46.

The Portuguese and Hispanic monarchies shared the practice of appointing men with experience in various overseas territories to councils and courts. The Lisbon Overseas Council proved to be no exception, since those with experience in Brazil, Africa, or Asia held positions on it. Magistrates of the Spanish American *audiencias*, for their part, might look for promotion to the Council of the Indies in Madrid, although they would not always be successful in so doing. Myrup calculates that 146 individuals, whether noblemen or lawyers, manned the Overseas Council during the almost two centuries of its existence. Nobles predominated from 1643 until 1700, whereas lawyers formed the majority from 1751 until 1807, an indication of preference for professionals, especially for those with prior experience on the *Casa de Suplicação*. He makes the significant point that Portuguese lawyers "never gained the prestige and power of their Spanish counterparts and cannot necessarily be considered a separate lettered class."[42]

In both Monarchies, we should be wary of assuming that those who manned the formal institutions in the overseas territories constituted a caste apart from the local élites. Myrup's central argument concerning the function of local power networks and their wider linkages not only corroborates other studies of the Lusitanian Monarchy but also provides a viable basis of comparison with the Hispanic Monarchy, at least until the second half of the eighteenth century. Patronage networks of varying types, such as those that Cañeque has identified as stemming from the viceregal court in Mexico City, and personal relationships complemented the formal institutions. Such linkages bound the Portuguese Monarchy together, thereby enabling its long survival through tempestuous times.[43] Mercantile, financial, and family linkages were not exactly informal; they were conventional, involving trust earned through knowledge and personal contacts.[44] Beneficiaries of such linkages wanted government to bend in their direction.

[42] Myrup, *Power and Corruption*, 43–44, 50–53.
[43] Myrup, *Power and Corruption*, 34, 38, 71. Cañeque, *The King's Living Image*, 158–59: "Although relations of patronage and clientage were central to the functioning of colonial society, these are, however, aspects that have hardly been studied by historians ... Patron-client ties and networks were a way of organizing and regulating power relationships in a society where the distribution of power was not completely institutionalized."
[44] Xabier Lamikiz, *Trade and Trust in the Eighteenth-Century Atlantic World. Spanish Merchants and Their Overseas Networks* (Woodbridge 2010), on the trust and friendships among merchants of common peninsular-provincial ancestry.

FAMILIES, PROPERTIES, OFFICES, BUSINESS

Incoming peninsular officials tended to become co-opted into these American networks, the members of which often had different ways of thinking to metropolitan policy-makers. If in-coming administrators wished to avoid conflict – and most did – they would have to take these interests and views into consideration. The financial and military capacity of metropolitan Spain and Portugal rarely permitted direct repression. Instead, the long duration of Iberian rule in the Americas may be explained more by negotiation than by force or fear.[45]

Members of the Hispanic-American élite found informal ways of gaining access to positions technically reserved for *peninsulares*. The municipal councils of Mexico City and Puebla, however, failed in 1636 and 1637 to persuade Olivares that one-half of *audiencia* positions in Mexico City, Guadalajara, Guatemala, and Manila should be reserved for Americans in return for a vote of funds. Although Atlantic transit between Spain and the Indies considerably diminished in the periods from 1606–10 and 1646–50, the American Empire did not drift apart. Even when Spain was at its weakest, between the 1650s and the 1680s, the Monarchy as a whole remained intact. Delgado Riba argues for the successful establishment of equilibrium between governmental objectives and colonial interests, that is, between official policy and local perceptions.[46]

Metropolitan financial needs in the long run overruled prohibitions. Between 1701 and 1750, the Crown appointed 108 Americans to 136 *audiencia* positions in Lima. In 1767, eight of the twelve *oidores* (magistrates) in the Audiencia of Mexico were Americans.[47] Such a situation suggests that it might have been more rewarding to reformulate Spanish monarchical government in the Americas less in terms of absolutist theory and more with respect to what was actually happening on the spot.

Traditionally, *audiencia* positions had not been up for sale. Sales had, however, taken place. Proof of this was the Crown's prohibition of sales of

---

[45] Note the essays in Christine Daniels and Michael J. Kennedy (eds.), *Negotiated Empires. Centre and Peripheries in the Americas, 1500–1820* (New York and London 2002).

[46] Joseph M. Delgado Riba, *Dinámicas imperiales (1650–1796). España, América y Europa en el cambio institucional del sistema colonial español* (Barcelona 2007), 18–22.

[47] Guillermo Lohmann Villena, *Los ministros de la Audiencia de Lima en el reinado de los Borbones (1700–1821)* (Seville 1974), xxii–xxvii. M. A. Burkholder and D. S. Chandler, "Creole Appointments and the Sale of Audiencia Positions in the Spanish Empire under the Early Bourbons, 1701–1750," *JLAS*, 4, ii (November 1972), 187–206.

judicial and fiscal offices in 1689. The financial needs of the war against France led to royal permission for sales in 1692. Philip V, inheriting a hard-pressed treasury, sold both vacant positions and the rights to future offices. The Crown also created a fluid number of "supernumaries" and auctioned access to them. These individuals would then have the right to take places that subsequently became vacant. The largest number of sales took place in 1706–11, grim war years, and in 1740–50, during the War of the Austrian Succession and its aftermath. Between 1707 and 1711, seven Americans born in New Spain purchased judicial office on the Audiencia of Mexico. During the 1740s, one half of the membership of the Audiencia of Mexico consisted of Americans. By 1750, the Crown had earned one million pesos from the sale of one-quarter of all American *audiencia* positions.[48]

Family and commercial networks penetrated senior and junior administrative positions. Joseph Joaquín de Uribe y Castrejón, for instance, was a product of the *Colegio Mayor del Arzobispo* in the University of Salamanca. Appointed *oidor* of the Audiencia of Mexico in 1701, he took a Mexican wife, a hacienda-owner in the Puebla district of Huejotzingo. By 1716, Uribe had become the owner of the Hacienda de San Juan Molina and the Rancho de Aitic in the Tlaxcala district of Iztacuixtla, with adjacent mills. He became *alcalde mayor* of Puebla between 1723 and 1726. A royal license on December 22, 1734 permitted the married couple to found an entailed estate from their joint properties. Uribe died in 1738 on another of his properties, the Hacienda de Atoyac in Puebla. The Archbishop-Viceroy's report on his death to the metropolitan government apparently saw no reason to mention the late *oidor*'s matrimonial and property connection, perhaps because they were not unusual. Uribe's three daughters married men holding administrative positions. The first married into the Lardizábal family; the second's husband became an *oidor* of the Audiencia of Guadalajara in 1740; the third married into a Venezuelan cacao-planting family, and her husband, son of the Marqués del Toro, purchased the office of *oidor supernumerario* in the Audiencia of Mexico in 1741, and took office two years later. Joseph Rodríguez del Toro, born in 1715 and educated at the University of Salamanca, still held this office in 1770, when his daughter

---

[48] J. H. Parry, *The Sale of Public Office in the Spanish Indies under the Habsburgs* (Berkeley 1953), 24–25. Mark A. Burkholder and D. S. Chandler, *From Impotence to Authority. The Spanish Crown and the American Audiencias, 1687–1808* (Columbia, Missouri, and London 1977), 28–29. Burkholder and Chandler, "Creole Appointments," 189–92, 202.

married, with special royal license, the Corregidor of Oaxaca (1769–74), Pedro de Pineda. One of Uribe's sons married the daughter of Domingo Válcarcel, *alcalde del crimen* (from 1728) and *oidor* of the Audiencia of Mexico (from 1736).[49] Valcárcel had been a product of the Colegio Mayor de San Ildefonso at the University of Alcalá de Henares. His father and grandfather had served on the Council of Castile. From his position as *oidor* in Mexico, Valcárcel purchased a royal dispensation to marry in 1732 the daughter of the Conde de Santiago de Calimaya, one of the Mexican nobility, whose title originated in 1616. Viceroy Conde de Revillagigedo the Elder (1746–55) described Valcárcel, candidate for promotion to the Council of the Indies, as too involved in Mexican family interests to have an impartial judgment. His wife, in any case, opposed transfer to the peninsula. Valcárcel retired in 1778.[50]

The Lardizábal family descended from Colonel Miguel de Lardizábal, a Basque immigrant from Guipúzcoa, whose four sons made good marriages and secured high positions. His first son married the daughter of the President of the Audiencia of Santo Domingo. Their son, born in Veracruz in 1733, became *alcalde mayor* of Tehuantepec in 1766. Lardizábal's second son became senior councilor on the Council of the Indies; his third son, José Antonio Lardizábal y Elorza, became Bishop of Puebla in 1723–33. The fourth son, Francisco, married into the Uribe family of landowners in Tlaxcala and Puebla. He was the father of two brothers who would gain importance during the crisis years of the Monarchy at the beginning of the nineteenth century. Manuel de Lardizábal y Uribe, born at the Hacienda de San Juan Molino, rose to become *fiscal* of the Council of Castile under Charles IV. Miguel de Lardizábal y Uribe, born in Puebla, represented Mexico on the Supreme Central Junta in 1809, which led Spanish Patriot resistance to Napoleonic rule in Spain. He was a member of the First Regency Council of 1810–11, a bitter opponent of the Liberals in the Constituent Cortes of 1810–13,

---

[49] Archivo General de Indias (Seville), Audiencia de México, legajos 452; 638; 1128, *consultas*, license granted on 31 May 1770; and 1506. AGI Escribanía de Cámara, leg. 191ª. Archivo General de la Nación (Mexico City), Ramo Virreyes, Primera Serie, tomo 4, no. 458, 16 March 1759. Isabel González Sánchez, *Haciendas y Ranchos de Tlaxcala en 1712* (Mexico City 1969), 17, 160, 165.

[50] AGI México 452. J. Ignacio Rubio Mañé, *Introducción al estudio de los virreyes de Nueva España*, 4 vols. (Mexico City 1959–61), vol. II, 65. Doris M. Ladd, *The Mexican Nobility at Independence, 1780–1826* (Austin 1976), 215–16.

and duly became Ferdinand VII's Minister of the Indies in 1814–15, at the beginning of the first restored absolutist regime.[51]

Many *peninsulares* married American wives and thereby integrated into their families. Robert Ferry has drawn attention to the habit in Venezuelan landed and business families of seeking immigrant husbands from Spain for their American daughters in the case of Caracas and its agricultural zone. In such a way, they hoped to distinguish the family and at the same time bring in further commercial contacts.[52] Although Venezuela was not one of Spain's principal American territories, cacao production from the 1630s to 1740s had created substantial fortunes among hacienda-owners in the Province of Caracas, using African slave labor, through the lucrative trade to New Spain and the contraband trade to Dutch Curaçao. The metropolitan government's efforts to re-channel trade toward the peninsula by creating the monopoly Guipúzcoa Company in 1728 and forcing down prices aroused hostility among a range of planters. A brief protest movement in 1749 was treated as rebellion and repressed in 1750–53, with long-lasting and bitter memories. The élites salvaged their position by coming to an accommodation with the Ensenada administration in Madrid.[53]

Credit and family ties tended to be interconnected; they lay at the heart of these linkages. Merchants in the Hispanic dominions acquired a range of interests, which extended from import of European goods through Veracruz or Callao to the financing of mine-production, the textile trades, and internal commerce. Essentially, the interests of the networks operating in Spanish America were American-oriented; merchants of peninsula origin did not usually aspire to return to the peninsula in the way senior ecclesiastics or administrators did in order to further their careers. Mercantile interests spread through New Spain, for example, and outwards from Mexico City during the course of the seventeenth century.[54]

---

[51] AGI Indiferente General 172, *memoriales de pretendientes a corregimientos y alcaldías mayores* (no dates). Archivo General de Notarías (Puebla) [AGNP], legajo 235 (1759–65), Registry of Deeds, Puebla 25 August 1759, 30 December 1760; Registry of Wills, Puebla 20 January 1758.

[52] Robert J. Ferry, *The Colonial Elite of Early Caracas. Formation and Crisis, 1567–1767* (Berkeley, Los Angeles, London 1989), 8.

[53] Ferry, *Colonial Elite*, 45–46, 63–71, 139–74, 184–92, 252–56.

[54] Louisa Schell Hoberman, *Mexico's Merchant Elite, 1590–1660. Silver, State and Society* (Durham, NC 1991), 273, notes 17 and 18. John Kicza, *Colonial Entrepreneurs: Families and Business in Bourbon Mexico City* (Albuquerque 1985). Guillermina del Valle Pavón (coordinator), *Mercaderes, comercio y consulados de Nueva España en el siglo XVIII* (Mexico City 2003), 8.

Eighteenth-century linkages broadened and deepened in response to population recovery and the growth of the economy. In New Spain, which provided the most striking instance of both, merchant-financiers took the lead in forming contracts and associations, not only with one another but also throughout the economy and the royal administration. Francisco Ignacio de Yraeta was one of the most important figures. His company involved two other key Spanish merchants, José de Yraeta and Gabriel de Iturbe, both of Basque origin. This company regularly traded with commercial houses in Cádiz and with two in Bilbao, although not as their subordinates. The company also operated the sugar refinery of San Nicolás Tolentino in the Puebla district of Izúcar, the largest of the Hispanic properties in the area. Since the sugar plantation was surrounded by Indian *pueblo* lands, there were constant disputes between the proprietors and the villagers over land usage and access to the waters of the Río Atoyac, especially from the 1790s. Yraeta at that time had become interested in the techniques employed in sugar production in Cuba.[55] This merchant also had financial and commercial interests in Oaxaca through the mediation of the district administrators. Yraeta and his heirs traded along the Pacific coast, above all to Guayaquil and Callao, across the Pacific to Manila, and through the Caribbean to Havana, New Orleans, and other positions. They exported Oaxacan cochineal dye and Guatemalan indigo, and marketed the cotton cloth of the Oaxaca sierra. Rumor had it that they also took part in the clandestine trade with British Jamaica.[56]

Iturbe and Iraeta happened to be the only two Mexico City merchants in favor of the metropolitan government's *comercio libre* policy. It is not entirely clear why this should be so. Evidently, they did not feel threatened by it, as did most members of the Consulado. Perhaps the scale of their operations secured them from unexpected reverses of fortune. In the port of Veracruz, Iraeta's contacts were Pedro Miguel de Echeverría and Francisco Guerra y Agreda, who would become leading members of the newly established Consulado there after 1795. Their commercial interests within New Spain extended to the struggling Oaxaca mining industry, which operated on a much smaller scale than the industry of central and

---

[55] Maria Cristina Torales Pacheco (co-ordinadora), *La Compañía de Comercio de Francisco Ignacio de Yraeta (1767–1797)*, 2 vols. (Mexico City 1985), vol. 1, 131–59, 185–202.

[56] John Kicza, "Mexican Merchants and their Links to Spain, 1750–1850," in Kenneth J. Andrien and Lyman L. Johnson (eds.), *The Political Economy of Spanish America in the Age of Revolution, 1750–1850* (Albuquerque 1994), 115–36: see pp. 117–19.

north-central Mexico. In Oaxaca, they did business with the Yrizar brothers and Colonel Victores de Manero, dependent of Juan María García,
business associate of Fausto de Corres, *alcalde mayor* of the cochineal
district of Miahuatlán, south of the central valleys of Oaxaca. Iraeta
guaranteed the financial operations of García and Manero in Mexico
City, while these two merchants attended to the payment or collection
of Iraeta's bills of exchange in Oaxaca. Iraeta's main contact in Oaxaca,
over three decades, was Alonso Magro, from 1769 to 1797. Magro, with
his political base on the city council in the 1770s and 1780s, was one of the
city's most powerful merchants. He became the Consulado of Mexico's
agent in the city in 1793. Pablo Ortega, *alcalde mayor* of Villa Alta from
1784 to 1789, subsequently acted as Iraeta's business administrator in the
cotton-textile trade for the Bajío and the mining districts. This would be
continued by Bernardino Bonavía, Subdelegate under the Intendant system from 1790 to 1796. Magro, for his part, played the role of intermediary between Iraeta and the Guatemalan merchants and the cacao traders
of Soconusco.[57]

Another peninsular merchant of Oaxaca, Tomás López Ortigosa, similarly had an extensive commercial network. He imported European textiles through Veracruz and re-exported them to Guatemala, where his
business associate was none other than the Marqués de Aycinena, the
most powerful merchant in that Kingdom. López Ortigosa also imported
iron products from Vizcaya through Veracruz for use in the mines at
Ixtepejí, in the sierra north of Oaxaca City. The return cargo would be
cochineal dye from the Pacific district of Jicayán.[58]

LOCAL ÉLITES AND MUNICIPALITIES

Town and city councils became expressions of local élite interests.
The royal authorities in both Monarchies sought to control them as best
they could at long distance. The municipalities reflected *ancien régime*
juridical and political structures, since they boasted royal charters and
delineations of privileges. The town authorities in Spain collected the

---

[57] Archivo General del Poder Ejecutivo del Estado de Oaxaca [AGEPEO formerly AGEO],
Real Intendencia, Section 1, leg. 10 (1792–1810), exp. 37, *liquidación de los débitos de
D. Bernardino Bonavía, subdelegado que fue del partido de Villa Alta (1799)*. Torales,
Compañía de Comercio, I, 58.

[58] Ana Carolina Ibarra, *El cabildo catedral de Antequera, Oaxaca, y el movimiento insurgente* (Zamora, Michoacán, 2000), 47. His son, José López Ortigosa, was Governor of
the State of Oaxaca six times between 1830 and 1846.

indirect and consumption taxes upon which the royal government so greatly depended.[59] It is important to throw the focus on their American counterparts because they weathered the crisis of the colonial regime through the 1810s and early 1820s, although not unchanged.

Municipalities (*senados da câmara*) in the Portuguese imperial world generally acquired greater political weight than their Spanish American counterparts (*cabildos* or *ayuntamientos*), largely because of the long absence of higher bureaucratic and judicial structures in the former. C. R. Boxer compared the Spanish and Portuguese colonial municipalities in the following way:

Whereas in Spanish America by the beginning of the seventeenth century most municipal posts had become proprietary and hereditary through the sale of office, this transformation never occurred in the Portuguese *câmaras*. Nor were the Portuguese colonial *câmaras* subjected to frequent inspection by visiting Commissioners, as were many of the Spanish colonial *cabildos*. The Spanish American *Audiencia*, or High Court, with its *oidores* exercised much closer financial and administrative supervision over the *cabildos* than did the Portuguese colonial *Relação* over the *câmaras*.[60]

The Portuguese Crown initiated the process of regulating the municipal councils in the Lusitanian Monarchy in accordance with its General Rules of 1504. This provided for the annual election by ballot of their members – but in the presence of a royal magistrate. Outside Portugal, the overseas councils were modeled on those of Lisbon and Oporto, and they had the right to correspond with the Crown directly, rather than through the governors of provinces or viceroy. There would be fifteen of these *ouvidores* in each of the Brazilian provincial Captaincies. In many respects, the Crown sought to counterbalance the *senados da câmara* and the senior royal officials. The councils, for instance, had a marked tendency to encroach on functions technically the preserve of the royal administration and judiciary, resulting in a repeated jockeying for position. In Brazil, the functions of the *senado da câmara* also extended to slave control.[61]

In both empires, royal officials might come and go, as they followed their career patterns throughout their respective Monarchy's territories,

[59] Grafe, *Distant Tyrannies*, 243–44.

[60] C. R. Boxer, *Portuguese Society in the Tropics: The Municipal Councils of Goa, Macao, Bahia and Luanda, 1510–1800* (Madison 1965), 148.

[61] António Manuel Hespanha, *História de Portugal Moderno: político e institucional* (Lisbon 1995), 155–73 deals with the municipalities. A. J. R. Russell-Wood, "Local Government in Portuguese America," *CSSH*, 16, no. 2 (March 1974), 187–231: pp. 188–89.

including those of the peninsula. Municipal councils, however, always remained and with a certain amount of continuity of personnel. Russell-Wood rightly stresses the municipal councils' stabilizing effect:

> They offered stability in a highly mobile empire, a voice at Court for local interests, and reassurance of Portuguese citizenship for the large number of soldiers, sailors, and merchants who composed the human factor in the demographic flux and re-flux which characterised the Portuguese seaborne empire.[62]

Portuguese merchants in Bahia were involved in the processes of sugar production by extending credit to planters and overseeing marketing. Their capacity for diversification through the various sectors of the local economy, from sugar refining-plants to urban-property ownership, remained a striking feature. Activities such as these helped to explain the absorption of merchants into the landed elites. The Crown specifically stated in 1740 that merchants were eligible for municipal and bureau-cratic office. In the municipal councils of Bahia, they gained greater influence in the latter part of the eighteenth century. There were some 150 merchants, most of them of Portuguese origin, in Salvador, out of a total city population of around 7000. A large proportion (c. 45 percent) were converted Jews (*cristais nôvos*). Such diversification helps to explain why the Portuguese colonial councils were never as closed as the oligar-chies dominating Spanish American municipalities until at least the latter part of the eighteenth century. The Portuguese Crown's insistence that Portuguese-born residents should have an equal footing on the electoral lists to Brazilians significantly needed to be repeated at least three times, in 1709, 1711, and 1746.[63] As the gold boom from the 1690s onward drew population inland, the Crown authorized the establishment of municipal councils in the interior provinces of Minas Gerais, Mato Grosso, and Goiás and inland in Bahia. The two Minas Gerais towns of Vila Rica (the future Ouro Preto from 1823) and Sabará, for instance, received councils in 1711.[64]

The municipalities appointed ordinary justices (*juízes ordinarios*) to cope with local cases. The Portuguese Crown, however, instituted a higher

---

[62] Russell-Wood, "Local Government," 188–89. The *pelourinho*, or whipping-post, became the symbol of municipal authority in Brazil.

[63] C. R. Boxer, *Portuguese Seaborne Empire*, 273, 285. R. Flory and D. G. Smith, "Bahian Merchant Planters in the Seventeenth and Eighteenth Centuries," *HAHR*, 58, iv (November 1978), 571–94: see pp. 574, 576, 585. J. N. Kennedy, "Bahian Elites, 1750–1822," *HAHR*, 53, iii (August 1973), 415–39: see p. 421.

[64] Russell-Wood, "Local Government," 192–93, 196.

level above them, in order to prevent collusion between existing administrators and the principal families of Bahía. The first was the *juíz de fora* of Salvador in 1695, the title implying an appointment from "outside." Others would follow in Olinda, Minas Gerais, and Rio de Janeiro. In the following year, the crown sought even greater control over the Salvador municipality by authorizing the *Relação* to select its members. Relations between the municipality and the High Court, located in the same city, had for long been uneven, although the cost of referring cases to Lisbon outweighed opposition to having a High Court in Brazil. Similarly, in 1696, the Crown appointed an *ouvidor geral* to supervise judicial administration in the Captaincy of Bahía. Others followed in response to repeated unruliness in the mining zones and on the expanding southern and western frontiers, but soon there appeared to be a conspiracy between royal officials and freebooters to disobey laws emanating from above. By 1714, there were four in Minas Gerais.[65]

The degree of effective royal supervision varied according to empire and to the social and economic utility of the component provinces. A Spanish official, the *corregidor*, convened and presided over the *cabildos*, with the intention of denying the élites free control of political space. This official became the essential channel for the assertion of royal control. Although viceroys generally appointed them, the Crown reserved the right to appoint to the most important *corregimientos*, such as Mexico City and Zacatecas, Cuzco and Arequipa. The royal government codified regulations in the Laws of the Indies.[66] Even so, the city council of Mexico City was controlled, by the late 1620s, by a tightly knit group of families, who had inherited or purchased their offices. The seventeenth-century councilors of Popayán in southern New Granada had either purchased their offices from the Crown or been elected (annually) by proprietary members and outgoing councilors. By the 1630s, leading families were in control there, even though the composition of the council still fluctuated, since membership, which was honorary, proved to be inconvenient for landowners and long-distance traders.[67] In 1696, the Lisbon government attempted to clip the freedom of action of the *senados da câmara* by

---

[65] Schwartz, *Sovereignty and Society*, 257–59, 264–67.

[66] J. M. Zamora y Coronado, *Biblioteca de legislación ultramarina en forma de diccionario alfabético*, 6 tomes (Madrid 1844–49), Tomo II, 450, 454, 459–60: Laws II, 12, and 14 of Title 10, Book IV, dated from 1528–1587. Mark A. Burkholder and Lyman L. Johnson, *Colonial Latin America* (New York 1990), 76–77.

[67] Louisa S. Hoberman, "Merchants in Seventeenth-Century Mexico City: A Preliminary Portrait," *HAHR*, 57, no. 3 (1977), 479–503: p. 482. Peter Marzahl, "Creoles and

specifying that councilors were to be annually selected by governors on
the basis of three-yearly voting lists by heads of households. A royal-
appointee would preside over the councils.[68]

THE EXAMPLE OF THE CITY OF PUEBLA

In Puebla, a city that was in this respect no exception, an intimate relationship between landowning families, merchants, and municipal office-
holders developed from an early date. We could compare it, for instance,
with the capital city of the Kingdom of Guatemala, or with Medellín in
New Granada.[69] Situated in the heart of what had been a densely populated area of indigenous villages at the time of Conquest, the city of Puebla
lay relatively close to Mexico City. A Hispanic foundation, Puebla had its
own characteristics and networks, which prevented it from ever becoming
a subsidiary of Mexico City. Its immediate linkage was to the port of
Veracruz, and thence to Havana and Spain. Several other major cities –
Jalapa, Orizaba, Córdoba – stood along the two routes to Veracruz, each
with their own councils, principal families, and connections.
The economic interests of its city notables explain this clearly when we
look at textile production in New Spain and the areas of cotton supply on
the Gulf and Pacific coasts.[70]

By 1797, the city of Puebla reached an estimated total of 52,717
inhabitants. The Intendancy, established in 1786, contained as many as
811,285 inhabitants, of which around two-thirds were officially classified
as "Indians." The diocese, extending beyond the Intendancy boundaries,
yielded the second largest revenues after the Archdiocese of Mexico.
The large number of haciendas (764) suggested small or medium size,
especially since there were even more ranches (911) formed in the seventeenth and eighteenth centuries on less fertile soil on the highland slopes.

Government: the Cabildo of Popayán," *HAHR*, 636–56: pp. 650–51. Russell-Wood,
"Local Government in Portuguese America," 189–90.

[68] Stuart B. Schwartz, *Sugar Plantation in the Formation of Brazilian Society, 1550–1835*
(Cambridge 1985), 277.

[69] José Manuel Santos Pérez, *Élites, Poder Local y Régimen Colonial. El cabildo y los
regidores de Santiago de Guatemala, 1700–1787* (Cádiz and South Woodstock,
Vermont, 1999), which deals with the sale of municipal office, 65–122, and matrimonial
connections, 125–64; Anexos, 329–63. See also Ann Twinam, "Enterprises and Elites in
Eighteenth-Century Medellín," *HAHR*, 59, no. 3 (August 1979), 444–75.

[70] See Frances J. Ramos, *Identity, Ritual, and Power in Colonial Puebla* (Tucson 2012), and
Ida Altman, "Reconsidering the Center. Puebla and Mexico City, 1550–1650," in
Daniels and Kennedy, *Negotiated Empires*, 43–58.

The main cereal zones lay in the central valleys. The towns of Huejotzingo and Atlixco, both with a mild climate and access to water, produced the best wheat and attracted Hispanic settlement.[71]

Puebla's connection with the upland city of Orizaba and the port of Veracruz explained the careers of several of its key merchants. Joseph de Bringas Manzaneda and Pablo Escandón, merchants from Orizaba, joined the Puebla élite in the 1760s and 1790s, respectively. The former's marriage into the Puebla family of José Antonio de Ravanillo, another merchant, deepened his business activities. Ravanillo's financial guarantor had been Francisco Lardizábal y Elorza, the Bishop's brother. Escandón originated from Asturias, arriving in New Spain in his twenties during the 1790s. He married into Jalapa's Garmendia family, which administered the Royal Tobacco monopoly. His principal activity was investment in cotton cultivation in three of the Gulf coast districts. He became town councilor and constable (*alcalde ordinario*) of Orizaba and captain of the Patriotic Militia during the counterinsurgency of the 1810s. In Puebla, he became consular deputy and a leader of the business community, along with Joaquín Haro y Portillo, future deputy to the Madrid Cortes in 1820. The latter had come from Santander on the Cantabrian coast of northern Spain in 1777 and married into the long-established Tamariz family of Puebla in 1797. Haro owned five estates of his own and acquired control of his wife's entail in the maize-producing district of Tepeaca plus a flour mill and bakery. He held municipal office in Puebla from 1802 until his death in 1825. By 1807, he had become one of Puebla's principal cotton dealers, importing from the Gulf zone, and distributing cotton textiles. The Escandóns continued to be active businessmen well into the nineteenth century.[72]

---

[71] Archivo General de Notarías (Puebla), legajo 68 (1772–90): Registro Atlixco, Villa de Carrión 31 December 1779 and 19 June 1780. Enrique Florescano and Isabel Gil Sánchez (eds.), *Descripciones económicas regionales del centro, sureste y sur, 1766–1827* (Mexico City 1976), 162–68, 172–73. Juan Carlos Garavaglia and Juan Carlos Grosso, "La región de Puebla/Tlaxcala en la economía novohispeana (1670–1821)," *HM*, XXXV (1986), 549–600.

[72] AGNP legajo 146, caja 2 (1806–7), notaría. 2, Puebla 10 July 1806; legajo 235 (1759–65): Registry of Deeds, Puebla 17 September and 30 October 1760; legajo 170, caja 1 (1822–23); legajo 241 (1786–88), Legal Titles, Puebla 20 October 1787. Archivo del Registro Público (Puebla): Libro de Censos, no. 40 (1811–15), ff. 31v-37v, Puebla 30 August 1811: no. 41 (1811–15), ff. 196–98v, Puebla 4 June 1813. Archivo Histórico Municipal (Puebla) [AHMP], Tomo 113 expediente sobre alhóndigas (1800–10), L. 1211 (1804), f. 118; Tomo 169, expediente sobre abastos (1810–16), L. 1684 (November 1810),

The Ovando family entail of four Tepeaca haciendas dated from 1728. This family had a tradition of municipal office-holding: Agustín Ovando, born in Puebla in 1745, held office in 1773–92 and his son, Joaquín, was elected constable for 1797–98. He was one of the 140 estate-owners and merchants who, in 1811, contributed a substantial sum toward the maintenance of the "Volunteers of Ferdinand VII" for the defense of the city against encroaching insurgents.[73] James Furlong, a Catholic refugee from Belfast in the 1760s, married in Puebla in 1772. His son, José Sebastián, city councilor in 1811–12, was listed in 1813 as a leading merchant and owned a bakery. His grandson, Vicente, became an *alcalde ordinario* in 1818, 1823, and 1824, serving also as a militia captain. Patricio and Cosme Furlong both became Governors of the State of Puebla under the First Federal Republic, the former in 1829 and 1833, the latter in 1834 and 1853. Patricio had been one of eight city councilors in 1823.[74]

Combatting the Insurgency, members of the Puebla élite assisted in managing the transfer from Spanish dependency to independent state after 1821, staffing not only the city council but also the institutions of the Federal Republic, while continuing to uphold their business interests. The ease with which peninsular merchants merged into the prominent families never ceases to impress. Continuity over several generations points to an integrated and self-renewing élite, perhaps in contrast to a perceived instability in the mining districts further to the north of Mexico City.

THE BUSINESS COMMUNITIES OF PERU

In the Viceroyalty of Peru (before the division of the Perus in 1776), the dominant nexus was between the mercantile community of Lima, as creditors, and the silver-miners of Potosí in Upper Peru.

ff. 1–2v; Libro de Cabildos 82 (1813), ff. 231–33v, Puebla 3 May 1813; 92/1 (January–June 1823), ff. 86–86v, 459.

[73] AHMP, Tomo 117, expedientes sobre servicio militar (1810–11),L. 1288, ff. 206–18v, 240–56, Puebla 25 May 1811; Libro de Cabildos 83 (1814), *alcaldes ordinarios* (1788–1814), and cabildo members (1814).

[74] AHMP, Tomo 117, servicio military, f. 72, Puebla 19 December 1810; Libro de Cabildos 80 (1811), ff. 1–18, Puebla 2 January 1811; 81 (1812), ff. 14v-16, 23, 29, 79–83; 82 (1813), ff. 231–33v; 92/1 (January–June 1823), ff. 1–17; 92/2 (July–December 1823), f. 406v; 93/1 (January–June 1824, ff.3v-4.

For generations, the peninsular merchants who carried goods to Peru from Spain, and their agents in Lima, had enjoyed the profits to be reaped from a market in which artificial scarcity, and consequent high prices, had gone hand-in-hand with the various forms of production from competition, including forced sales to rural populations (the *repartimientos*) and regulations forbidding some forms of local manufacture and intercolonial trade. The advent of uncontrolled imports, first with the implementation of the *Reglamento de comercio libre* and later with the growth of contraband trade carried directly to the Pacific by foreign merchants, fundamentally disrupted this system.[75]

The vital sub-link was the mercury mine of Huancavelica in Lower Peru for the so-called amalgamation (or "patio") process in extracting silver from the ore. Related to this central-southern Andean complex were the cereal and clothing suppliers of Cuzco (Lower Peru) and Cochabamba and other Upper Peruvian localities. Cotton came from the Santa Cruz district in the eastern lowlands beyond the Andean chain.[76] Marks argues for a division between Atlantic and Pacific interests in the later eighteenth and early nineteenth centuries: "metropolitan merchants" – ship-owners and agents largely resident in Spain, though sometimes in Lima for long periods, had direct ties with the Consulado of Cádiz; "*limeño* merchants," by contrast, were Lima residents, usually *peninsulares*, many of whom had crossed over to Peru in the 1750s and 1760s, primarily engaged in the Pacific trade. By the 1780s, their leading figure was the Conde de San Isidro, who had strong interests in the interior trade, particularly the *repartimientos* distributed to Indian communities by their *corregidores*.[77]

Bourbon Ministers intended to tighten Peru's administration and break open the commercial monopolies and inland trades. They sought to do this by enabling the *Cinco Gremios Mayores de Madrid*, an association of five trading corporations at the center of the imperial capital's commercial and (informal) banking system, to trade in Peru. The royal government, in 1784, authorized the *Cinco Gremios* to commence operations in the prosperous southern city of Arequipa, and two years later in Lima. By 1795, the *Cinco Gremios* controlled one-third of the trade of Peru.[78]

---

[75] Marks, *Deconstructing Legitimacy*, 345.
[76] Brooke Larsen, *Colonialism and Agrarian Transformation in Bolivia. Cochabamba, 1550–1900* (Princeton 1988), 67–74, 85.
[77] Marks, *Deconstructing Legitimacy*, 37, 44 note 83, 55–115: see pp. 69 and 101.
[78] Miguel Capella Martínez y A. Matilla Tascón, *Los Cinco Gremios Mayores de Madrid. Estudio crítico-histórico* (Madrid 1957). José Miguel Medrano y Carlos Malamud Rickles, "Las actividades de los Cinco Gremios Mayores en Perú. Apuntes preliminares," *RI*, XLVIII, núms. 182–183 (enero-agosto 1988), 421–34, see pp. 427–28, 432. Jorge Pinto Rodríguez, "Los Cinco Gremios Mayores de Madrid y el comercio

With the same objective in mind, the royal government authorized the formation of the Royal Philippine Company on March 10, 1785 and sanctioned its trading with Peru. This enabled Lima merchants to send domestic (and imported) produce across the Pacific to Manila in Company ships in return for Asiatic goods, despite recurrent protests from the transatlantic merchants. Pedro de Abadía, the Philippine Company Factor in Lima, became one of the most influential figures in the city by 1806.[79] Commercial and institutional changes apart, the role of the Consulado of Lima continued to be of the utmost significance to the royal government.[80]

Lima, by the last decades of the colonial era, no longer held the monopoly of commercial activity in Peru. Several merchants took up residence in Arequipa, and maintained contacts in Cádiz. This city did not have disparities of wealth and status comparable to those in Lima or Mexico City. It had few exceedingly rich families and there was a good deal of interconnection between land-ownership, commercial activity, and professional status. The three most important of the Arequipa families were the Moscosos, the Goyeneches, and the Tristáns. Members of all three families played active roles in the political, economic, religious, and military history of the late colonial and early republican periods in Peru.[81] Juan Manuel Moscoso was Bishop of Cuzco at the time of the Tupac Amaru Rebellion of 1780–81. His nephew, Lieutenant-Colonel Josef Gabriel Moscoso, became Intendant of Arequipa in 1810 and strongly supported Viceroy Abascal's opposition to the South American autonomists and separatists during the following years. The Cuzco Rebellion of 1814–15, however, spread rapidly through the southern Andes and he was seized by the rebels and executed in January 1815 after they had taken control of Arequipa.[82]

---

colonial del s. XVIII," *RI*, LI, núm. 192 (mayo-agosto 1991), 293–326: see pp. 294–95. Patricia H. Marks, "Confronting a Mercantile Elite: Bourbon Reformers and the Merchants of Lima, 1765–1795," *The Americas*, 60, no. 4 (April 2004), 519–58: p. 541.

[79] Marks, *Deconstructing Legitimacy*, 82–83. Note the comparison with New Granada's growing city of Medellín: see Twinam, "Enterprise and Élites," 444–75, for the Arango, Jaramillo, Restrepo, and Uribe families.

[80] Guillermo Cespedes del Castillo, "Lima y Buenos Aires. Repercusiones económicas y políticas de la creación del virreinato del Plata," *AEA*, iii (1946), 669–874: p. 736.

[81] Alberto Flores Galindo, *Arequipa y el sur andino: ensayo de historia regional: siglos xvii-xix* (Lima 1977). Sarah C. Chambers, *From Subjects to Citizens: Honor, Gender, and Politics in Arequipa, Peru, 1780–1854* (Pennsylvania 1999).

[82] Chambers, *From Subjects to Citizens*, 36–37, 50–59.

The Goyeneche family illustrated the depth of the ties between Spain and Peru, and it also maintained close connections to the Gárates, discussed below. The prime Cádiz connection was with the merchant house of Juan Miguel de Aguerrevere, who with Juan Miguel de Lestre also became a supplier of Juan Bautista Gárate. The Goyeneches were also by origin Navarrese, and the first Goyeneche in Peru married into a prominent Arequipa family. The importance of the Navarrese in the Castilian administration before 1700 and under the Bourbons in Spain and the Indies could be seen when Juan de Goyeneche (b. 1656) became a financial advisor to both Charles II and Philip V, and enjoyed the patronage of the Conde de Oropesa, President of the *Casa de Contratación*. His descendant, José Manuel de Goyeneche (b. 1776), went to the University of Seville for his further education. One of his uncles happened to be the General Administrator of the Royal Customs House there, and another, in Cádiz, managed the House of Aguerrevere's trade with Peru. Gárate in 1779 referred affectionately to Juan Miguel de Aguirreb[v]ere, who had been seventeen years in Peru, as his "patrón."[83]

The decline of silver-mining in Upper Peru at the beginning of the eighteenth century adversely affected Arequipa's trade. Landowners like the Goyeneches diversified into importing, which had greater profits. At the same time, several of them invested directly or indirectly in local mining in the districts of Tarapacá and Puno. In 1780, for example, Goyeneche joined Manuel de Cossío and Antonio Alvizuri in forming a company to exploit the Lampa mine in the latter district. However, their broader venture, the Arequipa Mineralogical Society of 1792, designed to promote mining investment, had little success.[84]

José Manuel Goyeneche rose through the army under Charles IV to become in 1809 the Seville Supreme Central Junta's commissioner to the Viceroyalty of Peru, returning there as a Brigadier. Abascal promptly employed him in the suppression of the autonomy movement in La Paz. Goyeneche became Commander of the Army of Upper Peru between 1810

---

[83] Stein and Stein, *Silver, Trade, and War*, 164–66. Xabier Lamikiz, "Transatlantic Networks and Merchant Guild Rivalry in Colonial Trade with Peru, 1729–1780: A New Interpretation," *HAHR*, 91, ii (May 2011), 299–331: see p. 324.

[84] Ramiro Flores Guzmán, "La complejidad del proceso de construcción regional: los casos de Trujillo y Arequipa durante la época colonial," in Cristina Mazzeo de Vivó (ed.), *Las relaciones de poder en el Perú. Estado, Regiones e Identidades: Siglos XVII-XIX* (Lima 2011), 39–85: pp. 79–80.

and 1813.[85] Juan Mariano, his brother, remained to manage the family estates in the province of Arequipa. During the second Spanish Constitutional Period (1820–23), he served as a member of the Provincial Deputation in 1822.[86] José Sebastián Goyeneche, a product of the Royal College (*Convictorio*) of San Carlos and the University of San Marcos in Lima, became the first Bishop of Arequipa in 1817 and Archbishop of Lima in 1859 at the age of 75.[87]

The Tristán family remained ardent Royalists right through the 1810s and the first half of the 1820s. Pío Tristán y Moscoso only rallied to the republican cause after the defeat at Ayacucho on December 9, 1824. He had fought in Spain against the French Revolutionaries in 1793–95 and returned to Peru with Goyeneche in 1808, fighting with him in the Army of Upper Peru until 1813. The son of a Corregidor of Larecaja in the early 1780s, Pío Tristán became Intendant of Arequipa in 1815 and President of the Audiencia of Cuzco in the following year. For a few days after Ayacucho he became interim Viceroy of Peru, technically the last occupant of that office. His career continued in Republican Peru as Prefect of Arequipa from 1836 and then as president of the Southern State in the Peru-Bolivia Confederation of 1836–39.[88]

The Gárate family of Arequipa originated from another such metropolitan merchant, who had come from Navarra to Peru before 1770, and combined bullion export with refining. He became the owner of the Hacienda de Tingo, near the city. By 1803, Juan Bautista Gárate y Zelayeta, "was one of the most powerful merchants in Peru, and as such served as both prior (1807–8) and consul of the consulado. He maintained offices in Lima, Cuzco, Arequipa, La Paz and Cochabamba in addition to correspondents in Cádiz," and trading with thirty-one merchant houses in the peninsula. He dealt in cotton, clothing, hosiery, spices and confectionary, cacao and chocolate, and wine, and was a major importer of European produce. Family ties linked the Arequipa family to business associates in Spain. In the elections to the Constitutional City Council of Lima, held on December 9, 1812, Juan Bautista Gárate was

---

[85] Manuel de Mendíburu, *Diccionario histórico-biográfico del Perú*, 15 tomes (Lima 1931–5), tomo XI, 26–28.

[86] Chambers, *From Subjects to Citizens*, 50–59.

[87] Ernesto Rojas Ingunza, *El báculo y la espada. El obispo Goyeneche y la Iglesia ante la 'Iniciación de la República,'* Peru 1825–1841 (Lima 2006). The College of San Carlos in Lima had been a center of the Peruvian Enlightenment.

[88] Chambers, *From Subjects to Citizens*, 50–59. Pío Tristán's brother was secretary to the Bishop of Tucumán, another Moscoso.

chosen as one of the sixteen *regidores*, along with the Conde de San Isidro. Both were elected to the renewed Constitutional City Council on December 7, 1820, after the fall of Ferdinand VII's first absolutist regime in Spain.[89]

Tadeo Gárate (b. La Paz, 1774) became Peruvian deputy in the Cortes Extraordinarias. Elected deputy for Puno in July 1812, he arrived in Cádiz in July 1813. Gárate had been educated at the University of San Antonio Abad in Cuzco and had been the secretary of Bishop Las Heras in the same city from 1801 to 1806. A qualified lawyer from 1797, he became Subdelegate of Chucuito in 1807. He was a trusted figure in the confidence of Abascal. Gárate served with Goyeneche's forces in the suppression of the La Paz movement in 1809. Luis Miguel Glave describes him as "linked to the reactionary local aristocracy of Cuzco." He became an opponent of the Spanish Liberals and of the Constitution of 1812, signing the "Manifesto of the Persians" in 1814 and welcoming the restoration of absolutism by Ferdinand VII. As such he was a close ally of the notorious Blas Ostolaza, one of the king's intimates, who originated from the prominent Trujillo family to which we shall refer in a moment. Ferdinand appointed Gárate Intendant of Puno, where he arrived in 1816, but after the collapse of Peruvian Royalism with Sucre's victory at Ayacucho in 1824, Gárate emigrated to Spain.[90]

Mariano Rivero, the deputy sent by the Cabildo of Arequipa to the Constituent Cortes in Spain, proved to be no unquestioning partisan of Abascal's policies. Rivero delivered a virulent attack on the viceroy for "despotism" on March 1, 1813, complaining of his suspension of liberty of the press. This, however, did not make him a separatist. Such views represented one element in the wider perspective of regional dislike of the

---

[89] Timothy E. Anna, *The Fall of the Royal Government in Peru* (Lincoln and London 1979), 168. Juan Ignacio Vargas Ezquerra, *Un hombre contra un continente. José Abascal, rey de América (1806–1816)* (Astorga 2010), 95, 202–4. Marks, *Deconstructing Legitimacy*, 41–42.

[90] Marie-Laure Rieu-Millán, "Rasgos distintivos de la representación peruana en las Cortes de Cádiz y Madrid (1810–1814)," *RI*, XLVIII (1, 2), nos. 182–83 (January–August 1988), 475–515: see pp. 478, 507. Luis Miguel Glave, "La Ilustración y el pueblo: el 'loco' Bernardino Tapia. Cambio y hegemonía cultural en los Andes al fin de la colonia. Azángaro, 1818," *Historias*, 60 (enero-abril 2005), 93–112: see pp. 98–103. J. R. Fisher, *Government and Society in Colonial Peru. The Intendant System, 1784–1814* (London 1970), 98, 242. Anna, *Fall of the Royal Government*, 105, advocating, in June–July 1814, regular salaries for subdelegates; 228, welcoming the abolition of the 1812 Constitution in Peru in 1823–24. Brian R. Hamnett, *Revolución y contrarrevolución en México y el Perú. Liberales, realistas y separatistas (1800–1824)* (second edition, Mexico City 2011 [1978]), 208, 215–16.

predominance of Lima. Rivero and the City Council both favored removing Arequipa from the jurisdiction of the Audiencia of Lima, and
on November 10, 1812 requested its inclusion in the jurisdiction of the
Audiencia of Cuzco. He would repeat this request, writing to the restored
Ferdinand VII on June 17, 1814. He also requested the foundation of
a university in Arequipa.[91]

The connection between the leading families and the *corregidores*
engaged in the *repartos* to the southern-Andean Indian communities has
been clearly established by David Cahill. The Crown legalized this distribution between 1754 and 1780, which has frequently been seen as one
of the causes of popular support for the Tupac Amaru insurrection.
The *reparto*, with roots back in the seventeenth century, became
a fundamental part of the economic life of southern Peru and the regions
of Upper Peru connected to it. In Peru, the *reparto* represented a combined
attempt by district administrators and their merchant-backers to oblige
Indian communities to take commodities they might otherwise not need –
Spanish imports, workshop-clothing, or mules, for instance, instead of
local Andean pack-animals and home-produced clothing. In order to pay
for such items, community Indians would be obliged to work as laborers
on private estates, workshops, or in the mines. In such a way, the *reparto*
broke open indigenous self-sufficiency and local intermarket linkages,
binding indigenous peasant-artisans to a wider market chain. Cuzco's
leading families, several dating from the time of Conquest, presided over
these activities. The Ugarte, Concha, Xara, Esquivel, Moscoso (with connection to Arequipa), and Peralta families were often connected with one
another through matrimony and business. They derived their wealth from
a combination of sources – usually agriculture, or ownership of *obrajes*.
Credit was available through access to ecclesiastical corporations, in
which sons and daughters were frequently members. Other family daughters married *corregidores* involved in the *reparto*, or strengthened the
business network through intermarriage with other families.[92]

Cahill suggests a "golden age" of the Cuzco élites from the second half
of the seventeenth century through the first three-quarters of the
eighteenth century. This derived from the prosperity of the internal

---

[91] Chambers, *From Patriots to Citizens*, 50–59. Rieu-Millán, "Rasgos distintivos,"
   491, 504.
[92] David P. Cahill, "Repartos ilícitos y familias principales. El sur andino: 1780–1824," *RI*,
   XLVIII (1, 2), nos. 182–83 (January–August 1988), 449–73: see pp. 449–55, 461.
   The *corregimientos* of Tinta, Abancay, Chumbivilcas, and Quispicanchis were particularly involved.

trade in grains and textiles, connected to the mining industries of Lower and Upper Peru. The *repartos* helped supply the mining districts of Oruro and Potosí. Several factors, operating together from the late 1770s, contributed to the collapse of this earlier prosperity. The impact of the Tupac Amaru rebellion undermined the commercial networks, damaging some of the workshop installations, a rebel target, and impoverishing the credit supply and thereby hindering subsequent recuperation. Other textile centers, such as Huamanga, Arequipa, and Cochabamba, were better able to compete in the same market. The Crown's decision to outlaw the *reparto* in 1780 compounded this problem. More important still were the structural alterations in the administration and commerce of the entire southern-highland region with the separation of Upper Peru from the government in Lima and its attachment to the new Viceroyalty in Buenos Aires in 1776. The opening of Buenos Aires to the transatlantic trade in 1778 drew Upper-Peruvian silver away from Cuzco and enabled the import of Catalan and other European commodities, particularly better-quality textiles, through the newer market network from Buenos Aires into Upper Peru. When transatlantic warfare was renewed after 1796, Cuzco's textile industry had become too weak to take much advantage of the opportunity.[93]

The Andean south of Peru has received much attention in the historical literature, in part because it had been the heartland of the Inca Empire. Northern Peru also had a distinctive perspective. The social and ethnic composition of the north contributed another variant to the Peruvian whole. Ethnic distinctions were not as sharp in the north as in the Andean south; the neo-Inca tradition was not as prominent. Rising population, the growth of the internal market and interregional competition explained the increased economic activity, local specialization and product improvement. Polarization between the inland textile-producing cities and the ports and coastal cities became striking in their opposing reception of *comercio libre* during the 1770s. Northern merchant communities developed strong links with inland cities stretching into southern Quito and welcomed liberalization of the coastal trades from Panama and Guayaquil to Callao and Valparaíso. They benefited considerably from the opening of the port of Huanchaco in 1796, giving access to the sea for Trujillo, through which the city merchants exported sugar and *obraje*-produced woolens. Relatively close connection to Quito, Cuenca, and

---

[93] Cahill, "Repartos ilícitos," 459–60, 462, 464–72: illicit *repartos* after 1780 were at a lower level than before, and Andean textiles were virtually absent in them.

Loja pointed to what Elizabeth Hernández has described as "el gran espacio sur-ecuatoriano–norteperuano."[94] The northern regions of Peru also had sugar-estates, but they were not large-scale and they used a mixed system of labor, drawing from Indian communities, having resident Indian *yanaconas* on their lands, but also using Negro slaves. Slavery, however, did not predominate as it did on the haciendas of the coastal valleys south of Lima. Mining in the north did not predominate as it did in the Andean central core and the highlands of Upper Peru.[95]

During the second half of the eighteenth century, the cities of Trujillo, Lambayeque, and Piura grew in commercial importance. The relationship of their predominant groups to the Consulado of Lima remained complex. Family networks characterized local commerce, with the Ostolaza family in the lead in Trujillo. Such families eclipsed the more superficial presence of the royal bureaucracy, even despite the introduction of the Intendant system in 1784. They traded in cacao, cotton, tobacco, hides, and the quinine of Loja. Cristóbal Ostolaza and other *hacendados* like him had strong connections with the merchants, since *aguardiente*, produced from sugar-cane, was one of his principal products. Ostolaza also owned several shops in the city of Trujillo and a number of ships. Neither he nor his compatriots ignored developments in Lima, where his son, Juan, managed the family's interests in association with none other than Pedro de Abadía. Juan Ostolaza was a friend of another Trujillo native resident in Lima, José Faustino Sánchez Carrión, at that time a teacher at the Royal College of San Carlos, who would rise to political prominence during the 1820s in association with the Liberators, José de San Martín and Simón Bolívar. The combination of interests suggests that some *hacendados* and merchants may be referred to as one group, while others remained apart. After Independence, merchants extended their interests as the consignees of foreign, mainly British, suppliers.[96]

Piura formed one of the ten *partidos*, or districts, of the Intendancy of Trujillo, which were administered by subdelegates. The city was linked to

---

[94] Elizabeth del Socorro Hernández García, *La Elite piurana y la Independencia del Perú: la lucha por la continuidad en la naciente república (1750–1824)* (Lima and Piura 2008), 55.

[95] José Antonio García Vera, *Los comerciantes trujillanos (1780–1840)* (Lima 1989), 17–18, 22, 27, 31–33, 36. Susana Aldana Rivera, *Poderes de una región de frontera. Comercio y familia en el norte, 1700–1830* (Lima 1999) and the same author's "Un norte diferente para la Independencia peruana," *RI*, 57, no. 209 (1997), 141–64. See also Scarlett O'Phelan and Yves Saint-Geours (compilers), *El Norte en la Historia Regional. Siglos XVIII-XIX* (Lima 1998).

[96] García Vera, *Los comerciantes trujillanos*, 16–20, 22, 36. Aldana Rivera, "Un norte diferente," pp. 141–64: see 150–55, 162–63.

the Pacific through the small port of Paita. Two rivers, the Paita and the Chira, flowed down from the Andean sierra part of the district. Along their fertile banks the principal of the forty or so haciendas in Piura had formed. These estates combined with local commerce, and the distribution of European goods as consignees of merchants of the Consulado of Lima formed the basis of the wealth and influence of the Piura élite. Piura and Paita participated in the linkages that formed the Pacific trade network from Panama and Guayaquil to Chile, up to New Spain and across the Pacific to Manila and beyond. Parallel to this and an essential part of it was the inland trade to Cajamarca and northwards into Quito. Business and family connections linked local Americans to peninsula immigrants, often regarded as eligible husbands for the daughters of the élite, which was concerned to perpetuate the social dominance of a European-derived population that formed just under 7 percent of the total in the district. As a result, no divide could be perceived between the different origins of creole and peninsular. This would explain much of the political conduct of the Piura élites during the dynastic crisis after 1808, in the struggles over independence from Spain, and after the formation of the Republic in 1821. The élites remained committed monarchists, loyal to Spain and supporting the policies of Abascal. As in the case of the Royalist élite in Arequipa in 1824, they only changed sides, although earlier, in 1821, in order to preserve their social position and traditional local hegemony.[97]

Local production of sugar, cotton, and livestock would be discreetly supplemented by the contraband trade through Paita with administrative collusion. This enabled trade from Acapulco in Chinese products, distributed through Guayaquil and lesser ports, to pass into the Peruvian economy. When the northern Isthmus ports of Chagres and Portobelo were legitimized for commerce by the Crown in 1780, they proved to be further means of access for British contraband, usually from Jamaica, to pass down into Peru.[98]

The northern region did not develop its own political project as the southern Andes did, which we shall examine in the following chapter, during the eighteenth century and up to 1815. Trujillo proclaimed the Independence of Peru from the Hispanic Monarchy on December 29, 1820, the first Peruvian city to do so. This action expressed the desire of the dominant élites to salvage as much as they could from further

---

[97] Hernández, *La Élite piurana*, 19–20, 27–34, 38 56–61, 66–72, 80–91, 395–403 for family genealogy, 380–84.
[98] Hernández, *La Élite piurana*, 59, 98.

maritime raids by the Patriots. Rather than separatist tendencies from the Peruvian successor state, northern regional sentiment expressed itself in the determination of its leading personalities to compete for influence and power in Lima. Sánchez Carrión certainly reflected such a strategy. Furthermore, the son of another Trujillo merchant family, Luis José de Orbigoso, became President of Peru from 1829–35. Martín Ostolaza became a deputy in the Constituent Congress of 1825. The brothers Santiago and Francisco Távara became leading figures among the northern merchants during the 1830s, the former a consignee on behalf of French mercantile interests.[99]

The capacity of the American élites for survival through the economic and political changes of the 1770s into the 1820s was remarkable. Their penetration of the royal bureaucracy was not entirely reversed by metropolitan policies during the eighteenth century. In any case, they continued to retain strong positions in the municipalities. Their interests spread over a range of activities – land, mining, commerce, industry, and civil, ecclesiastical, and military office-holding. Leading families were characteristically interlocked through matrimony and business. This did not exclude mutual rivalries and, particularly after 1808, political divisions. Even so, they presided over the transition from colony to sovereign state, in one form or another, allowing for entrants from other social categories. Yet, their position did not go without challenge.

---

[99] José Antonio García Vera, "Aduanas, comerciantes y nación mercantil: Trujillo, 1776–1836," *RI*, XVIII, nos. 182–83 (January–August 1988), 435–47. Aldana Rivera, "Un norte diferente," 162–63. García Vera, *Los comerciantes*, 19, 25–26.

An Alternative Vision? Andean Perceptions of the Hispanic Monarchy

Since the colonial bureaucracy had become permeated by mercantile interests, concern with conditions and sentiments in the localities would have been paramount. With an Indian political structure intact through the *curacas* and the *ayllu*, much depended on the relationship between belief systems and capacity for revolt. Before we jump to conclusions, however, we should bear in mind that Andean society was wrought by family, local, and social rivalries, which would have thwarted attempts at a central leadership or a superimposed ideology.[1] The main issue is whether a neo-Inca or *Inkarri* myth would have been strong enough to provide unification and coherence for any movement of dissent. The messianic and millenarian elements in it were powerful. Classic millenarian sentiment presupposed that one violent act could overthrow the existing system and install the desired new world of justice and harmony – or restore the yearned-for old one. A neo-Inca myth infused the three great eighteenth-century rebellions of Juan Santos Atahualpa,

---

[1] David T. Garrett, *Shadows of Empire. The Indian Nobility of Cusco, 1750–1825* (Cambridge 2005), 4–5, 16, 25–30: the *cacique* or *curaca* represented "a cross between local lord, tax collector, and justice of the peace, who personified the point of contact between the Indian community and the Spanish colonial order, and organised the flow of tribute into the royal coffers and the market economy of Peru"; the *ayllu*, defined by common ancestry, was the basic social unit from Pre-Columbian times onward. Viceroy Toledo's policy of forming "reductions" regrouped population into Spanish-model *pueblos*, which taken in entirety constituted the "*república de indios*," as opposed to the other sociocultural division, the "*república de españoles*." *Ayllus* became subsumed into the *pueblos*. Most *pueblos* contained several *ayllus*, viewed henceforth as distinct districts with corporate identity and lands. The Spanish authorities recognized no Indian political unit above the level of the *pueblo*.

Tupac Amaru, and Tupac Katari.[2] Karen Spalding has drawn attention to the spread of neo-Inca sentiment to areas that had been beyond the direct control of the Inca rulers. The forest slopes of the eastern Andes, known as the *montaña*, were one such region. In this zone, the local population accepted "Juan Santos Atahualpa" as a descendant of the Inca royal lineage.[3]

The description of the sentiment as "Inca nationalism" has been misleading. I should prefer to refer to it as a group consciousness of "Indianness," just as Irene Silverblatt has done. She explains this as a long-term and deeply rooted consequence of the earlier division of the former Inca Empire into two "republics" of "Spaniards" and "Indians." The notion of "Indians" resulted from the colonial situation – all previously distinct ethnic groups were henceforth lumped together as one subordinated entity by the Spanish rulers. It appeared to emerge from the middle of the seventeenth century:

Indianness seemed to command a powerful grip on some Andean imaginings. Along with its promise to transcend ethnic orders, Indianness galvanised allegiances across gender and province ... Although the language of Indianness was ferociously anti-Spanish, it was, at the same time, pervasively (if unconsciously) Hispanicised.

While it did not necessarily reject the Spanish Crown, it did oppose the colonial order and acted as a surrogate ideology of resistance.[4]

Emphasis on the issue of whether the insurrections of the early 1780s, such as those of Tupac Amaru and Tupac Katari, foreshadowed those of the 1810s has receded in favor of greater concentration on ethnic and social components. In pursuing this, the findings of Sergio Serulnikov, David Garrett, Luis Miguel Glave, Charles Walker, David Cahill, Nuria Sala, Sinclair Thomson, and others have opened new dimensions of local and provincial history, which show the depths and extent of profoundly anticolonial struggles. If transported back to the Andean 1810s and 1820s, the contemporary historians who argue that the real revolution was constitutional would be hard-pressed to explain to the peasants, artisans, and small traders of the Peru's that their struggle against the

---

[2] Leon G. Campbell, "Ideology and Factionalism during the Great Rebellion, 1780–1782," in Stern, *Resistance, Rebellion*, 110–39: see pp. 113–15, 134.

[3] Karen Spalding, *De indio a campesino: cambios en la estructura social del Perú colonial* (Lima 1974), 130.

[4] Irene Silverblatt, *Modern Inquisitions. Peru and the Colonial Origins of the Civilized World* (Durham and London 2004), 196–97, 207, 210–11.

mita, obraje, hacienda, and tribute tax was not the real one but simply an overrated sideshow.[5]

OFFICIAL RELIGION, POPULAR RELIGION, AND NEO-INCA SENTIMENT

The eighteenth- and early nineteenth-century rebellions conceived of themselves within the Christian context established by the Spanish Conquest. Yet, at the same time, Christian evangelization proved to be a long and contested process in Peru. In effect, the official and the clandestine existed together. The impression is of an Indian population desperately trying to preserve what it could of its own and resisting as much as it could of the European imposition.[6]

The memory of the Inca past remained a living reality in the Andean world. Steve Stern has suggested that by the 1680s the balance of interests established in Peru in the aftermath of the stabilization policy of Viceroy Francisco de Toledo (1569–81) had begun to break down. In his view, the unrest of the decades from the 1730s to the 1780s resulted from new tensions and pressures between the dominant élites and the various peasant groups in the viceroyalty:

The changing political economy of mercantile exploitation undermined pre-existing strategies and relations of colonial rule and Andean resistance, by the 1730s, across virtually all of highland Peru-Bolivia. The changing relations of mercantile exploitation directly threatened the continuity of colonial political authority, and its rather fragile and partial legitimacy among Andean peasants.[7]

---

[5] Núria Sala i Vila, *Y se armó el tole tole. Tributo indígena y movimientos sociales en el virreinato del Perú, 1784–1814* (1996); Walker, Charles F., *Smoldering Ashes: Cuzco and the Creation of Republican Peru, 1780–1835* (Durham and London 1999); Sinclair Thomson, *We Alone Will Rule. Native Andean Politics in the Age of Insurgency* (Madison 2002); Sergio Serulnikov, *Subverting Colonial Authority: Challenges to Spanish Rule in Eighteenth-Century Southern Andes* (Durham and London 2003); Charles F. Walker, *The Tupac Amaru Rebellion* (Cambridge, MA 2014).

[6] Nathan Wachtel, *La vision des vaincus. Les Indiens du Pérou devant la Conquête espagnole, 1530–1570* (Paris 1971), 213–18, 223–41, 249–50, 269–75. Manuel Burga, *Nacimiento de una utopia. Muerte y resurrección de los incas* (Lima 1988), v. Sabine MacCormack, *Religion in the Andes. Vision and Imagination in Early Colonial Peru* (Princeton 1991). Nicholas Griffiths, *The Cross and the Serpent. Religious Repression and Resurgence in Colonial Peru* (Norman and London 1996). Kenneth Mills, *Idolatry and Its Enemies: Extirpation and Colonial Andean Religion, 1640–1750* (Princeton 1997).

[7] Steve Stern, "The Age of Andean Insurrection, 1742–1782: A Reappraisal," in Stern, *Resistance, Rebellion*, 34–93: see pp. 72–75.

The Indian majority faced diminished "institutional space" within the colonial structure. This resulted from the alliance between the official colonial power and what he describes as the mercantile interest in Lima. The key phenomenon appears to have been the subordination of the royal district official, the *corregidor*, to the material interests of the merchants. That official, accordingly, became the business agent of merchants who were intent upon subordinating the local villagers to a commercial monopoly. This development took place at a time when the Indian population was recovering, placing increased pressure on subsistence lands. Increased fiscal and mercantile burdens on the peasant-artisan population of the highland villages, along with the tightening of tribute and the *mita*, contributed to the rupture of social relations.[8]

The rising economic and political significance of the Consulado of Lima took place at a time of relatively weak metropolitan power. Furthermore, the agricultural crisis through the coastal valley in the latter part of the seventeenth century may also have reduced the importance of landholding interests linked to the Lima market as food suppliers. That, in turn, implied a need to tighten control of the interior by the Lima merchants, expanding markets there, and to ensure the supply of grains by sea from Chile.[9]

The colonial authorities in the 1720s were already receiving abundant notification of abuses by district administrators. The basic social grievances – violation of land rights, coercive labor drafts for the Potosí silver mines, oppressive conditions in the textile manufactories, and fiscal pressures – recurred as component elements in all the outbreaks from 1730 to 1815, despite their specific features. In 1730, a young mestizo led a rebellion in Cochabamba, a Quechua zone in Upper Peru and center of prosperous agriculture and textile workshops. Forty-two executions occurred in the repression. A *cacique*, Andrés Ignacio Ccama Condori, led a conspiracy for a series of uprisings in the latter part of the decade across southern Peru. A rebellion in Azángaro, in 1736–38, extended into Upper Peru. A mestizo from Moquegua led the Oruro conspiracy of 1739. He later claimed descent from the Inca Huascar and gained the support of fifteen *caciques* before betrayal.[10]

[8] Stern, "Age of Andean Insurrection," 72–75.

[9] For the development of this trade, see Demetrio Ramos, *Trigo chileno, navieros del Callao y hacendados limeños entre la crisis agrícola del siglo XVII y la comercial de la primera mitad del siglo XVIII* (Madrid 1967).

[10] Burga, *Nacimiento de una utopia*, 164. Leon G. Campbell, "Recent Research on Andean Peasant Revolts, 1750–1820," *LARR*, XIV, i (1979), 3–49.

In Spalding's view, the eighteenth-century rebellions revealed that the process of constructing an Andean identity had already been in motion: furthermore, memory of the Pre-Columbian past combined with present-day exploitation to shape consciousness. This explained how resentment cut across social groups.[11] Spalding's later study of colonial Huarochirí, the highland district located above Lima, draws attention to the colonial authorities' wariness of any signs of opposition in the localities:

the colonial authorities were thoroughly frightened by any sign of organized resistance to the system they maintained. The cycle of revolt that began in the viceroyalty of Peru within a century after the construction of the colonial state apparatus eroded their security and their fortunes. From the 1660s on, the antennae of the state were more and more sharply turned to receive any sign or rumour of Indian revolt.[12]

Divisions within Andean society, however, still remained as deterrents to collective action. Cahill stresses this in his study of late-colonial Cuzco society: "internal differentiation within each racial category impaired any possible unanimity based on racial identification." Within Indian society "kinship and land were the two fundamental determinants of peasant differentiation."[13] Such internal divisions may explain the mixed nature of the leadership of the eighteenth-century rebellions. The involvement of members of the Indian nobility from the 1730s onward remained significant and at times decisive. The leadership of mestizos suggests a bridge between Indian society and dissident upper echelons of local society. It also points forward to the mestizo, who in 1780 became Tupac Amaru II, able to appeal to both Inca descent and to dissident creoles. The principal underlying factor linking all these movements together was the attempt to bring together dissident social groups generally believed to have been antagonistic. By implication, then, the *Inkarri* myth was not uniquely an Indian affair but a more generalized attempt to supply an alternative legitimacy to colonial rule.[14]

---

[11] Spalding, *De indio a campesino*, 190.

[12] Karen Spalding, *Huarochirí. An Andean Society under Inca and Spanish Rule* (Stanford 1984), 270–71.

[13] D. P. Cahill, "Crown, Clergy, and Revolution in Bourbon Peru: the Diocese of Cuzco, 1780–1814," unpublished Ph. D. dissertation, University of Liverpool [1984], 156–58.

[14] Scarlett O'Phelan Godoy, "El mito de la 'Independencia concedida:' los programas políticos del siglo XVIII y temprano XIX en el Perú y Alto Perú, 1730–1814," in Alberto Flores Galindo (comp.), *Independencia y Revolución*, 2 vols. (Lima 1987), II, 145–99: see pp. 146–47, 169–71.

THE JUAN SANTOS ATAHUALPA REBELLION AND ITS CONTEXT

The emergence of a widespread opposition movement and deepening insurgency during the 1740s took the Lima authorities by surprise. Inca symbolism became intermingled with Christian messianism in the Juan Santos Rebellion. Sparse source materials hamper our understanding of this movement, explained partly by its core location in the *montaña* beneath the eastern cordillera. Juan Santos was able to establish a base area there and take territory away from government control – if it had ever effectively been controlled at all. Juan Santos insisted upon his Cuzco origins and Christian orthodoxy, and it seems that he may well have been of noble birth. Beyond that, there are problems concerning his identity. It has been said that he originated from Cajamarca and was a pupil of the Cuzco Jesuits and educated in the school for sons of *curacas*. Juan Santos appears to have taken over the cause of Indian vindication, condemning colonial abuses in the name of the Christian God. Pursuing this objective, he lived among the Indian tribes of the *montaña* and the forests beyond the cordillera, wearing simple clothes, chewing coca leaf, and using other narcotics, perhaps taking part in Indian magic cults. It is possible that the forest tribes regarded him as a shaman.[15] The rebellion appears to have begun in May 1742 in and beyond the Franciscan-mission territories of the *Gran Pajonal* plateau, parts of the provinces of Tarma and Jauja remote from official authority. Apparently, his project was the reconquest of Peru from the Pizarros and Spaniards, and the establishment of a Christianized Inca Empire.[16]

The rebellion came to control a large extent of territory, obliging Franciscan missionaries and local estate-owners to evacuate the area. The heartlands were the *Campa*, where, whether by coincidence or not, Vilcabamba had been located and from which effective guerrilla warfare

---

[15] Jay F. Lehnertz, "Juan Santos: Primitive Rebel on the Campa Frontier (1742–52)," in Actas y Memorias del XXIX *Congreso Internacional de Americanistas*, 6 vols. (Lima 1972), vol. 4, 111–23: see pp. 116–17. Lehnertz stresses the Franciscan evangelizing of the *Campa* Indian zones in the early eighteenth century. More than twenty mission stations had been established. The first rebels came not from the *Campa* but from the *Pajonal*, where evangelization had had the least impact. Many mission Indians opposed the rebellion. See also M. Castro Arenas, "La rebelión de Juan Santos Atahualpa," *Cuadernos Americanos*, 199 (1975), 125–45. Leon G. Campbell, *The Military and Society in Colonial Peru, 1750–1810* (Philadelphia 1978), 11–12.

[16] Lehnertz, "Juan Santos," 115–16; Stern, *Resistance, Rebellion*, 78–79 n. 11, p. 82 n. 39. Castro Arenas, "La rebelión," 126–27. Michèlle Colin, *Le Cuzco à la fin du XVIIe et au début du XVIIIe siècle* (Paris 1966), 173–75, 180–81. Colin identifies the Chancamayo Indians of Cuzco as initial supporters of the rebellion.

had been waged from the 1540s against the Spanish Conquerors. By the end of 1742, Juan Santos had already moved the vanguard into the Chanchamayo Valley, which became his base of operations from 1743 to 1751. From there his forces raided upland into highland Tarma. The colonial militia, mainly composed of coastal blacks and mulattoes, was useless against rebels moving up from forest bases and with an intelligence network in the highland zones. The colonial authorities lost control of huge swathes of territory in central and eastern Peru for decades.[17]

Despite the geographically peripheral origins of the rebellion, it proved sufficiently resilient to defy eradication. Military expeditions in 1742, 1743, 1746, and 1750 failed to dislodge the rebels. The colonial authorities resigned themselves to a policy of containment, attempting to stop the spread of the movement into the sierra. This was particularly their concern in the central highland provinces of Jauja and Tarma, strategically located above Lima, where a strong military presence remained from the 1740s into the 1780s. However, the continuing existence of an undefeated opposition movement proposing an alternative political and social order reinforced the already existing tradition of defection from the sierra zones to the *selva*. Juan Santos could draw on a multi-ethnic component, which became less a reaction in the *Campa* to outside penetration than an attempt to spread a neo-Inca gospel throughout the sierra. The adoption of the name of the murdered Inca laid claim to all the lands of the Inca *Tahuantinsuyo*. The possibilities of mass mobilization, which that claim implied, preoccupied the authorities in the 1740s and 1750s. The threat, nevertheless, did not materialize, and a shaken colonial regime survived.[18]

Before the Juan Santos Atahualpa rebellion had disintegrated, the colonial authorities faced a serious rebellion in Huarochirí in July–August 1750. Although this rebellion was directed against colonial abuses and appealed to the Pre-Columbian era as an ideal, it saw redress in terms of the application of Christian law and justice. Six *curacas* were involved and the rebellion seems to have been linked to a conspiracy in Lima by a group of Indian noblemen, whose intention was to link up with Juan Santos Atahualpa's movement. The conspiracy aimed to seize control of the viceregal palace and kill all the Spanish with the exception of members of the clergy.

---

[17] Castro Arena, "La Rebelión," 126–27. Stern, *Resistance, Rebellion*, 43, 78–79 n. 11.
[18] Lehnertz, "Juan Santos," 112, 1126–28. Stern, *Resistance, Rebellion*, 34, 36, 44–50, 56, 80–81 n. 29.

The discovery of this plot sparked the rebellion in Huarochirí. That, in turn, collapsed within twenty days, when the leaders were handed over to the authorities and a force of 600 disciplined troops from Lima occupied the town. The collapse of this rebellion did not, however, signify a generalized pacification of the sierra, where a series of rebellions occurred in the following decades, provoked by local hostility to *repartimientos*, conditions in the *obrajes*, and the pressure of tithe levies, for example in the wealthy and populous district of Sicasica (between La Paz and Oruro) in 1770–71, in Pacajes in 1771 in the vicinity of La Paz, and in the Lower Peruvian towns of Huamachuco in 1773 and 1774, Chumbivilcas in 1776, and Huamalíes in 1777.[19]

Even so, too stark a dichotomy should not be asserted between the differing character of Indian communities and the Hispanic world to which they were often linked. Deep divisions and rivalries frequently existed within the former, and, furthermore, many Indian noble families and local interests had become integrated into the ways in which Spanish colonialism functioned in the Perus. This might take the form of hierarchical rank, social function, economic activities, or matrimonial connections. Intermarriage produced *mestizos* rather than pure Indians, a cultural dimension that considerably complicated identities and loyalties:

[T]he front-line troops of the colonial system were not soldiers, but the people who spoke the language of the Indian people, who were willing to stand as godparents to their children or sponsors at their marriages, and who would do small favours for their ritual kinsmen – favours that generally proved to be to their own benefit. These people were often sympathetic to the Indians who worked for them and among whom they lived, as long as the Indians showed them respect and submission due to a superior from an inferior.[20]

The role of the clergy in sustaining the eighteenth-century colonial system should on no account be overlooked. Even so, fear of spreading dissident sentiment inhibited the official sanction of the training of an indigenous, Indian clergy.[21]

THE TUPAC AMARU REBELLION, 1780–1781

The keys to the destabilizing of the southern Andes and the Upper Peruvian zones linked to it on the opposite shores of Lake Titicaca were

[19] Spalding, *Huarochirí*, 272–78, 284–85.
[20] Spalding, *Huarochirí*, 286–87. Garrett, *Shadows of Empire*, 2 note 3.
[21] Spalding, *Huarochirí*, 287.

the activities of the *corregidores* and their agents in the *repartos* to Indian communities. The declining significance of the 2300 or so *caciques* or *curacas*, the Indian noblemen, in the truncated, post-1776 Viceroyalty of Peru compounded this problem. It may well be that accelerated royal patronage of these nobles responded to awareness of their increased marginalizing within their communities and the danger that such a development posed to the type of indirect rule practiced through them by the viceregal authorities. The Spanish Crown singled out for special honors those Indian noblemen who could accredit their descent from the Inca royal house. One of the most powerful of these, Diego Choqueguanca, combined royal recognition of his status as *cacique* of Azángaro in 1754 with the rank of Colonel of the Infantry Regiment of Natives of his province. His sons and those of two other *caciques*, Tito Atauchi and Sahuaraura, whose pedigree was recognized in 1742, gained positions in the clergy, perhaps as a result of training in the Cuzco Seminary of San Bernardo Abad. Scarlett O'Phelan sees this as a parallel to royal patronage of the Lima élite, several of whose number received noble titles in the 1740s and 1750s. By such methods, the metropolitan government sought to bind the most influential individuals and their families to the viceroyalty and the colonial system. Few Indian nobles supported the Tupac Amaru rebellion. Choqueguanca's opposition proved crucial to the rebellion's defeat.[22]

A major explanation for the decline in local prestige of the *curacas* was their connection with the *corregidores* in the attempt to create commercial monopolies and thereby raise prices in their districts. Rough treatment by these royal administrators and their agents combined with the distortion of weights and measures in the villages had already become a source of widespread discontent during the 1740s, with complaints in Upper Peru reaching the Audiencia of Charcas in the capital, Chuquisaca. They dee-pened, when the Crown was persuaded to legalize the *repartos* in 1754. Attempted monopolies in the coca trade in the sub-tropical *yungas* of the province of La Paz inflamed peasant communities. The president of the Audiencia warned the government in 1766 of the potential consequences of the abuses. An uprising in Sicasica followed in 1769, followed by the more serious outbreak in 1771. Sinclair Thomson had drawn attention to

---

[22] Scarlett O'Phelan Godoy, "Repensando el movimiento nacional Inca del siglo XVIII," in Scarlett O'Phelan Godoy (compiladora), *El Perú en el siglo XVIII: la era borbónica* (Lima 1999), 263–77: see pp. 363–67, 276–77.

the violence spreading across the province of La Paz between the 1740s and the 1770s.[23]

Minister of the Indies Gálvez, sent José Antonio Areche, previously his deputy in New Spain, to Peru as Visitor-General, entrusted with the revision of the processes of government within the viceroyalty and maximizing its tax revenues to the advantage of the metropolis. Areche arrived in Lima in June 1777. The Visitor-General immediately increased the sales tax from 4 percent to 6 percent. Riots in Arequipa and Cuzco were the response. The Tupac Amaru rebellion began in the southern Andean countryside and smaller towns in November 1780 at a time of deep conflict within the colonial administrative structures.[24]

The depth of community resistance to long-lasting abuses explained the spread of insurrection across southern Peru and related territories in Upper Peru from the late 1770s into the first years of the 1780s. Until that time communities continued to appeal against abuses through the medium of the colonial legal system. The repeated inability of metropolitan administrations, viceroys, audiencias, bishops, and clergy, all of whom were well aware of what was going on, to remedy the situation and punish the perpetrators threw into question the legitimacy of colonial rule. This questioning rose to a climax in 1780–81. The protest movement in Upper Peru that gathered around Tomás Katari from 1777 onward formed part of this process. At that time, no Inca identification was made. Tomás Katari came from Pacajes and was a tribute-payer who originated in the village of Ayoayo. He had journeyed first to Buenos Aires in order to put complaints of abuses before the viceregal administration, though to no avail. No help came from the Audiencia of Charcas. As a result, a large swathe of territory slipped from the Audiencia's control. Into this situation came news of the Tupac Amaru rebellion in the Cuzco district and the claim of an Inca alternative legitimacy.[25]

José Gabriel Condorcanqui was a *mestizo curaca* who claimed the Inca succession. The indigenous nobility of Cuzco rejected him as an imposter

---

[23] Alfredo Moreno Cebrián, *El Corregidor de Indios y la economía peruana del siglo XVII: los repartos forzosos de mercancías* (Madrid 1977). Jürgen Golte, *Repartos y rebeliones: Tupac Amaru y las contradicciones de la economía colonial* (Lima 1980). Thomson, *We Alone Will Rule*, 107–08, 111–13, 116, 130–38.

[24] See for instance: David Cahill, "Taxonomy of a Colonial 'Riot': the Arequipa Disturbances of 1780," in John R. Fisher, Allan J. Kuethe and Anthony McFarlane (eds.), *Reform and Insurrection in Bourbon New Granada* (Baton Rouge and London 1990), 255–91.

[25] Thomson, *We Alone Will Rule*, 124–25, 142, 163.

and competitor. Designed to be the rallying call for unity, the Inca claim proved to be divisive. Since Condorcanqui found it impossible to work within the structure of Indian noble power, he was obliged to nominate substitute *caciques* and governors in areas that fell under rebel control.[26]

Tupac Amaru intended to construct a broad, multi-ethnic, and cross-social group alliance. Early support came from creoles rather than the Indian majority. Once violence began, initial creole support and clerical sympathy evaporated. Most historians agree on that but they differ on the movement's objectives – whether it was directed toward a righting of wrongs within the colonial structure or aimed to overthrow it and establish a separate neo-Inca state. Pablo Macera sees the rebellion as "fundamentally a peasant movement, revolutionary and messianic, which questioned the structure of the colonial system." O'Phelan considers that Tupac Amaru's retention of Tribute and *mita*, abolishing only the *repartos* by the *corregidores*, vitiates any argument that he was revolutionary. Along with most historians of the eighteenth-century Andean zone, she identifies hatred of the *repartos* as the center of virtually all the rebellions. Thomson draws attention to the social and ideological limitations of the insurrection on the question of land redistribution.[27]

Insurrection resulted from Condorcanqui's failure to secure redress for the Indian population within the existing system. The execution of the Corregidor of Tinta marked the symbolic act of rebellion. This made the establishment of an alternative legitimacy urgent. The scale of mobilization, however, may have surprised the leadership. In response, neo-Inca messianism assumed greater significance in the movement's ideology. A Christian theme of deliverance or redemption permeated the movement.[28] Cahill argues that Tupac Amaru led a rebellion pressing for redress within the colonial structure, rather than a revolutionary movement trying to overthrow it. He regards it as neither a peasant movement nor as an inter-class revolutionary attempt, still less as a precursor of the South American insurrections of the 1810s. In his view, the role of the

---

[26] Scarlett O'Phelan Godoy, "Elementos étnicos y de poder en el movimientos tupacamarista, 1780–81," *Nova Americana*, 5 (1982), 79–101. Campbell, "Ideology and Factionalism," 115–19, 121. Stern, *Resistance, Rebellion*, 59–62, 65–66. Condorcanqui had been pressing for Spanish recognition of his Inca descent during the 1770s but the Crown had already declined to recognize his claimed cacicazgo in 1766. Garrett, *Shadows of Empire*, 184–89, discusses historiographical interpretations.

[27] Pablo Macera, *Visión histórica del Perú, del paleolítico al proceso de 1968* (Lima 1978), 159–61. Scarlett O'Phelan Godoy, *La Gran Rebelión en los Andes: De Túpac Amaru a Túpac Catari* (Cuzco 1995), 186–96. Thomson, *We Alone Will Rule*, 170.

[28] Walker, *Tupac Amaru*, 65–85, discusses the relationship to the Catholic Church.

diocesan clergy of Cuzco proved to be decisive in determining the nature and outcome of the Tupac Amaru rebellion. Its leader had expected the support of the local clergy and the hierarchy as well, hardly the characteristic of a revolutionary movement. The Bishop of Cuzco, Juan Manuel Moscoso, from the influential Arequipa family, ensured the loyalty of the overwhelming majority of the diocesan clergy to the colonial regime, but his initial sympathies for the opposition movement and his creole origin brought him under suspicion of collusion with the rebels.[29]

A major problem of interpretation has been where to place the Tupac Amaru rebellion in the context of its time. Durand Flores, for instance, identifies it with the *comunero* rebellion of 1781 in New Granada and the Katari movements in Upper Peru. He argues that these movements, in effect, inaugurated the struggle for emancipation, which lasted over the period from 1780 to 1825, and that the Tupac Amaru rebellion was "nationalist, all-embracing, and anti-colonialist." Tupac Amaru's bid for widespread support differentiated his movement from the sixteenth-century opposition to Spanish rule, which sought to restore what had been overthrown. By contrast, the 1780–81 rebellion pointed forward to the Cuzco rebellion of 1814–15, although the external conditions and intellectual currents were radically different. Both insurrections, however, were Andean movements designed to impose political change on Lima. The two defeats of 1781 and 1815 thwarted this objective and left the field open for the creole circle in the capital and other cities to substitute peninsular rule for their own. It is essential to place the Andean rebellions within the broader context of the movements against colonial rule across Ibero-America from the 1780s into the 1820s, and not leave them aside as distinct phenomena.[30]

Condorcanqui was portraying himself as the Inca Tupac Amaru II by January 1781. Clearly, there could not be two legitimate monarchs in Peru. By the adoption of the Inca title he must surely have regarded the Viceroyalty of Peru as no longer legitimate in its claim to be the successor entity to the Inca Empire, ruled by the usurping Kings of Spain. Creole and clerical opposition to the rebellion exposed the division between a noble-

---

[29] Fisher, "Rebelión," 414–15: "a fruitless effort to redress grievances by legal means, followed by a sudden and violent uprising." Cahill, "Crown, Clergy," 200–4, 208–9, 215, 249–51, 255–59, 263, 269.

[30] Luis Durand Flores, *Independencia e integración en el plan político de Tupac Amaru* (Lima 1973), 9, 15–17, 36, 159. Tupac Amaru's forces failed to take the city of Cuzco in January 1781. See Sergio Serulnikov, *Revolution in the Andes: The Age of Tupac Amaru* (Durham, NC 2013).

derived leadership, competing for power with the viceregal authorities, and a peasant following, determined to end colonial abuses. In Jan Szeminski's view, these peasant followers regarded creoles as enemies. Szeminski examines the question of whether or not Condorcanqui had himself crowned in Tungasuca as King José I on November 26, 1780, following the rebel victory at Sangarará – "by the Grace of God Inca King of Peru, Santa Fe, Quito, Chile, Buenos Aires, and the continents of the Southern Seas ..." – when the fall of Cuzco seemed probable. No concrete evidence of any such coronation has come to light.[31] Even so, the impact of the government defeat at Sangarará should not be underrated. Garrett, for instance, sees this as the "most significant defeat dealt to Spanish rule by Indian forces since the 1530s, and it shook Cusco's colonial society correspondingly."[32]

Condorcanqui's letter to Areche on March 5, 1781 made the economic and social grievances explicit, but, as Magnus Mörner pointed out, it is hard to relate the existence of abuses to the decision to take up arms in rebellion.[33] In O'Phelan's view, the Bourbon fiscal measures provided the "detonator" for the rebellion of 1780. Many *mestizos* joined the rebellion through opposition to increased taxation and fear of demotion to the status of Tribute-payers.[34] The original base of the rebellion lay in the highlands south of Cuzco, Quispicanchis, Tinta, and Chumbivilcas, where the *reparto* combined with Tribute and *mita* to press heavily on the local working population. Indians in the fertile valley of the Cuzco area, however, resented the descent of highlanders through their fields and opposed the rebellion. Despite this hostility, some 50,000 followers had accumulated by early December 1780 and the whole region as far as the city of Puno lay in rebel hands. The scale and geographical location of the rebellion went beyond those of the Juan Santos Atahualpa rebellion. They shared, however, a cultural connection, which was the political use made of Inca symbolism.[35]

---

[31] Jan Szeminski, *La utopia tupamarista* (Lima 1984), 221–24, 284–86. Thomson, *We alone will rule*, 164, 167, 169, 179, nevertheless, points to the coronation edict, denouncing three centuries of usurpation and describing Areche as a "second Pizarro." He views it as an attempt to create a "new order" in Peru.

[32] Garrett, *Shadows of Empire*, 191.

[33] Magnus Mörner, "La rebellion de Tupac Amaru en el Cuzco desde una perspectiva nueva," in Jorge Flores Ochoa and Abraham Valencia E., *Rebeliones indígenas quechuas y aymaras* (Cuzco 1980), 5–34: see pp. 6–28.

[34] Scarlett O'Phelan Godoy, "Las reformas borbónicas y su impacto en la sociedad colonial del Bajo y el Alto Perú," in Jacobsen and Puhle, *Economies of Mexico and Peru*, 340–56: see pp. 342–43, 351–53.

[35] Garrett, *Shadows of Empire*, 187, 191, 209.

The decisive element in the collapse of the rebellion was its internal contradictions and the divisions within Indian society. We shall see similar problems in the Cuzco Rebellion of 1814–15, although in a completely different historical context. Cahill stresses the competition within the Indian élite for control of wealth and population resources in Andean southern Peru. *Curaca* hostility to Condorcanqui's pretentions proved to be part of his undoing. With few exceptions, no *curaca* on either side of Lake Titicaca supported him. The majority, as is well known, placed their services (and their manpower) at the disposal of the colonial authorities. In such a way, they sought to sustain their position as the instruments through which Spain ruled the local population. The neo-Inca myth proved to be insufficient to recruit the nobility into open revolt. Family rivalries of long standing played their part. The Pumacahua family, *caciques* of Chincheros, were also hostile to the Condorcanquis, and, although their head, Mateo García, had been educated at the same college as Tupac Amaru, opposed the rebellion. Choqueguanca, for his part, reinforced the viceregal defense of Cuzco at the head of 12,000 men. By way of retaliation, the *tupamaristas* destroyed eleven of the sixteen haciendas possessed by the Choqueguanca family in the Puno district. The *cacique* of Anta, in Abancay, secured the viceregal supply route from Lima to Cuzco across the Apurímac River. In this way, *cacique* loyalty was vital to the final success of the colonial authorities. Accordingly, the viceregal government was able to eliminate a radical threat through the use of Indian armies.[36]

The capture and then execution of Condorcanqui and his immediate family in Cuzco on May 18, 1781 did not end the rebellion. Failure to take Cuzco, furthermore, pushed the focus of the movement southward to the Titicaca basin and the Altiplano. Diego Cristóbal, Tupac Amaru's cousin, made his headquarters in Azángaro and entered Puno in late May 1781. Another relative, Andrés, advanced along the eastern shore of the Lake. *Caciques* lost control over their communities. Massacres of creoles and

---

[36] C. Daniel Valcárcel, *Tupac Amaru. Precursor de la independencia* (Lima 1977), 54–60. Campbell, *Military and Society*, 126, 129, estimated that some 100,000 persons took part in the rebellion, although by the end of December 1780, this had shrunk to 40,000. Cahill, "Crown, Clergy," 142–44, 252–53. Ward Stavig, "Ethnic Conflict, Moral Economy, and Population in Rural Cuzco on the Eve of the Thupa Amaru II Rebellion," *HAHR*, 68: iv (November 1988), 737–70: see pp. 768–70, points out that the only territory supporting the rebellion were Tupac Amaru's home areas of Quispicanchis and Canas y Canchis, from which he drew on family, kinship, and dependency bonds, in defense of the moral economy and traditional way of life of the Indian communities.

caciques, seeking refuge in churches in Sangarará and Juli, showed that in the Titicaca basin "the rebellion had become an open assault on all aspects of colonial authority." There social tensions within Indian society accumulated against rich *caciques*, collectors of Tribute revenue and suppliers of labor for the mining zones.[37] During February 1781, following the assassination of Tomás Katari in the previous month, the La Paz movement converged with the Tupac Amaru uprising, as we shall see shortly. The La Paz peasant communities strove for land reform, peasants for the vindication of lost lands from the haciendas, and their peons for seizure of these estates, both in the expectation of the imminent collapse of Spanish authority in Upper Peru.[38]

THE KATARI REBELLIONS IN UPPER PERU

We should now throw the focus on Upper Peru, still under the jurisdiction of the Audiencia of Charcas after 1776 but thereafter within the Viceroyalty of the River Plate. Metropolitan-government tax policies combined with dislocation of local economies to place renewed burdens on the peasant-artisan population and provide extended grounds for protest. Tomás Katari's protest against abuses had led to eight months' imprisonment in Chayanta (in the district of Potosí) from September 1779, awaiting trial by the *corregidor*. An insurrection broke out in Chayanta, where tensions had been building up, on April 26, 1780. It was joined by *caciques* from Cochabamba, Oruro, La Paz, Pacajes, Omasuyos, Larecaja, Chucuito, Carangas, and Sicasica, and spread to the *yungas*. The movement began, as Sergio Serulnikov argues, "as a routine legal protest but became the most powerful challenge to colonial rule in the southern Andes [i.e. Upper Peru] since the Spanish Conquest." Divisions within the dominant élites over government policy provided openings for popular mobilization.[39]

The rebellion, initially directed against the Audiencia of Charcas, the *corregidores* and their commercial connections to the Lima élite, covered the period from August 1780 until May 1781. The Upper Peruvian

---

[37] Garrett, *Shadows of Empire*, 208–9. Thomson, *We Alone Will Rule*, 222–26, draws attention to the distinction between the free communities of the *altiplano*, active in commerce between localities and with the *yungas*, and these lower-altitude valleys and the valleys of Cochabamba, where the bulk of the haciendas were located, mestizos had penetrated villages, and market forces had undermined community cohesion.

[38] Thomson, *We Alone Will Rule*, 167, 171–75.

[39] Serulnikov, *Subverting Colonial Authority*, 120, 123.

outbreaks anticipated the Tupac Amaru insurrection by two months. From August, the rebellion led to "the sweeping demise of colonial power in the countryside." The Audiencia managed to seize hold of Tomás Katari in mid-December 1780 and, after transfer to Chuquisaca, seat of the Audiencia of Charcas, he was murdered on January 7, 1781. The second phase of the rebellion focused on Chuquisaca, forcing peninsular authorities from strategic positions such as Oruro, another main mining town.[40]

The third phase involved "Tupac Katari," the pseudo-Inca title adopted by Julián Apasa, an Aymara-speaking former trader in coca and baize between La Paz and the *yungas*, who, though physically infirm, demonstrated an instinct for military strategy. Both Apasa and his wife, Bartolina Sosa, also a skilled military commander, originated from Sullcavi in the district of Sicasica. He may have worked in the *mita* for the Oruro mine. Bartolina had been a washerwoman and weaver. Apasa claimed to have been commissioned by Tupac Amaru to lead rebellion in Upper Peru, and his adoption of the name Katari provided a supposed connection with the late Tomás Katari and the possibility of a confusion of identities. In this way, his leadership sought political legitimacy and a relation to the Inca nobility. Apasa had little knowledge of Hispanic culture and did not know how to write. *Mestizo* or creole secretaries wrote his letters and proclamations. On the other hand, his background meant that he had experience of a wide range of social groups. At the same time, his adoption or practice of Andean village rituals gave a spiritual and supernatural dimension to his leadership.[41]

The Katari movement differed considerably from that of Tupac Amaru. All the leaders came from among the Aymara-speaking Kolla villages and were delegates of the Indian communities. The movement had a double objective – to free the Aymara peoples from the colonial power but also from the original leadership of Cuzco. The *Kataristas* were far more radical than the *tupamaristas* in that their movement was based on the vindication of popular grievances and the assertion of Indian rights. Leaders had to pay attention to sentiments from below and were repeatedly subjected to pressures from those they commanded. Apasa and his wife's siege of La Paz, which began on March 14, 1781, posed a dire threat to the colonial order in Upper Peru at the time of the Tupac Amaru

---

[40] Serulnikov, *Subverting Colonial Authority*, 126–27, 131, 158–59, 162, 176–77, 186.
[41] María Eugenia Valle de Siles, "Tupac Katari y la rebelión de 1781," *AEA*, XXXIV (1977), 633–64: see pp. 645, 648, 653–55. Thomson, *We Alone Will Rule*, 203, 221–22.

rebellion on the other side of the Lake. The siege lasted until the end of June. A second siege lasted seventy-five days, from August 5 until October 17, 1781. Serulnikov describes this phase as "full-blown anti-colonial warfare," a direct challenge to the colonial order in Upper Peru.[42] Despite Tupac Katari's personal devotion to the Virgin of Copacabana and his reluctance to confront Church and clergy, the latter generally shied away from the rebellion.[43]

Szeminski sees a distinct social dimension of the rebellion, suggesting that, if it had been successful, then the disaggregation of the haciendas, which had arisen during the seventeenth and eighteenth centuries on lands claimed as theirs by the Indians, would have resulted. The peasant dimension took second place in the Tupac Amaru rebellion to the political aspirations of one family of the nobility. This nobiliar objective was largely absent in the Tupac Katari movement.[44] When Tupac Amaru failed to take Cuzco in January 1781, the balance in the rebellions began to shift to Upper Peru. This corresponded to the rise of Apasa, who at his height commanded an army of 40,000 followers, and the opening of the siege of La Paz. *Tupamarista* forces, under Andrés Tupac Amaru and Miguel Bastidas, converged on La Paz to cooperate with Apasa. They sought, however, to undermine his authority by removing all his appointees. They did this under instructions from Diego Cristóbal, who referred to Tupac Katari as Apasa and denied him any right to Inca status.[45]

The continual social tension in the Andean zones from the 1730s onward demonstrated the vulnerability of Spanish colonial rule in those areas. The rebellions accompanied or followed attempts to put right abuses by means of the colonial legal system, exploited by the Indian population in Peru as in New Spain. They represented repeated challenges to the structure of ethnic relationships put in place from the time of Viceroy Toledo. Indian nobles sought a broader rule for themselves within the colonial system. The remarkable regional variations in these challenges were a striking aspect of the period and indicated that different dynamics were at play. This could be clearly seen in the cases of the Tupac Amaru and Katari movements.[46]

---

[42] Serulnikov, *Subverting Colonial Authority*, 208. Thomson, *We Alone Will Rule*, 182–89, 199–200, 206, 213. In all, the siege lasted for 101 days until relief came from official forces.

[43] Alipio Valencia Vega, *Julián Tupaj Katari* (Buenos Aires 1950), 39–44, 49–53.

[44] Szeminski, *La utopia tupamarista*, 248, 282, 284.

[45] Valle de Siles, "Tupac Katari," 644, 650–51, 657–58, 661–63.

[46] Serulnikov, *Subverting Colonial Authority*, 215–19, 222, 224–45. Garrett, *Shadows of Empire*, 196, 198.

Fear of the breakup of the Viceroyalty of Peru and the consequences of insurrection across the Upper Peruvian sector of the Viceroyalty of the River Plate explained the savage penalties meted out to the rebel leaders and their immediate associates by the official power. Spanish responses to the Tupac Amaru rebellion, moreover, fell heavily on the Indian nobles, punishing the caste as a whole rather than simply the supporters of the rebellion. The colonial regime used the defeat of the rebellions as a pretext to overhaul the political structure of Andean society, transferring what remained of autonomous *cacique* power to royal officials. The Spanish determination to stamp out all memory of the Inca tradition in the Andes showed how serious a threat the rebellions were considered by the colonial authorities. The rebellions revealed the structural flaws in the Spanish colonial system, never able to reconcile exploitation with the administration of justice.[47]

The question of whether the Tupac Amaru Rebellion in 1780 initiated the process of Independence in Peru has long been a topic of discussion.[48] As Cecilia Méndez points out, only during the military regime of General Juan Velasco Alvarado (1968–75) was Tupac Amaru portrayed as a national hero, precursor of Independence, and the Great Rebellion as the prime national epic, superseding in impact the War of the Pacific (1879–83), a saga of Peruvian and Bolivian defeat by Chile.[49] The rebellions before and during the 1780s took place in different historical times from those that broke out in 1809 and 1810 in Upper Peru, and in 1812 and 1814–15 in Lower Peru. In that respect, they were qualitatively distinct. Yet, they shook two viceregal regimes with their threat to overturn the colonial order as it had developed since the 1570s.

The version of Independence that triumphed in Peru and Upper Peru in 1824–26 did not correspond to the alternative vision that emerged during the course of the Andean eighteenth century. A narrower,

---

[47] Tupac Amaru and his wife, Micaela Bastidas (b. 1744), were executed on May 18, 1781, Tupac Katari on November 14, 1781, and Diego Tupac Amaru on July 19, 1783, Walker, *Tupac Amaru*, 152–67. Serulnikov, *Subverting Colonial Authority*, 223–24, 227. Garrett, *Shadows of Empire*, 187, 193–94, 206.

[48] *Colección Documental de la Independencia peruana [CDIP]*, 86 vols. Comisión Nacional del Sesquicentenario (Lima, 1971–76), corresponding to the period of nationalist-military rule.

[49] Cecilia Méndez, "La Guerra que no cesa: Guerras civiles, imaginario nacional y la formación del estado en el Perú," in Clément Thibaud, Gabriel Entin, Alejandro Gómez y Federica Morelli (comps.), *L'Atlantique révolutionnaire. (Une perspective ibéro-américaine* (Paris 2013), 379–420: see p. 381.)

creole-mestizo perspective became superimposed on a defeated and divided, ethnically diverse majority in the two new republican states of Peru and Bolivia. These became "nations" in which, officially, the majority of the population did not directly participate – except as tax-payers and laborers.

3

The Idea of Metropolis and Empire as One Nation

By the mid-eighteenth century three factors had become evident in the Hispanic Monarchy: the penetration of governing organs by Spanish Americans in their home territories; the metropolitan government's uncertain response; and Spain's continued inability to mobilize peninsular resources sufficiently to compete effectively with rival European Powers as an imperial Monarchy. Centralizing policies may have been seen as negative from an American point of view, but they did demonstrate that the metropolitan government was by no means moribund. Madrid's policies were frequently infused with constructive intentions. Many of the reforms benefited interested segments of the American population, as they also did in European Spain.[1] They tended, however, further to fragment American society by creating fresh polarities, particularly among the *peninsulares*. This latter was a major issue, and one which has not received sufficient attention in the historical literature. It meant that peninsular groups, powerful though numerically small, became increasingly divided in the decades after c. 1770, at precisely the time when American corporations were demanding a greater say in their destinies. Vested peninsular interests in the older *consulados* were often in opposition to metropolitan-government policies.[2]

Much of the history of the later seventeenth and eighteenth centuries deals with metropolitan efforts to recover control in the overseas territories. To do so, ministers in both Monarchies would either have to enlist

---

[1] See, for instance, Gabriel B. Paquette, *Enlightenment, Governance, and Reform in Spain and Its Empire, 1759–1808* (London 2008).
[2] Hamnett, *Politics and Trade*, 41–120.

the support of local interest groups and work through them or subordinate them. Although the Portuguese Monarchy appeared more willing to adopt the former policy, neither government succeeded entirely in pursuing either policy. The explanation lay in the two overriding factors: the growing determination of American poles of power to maintain and expand the positions they had already acquired within their home territories, and the inability of both metropoles to mobilize sufficient resources in order to assert effectively the plenitude of power that they claimed. As the course of events from the 1790s to the 1820s would demonstrate, it was the metropoles that collapsed.

"ONE SOLE NATION" – A MODIFICATION OF METROPOLITAN CENTRALISM?

Some metropolitan ministers in Madrid were aware of the negative aspects of their policies in the Indies, and, after 1768, began to suggest, as it turned out unsuccessfully, that the Hispanic Monarchy really constituted one "Nation." The contradiction between increased subordination of the American territories and the potential emergence of a pan-imperial national sentiment were, however, obvious.

The first intimation of a moderated policy appeared in March 1768 during the period of the Conde de Aranda's primacy. The historical literature has identified Aranda, whether justifiably or not, as an advocate of a looser form of imperial monarchy than that envisaged by his predecessor, Esquilache, although not one that might jeopardize its unity. A meeting of the combined Councils of Castile and the Indies in Madrid, following the controversy over the expulsion of the Jesuits, recommended a policy of union of sentiment among the king's vassals. This Council proposed to inculcate a belief that the Hispanic Monarchy as a whole constituted "One Sole Nation."[3]

The fiscals of the Council of Castile, José Moñino and Pedro Rodríguez de Campomanes, both of them initially protégés of Aranda who later dominated political life in the peninsula, argued that by such a method Spain could avoid the tension between metropolis and overseas territories evident in the relationship between Great Britain's Thirteen North American Colonies and the London government. No practical policies

---

[3] Rafael Olaechea, S. I. y José A. Ferrer Benimeli, *Aranda*, 2 vols. (Madrid 1978), II, 46–50. Luis Navarro García, "La crísis del reformismo borbónico bajo Carlos IV," *Temas Americanos*, 13 (Sevilla 1997), 1–8.

seem to have resulted from the meeting. Aranda's political eclipse, between 1773 and 1792, aborted any further vague consideration of a "contractual monarchy" or a "monarchy of estates," in which the nobility might participate directly and institutionally in governmental decisions as a "constituted body of state."[4]

Accordingly, the initiative in proposing constitutional changes passed from the metropolitan government to the American corporate institutions. Late in 1771, Charles III received a Representation from the Ayuntamiento of Mexico City, dated May 26. This amounted to a complaint against the metropolitan government's neo-absolutism. The City Council, composed of both *peninsulares* and Americans, requested a form of power-sharing between these two categories within the élite. The metropolitan government ignored this Representation, Mexico City Council's response to the policies of Visitor-General Gálvez.[5] A keen exponent of Caroline policy, Visitor-General Gálvez believed that New Spain had fallen prey to vested interests whose particular concerns conflicted with those of the Monarchy as a whole. He sought to restrict what he believed to be the unwarranted independence of the Mexico City Council by imposing six new *regidores honorarios* (ex-officio councilors) appointed by the viceroy. H. I. Priestley made the largely unnoticed comment that if the objective of metropolitan policy had been to strengthen the powers of the municipal councils, then the history of the separation of Mexico from Spanish rule might have been written with less bitterness than actually became the case.[6]

Aranda, during his time as Spanish Ambassador to the Court of Versailles, sent a confidential recommendation to Charles III in the aftermath of British-American Independence in 1783. In his view, the virtual elimination of France from the Americas opened the way for a new power in the form of the United States of America to challenge Spain's position in the continent. The Family Compact, he went on, had drawn Spain into a war with Great Britain that was not in its interests, which compounded the problem of retaining control of its extensive possessions. If the Floridas should fall to the USA in its attempt to control the Gulf of Mexico, New Spain would face great danger. Aranda maintained that

---

[4] Antonio Ferrer del Río, *Historia del reinado de Carlos III en España*, 4 vols. (Madrid 1856), II, 13, 52, 55, 83–116; III, 165–80.

[5] Juan Eusebio Hernández y Dávalos, *Colección de documentos para la historia de la guerra de Independencia de México*, 6 vols. (Mexico City 1877–82), vol. 1, 427–55.

[6] H. I. Priestley, *José de Gálvez. Visitor-General of New Spain (1765–1771)* (Berkeley 1916), 300–2. Philippe Castejon's research on Gálvez should provide fresh insights.

he had thought long and hard about this. Accordingly, the metropolitan government should take measures to prevent a catastrophe by placing three Princes Royal on the thrones of Mexico, Peru, and Spanish northern South America. These three new kingdoms would all recognize the authority of the Kings of Spain and send annual contributions to the metropolitan exchequer. Spain itself would govern directly only the islands of Cuba and Puerto Rico and two ports on the northern and southern mainland. The Spanish king and government, however, opposed such a course.[7]

The recommendation to hold on to Cuba and Puerto Rico directly had considerable foresight, since there was a possibility that Spain might actually be able to defend them. The Memorandum, however, foresaw neither the impending collapse of Bourbon France nor the strategic possibilities resulting from the strength of the British economy. Furthermore, no attention was given to American views on the subject of how the empire was to be governed. The preoccupation in Madrid with American contributions to the imperial treasury, already an irritant in the Americas, showed no sign of diminishing. Aranda, in fact, advised Floridablanca in May 1786 that the American territories should be exploited to the maximum so that metropolitan Spain would be in a better position, should they be lost altogether.[8]

When Charles III's government decided to assist the French in supporting the rebel Thirteen Colonies, Gálvez, promoted Minister of the Indies, secured the appointment in June 1780 of an outstanding member of his team, Francisco de Saavedra (1746–1819), as Royal Commissioner to the Caribbean, which had become a major theatre of war. Spain hoped to recover West Florida, expel the British from Central America, and possibly take back Jamaica, lost in 1655.

Saavedra wrote a diary of his experience, which revealed his thoughts on the tenuous nature of Spain's hold on the American possessions, especially if policy remained unchanged in the aftermath of the Independence of British North America. Independence was in the air from the 1780s onwards, and the scent of it drifted down to Spanish America. Saavedra arrived in Havana at the time of Bernardo de Gálvez' campaigns to drive the British from Florida in 1781. In November

---

[7] Centro de Estudios Históricos Mexicanos (CONDUMEX), Mexico City: Fondo XCII (1783), *Memoria secreta que el Conde de Aranda remitió a Carlos III sobre la independencia de las colonias inglesas.*

[8] Delgado Ribas, *Dinámicas imperiales*, 526–27.

and December, he crossed to New Spain, where Viceroy Martín de Mayorga warned him of the discontent caused in the viceroyalty by constant metropolitan fiscal pressure. While in the Indies, Saavedra became aware of the widespread dissemination of contemporary European ideas and literature, despite royal prohibitions. On return, he advised the home government to modify exclusive peninsular control by treating the Americans as responsible partners in the administration of their territories. He recommended the deepening of ties at all levels: irreproachable administration and mutual respect, intermarriage, the education of the sons of American notables in Spain, more colleges in the Indies, and treating the American territories exactly as though they were provinces of Spain. He went as far as to suggest that the liberalization of trade would finish off contraband once and for all. Saavedra expressed the "One Sole Nation" position at its clearest. He mentioned nothing, however, about representative institutions in the Americas, because there were none at the center of government in absolutist Spain. Although he advised the government to change tactics, the strategy remained the same. All decision-making remained concentrated in Madrid and there would be no representative bodies anywhere in the political system beyond the largely closed *cabildos*. Gálvez was pleased with Saavedra's conduct in the Indies, and secured his appointment as Intendant of Caracas in 1783.[9]

Saavedra remained a respected figure, appointed to the Council of War in Madrid in 1788. Only when financial crisis brought the Monarchy to its knees did Saavedra gain appointment to the highest offices of state as Secretary of Finance in 1798.[10]

Aranda criticized Gálvez' domination of the Ministry of the Indies on the grounds that it separated American administration from European, when both formed part of the same nation. For that reason, he wrote to Floridablanca, advising the abolition of the office after Gálvez' death in 1787 and the redistribution of its functions among the remaining five

---

[9] *Diario de D. Francisco de Saavedra durante la comisión que tuvo a su cargo desde 25 de junio de1780 hasta 20 del mismo mes de 1783*, edited by Francisco Morales Padrón (Seville 2004). Navarro García, "La crísis del reformismo," 6. Saavedra was a native of Seville, who joined the Army in 1768, rising to become secretary to General Alejandro O'Reilly, but was wounded in the siege of Algiers in 1775, the disaster which brought down O'Reilly. Saavedra, already friendly with Bernardo de Gálvez through common interest in American policy, moved into the Gálvez camp. In 1778, he was briefly Ambassador in Lisbon.

[10] See Morales Padrón's Introduction to the *Diario*.

secretariats of state. In any case, both Aranda and Floridablanca disliked the concentration of so much power and influence in Gálvez' hands, which the former saw as a source of nepotism and corruption.[11]

The collapse of the French political system in the course of 1789 left the Spanish government in a state of panic, fearing the spread of revolution to the peninsula. Into this context came the two further Representations from the *Ayuntamiento* of Mexico City on May 2, 1792 and May 27, 1800, addressed to the King. In effect, they repeated what the first Representation had said back in 1771. Grievances had deepened between 1771 and 1792, however, since Americans had lost their majority in the Audiencia of Mexico as a result of Gálvez' policies. The contents of the two Representations must have seemed to ministers in Madrid almost subversive against the background of events on the continent of Europe. As in 1771, the metropolitan government ignored them. In such a way, the last opportunity for an accommodation with American élites on the basis of power-sharing within the context of the old regime was lost.[12]

The reforms proposed in 1797 by Victorián de Villava, *fiscal* of the Audiencia de Charcas, also fell on deaf ears in Madrid. The objective was the preservation of the unity of the Monarchy. Villava, born in Zaragoza in 1747, was, like Saavedra, another important figure in the Spanish Enlightenment. Villava originated not from the Castilian tradition but from a dynasty of Aragonese magistrates. Charles IV appointed him fiscal of the older Audiencia of Charcas in 1789. Villava finally arrived in the capital, Chuquisaca, in June 1791.[13]

Villava advised the admission of Americans to the political process in their own territories. This advice was exactly the opposite of the strategy adopted by the metropolitan government since the accession of Charles III in 1759. Showing further his dissent from the neo-absolutist policies pursued, Villava recommended the convocation of a congress or *cortes* in Madrid representing the entire Hispanic Monarchy and to which American representatives would also be invited. At the same time, he recommended the reduction of the *audiencias* to purely judicial functions, stripping them of their immense and long-standing political authority. Such a departure, which anticipated the actions taken by the Constituent Cortes of 1810–13, would have devolved much of the administration to local bodies and introduced a representative body at the center of power in

[11] Delgado, *Dinámicas imperiales*, 522–23.
[12] Hernández y Dávalos, *Colección de documentos*, I, 429–40.
[13] Portillo, *La vida atlántica*, 14–24, 49–50.

Madrid. Villava's proposals were greeted with silence by the metropolitan government. Powerful as Villava's recommendations might seem, it is important to recall that he was making them in 1797, that is to say, at least fifty years after they might have been due.[14]

The combination of defeat in war, naval blockade, stagnation of the transatlantic trade, two series of concession to neutral traders in 1797–99 and 1805–08, and the imperial-level financial crisis, not to mention the revolutionary examples of France and the United States, finally brought home to the metropolitan government the precariousness of its hold on the American territories. The king was alarmed.

In 1806, Charles IV appeared to be considering the possibility of a new structuring of imperial government. Since this was a deeply sensitive issue for the monarch, his prime point of consultation was not his ministers but his confessor. This happened to be the Abbot of San Ildefonso de La Granja, Félix Amat, one of the leading reformers in the Spanish Church. The king wrote to Amat on October 6, expressing his preoccupation with the problem of how Spain might hold on to the Americas while, at the same time, being unable to defend them. The king's proposed solution was to transform the four viceroyalties into hereditary offices held by his two younger sons, D. Carlos and D. Francisco de Paula, his brother, D. Antonio, and his chief minister, the Prince of the Peace, Manuel Godoy. They would become vassals of the crown and contribute financially and militarily to the upkeep of the Monarchy. The resemblance to Aranda's supposed program of the late 1760s was striking. Amat thought that these were feasible proposals. However, nothing was done. It was far too late to give any semblance of reality to such an idea. In the following year, in any case, the Royal Family was torn apart by the Escorial Conspiracy of Ferdinand, Prince of Asturias, heir to the Throne.[15]

DIVISIONS AMONG THE PENINSULARES

The predominant groups in the capital cities of the Monarchy, regardless of whether they were of American or peninsula origin, frequently viewed their commercial interests in different ways. Madrid and the older

[14] Ricardo Levene, *Obras* (Buenos Aires 1942), vol. III, 296–303. For the revised text, see Portillo, *La vida atlántica*, 57–163.
[15] Ramón Corts, *L'arquebisbe Fèlix Amat (1750–1824): l'última Il.lustració espanyola* (Barcelona 1992), 214–17.

viceregal cities of Lima and Mexico City viewed policy from diverging perspectives.[16]

Commercial reforms in the Hispanic Monarchy were intended to reduce the dominance of the three Consulados of Cádiz, Mexico City, and Lima. The *comercio libre* policy, beginning with Cuba in 1764, only applied within the Monarchy; it did not envisage extension to foreign ports. Even after the implementation of the *"Reglamento para el comercio libre de España e Indias"* in 1778, the perils of transatlantic navigation and the cost of transit, insurance, and commissions still kept prices high in American markets. Barcelona merchants were still complaining in 1787 and 1788 of competition from American textile manufacture and requesting its suppression.[17]

Viceroy Revillagigedo the Younger (1789–94) of New Spain, protagonist of the Caroline commercial and administrative reforms, drew the metropolitan government's attention, in his *Instrucción Reservada* of 1794, to the decay of the trans-Pacific trade from Mexico to Manila. He attributed this to competition from the Royal Philippine Company.[18] The Crown had awarded this Company the monopoly of trade with Asia, bypassing New Spain.[19] As in the case of the Caracas Company of 1728, this formed part of the Madrid government's strategy of drawing trade away from the colony to colony exchange in favor of metropolitan trade. The aim was to send European manufactures directly from Cádiz to Manila, thereby cutting out the export of Mexican silver to Asia in return for Chinese silks, porcelain, and other Asiatic products traded through Manila.[20]

---

[16] Mathilde Souto Mantecón, *Mar abierto. La política y el comercio del Consulado de Veracruz en el ocaso del sistema imperial* (Mexico City 2001), 187–90, 225–26, 241–42, showing the growing polarities between Veracruz and Havana in the 1800s and 1810s.

[17] AGI Indiferente General 2436, Juan Gispert, Barcelona, 19 Septiembre 1787; Mariano Font, Barcelona, 24 Octubre 1787. José María Quirós, *Memoria de Instituto* (Havana 1814), read to the Consulado of Veracruz, 10 January 1814, p. 13, refers to a report from the Consulado of Barcelona on February 9, 1788, with the same sense. Bibiano Torres Ramírez y Javier Ortiz de la Tabla (eds.), *Reglamento y aranceles reales para el comercio libre de España a Indias de 12 de octubre de 1778* (Sevilla 1979). See also, Carlos Martínez Shaw, *Cataluña en la carrera de Indias* (Barcelona 1981); John Fisher, *Commercial Relations between Spain and Spanish Americas in the Era of Free Trade, 1778–1796* (Liverpool 1985).

[18] Conde de Revillagigedo, *Instrucción reservada, en Instrucciones que los virreyes de Nueva España dejaron a sus sucesores*, 2 vols. (Mexico City 1867–73), 416–18.

[19] Patricia H. Marks, *Deconstructing Legitimacy*, 539. Company ships were authorized to call in at Buenos Aires and Callao, discharge European products, and secure funds necessary for the Manila trade.

[20] Revillagigedo, *Instrucción reservada*, ibid.

Metropolitan ministers attributed the backwardness of the Indies to the traditional Consulados of Mexico City and Lima. New consulados were also established in Manila in 1769, Guatemala in 1793, and in Santiago de Chile, Buenos Aires, Havana, Cartagena, and Caracas in response to the requirements of local merchant communities and as a reflection of the metropolitan policy of diversification.[21] The metropolitan attempt to diminish the existing *consulados* had its roots earlier in the century. Between 1644 and 1753, the Consulado of Mexico City had generally administered the sales tax for the capital and its immediate environs, but the Crown in 1746–47, preoccupied with low yield, empowered the viceroys to transfer this to the civil bureaucracy. Accordingly, Revillagigedo the Elder did this in New Spain in 1754.[22] Viceroy Bucareli completed this process by terminating the lease for the rest of the viceroyalty in 1776. The establishment of the *Administración General de Alcabalas* came in the following year.[23] The effect of these measures on the prestige of the Consulado and the merchants' morale appears to have been drastic.[24]

Conflict within the Madrid government over what measures to adopt explained the checkered nature of decision-making during the course of the eighteenth century. Although Philip V's ministers had decided to terminate the fleets system at the end of the 1730s in favor of individual, registered ships (*registros sueltos*), the Consulados of Mexico City and Cádiz, which had an agent in Madrid, remained powerful enough to secure the reversal of this policy in 1754. Accordingly, six fleets arrived in Veracruz between 1757 and 1776.[25]

---

[21] See the wide-ranging discussion in Gabriel B. Paquette, "State-Civil Society Cooperation and Conflict in the Spanish Empire: The Intellectual and Political Activities of the Ultramarine Consulados and Economic Societies, c. 1780–1810," *JLAS*, 39 (2007), 263–98. José Ramírez Flores, *El Real Consulado de Guadalajara: notas históricas* (Guadalajara 1952). Ralph Lee Woodward, Jr., *Class Privilege and Economic Development. The Consulado de Comercio of Guatemala, 1793–1871* (Chapel Hill 1966), 119–20, 130, the Aycinena family spanned both Consulado and Cabildo and held the only noble title in Central America. Juan Fermín, the Marqués, became the first Prior of the Consulado in 1794 and a consul in 1803. Mariano Aycinena was Prior in 1824 and 1850.

[22] AGI México 1506, Revillagigedo to Ensenada, Mexico City 6 December 1751. AGI México 2502, Consulado to Viceroy, Mexico City 4 January 1753.

[23] AGI México 2347, Bucareli to Gálvez, no. 2959, Mexico City 27 May 1777.

[24] Hipólito Ruiz y Villarroel, *Enfermedades políticas que padece la capital de esta Nueva España en casi todos sus cuerpos de que se compone* (Mexico City 1785–87), ff. 20–21.

[25] Antonio García-Baquero, *Comercio colonial*, I, 90–1, 163–70, 330. Stein, "Bureaucracy and Business," 7–8.

Despite the crucial role of the Consulados of Lima and Mexico City in sustaining Spanish rule in the Indies, the Bourbon government persisted in identifying them as two of the principal sources of the Monarchy's problems. When Veracruz merchants, exasperated by the costly delays in Mexico City, requested a *consulado* in the Gulf port, Revillagigedo the Younger supported them. They requested that the proposed *consulado* should include the salubrious upland town of Jalapa in its jurisdiction, where many of them lived and conducted their business. The Veracruz merchants, Revillagigedo pointed out to the ministry, ardently supported the government's *comercio libre* policies, extended to New Spain in 1789 in face of strong opposition from the Mexico City merchants.[26] Some 300 merchants were doing business in the port at any given moment between 1796 and 1824.[27]

Equally, the viceroy supported the Guadalajara merchants' request for a *consulado in* 1791. The merchants took their stand on the economic potential of their vast region, especially with the recent expansion of cotton-spinning. New Galicia was also a rich mining area with a strong agricultural base, although its economy, they argued, was underexploited and starved of investment. They stressed the distinct interests and perspectives of the Guadalajara business community to that of Mexico City. Mercantile capital was spreading into the districts. Shops and warehouses in the Lake Chapala area, Sayula, Zacoalco, and the mining zones of Bolaños, Etzatlán, and Rosario (in Sinaloa) became linked to the city merchant houses, while district administrators usually operated in concert with them. The names of seven families recur throughout the primary sources for this period: the Vizcarra, Basauri, Echaurri, Sánchez Leñero, Porras Baranda, Sánchez de Tagle, and Cañedo.[28]

Leading the forty-eight signatories of July 12, 1791, were three militia captains who were also hereditary members of the city council, Juan López Portillo, Francisco Escobedo y Daza, and Patricio de Soto. The López

---

[26] AGI México 2506, Revillagigedo to Charles IV, no. 119 (reservada), Mexico City 11 November 1789.

[27] Souto Mantecón, *Mar Abierto*, 135. Jackie Brooker, *Veracruz Merchants, 1770–1829. A Mercantile Elite in Late Bourbon and Early Independent Mexico* (Boulder, Colorado 1993).

[28] AGI México 2506, Merchants to Jacobo Ugarte y Loyola, Guadalajara 12 July 1791; Merchants to Ugarte, Guadalajara 20 August 1791; Ugarte to Minister of Finance (Madrid), Guadalajara 4 February 1792. Van Young, *Hacienda and Market*, 67, 79–81, 88, 284. Antonio Ibarra, "Mercado global, economías coloniales y corporaciones comerciales: los Consulados de Guadalajara y Buenos Aires," *HM*, LXII, no. 4 (April–June 2013), no. 248, 1421–58.

Portillo were a prominent Guadalajara family, which had supplied magistrates of the Audiencia of Guadalajara in the eighteenth century and would provide political officials of the State of Jalisco in the nineteenth century. Escobedo's brother was also one of the leading city merchants. Soto, who originated from Spain, had used mercantile wealth to become a landed proprietor and warehouse-owner in the late eighteenth century, dealing in wheat flour. Miguel Sánchez Leñero, a member of one of the city's rising families from the 1730s, originating from Toledo, also joined the signatories. His brother Gabriel Sánchez Leñero, son of a former *alcalde mayor* of Aguascalientes, had married the heiress of the Santa Lucía Hacienda in the district of San Cristóbal de la Barranca near the Zacatecas border, secured municipal office and engaged in mine-financing and livestock-marketing. With matrimonial connections in Tepic, San Blas, and Compostela, the family extended its business network through outlying districts, particularly in cattle-raising zones. On the death in 1794 of Gabriel Sánchez Leñero's nephew Juan Alfonso, a Spaniard who appears to have joined his uncle in the 1750s, the total estate was valued at 500,000 pesos. One of the wealthiest merchants, José Monasterio, came from the Santander region of Cantabrian Spain. A bachelor during the 1790s, he would become Prior of the new *consulado* in 1802 and a hereditary city councilor. He was murdered by Hidalgo's insurgent forces after their occupation of Guadalajara in 1810–11 and his property confiscated.[29]

Revillagigedo took advantage of these requests to draw the Council of the Indies' attention, on August 31, 1793, to the Mexico City merchants' hostility toward *comercio libre*. He saw *comercio libre* and the creation of the two new *consulados* in New Spain as aspects of the same policy. The viceroy recognized, however, that the Crown would shrink from outright abolition of the Consulado of Mexico.[30] At the same time, he

---

[29] AGI México 1818, *expediente sobre la extinción de los consulados of Veracruz y Guadalajara*, cuaderno no. 3 (1797), ff. 1–1v, Merchants' Petition, casas consistoriales, Guadalajara 12 July 1791. Archivo de Instrumentos Públicos (Guadalajara), Protocolos 3 (1795–96), ff. 1–2v, Guadalajara 20 January 1796; AIPG Protocolos 9 (1806–7), no folio numbers, Guadalajara 19 June 1806; Protocolos 11 (1810–11), Guadalajara 22 August 1810; AIPG Protocolos 17 (1818), Guadalajara 20 May 1818. Archivo Histórico Municipal (Guadalajara), Paquete 36 (1820), Guadalajara 28 August 1820. Burkholder and Chandler, *From Impotence to Authority*, pp. 150, 174, 197, 212. Moisés González Navarro, *Anatomía del poder en México (1848–1853)* (Mexico City 1977), 279, 282–85. Francisco López Portillo was *oidor* from 1747. Jesús López Portillo, a moderate Liberal, became State Governor in 1851.

[30] AGN Virreyes 26, f. 42, Revillagigedo to Council of the Indies, no. 627 (reservada), Mexico City August 1793.

pressed the Mexico City Consulado for loans to the metropolitan government for the war effort against Revolutionary France. For their part, these
merchants attributed the dearth of circulating medium in New Spain to
comercio libre, particularly when imported manufactures were paid for in
bullion or specie. Accordingly, when they volunteered a loan of
one million pesos, they warned that capital would quickly dry up. They
appealed to ministers to reverse the policy of creating new *consulados*.[31]

This type of conflict reflected the intensity of debate over metropolitan
government attempts at reform. The issues touched upon wider questions
of the competition for wealth, its distribution, and how to create it, as well
as the increasingly controversial subjects of how power was managed in
Spain and its overseas territories, and who took the decisions that affected
the most influential groups in society, and for what motive. They divided
the peninsular merchants in New Spain, as elsewhere in the Monarchy,
with potentially destabilizing results.

Charles IV's ministers saw the incorporation of new *consulados* as a
contributory factor in the economic development of their prime American
territory. This accounted for their placing of a significant area of Gulf
coast and hinterland territory under the jurisdiction of the Consulado of
Veracruz, with the object of stimulating cotton production. They highlighted the Consulado of Mexico's failure, over two centuries, to construct
the long-projected highway between Jalapa and the port. Accordingly,
they commissioned the new *consulado* to make this a priority.
The accompanying objective would be settlement of small farms along this
road.[32] The Consulado of Mexico specifically objected to the funding of
the new *consulado*.[33]

The port of Veracruz, although Spain's main entry point into its viceroyalty, was, however, little more than a landing stage, where dangerous
north winds threatened to wreck shipping moored off coast. The port had no
lighthouses and the city still had no proper supply of fresh, running water in
1802. Yellow fever could be rampant during the rainy season, and travelers
and merchants hurried through, once they had secured permission to

---

[31] AGI México 2506, Consulado to Charles IV, Mexico City 28 November 1793; ibid to
ibid, Mexico City 28 April 1794.

[32] AGI México 2506, Real Cédula, Aranjuez 17 January 1795, articles 22–30; Real Cédula,
Aranjuez 6 June 1795, awarded the Consulado of Guadalajara jurisdiction over a huge
swathe of the north-west. See also José Ramírez Flores, "El Real Consulado de
Guadalajara. Notas históricas," in Robert S. Smith and José Ramírez Flores, *Los
Consulados de comerciantes de Nueva España* (Mexico City 1976 [1952]), pp. 88–92.

[33] AGN México 2512, Real Orden to Consulado of Veracruz, 27 October 1795.

proceed inland. In Jalapa they would then apply for a passport, which would allow them to continue into the country proper. In this sense, Jalapa became a surrogate frontier: in effect, an inland port at 1500 meters above sea level in the *tierra templada*. In 1806, the government established a quarantine zone just outside Jalapa in order to contain the spread of disease inland.[34]

Between 1795 and 1808, the bitter conflict over the new *consulados*, incorporated in 1795, deepened peninsular-merchant divisions. The governing boards of the two new *consulados* represented the most prominent merchants of their regions. In the case of Veracruz, at least two members were Mexicans: Andrés Gil de la Torre and Miguel Ignacio de Miranda. Merchants like Pedro Miguel de Echeverría (from Navarra) and Tomás Murphy (from Málaga) also came to exercise a leading role in internal and transatlantic trades through their position in Veracruz.[35] Souto Mantecón estimates that the Veracruz merchants controlled 59 percent of all imports and 78 percent of all exports (excluding sugar and silver) from New Spain, and played a major role in the dissemination of information concerning commerce and the economy in general.[36]

Revillagigedo's replacement, the Marqués de Branciforte, described the new consulados as "little monsters," which should be abolished immediately. Whether this was because of the deepening financial difficulties of the metropolitan government or because the incoming viceroy wished to ingratiate himself with New Spain's most powerful corporation, remains difficult to determine. Branciforte praised the Consulado of Mexico's long-standing role as creditor to the imperial government.[37]

---

[34] AGI Indiferente General 2437, ff. 15vta -16 vta, audiencia gobernadora to José de Gálvez (Minister of the Indies), no. 317, Mexico City 24 March 1785. AGI México 2511, Consulado to Miguel Cayetano Soler (Minister of Finance), Veracruz 26 November 1802. Alexander von Humboldt, *Essai politique sur la Nouvelle Espagne*, 5 vols. (Paris 1811), vol. 2, p. 355. Rachel A. Moore, *Forty Miles from the Sea. Xalapa, the Public Sphere, and the Atlantic World in Nineteenth-Century Mexico* (Tucson 2011), 2, 4, 28, 45–46, 51–52, 74.

[35] Javier Ortiz de la Tabla, *Comercio exterior de Veracruz, 1778–1821: crisis de dependencia* (Seville 1978), 205. Souto Mantecón, *Mar Abierto*, 287–9, 311–13. Susan Deans Smith, *Bureaucrats, Planters, and Workers. The Making of the Tobacco Monopoly in Bourbon Mexico* (Austin, Texas 1992), 65, 103, for Murphy.

[36] Souto Mantecón, *Mar Abierto*, 115, 157, 169.

[37] AGI México 1144, Branciforte to Diego de Gardoquí (Minister of State and Finance), no. 368 (reservada), Mexico City 31 May 1795; Branciforte to Gardoqui, no. 805, Mexico City 27 August 1796; ibid to ibid, no. 856, 27 September 1796; ibid to ibid, no. 891 (reservada), 27 December 1796. *Instrucciones que los virreyes de la Nueva España dejaron a sus sucesores*, 2 vols. (Mexico City 1877 and 1882), vol. II, *Branciforte*, paragraph 96, p. 569: he placed his faith "In the Royal Tribunals of the Consulado of Mexico and the Mining Tribunal, two firm columns which admirably uphold the most important branches

The Prior and Consuls of the Consulado of Veracruz defended their position.[38]

The new *consulados* both had agents in Madrid to press their case before the Council of the Indies. The Veracruz agent pointed to the advances made in road construction in the direction of Perote. He drew attention to increased cotton production on the Gulf coast in Tlalixcoyan and Medellín and to cattle-raising and timber-cutting in Tlacotalpan, Alvarado, and Boca del Río. Added to this, was the recruitment of a force of 1000 men to protect the port in the event of a British attack.[39] The Guadalajara agent welcomed the increased competition within New Spain and roundly defended the beneficial effects of *comercio libre*. In his view, the Mexico City merchants longed for the return of the old Fleet System with high prices and large profits for themselves.[40] The *consulados'* defense anticipated much of the argument that would subsequently appear during the pressure for a federal system of government in 1823–24.

The Consulado of Mexico found itself in continuous opposition to metropolitan policy during the 1790s and the first half of the 1800s. Despite the commercial and administrative changes since 1778, however, Cádiz did not lose its predominance in the American trade.[41]

The mercantile community and municipal authorities of Puebla unsuccessfully pressed for the incorporation of a *consulado* in their city in the same period. Puebla merchants similarly complained of delays, abuses, and costly litigation in Mexico City. All they secured, however, was a provincial committee in 1796, in face of strong Mexican opposition. Undeterred, they pressed in 1805 for a proper consular or outlying deputation, which was granted in 1807, although subordinated to the Consulado of Mexico and with little prestige or power. Similar *diputaciones consulares* also existed in Valladolid, Guanajuato, Querétaro, Orizaba, and Oaxaca.[42]

---

of government responsibility, and upon which the viceroys can depend in their effort to assist the Crown in times of urgent financial need."

[38] AGI México 1144, Andrés Gil de la Torre (Prior), Miguel Ignacio de Miranda, and Remigio Fernández to Diego de Gardoqui, Veracruz 15 October and 3 November 1796. AGI Estado 28, no. 104, doc. 42, *Representación del Consulado de Veracruz*, 10 October 1798.

[39] AGI Mexico 1144, *apoderado* to Council of the Indies, Madrid 4 June 1804.

[40] AGI Mexico 1144, *apoderado* to Council of the Indies, Madrid 11 August 1804.

[41] García Baquero, *Comercio colonial*, I, 147–52.

[42] Archivo Histórico de Hacienda: *Diputaciones foráneas*, leg. 463, exp. 3, f. 5, Real Orden, Madrid 8 July 1807. Robert S. Smith, "The Puebla Consulado, 1821–1824," *Revista de Historia de América*, no. 21 (1946), 151–60.

The Consulado of Veracruz had good fortune right from the beginning in its choice of administrators, particularly its secretaries, Vicente Basadre, Juan Donato de Austria, and José María Quiroz. Their annual reports to the Consulado's Central Committee explain a great deal about the issues of their day and the problems encountered by the new corporation. Basadre (1750–1828), who took office on August 3, 1795, was a partisan of the reforming policies in the spirit of Jovellanos and Saavedra. He knew the empire well, having been in the Philippines and travelled to the Chinese Empire in the years before his return to Spain in 1789. From that time until his appointment in Veracruz, he had served as a member of the Governing Board of the Royal Philippine Company. In 1809, he would take office as Intendant of Venezuela at Saavedra's recommendation.[43]

Back in Madrid from 1802, Basadre in 1807 strongly denounced the Consulados of Cádiz, Mexico, Lima, and Manila. He saw the Mexico City Consulado as "a monstrous, tyrannical, oppressive and destructive body," and singled out its lack of concern for the improvement of conditions in the port of Veracruz. In Basadre's view, the *comercio libre* legislation had benefited all the provinces of New Spain and led to the disappearance of foreign woolens and silks from the list of imports through Veracruz, although linens had overtaken the more sluggish peninsular industry. Five years of warfare up to 1802 hit Spanish industry badly. During the brief period of peace from 1802 to 1804, Catalan textiles had managed to supersede foreign competition, although the renewal of war in 1804 again hurt Spanish industry. A second round of concessions to neutral shippers had brought in more English cottons, which proved highly popular in New Spain, competing with home products, since they were light and made in imitation of the cottons of India.[44]

---

[43] Saavedra had been the second Intendant of Venezuela. Following the Venezuelan Revolution of April 19, 1810, Basadre arrived back in Spain on July 4. Basadre's secret dealings in 1808 with Joseph Bonaparte's Minister of Finance, Miguel de Azanza, former Viceroy of New Spain (1798–1800), did not become known until 1814, while he was in New Spain, where he had returned in 1812 in the expectation of an appointment to an Intendancy. On arrival in Cádiz in 1818, he was arrested as an "*afrancesado*" and found guilty by Ferdinand VII's Council of the Indies. In La Coruña, in 1824, he was accused of being a "constitutionalist" by Ferdinand's partisans, and died without exoneration in 1828. In such a deplorable way Ferdinandine Spain treated one of the country's most intelligent and able public servants. See Manuel Lucena Salmoral, *La economía americana del primer cuarto del siglo XIX, vista a través de las memorias escritas por D. Vicente Basadre, Intendente de Venezuela* (Caracas 1983), 14.

[44] AGI Indiferente General 2439, Basadre to Godoy (Prince of the Peace), Madrid 21 July 1807. He stated that English cottons had been arriving in increasing quantities

Despite the contradictory nature of these arguments, the metropolitan government, also under threat at home from traditionalist opponents of all types, kept its options open right throughout the war with Great Britain. When the government of Charles IV and Godoy collapsed in March 1808, still no decision had been reached. It seemed out of the blue when the new ministry, on April 2, 1808, upheld the reform, rejected the position put forward by Branciforte in the previous decade, and refused the Consulado of Mexico's call for abolition.[45]

CUBA: A DIVERGENT VIEW OF THE EMPIRE

The metropolitan government and the circles surrounding it were acquiring a view of the overseas territories that prioritized Cuba. This probably originated with the group around Alejandro O'Reilly and the Conde de Ricla, during the first part of Charles III's reign. They saw Cuba and the Caribbean as the first line of imperial defense.[46] As a result, Cuba became the experimental laboratory to test the feasibility and efficacy of the two distinctive aspects of Caroline imperial policy: the introduction of the Intendant system and the *comercio libre* concessions to a range of ports in the Monarchy. The militarization of the island accompanied their implementation, with the result that taxes had to rise, the *alcabala* rising from 2 percent to 6 percent. A range of concessions to the creole and resident Spanish population made this more palatable.[47]

Possibly, the plan attributed to Aranda may have reflected such a view. In all events, two overriding questions faced the ministers of Charles III: the defense of the American possessions in the light of the British seizure of Havana in 1762–63; and how to respond to the escalating tensions evident within the continental American territories from 1765 through to the Highland Peruvian rebellions of 1780–83.

---

since 1792. Basadre advocated legitimizing the contraband trade in cottons by taxing them. The competition, he believed, would force Spanish producers to adapt to market demand.

[45] AGI México 1144, Council of the Indies, Madrid 2 April 1808. See also AGI Mexico 1818, *expediente sobre la extinción de los consulados de Veracruz y Guadalajara*. AGI Mexico 1819, Consulado to Antonio Porcel, Guadalajara 12 May 1809. Seventeen members of the *consulado* were listed in 1809.

[46] The work of Allan Kuethe has pioneered the emphasis on the defense of Cuba.

[47] Allan J. Kuethe and G. Douglas Inglis, "Absolutism and Enlightened Reform: Charles III, the Establishment of the *Alcabala*, and Commercial Reorganization in Cuba," *Past and Present*, 109 (1985), 118–43.

As we have seen, ministers from the time of Patiño had appreciated the urgency of drawing the entire edifice of the Hispanic Monarchy more tightly together through commercial, administrative, and military reforms. A consciousness that something was radically wrong in the Americas permeated government circles and preoccupied the politicized intellectuals who sought to influence policy. The shock of the strategic vulnerability of Manila and Havana – especially Havana at the center of the Caribbean-Gulf of Mexico network – galvanized the ministry into resuming earlier reform projects and taking them to a more intensive stage.[48]

During the course of the events that played out in the four decades from 1780 to 1820, two propositions emerged, which must have seemed alarming at first appearance. Yet, neither was entirely new. The first of these was the view that the continental territories presented more trouble than they were worth, and the second, an old cry from the early seventeenth century, was that the explanation for Spain's perceived backwardness in relation to its imperial rivals lay in the false promise of the overseas empire's wealth. This myth, it was said by the *arbitristas* and again at the end of the 1810s, accounted for Spanish poverty.[49]

A view began to emerge at the end of the eighteenth century that Spain might well be better off concentrating her interests and resources in the defense of the defensible, namely the position in the Caribbean, with Cuba as the strategic core. The metropolitan government's Cuban policy began to reflect this objective from the middle of the 1760s with the careful reconstruction of the Spanish military presence on the island and the attention to its defenses.[50] In the view of Sherry Johnson, this policy led to both a social transformation of the island through the immigration of new groups associated with these aims, and a binding together of the ties between leading Cuban families, the new military, and the Spanish metropolis in the following decades. This is a powerful argument, which reshapes our knowledge of Cuba in the later eighteenth century, and, by

---

[48] See Johanna von Grafenstein Garcis, *Nueva España en el circuncaribe, 1779–1808. Revolución, competencia imperial y vínculos internacionales* (Mexico City 1997), 79–195, for a detailed explanation of the importance of this network and the role of New Spain, as supplier of large funds, within it.

[49] This was the view of a representative group of Madrid merchants: Archivo de Palacio Madrid], *Papeles Reservados de Fernando VII*: tomo 16, ff. 35–45 obv., Junta de diputados to the King, Madrid 18 June 1816.

[50] For the context, see Allan J. Kuethe, *Cuba, 1753–1815. Crown, Military, and Society* (Knoxville, TN 1986).

so doing, transforms our understanding of Cuba's relationship to the rest of the Spanish American empire.[51]

As Johnson argues, these earlier factors have largely been overlooked in the historical literature. This has focused on the subsequent economic transformation of Cuba from the 1790s through the intensification of sugar cultivation and the expansion of slavery in response to it. The Cuban sugar economy, developing in response to the crisis of French rule in Saint-Domingue (Haiti), led to further metropolitan focus on the interests of the island.[52] This represented the second phase of a policy putting emphasis on Cuba that was already in place from the mid-1760s. It led to considerable rivalry between Havana and Veracruz, until then the prime locus of Hispanic mercantile influence in the Gulf region, until the latter port by 1812 lost its primacy, a situation made worse by Mexican-insurgent operations across the main routes from Mexico City in the port hinterland.[53]

The singularity of the Caribbean in Spain's strategic calculations became evident as the prospect of a general European war drew nearer. In May 1793, Diego de Gardoqui, Finance Secretary, first appointed during Aranda's final ministry, outlined for the benefit of the Council of State the implications of French isolation and financial weakness for the Spanish alliance and defense of the overseas territories. Gardoqui envisaged a Spain on its own, appealing for a reinvigoration of earlier Caroline policies of boosting industrial production in the metropolis and for financial restraint. This situation highlighted the crucial importance of maintaining Spain's position in the Caribbean. The Council of State responded to Colonial Secretary Antonio Valdés' report that Guanatánamo Bay, in south-east Cuba, should become a major naval base. In mid-October, Cuban planters, through their agent in Madrid, requested special tariff privileges with foreign ports, designed to stimulate primary exports and the re-export trade. Such a demand reflected the growing level of trade between Havana and the United States' port of Baltimore. The metropolitan government viewed this favorably, an indication of the growing significance of Cuba in its policy calculations, regardless of the doctrine of commercial monopoly.[54]

---

[51] Sherry Johnson, *The Social Transformation of Eighteenth Century Cuba* (Gainesville 2001): particularly the first four chapters. See also Allan J. Kuethe, "The Development of the Cuban Military as a Sociopolitical Élite, 1763–83," *HAHR*, 61 (November 1981), 695–704.

[52] Franklin W. Knight, "Origins of Wealth and the Sugar Revolution in Cuba, 1750–1859," *HAHR*, 57 (May 1977), 231–53.

[53] Souto Mantecón, *Mar Abierto*, 213–24, 216, 219, 221–23, 227–28.

[54] Stein and Stein, *Edge of Crisis*, 36–38.

THE IDEA OF A "VASTO IMPÉRIO LUSO-BRASILEIRO"
AS THE REUNIÃO DE "UM SÓ É ÚNICO REINO."

There was no Viceroy of Brazil until 1720, and even then he was little more than *primus inter pares* among the provincial captains general, and did not possess the faculties of the Spanish American viceroys. In reality, each of the captaincies-general continued to be more closely linked to Lisbon than to each other. Despite the fact that by the 1730s Brazil became Portugal's most important overseas territory, no distinct body presided in Lisbon over its general administration. Brazilian affairs continued to form part of the duties of the Overseas Council, which also dealt with Portuguese Africa and Asia.[55] No separate ecclesiastical hierarchy existed until the institution of the Archbishopric of Bahia in 1676, separate from the original metropolitan see of Lisbon.[56] Large territories in northern Portuguese America, furthermore, did not form part of Brazil at all. Between 1621 and 1777, the *Estado do Maranhão e Grão Pará* was administered directly from Lisbon. At least until the 1760s, that territory remained largely beyond the orbit of the slave-plantation economy and was overwhelmingly Indian in ethnic composition. Jesuit pressure on the Madrid and Lisbon governments to protect resettled Indian communities from white slavers helped to explain this separation. The strategic importance of Amazônia and the presence of the English, Dutch, and French in Guiana reinforced these policy decisions. The metropolitan government, from the 1620s, constructed a line of forts to safeguard its position on the river systems as far up the Amazon as Belém and Santarém, and by 1669 at São José de Manaus. At Santo Antonio do Gurupá, the fort built in 1623 guarded the mouth of the River Xingú. The Alcântara fort opposite São Luis protected the capital of Maranhão.[57] Until the mid-eighteenth century, Portuguese America "can be seen as three distinct colonies."[58]

---

[55] Schwartz, "Formation of Colonial Identity," 33–35.
[56] Schwartz, "Colonial Brazil: The Role of the State," 1–23, and "The Formation of Colonial Identity," 32–33. Francis A. Dutra, "Centralization versus Donatorial Privilege: Pernambuco, 1602–1630," in Dauril Alden (ed.), *The Colonial Roots of Modern Brazil* (California 1973), 19–60.
[57] Manuel Nunes Dias, *Fomento e Mercantilismo: A Companhia Geral do Grão Pará e Maranhão (1755–1778)* (Pará 1970), 2 vols., vol. 11, 40–49.
[58] Luiz Toledo Machado, *Formação do Brasil e Unidade Nacional* (São Paulo 1980), 31, 63. Schwartz, "Formation of Colonial Identity," 33: "Nothing was done to give a sense of unity or real political cohesion to Portuguese America."

Metropolitan Portugal faced similar problems to those of Imperial Spain with regard to its deficiency of resources, despite the gold imports from Brazil.

For the first half of the eighteenth century, Portuguese Brazil experienced a spectacular cyclical boom in an imperial trade that had begun over three centuries before. By then, however, the limits of empire were plain to see. To maintain, govern, and defend an empire required an enormous investment, not only in money but also in personnel and technical support such as shipping. Portugal faced a chronic shortage of all three, plus a poor agrarian economy, that limited population growth.[59]

Portugal depended on imported grains from northern Europe during the eighteenth century and, by the end, from Virginia and the Carolinas.[60] The Brazil trade made sufficient profit for the metropolis to achieve a favorable balance of trade during the 1790s. Portugal achieved a trade surplus with Great Britain, partly through the revival of artisan textile manufacture – woolens, cottons, linens from the Minho and silks from Trás-os-Montes – exported through Oporto to Brazil. British textiles paid a tariff of 30 percent. Colonial re-exports, nevertheless, accounted for more than 60 percent of all metropolitan exports up to 1808. Portuguese government finance still remained in a precarious condition, since Brazil traditionally contributed little to remedy this. Increasing taxes there threatened further rebellions, while any attempt to increase customs revenue encouraged contraband. Portugal on the outbreak of war with Spain in 1801 could not rely on short-term loans. The extemporary solution proved to be, as in Spain from 1780, bills of payment, guaranteed by the merchants, and the creation of an amortization fund. The Treasury was momentarily saved, however, by the short duration and easy termination of the war, given Spain's own condition.[61]

As Portugal gradually became drawn toward the European conflicts of the twenty-year period 1789–1808, the strategic weakness of the Monarchy became the focus of ministerial discussion. This meant that the period of reforms associated with the Pombal era did not abruptly end, much as traditionalists might have desired. On the contrary, reform

---

[59] Carla Rahn Phillips, "The growth and composition of trade in the Iberian empires, 1450–1750," in Tracy (ed.), *The Rise of Merchant Empires*, 34–101: see p. 69.

[60] Kenneth J. Maxwell, "The Atlantic in the Eighteenth Century: A Southern Perspective on the need to return to the 'Big Picture'," *TRHS*, 6th series, 3 (1993), 209–36: p. 219.

[61] Valentim Alexandre, *Os sentidos do Império. Questão colonial na crise do Antigo Regime Portugués* (Oporto 1993), 319–29, 769–814. Adelman, *Sovereignty*, 115–16, 125–26, 129–30.

became all the more urgent, as, from the perspective of Lisbon, the European situation worsened. Accordingly, discussion extended to how best reforming polices would be able to uphold monarchical authority and the unity of the Empire. As in Spain, the idea of putting limits to absolute monarchy in Portugal did not come out of nowhere. Similarly, this problem became closely connected to the wider issue of restructuring the entire Lusitanian Monarchy.

The example of the British-American Revolution provided the idealized model for the Brazilian conspirators of the center south-eastern province of Minas Gerais. Nevertheless, the *mineiro* conspirators' goals in 1789 were provincial rather than potentially "national." They sought to dismantle the juridical structures of Portuguese colonialism and set up a parliament not in the capital of the viceroyalty but in their home capital city of Vila Rica (Ouro Preto). Their vision of a future society remained limited to the non-slave population in a province in which 45 percent of the population were in fact slaves. The conspirators came from the educated and propertied elite of the province, many of them slave-owners. Maxwell contrasts this group of "middle-aged lawyers, magistrates, and clerics" with the conspirators in Salvador in 1798. These "mulatto artisans, soldiers, sharecroppers and salaried school-teachers" exalted the French Revolution of 1789 rather than the American of 1776, which had been the *mineiros'* ideal.[62]

The Salvador conspirators, by contrast, called for the overthrow of the whites. Three *pardos* and one son of a slave led the Bahia plot. In the Bahian Recôncavo, the sugar-producing hinterland of Salvador and Brazil's most densely populated region, further attempted uprisings took place in 1807, 1809, and 1813. In this last uprising, some 600 slaves, mainly of Hausa and Dahomey origin, unsuccessfully attempted to seize control of the provincial capital.[63] István Jancsó sees the run of these conspiracies from 1789 onwards as recurrent aspects of the crisis of the

---

[62] Kenneth Maxwell, "The Generation of the 1790s and the Idea of Luso-Brazilian Empire," in Dauril Alden (ed.), *Colonial Roots of Modern Brazil* (California 1973), 114, 118–19.

[63] Luis Henrique Dias Tavares, *História da Bahia* (Salvador 1974), 153, and the same author's *História da Sedição intentada na Bahia em 1798.* ('A Conspiração dos Alfaiates') (São Paulo 1975), 9. Luis Viana Filho, *O Negro na Bahia* (Rio de Janeiro 1988 [1946]), 14–15, 172–73, 215–16, 219–20. João José Reis, *Rebelião escrava no Brasil. A história do levante dos malês* (São Paulo 1987 [1986]), 14–16. In 1808, the free population of Salvador and thirteen rural parishes have the balance between free and slave at roughly 60 percent and 40 percent, respectively, with whites at around 20 percent of the free population. In the city itself, the whites constituted some 28 percent of the population. The city grew rapidly between 1777 and 1807 (by 31 percent), increasing the

colonial *ancien régime* in Brazil. Emphasizing the size of the city, with an estimated population of 60,000 at the end of the century, he argues that the Salvador conspiracy of 1798 represented the first example of cross-class alliance directed toward a political objective.[64]

No serious thought was given by the Lisbon ministry to the convocation of the Cortes as participant in an agreed reform program. This was anathema in the eighteenth-century political context. When, for instance, the towns of Minas Gerais had set up a junta of representatives of their councils to discuss matters of taxation from 1710 onwards, the Crown managed to suppress it by the 1730s. Right through until the departure of the Royal Family for Brazil at the end of 1807 and during the Braganza dynasty's sojourn in Rio de Janeiro, no attempt was ever made to summon a Cortes. The hallmark of ministerial policy remained the maintenance of royal supremacy within the political processes combined with its religious mandate.[65]

The *Academia Real das Ciências* in Lisbon, founded under the influence of one of Portugal's principal noblemen, the Duque de Lafões, remained at the center of intellectual discussion of the unitary nature of the Lusitanian Monarchy and the interdependence of its component parts. The scientific expeditions across the Empire and attempts to improve mining in Brazil formed another essential aspect of this policy.[66]

Rodrigo de Souza Coutinho became closely identified with the policy gaining ground in Lisbon during the later 1790s that metropolitan Portugal needed to recognize with greater emphasis the important position of America within the Monarchy and, accordingly, accommodate the Brazilian élites. In common with many of his contemporaries in and around the Lisbon government, Souza Coutinho defended Portuguese hegemony within the Monarchy and sought to draw on Brazilian resources in order to uphold it. Not the least of this was the desire to sustain the Portuguese role as commercial entrepôt of the Monarchy and intermediary between the Empire and the world economy.[67]

---

proportion of the free and enslaved African and Afro-Bahian component from 64 percent to 72 percent.

[64] István Jancsó, *Na Bahia, contra o Império. História do Ensaio de Sedição de 1798* (São Paulo and Salvador 1996), 22, 38–9, 55–8, 65–71.

[65] Schwartz, "The Formation of a Colonial Identity," 33.

[66] Ana Rosa Cloclet da Silva, *Inventando a Nação: Intelectuais Ilustrados e Estadistas Luso-Brasileiros na Crise do Antigo Regime Português, 1750–1822* (São Paulo 2006), 233. Maxwell, "The Generation of the 1790s," 134–36.

[67] Biblioteca Nacional (Rio de Janeiro): Manuscript Collection: Coleção Linhares 1-29-13-16, Rodrigo de Souza de Coutinho, Memória sobre o Melhoramento dos Domínios na

Study of Portuguese policy from the 1770s to 1808 reveals the difference with Spanish policy in the era of Gálvez and Areche. Despite this tactical distinction, overall strategic aims remained similar. In both Monarchies, certain ministers pressed the urgency of reform, in order to preserve unity and provide for effective defense against foreign predators. Nevertheless, we should not forget that Spain and Portugal, despite royal marriages and treaties, remained bitter rivals in both the peninsula, where the two countries went to war in 1762 and 1801, and in South America. In fact, Spain represented the constant menace. Fortress towns like Tuy in Galicia and Valença in Portugal faced one another across the Minho, as did a range of other border positions in the peninsula. Hostile designs on both sides marked relations across the Rio de la Plata. The territorial expansion of Portuguese America westward challenged Spanish claims to territory in the remote interior.

Despite the policy objective of maintaining the unity of the Monarchy, the Portuguese government did little to promote unity within the disjointed territories of Portuguese America. This remained the case even beyond 1808. Provincial captaincies pursued their own interests and had little sense of coordination or of belonging to another broader polity than the Lusitanian Monarchy as a whole. "Brazil" in 1810 was in no sense a potentially coherent "nation." It would be erroneous to suppose that it was. Portuguese colonialism did not involve "nation-building" but fostering the interests of the metropolis. The Monarchy was conceived as an agglomeration of distinct provinces bound directly to Lisbon. This is what was meant by "unity." These provinces had different cultures and perspectives from one another – and there were many other such distinctions within them as well. Between 1670 and 1720, the Crown had increased the powers of provincial governors, giving them the right of direct correspondence with Lisbon, bypassing the Governor-General in Bahia. The north-eastern provinces of Portuguese America still looked more closely to West Africa and Lisbon than they did to Rio de Janeiro.[68]

During the period from the 1790s to the 1820s, issues such as these would come to a head. The catalyst was the question of metropolitan Portugal's continuing neutrality in the European conflict, in which Caroline Spain had become the ally of the French Directory in 1795. As early as October of that year, Souza Coutinho was preoccupied with

América, presented to the Prince Regent, Dom João, Lisbon (no date), ff. 8–17v. Souza later became Conde de Linhares.

[68] Schwartz, "Formation of Colonial Identity," 33.

this issue, in view of Spain's traditional enmity toward its Iberian neighbor. It seemed increasingly impossible to maintain neutrality. Yet, the country's financial situation required non-participation in the war. Hence, financial reform was his top priority, since only stable finances could provide the armed forces to defend frontiers and empire. This he recommended to D. João in his *Planos de Fazenda* of July 1798, thereafter calling for the rapid amortization of paper money and the public debt in January 1800. Souza Coutinho's position as President of the Royal Treasury from 1801 gave him greater authority. Quickly, the spotlight fell on the privileged structure of the old regime, viewed as an obstacle to reform and, therefore, to the survival of the Monarchy. As in the Spain of Charles IV, ecclesiastical revenues and properties fell under scrutiny. The principal obstacles to metropolitan Portugal's recovery continued to be the survival of feudal dues, the concentration of landownership in few hands, the large number of clerics, low productivity, and poor returns on invested capital. The continued influence of the nobility and clergy at the center of government further obstructed reform, even though, as a counterbalance, Pombal had sought to promote Portuguese mercantile interests.[69]

Great political skill would be needed: either the Monarchy would collapse under the strain of war and invasion or the ministry would collapse under fire from a conservative and clerical opposition at Court. Souza Coutinho's principal case rested on the continuation of the British connection and reform at home as protection against the French and security for the existing juridical structure in Portugal. He continued to warn the Prince Regent of Portugal's vulnerability in 1803, despite the brief period of peace between Great Britain and France. Portugal had already lost Olivença to Spain in 1801. The "French party" at Court, however, brought him down in 1803 and he spent four years in eclipse. With the renewal of war in 1805, the French grip tightened on Portugal.[70]

Insuperable as these problems were, Braganza Portugal still had one advantage over late Bourbon France and Spain. The function of kingship was not breaking down in Portugal, as it had been in the France of Louis XV and XVI or under Charles IV in Spain. Queen Maria I's incapacity had been taken care of by the smooth acquisition of her political faculties by D. João, who proved to be a capable ruler, disposed to paying attention to

[69] Coclet da Silva, *Inventando a Nação*, 173–84.
[70] BN (RJ) Col. Linhares 1-19-13-22, Souza Coutinho to D. João, Quinta de São Pedro, 11 August 1803.

intelligent ministers and advisers. In both Portugal and Brazil, the person of the monarch continued to be venerated, shrouded as it was in religious aura. Neither the Royal Family and Court nor the ministry were objects of a generalized disdain, as they had been in the France of Louis XVI or were in Spain under Charles IV and Godoy. Even when Souza Coutinho fell, able ministers sought an alternative way out for the Monarchy. When Souza Coutinho returned to primacy in 1807, he could depend on the support of strong colleagues, such as the Vizconde de Anadia as the Minister of Navy and Ultramar and Francisco José de Portugal as President of the Royal Treasury.[71] The Prince Regent trusted Souza Coutinho's judgment, most of all because of the successful policy *coup* of transporting the Royal Family to Rio de Janeiro in the very face of the French invaders. Maxwell argues that, "The fact that D. João arrived in Brazil so well prepared was important to the success of the establishment of monarchy in Portuguese America." He went along with his chief minister in encouraging Brazilians to share in the process of policy-making.[72]

The Council of State in Lisbon had spent several months, between August and November 1807, discussing metropolitan Portugal's dangerous situation. The disintegration of the Spanish Bourbon monarchy made this even more urgent, since French intervention in Spain seemed the likely outcome. The crunch came when the French Foreign Minister, Talleyrand, requested Portuguese adhesion to the Continental System imposed on occupied or allied Europe by the Berlin and Milan Decrees of December 21, 1806. This request also included rupture of relations with Great Britain, the expulsion of Lord Strangford, the British Minister, the exclusion of British trade, the arrest of all British subjects and the confiscation of their properties, a declaration of war on Great Britain, and the merging of the Portuguese fleet with the remnants of the Spanish Navy. Such demands would have reduced the Lusitanian Monarchy to abject dependency on France. At an urgent meeting of the Council of State at the Mafra Palace, Souza Coutinho on August 27 reaffirmed the Portuguese government's preference for the British alliance. It became urgent to activate his proposal, already conceived back in 1803, that, in order to preserve their security and the continued independence of the Lusitanian Monarchy, the Royal Family should proceed on British ships to the safety of Brazil. The "French party"

---

[71] Coclet da Silva, *Inventando a Nação,* 180–82, 201, 212.
[72] Maxwell, "Generation of the 1790s," 142–43.

feared that the transportation of the Royal Family to Rio de Janeiro would lead to the creation of an independent Brazilian state under British protection. They could not explain, however, how rupture with Great Britain would preserve Brazil within the Monarchy.[73]

The Council of State heard on November 24 that French troops had entered Portuguese territory through Spain, in order to force the Portuguese government to adhere to the Continental System. Spanish desire to see the partition of Portugal was well known in Lisbon. Five days later, the Royal Family, Court, and ministry left for Rio. The implications for the future balance of power within the Monarchy were far-reaching. The center of power would pass from Lisbon to the American city of Rio de Janeiro. Such a transfer would affect the political economy of metropolis and empire by resulting in the promotion of the interests of Brazil to the detriment to those of Portuguese commerce and industry, both of which had been fostered during the Pombal era. That, in turn, would weaken the Portuguese bourgeoisie, whose support Pombal had counted on for his reform policies designed to save the Monarchy.

THE FAILURE OF THE FIRST "ONE-NATION" EXPERIMENT AND THE COLLAPSE OF THE SPANISH METROPOLIS

It was not debt in itself that brought down the Spanish absolute monarchy during the decade before 1808, but the inability to manage it. Neither France before 1787 nor Spain before 1808 resolved this problem. Great Britain was also under intense financial pressure throughout the long war years, which produced no great successes until the naval victory at Cape St. Vincent in 1797. Home society felt the moral and financial strain. Although hardship and naval mutiny in that same year threatened social cohesion for a time, they did not presage the collapse of the political system. The British debt could be sustained largely for two reasons: first, banking institutions existed with a hundred years of history behind them, and, second, because the economy was not only strong and diversified but undergoing a technological transformation that increased productivity on the land and in industry. We should also add that British parliamentary institutions incorporated the tax-paying landed and commercial groups into the decision-making processes. The Spanish economy was in no way comparable, still weak even after the reforms of the eighteenth-century ministers. The reassertion of absolutism, particularly after 1759, meant

[73] Coclet da Silva, *Inventando a Nação*, 175, 184–87, 193.

that the Spanish political processes were moving away from any possibility of directly enfranchising taxpayers.[74]

Repeated failure of fiscal reform in 1750–56, 1760, 1766, and 1770–71 led Spanish governments to try extraordinary methods of raising revenue. For intervention in the American War of Independence in 1779–83, Spain resorted to the issue of government bonds known as *vales reales*. The idea for this came from Francisco Cabarrús, who himself would have preferred full-scale reform. Merchants and government officials were prepared to purchase the bonds in return for interest payments. The issue began in 1780. For some time the value of the bonds remained high, assuring public confidence in this new fiscal strategy. In order to maintain confidence, Cabarrús presided over the foundation of Spain's first bank, the *Banco Nacional de San Carlos*, in 1782, the purpose of which was to redeem the bonds issued.[75]

Between 1780 and 1799, the metropolitan government issued an enormous quantity of bonds to cover its costs. During the peace years, 1784–93, however, the Bank redeemed a large number of them, honoring thereby the original intent, and, accordingly, public confidence remained high. By the time of Charles III's death in 1788, the government had already issued bonds to the value of some 550 million reales and had set aside 22 million reales for interest payments. Financial confidence, however, depended on the maintenance of peace and that Spain did not become involved in more expensive wars.[76]

Spain's war against Revolutionary France in 1793–95 further frustrated any prospect of fiscal reform. Even so, the metropolitan government managed to finance the first nine months of warfare from ordinary revenues combined with short-term credits guaranteed against revenues from Spain and the Indies. Spanish American *consulados* and ecclesiastical bodies supplied considerable credits. Only in 1794 did the metropolitan government issue further *vales reales*. Until that time, the government still appeared to be strong. Continued warfare, however, exposed the

---

[74] These issues are discussed in Rafael Torres Sánchez, "'Las prioridades de un monarca ilustrado,' o las limitaciones del estado fiscal-militar de Carlos III," *Hispania. Revista Española de la Historia*, LXVIII, no. 229 (mayo-agosto 2008), 407–36.

[75] Juan Hernández Abreu, "Evolución histórica de la contribución directa en España desde 1700 a 1814," *Revista de Economía Política*, no. 61 (1972), 31–90: p. 77. Another attempted fiscal reform failed in 1784–85.

[76] Earl J. Hamilton, "Monetary Problems in Spain and the Spanish Empire, 1751–1800," *Journal of Economic History*, IV (1944), 21–48. Miguel Artola, "Estudio preliminar," *Memorias de tiempos de Fernando VII* (Madrid, Biblioteca de Autores Españoles 1957), vol. II, v–lvi.

fundamental weaknesses of the financial system. When, after 1795, Spain changed sides and a more devastating war resulted with Great Britain in the following year, the disintegration of the financial system began in earnest. Catalan manufacturers, moreover, viewed with alarm the prospect of warfare across the vital transatlantic trade routes. At first, though, commercial credits and the issue of bonds covered costs but soon revenues began to dry up in response to the depressed condition of trade and industry. The naval defeat of 1797 at Cape St. Vincent and the interruption of transatlantic commerce further contributed to the shortage of ordinary revenues. When further bonds were issued in 1798, their value had depreciated by 50 percent.[77]

The wars of 1796–1808 in alliance with Revolutionary and Napoleonic France against Great Britain increased the Spanish government's dependence on extraordinary revenues and shipments from the Indies. The Madrid government somehow had to find income to guarantee the value of the bonds. This was the problem facing Finance Minister Saavedra in 1798.[78]

The financial crisis explained growing pressure on American resources, particularly those of New Spain. It would certainly be possible to argue that metropolitan Spain bled its richest dependency white.[79] This had dramatic consequences in a Mexican economy already characterized by imbalance, in which overconcentration on mining led to the neglect of investment in the food supply at a time of continued population rise. The serious subsistence crises that hit the viceroyalty in 1785–86 and 1809–10 – the former worse than the latter – took a terrible toll on many populous areas.[80]

Metropolitan-government costs spiraled out of control after 1796. American-Treasury remissions to the peninsular government enabled the servicing of debt during the reigns of Charles III and Charles IV. American remissions increasingly formed one of the principal components of the income of the Imperial General Treasury. In the period from 1763 to

[77] Richard Herr, "Hacia el derrumbe del antiguo régimen: crisis fiscal y desamortización bajo Carlos IV," *Moneda y Crédito*, 118 (septiembre de 1971), 37–100.

[78] Artola, "Estudio preliminar," pp. xlvii–xlviii.

[79] This is the argument in Marichal, *Bankruptcy of Empire*, and Luis Jáuregui, *La Real Hacienda de Nueva España. Su administración en la época de los intendentes, 1786–1821* (Mexico City 1999).

[80] Enrique Florescano, *Precios del maíz y crisis agrícolas en México (1708–1810). Ensayo sobre el movimiento de los precios y sus consecuencias económicas y sociales* (Mexico City 1969), 111–95.

1783, the proportion had only come to an annual average of 15 percent. This rose to 25 percent during the 1790s. However, during the peace years, 1802–4, when shipments crossed the Atlantic unimpeded, the proportion rose to 40 percent and then to 50 percent in 1808–11, following the second reversal of alliances. The contribution from New Spain represented 75 percent of this total during the period 1790 to 1810.[81]

Increased fiscal pressure on New Spain occurred at a time of deepening economic weakness in the viceroyalty. John TePaske traces the roots of financial crisis in New Spain to the 1780s. While it was true that revenue from tax collection increased from around 2 million pesos in the 1700s to a peak of 28 million pesos in 1809, inflation was eroding its value. Furthermore, growing expenditure, particularly on defense, resulted in an increasing deficit, rising from around 3 million pesos in the early 1770s to 31 million pesos in 1810 and to 37.5 million pesos in 1811–15. In other words, the financial system in New Spain had already disintegrated before the outbreak of rebellion in September 1810 inflicted further damage on it. Total revenue had fallen to 8.7 million pesos in 1812, and in 1817 tax revenues appeared to be no greater than in the late 1770s. Much of this was explained by falling production in the main silver-mining zones, retention of revenue in provincial capitals for local needs, and disruption of communications between them and Mexico City. The Royal Mint, accordingly, was coining an annual average of only 8.5 million pesos in 1811–21, in contrast to the annual average of 23 million pesos in 1791–1810.[82]

The metropolitan government tapped the savings of private individuals and powerful corporations, such as the *consulados*. After 1790, such sources as these accounted for 31 percent of all revenues, a proportion that rose to 65 percent during the 1800s. Ordinary revenues were clearly insufficient to cover the costs of either the metropolitan or the viceregal government. Since the latter provided extensive subsidies to outlying positions in the Caribbean, including the administration in Havana,

---

[81] Jáuregui, *La Real Hacienda*, 79–184. Marichal, *Bankruptcy of Empire*, 104–18, and "Beneficios y costos fiscales," 491. Stein y Stein, *Edge of Crisis*, 277, 288–91.

[82] John TePaske, "The Financial Disintegration of the Royal Government of Mexico during the Epoch of Independence," in Jaime E. Rodriguez (ed.), *The Independence of Mexico and the Creation of the New Nation* (Los Angeles 1989), 63–83. See also Herbert J. Klein, "Resultados del estudio de las finanzas coloniales y su significación para la historia fiscal republicana en el siglo XIX," en José Antonio Serrano y Luis Jáuregui (eds.), *Hacienda y política. Las finanzas públicas y los grupos de poder en la Primera República Federal Mexicano* (Zamora y Mexico City 1998), 317–51.

a range of financial activities were reduced or curtailed. In that sense, the financial crisis at the center, and the parallel crises within New Spain, had a profound effect on the cohesion of the entire Monarchy.[83]

As a result, the Madrid government needed to devise a new method of holding up the value of the *vales reales*. Ministers recognized that the imposition of new taxes and the increase of existing ones would inflame popular discontent. The result was legislation on September 16, 1798 for the disamortization of a series of properties belonging to ecclesiastical bodies in the peninsula. Such a measure aroused intense hostility to the ministers of Charles IV from all those, clerical or otherwise, deriving incomes from them. Ministerial focus fell on the degree to which the supposed wealth of the Church was to be used in order to salvage the State. Even so, the peninsular disamortization still left the *vales reales* at only 25 percent of their original value by 1802. In the imperial government's view, further drastic measures were required. Its solution was the extension of its disamortization policy to the Indies on December 26, 1804. Known as the *Consolidación de los Vales Reales*, this policy stirred up vigorous opposition, particularly in New Spain. The *Caja de Amortización ("Consolidación,"* after 1800) received the proceeds of this revenue-raising device. In this way, the Indies became implicated in metropolitan Spain's financial crisis and would not be able to escape the consequences of disaster. The imperial government, moreover, given its ideological basis in the theory of absolute monarchy, had no intention whatever of convening the Cortes, in which there had never been any American representation, to assist in the process of resolving the financial crisis.[84]

The wealth of the Mexican Church was, however, largely illusory. It did not consist, in the main, of landed properties but in the receipt of revenues from donors intent upon securing safe passage from the earthly existence into the eternal through the funding of masses for their souls by means of *obras pías* and *capellanías*. These accumulated chantry funds were put to practical use by the Church as guarantees of credit at 5 percent annual interest for investment by private proprietors or merchants in their enterprises, commercial or agricultural. At the same time, such revenues

---

[83] Marichal, *Bankruptcy of Empire*, 32–47, 81–118.

[84] AGI Indiferente General 666, Real Cédula, Aranjuez, 26 de diciembre de 1804. Candelaria Saez Pastor y Javier Vidal Olivares, *El fin del antiguo régimen (1808–1868)* (Madrid, 2001), 197–98. William J. Callahan, "The Origins of the Conservative Church in Spain, 1793–1825," *European Studies Review*, 10 (1980), 199–223. Stein and Stein, *Edge of Crisis*, 277, 286–99, 379–80.

also provided small incomes for many otherwise impoverished sections of society, such as widows and orphans. The outcry was intense. Implementation of this policy, furthermore, depended on finding some feasible methods of calling in such invested funds and then paying the interest on them. The only way could be through conceding payment by instalments. The connection was thereby made between the question of government solvency and the continued wealth of the Church, a linkage which would have profound repercussions later in the nineteenth century in both Bourbon Spain and Independent Mexico.[85]

War expenses, already critical in 1795, tripled the metropolitan public debt up to the collapse of the Madrid regime in March 1808.[86] Inevitably, the strategic weakness of the Spanish government opened the way for the provinces of the Monarchy to trade directly with foreign states, whenever they were in a position to do so. Naval defeat in 1797 and at Trafalgar in 1805 obliged the metropolitan government to sanction trade between its overseas territories and neutral states, first in 1798 and again in 1805. Alongside this neutral trade came a complex series of maneuverings and connections between British commercial houses, US business interests, French and Dutch bankers, and the Spanish government, usually involving the *Caja de Consolidación*, at a time when Britain and Spain still remained at war. It was symptomatic of the drastic financial situation in Spain. The objective was to negotiate behind the scenes a way around the British blockade, which suited the needs of both governments. Regardless of opposition from the Consulado of Veracruz, the Spanish government permitted out of the ordinary concessions and gave contracts to foreign shippers. Veracruz merchants soon learned to accommodate themselves to this situation: Several of its most distinguished members became involved in the neutral trade and with concessions offered to British houses, with the result that large sums of money left the port between 1806 and 1809.[87]

---

[85] AGI México 3170, Tribunal de Minería al Virrey José de Iturrigaray, México, 16 de septiembre de 1805; Ayuntamiento de México, 28 de marzo de 1806; Consulado de Veracruz, 22 de Julio de 1806. Herr, "Hacia el derrumbe del antiguo régimen," pp. 41–56. Artola, "Estudio preliminar," xlviii.

[86] Guillermina del Valle Pavón, "Los empréstitos de fines de la colonia y su permanencia en el gobierno de Iturbide," en Serrano Ortega y Jáuregui (eds.), *Hacienda y política*, 51–53, 72.

[87] AGI México 2512, Consulado de Veracruz, *Expone los perjuicios que padece el comercio por las gracias concedidas a la consolidación de vales*, no. 271, Veracruz, 15 de noviembre de 1805. AGI Indiferente General 2439, Manuel Sixto Espinosa a Miguel Cayetano Soler

The Spanish government sank beneath its own complicated maneuverings. Bourbon reforms had not been able to stimulate productivity on the land or in industry sufficiently. The infrastructure remained woefully inadequate. The interior could not be relieved in times of dearth by imported grains from the coasts.[88] The Spanish metropolitan government was unable to wage war effectively. The fiscal measures had politically destabilizing consequences. Then, on December 12, 1806, Charles IV's ministers secured papal authorization to appropriate and sell a seventh-part of clerical properties in Spain in order to uphold the credit-worthiness of the *Caja* and pay the interest on the debt already incurred.[89]

At the root of the problem of explaining the collapse of metropolitan Spain between 1795 and 1808 was the breakdown of Bourbon ministerial absolutism. It must be stressed that Spain's difficulties had long-term origins in the incapacity of the State to mobilize sufficient resources and broaden its fiscal base in order to maintain its position at the core of a vast territorial empire. The more immediate problems of the debt question further incapacitated the metropolitan government. These problems all existed well before the Napoleonic intervention in 1808, which, in traditional narrative was supposed to have initiated the imperial crisis. Neither the impact of the French Revolution nor the intervention of Napoleon's Army brought down metropolitan Spain but irresolvable problems that long antedated them. Such problems, we should recognize, were also shared by other imperial powers, notably Great Britain, as the literature on the eighteenth-century fiscal-military state demonstrated. Britain, however, also locked into twenty-five years of bitter warfare in the Atlantic and on the European continent, managed to survive the social and financial strain partly through parliamentary institutions and a banking system established in the 1690s, and partly through agrarian and technological transformation.

The impact and breadth of the political and financial crisis running through the Hispanic Monarchy released other forces beneath the surface. The definition of relationships between provinces and also between them and the political center would become a major issue in Ibero-America

---

(Ministro de Hacienda), Madrid, 2 de Julio de 1806. Souto, *Mar Abierto*, 179–91, 205–36, 241–69. Barbier, "Peninsular Finance and Colonial Trade," 21–37.

[88] Gonzalo Anes, *Crisis agrarias en la España moderna* (Madrid, 1970), 319, 342. Manuel Ardit, *Revolución liberal y revuelta campesina. Un ensayo sobre la desintegración del régimen feudal en el País Valenciano (1793–1840)* (Barcelona, 1977), 51–58, 70–82, 106–10.

[89] Herr, "Hacia el derrumbe," 59–63, 76–77.

during much of the nineteenth century. In Portuguese America, as we shall see, this took a different form. Although the process proved to be remarkably similar, the component elements reinforcing fissure rather than homogeneity acted in response to issues intrinsic to Brazil. It is probably the case that readjustment between provinces and the centre, and among and within the provinces across Spanish and Portuguese America over the period from the 1770s into the 1830s, was the factor that shared prime significance with the more widely recognized separation of the American continental territories from their Iberian metropoles.

PART II

SALVAGING THE GREATER NATION – CONSTITUTIONALISM OR ABSOLUTISM?

4

Iberian Monarchies in Crisis: Juntas, Congresses, Constitutions

In Portugal, in contrast to Spain, the juntas established in 1808 did not mark the initiation of any new process of constitutional renewal. David Birmingham speaks of the events of 1808 in Portugal as a "failed revolution," neutralizing the middle classes, enabling the nobility to reassert its predominance, and allowing the *ancien régime* to survive in the former metropolis. The long British dominance of the Portuguese armed forces by Arthur Wellesley's colleague Major-General William Beresford and his British officers also facilitated this, but aroused enormous resentment among the Portuguese.[1] Such a view, if we should adopt it, would point forward to the revolution of 1820, in which officers with the support of merchants and lawyers took control of Portugal's political life, while the king still remained in Brazil. In Brazil, Braganza absolutism continued as before. While it was true that the Portuguese Royal Family, like that of Spain, was absent from the metropolis, it was not in captivity but in renewed safety and relative splendor in Rio de Janeiro. Spain failed to collapse entirely in 1808–9. Napoleon's attempt to occupy Spanish-peninsular territory early in 1808 – and subordinate the Indies to his rule – ultimately failed, despite the seizure of Madrid. The French defeat at Bailén on July 20, 1808, in the approaches to Andalusia, ensured the survival of an independent Spanish authority and opened the possibility of concerted resistance.

WARFARE IN THE PORTUGUESE HOMELAND

The departure of the government, Court, Treasury, some 10,000 members of noble families, and the Lisbon merchant community left Portugal, no longer the Lusitanian Monarchy's metropolis, exposed to deplorable

---

[1] David Birmingham, *A Concise History of Portugal* (Cambridge 1993), 103, sees the "Portuguese Revolution" as an intermittent process from 1820 to 1851.

social and economic consequences. Three attempted French invasions between 1807 and 1811, the first under Junot on November 19–30, 1807, devastated the north and center, with lasting consequences. Once in Lisbon, the French dissolved the Regency left by D. João, nullified the rights of the Braganza dynasty, and established military rule.[2] Unavoidable entry into the European war in 1807–8 destroyed Portugal's economic recovery during the preceding three decades. This had reinforced government finance and promoted capital accumulation in the Lusitanian metropolis. The rupture of direct contact with Brazil, however, undermined Portugal's intermediary role between Brazil and the world market. Furthermore, it led to the collapse of the linen trade and the destabilization of peasant-artisan society across the Minho. By 1814–19, Portuguese exports of manufactures fell to two-thirds of the level reached in 1802–6.[3]

The immediate and most striking response to the combined consequences of the departure of the government and the initial imposition of French rule in Lisbon was a series of local uprisings, not dissimilar to those in Spain during the summer of 1808. They began in the commercial hub of Oporto, where the Archbishop took control on June 18, then spread to Chaves on June 6, Braga and Bragança, and along the Minho to Melgaço. It took ten days for the rebellions to spread to the Algarve, where another junta was formed in Faro, and then on June 24 to Alentejo and Beira. Local notables took control, opposing the French and their supporters among the intelligentsia and upper orders and expressing loyalty to D. João. As a result, Junot's French Army of 26,000 men found itself isolated in Lisbon, its communications with other garrisons and with Spain broken. In despair, French soldiers sacked villages and towns such as Leiria, Évora, Beja, and Guarda on the route back to Spain. In the meantime, the Oporto Junta took the title of Supreme Governing Junta, implying superiority over the other juntas of insurgent Portugal. Responding to appeals from the juntas, a British Army of 40,000 men landed north of Lisbon and advanced southward. The result was the French defeat at Vimeiro on August 22, parallel to the victory of the Spanish Patriots at Bailén. The unfortunate Convention of Sintra

[2] Teresa Bernardino, *Sociedades e atitudes mentais em Portugal (1777–1810)* (Lisbon 1986), 26, 61–62. Neill Macaulay, *Dom Pedro: The Struggle for Liberty in Brazil and Portugal* (Durham, NC 1986), 16–25.

[3] Alexandre, *Os sentidos do Império*, 772–73, 780–87. Jorge Miguel Viana Pedreira, *Estructura industrial e Mercado colonial. Portugal e Brasil (1780–1830)* (Lisbon 1994), 65–191, 277–78, 281–82.

on August 30 allowed the French to withdraw peaceably from Portugal, thus nullifying Wellesley's victory. The defeat at Vimeiro, however, began the process whereby metropolitan Portugal, increasingly under British political and military tutelage, lost its independent capacity for action.[4]

Portuguese recovery of Lisbon led to the establishment of a second Regency: three members from the first with two representatives of the Oporto Junta. A second French invasion under Marshals Soult and Victor was delayed by the rising of Galicia and the resistance of the Portuguese fortress of Valença on the Minho. The remains of the Portuguese Army and its associated militias and Home Guard in Trás-os-Montes totaled only 12,000 poorly-armed men. The French took Oporto on March 29, 1809 amid horrendous scenes of panic on the Douro Bridge. Their attempted conquest of Portugal, however, became seriously compromised by failure to hold on to Asturias and Galicia in northern Spain and by the continued resistance of the Catalan city of Gerona. British forces, in the meantime, had seized hold of the Spanish Atlantic port of Vigo on March 27. Wellesley arrived back in Portugal in late April and began the defense of Lisbon, as Beresford remodeled the Portuguese Army. Unable to hold their position, the French finally withdrew to León in Spain, harassed on their way to the border by Beresford's forces and local peasant guerrilla-bands. Wellesley's Army crossed into eastern Spain and advancing up the Tagus defeated the French at Talavera on July 28, 1809. This second French invasion had compounded the destruction across northern Portugal and in Oporto and its environs. Napoleon's fury at this series of failures brought on the third invasion under Masséna with 65,000 men. Ney's capture of Ciudad Rodrigo on the Spanish side of the border on July 9 enabled the invasion. Wellesley, integrating the British and Portuguese forces, began toward the end of 1809 the complex process of establishing two parallel defensive lines blocking access to Lisbon – the Lines of Torres Vedras, provisioned from the sea. This involved stripping the countryside beyond the lines, in order to deprive the French Army of subsistence. Migrants from the devastated countryside sought refuge behind the Lines, where there were insufficient resources to feed them. For its part, the Portuguese Army, facing opposition to conscription, remained plagued by desertions. Elsewhere, banditry was rife across the countryside. Communications were appalling and the peasantry reluctant to supply the forces.[5]

---

[4] Esdaile, *The Peninsular War*, 26, 90–104.
[5] Esdaile, *Peninsular War*, 164–92, 295, 311–18. For Beresford (1768–1854), see Malyn Newitt and Martin Robson, *Lord Beresford and British Intervention in Portugal,*

On the political level, relations between the British and the Portuguese Regency were constantly tarnished by disputes over freedom of commerce, the slave trade, the role of British commanding officers, and the financing of the army. D. João, from Brazil, backed Beresford and remodeled the Regency in August 1810. Even so, civil government in the country remained largely ineffective.[6]

After the French defeat at Buçaco on September 22, unable to break through the Lines, frustration led to the burning of villages, pillage, massacre of inhabitants, and executions of members of the Home Guard. Masséna began his withdrawal on March 5, 1811, leaving whole areas of the countryside reduced to ruin, particularly in Beira. An estimate 25,000 French troops were lost and some 80,000 Portuguese civilians died. The withdrawal resulted in stalemate on the border for the rest of the year until Wellesley's Anglo-Portuguese forces opened their offensive early in 1812 by retaking Ciudad Rodrigo and then, in April, Badajoz. This opened the way into central Spain and came to a climax with the victory at Salamanca (Los Arapiles) on July 22 and the expulsion of the French from Madrid on August 12. On August 25, the French abandoned the siege of Cádiz. The Spanish Patriots recovered Seville two days later.[7]

THE SPANISH JUNTAS

No authority or legal document had given provincial factions in Spain the right to set up juntas. They had acted and retrospectively asserted their right to do so.[8] Two of the Spanish juntas, Asturias, which rejected the legitimacy of the Madrid government on May 9, and Seville, which rose on May 26 and was presided over by Saavedra, were claiming sovereign rights over the American territories in the absence of the king. Recovery of Madrid enabled the formation of the *Junta Suprema Central* in Aranjuez on September 25, under the presidency of Floridablanca, aged and very

---

1807–1820 (Lisbon 2004), 114–18. Beresford made two journeys to Brazil to consult the Prince Regent in the five years from 1810 to 1815. Beresford was the British officer who surrendered to Santiago Liniers in August 1806, after the collapse of the ill-advised British attempt to seize Buenos Aires. He finished his career as Governor of Jersey from 1821–54.

[6] Esdaile, *Peninsular War*, pp. 312–14.

[7] Esdaile, *Peninsular War*, 319, 328–33, 339, 367–70, 396–400.

[8] Breña, *El primer liberalismo español*, 218–19, argues that the swiftness of the collapse of Charles IV's government in March 1808, followed by the French Intervention and the uprisings in the peninsula, meant that there was no time to elaborate a program of government in advance. Accordingly, it had to be done on the spot and in response to prevailing realities.

conservative. Saavedra occupied the principal role. This body claimed to exercise sovereignty over the entire Hispanic Monarchy in the name of the captive king. The reality, however, was different. Large parts of the Spanish peninsula were already in open rebellion during the summer of 1808 against the Bonapartist seizure of Madrid.[9] The remaining political élite within the Patriot Zone struggled to establish some kind of acknowledged authority to contain centrifugalism. Many of these provincial movements had a mixed and contradictory character. They encapsulated the full extent of the grievances below the surface and gave the Patriot movement a traditionalist and even clerical character at its grassroots. The contrast with the reformist administration set up by the Bonapartes in Madrid would be striking.

The leaders of the Patriot cause had to take these sentiments into account.[10] Yet, at the same time, they planned for a durable transformation of the structure of the Monarchy and sought to resolve the outstanding problems, fiscal in particular, inherited from the previous regime.[11] A curious Manifesto appeared on November 10, 1808, apparently formulated by Jovellanos, Martín de Garay, and the poet, Manuel Josef Quintana, which exposed the deep contradictions within the Central Junta. It referred to a restoration of the "*antigua constitución*," "the traditional constitution," of the Hispanic kingdoms. Four months previously, the Napoleonic Constitution of Bayonne had on July 6 presented Imperial Spain with its first *written* Constitution conceived within the revolutionary tradition. It would take nearly four more years for the Patriot regime to produce a serious reply to this document. The Bayonne Constitution, however, emerged from a French not a Spanish context, and like its model, the French Constitution of the Year VIII [1800], it scrupulously avoided discussion of sovereignty. The Patriot Manifesto, furthermore, spoke of rescinding Charles III's expulsion of the Jesuits and terminating the sales of ecclesiastical property made during the reign of Charles IV. Most problematic was the call for the appointment of a new Inquisitor General. By contrast, the four Chamartín Decrees, issued by the Bonapartist regime in Madrid on December 4, abolished both seigneurial jurisdiction and the Inquisition. While such a goal might be desired by

---

[9] Esdaile, *Peninsular War*, 53. The Central Junta had twenty-five members (increasing to thirty-four) including sixteen representatives of the provincial juntas. There were seventeen noblemen and five bishops.

[10] Guerra, *Modernidad e independencias*, 146–47. Breña, *El primer liberalismo*, 219.

[11] Hamnett, *La política española*, 66–79.

leading *ilustrados* and Liberals within the Patriot Zone, they did not dare to propose such a drastic measure.[12]

The Patriot juntas could not ignore the Bonapartist measures. Sooner or later, they would have to be taken into account by the Supreme Central Junta, which regrouped in Seville on December 17, 1808, in the aftermath of the French military *révanche* in the peninsula. Like its predecessor in Aranjuez, the Supreme Central Junta of Seville sought to reduce the level of popular participation in Spain, subordinate the provincial juntas to its authority, and prevent the emergence of American juntas.

THE SUPREME CENTRAL JUNTA OF SEVILLE

The *Junta Suprema Central* of Seville, upholding the Bourbon vision of the Monarchy as one Nation and determined to maintain territorial unity, declared the imperial possessions to be integral parts of the Monarchy, equal in status to peninsular territories. Accordingly, it invited, on January 22, 1809, the Americans to elect representatives to the Central Junta, bringing American representatives into the central political processes for the first time. The impact on the American territories was profound. It would be one thing, however, to establish the principle of equality but quite another to give it practical effect. This issue, reappearing in the two constitutional periods, would never go away. As long as the extent of American representation in political bodies in the peninsular remained unresolved, the status of the Americans within the Monarchy also remained unresolved.[13]

The Supreme Central Junta provided for thirty-six representatives but only for nine from the overseas territories, even though the combined population of the Spanish American territories was greater than that of Spain. Capitals of Intendancies were to participate in the election of these American deputies. In New Spain, the city of Querétaro was one of several excluded cities, along with Monterrey, Chihuahua, Tlaxcala, and Campeche. Its Council claimed the right to participate in New Spain's election due to the city's special status as capital of a *Corregimiento de*

---

[12] Carlos Sanz Cid, *La Constitución de Bayona* (Madrid 1922), 417–40. Juan Mercader Riba, *José Bonaparte, Rey de España (1808–1813)* (Madrid 1971), 28–39, 83–84. Breña, *El primer liberalismo*, 78–80.

[13] Guerra, *Modernidad e independencias*, 178–89, 190–91.

Letras and third most populous city after Mexico City and Puebla.[14] Surprisingly, the Supreme Junta's decree made no provision for the election of representatives from the Kingdom of Quito and the territory of the Upper Peruvian Audiencia of Charcas. Guerra suggests that this omission may have encouraged their local élites to form their own distinct juntas, although there were many other reasons why locals would have decided to do that. Chuquisaca, the capital of Charcas, did so in May 1809 and La Paz, its rival city, in July. Quito set up its first junta in August. All three were stamped out by the intervention of viceregal forces from Lima and Buenos Aires.[15] The overriding intention of the Supreme Central Junta's American policy had been to prevent the emergence of juntas in the overseas territories by extending representation on the Central Junta in Seville. It was ironic that its failure or unwillingness to transform the principle of equality into reality provoked the formation of three further American juntas.

Selection of representatives to sit on the Supreme Central Junta did begin an electoral process in the Monarchy. Six of the nine American representatives were selected, representing New Spain, Guatemala, Puerto Rico, Venezuela, New Granada, and Peru. The Supreme Junta collapsed, however, before representatives could be selected for the River Plate and Chile and while the selection process was still continuing elsewhere. The blatant reality was that no elected American representatives ever formed part of the Supreme Central Junta.[16]

When, on October 28, the *Junta Suprema* set the date for the opening of the Cortes at January 1, 1810, it called for the election of American deputies along with those representing European Spain. This projected Cortes never had a chance to meet. The rout of the Spanish Army at Ocaña in La Mancha on November 19, 1809 left Andalusia defenseless against the advance of the French Army. The first Andalusian cities fell one after another in early January 1810 to a force of 60,000 French troops. The position of the Supreme Central Junta in Seville became untenable. Before its imminent collapse, the Junta attempted, on January 29, to define the structure of the Cortes, which would open on March 1. Responding to

---

[14] Hernández y Dávalos, *Colección de documentos*, vol. 1, 686–87, Ayuntamiento to Viceroy Garibay, Querétaro 22 April and 9 May 1809, signed by Corregidor Miguel Domínguez and ten councilors.

[15] Guerra, *Modernidad*, 146. Breña, *El primer liberalismo*, 99–104.

[16] Guerra, *Modernidad e independencias*, 190, 193, 219, 220–24. François-Xavier Guerra (ed.), *Revoluciones hispánicas. Independencias americanas y liberalismo español* (Madrid 1995), 21.

the pressures of traditionalists, this Cortes would consist of the three estates (*estamentos*) of the old regime. Curiously, this decree was never published by the succeeding Regency Council.[17]

The remnants of the Patriot regime fled to Cádiz to escape the rapid French advance through western Andalusia, which reached the Bay of Cádiz on February 6. The Regency Council of five, constituted on the Isla de León on January 31, superseded the Supreme Central Junta. No specific provision was made for American members, although one of the five Regents was Miguel Lardizábal y Uribe, but he was a Mexican who had been long-resident in Spain with distinctly traditionalist views. The collapse of the Supreme Central Junta, which had been recognized in the Americas as the interim repository of sovereignty, raised the question of the legitimacy of the Regency. This proved to be the stumbling block in Venezuela and New Granada, reviving the issues of representation and equality of status. Worst of all, the new location of the Spanish Patriot regime on the Bay of Cádiz exposed it to the powerful influence of the Consulado of Cádiz, long-time opponent of the Caroline *comercio libre* policies, and political ally of the Consulados of Mexico and Lima. None of these merchants viewed with sympathy American requests either for direct trade with friendly foreign states or for effective control of political institutions within the Americas. The *Junta Superior* of Cádiz, formed from among leading citizens in the aftermath of the collapse of the Seville Junta played a decisive role behind the Regency Council.[18]

The collapse of the Supreme Central Junta opened the way for greater pressure from the Liberal group in the Bay of Cádiz, which had already made itself evident in Seville. The Regency Council's Manifesto of February 14, 1810, written by the leading Liberal propagandist, Quintana, invited American deputies to the forthcoming Cortes on the basis of the principal of equality and unity. This looked better on paper than the reality would prove to be. The Manifesto set the number of American deputies at only twenty-eight, in contrast to more than 200 for the peninsula. Still no clear date was set for the opening of the Cortes.[19]

---

[17] Gabriel H. Lovett, *Napoleon and the Birth of Modern Spain*, 2 vols. (New York 1965), vol. I, 353–59. Esdaile, *Peninsular War*, 216–21.

[18] Daniel Gutiérrez Ardila, *Las vacilaciones de Cartagena. Polémicas neogranadinas en torno a la creación del Consejo de Regencia* (Bogotá 2012), 15. Anna, *Spain and the Loss of America*, 61–62.

[19] Guerra, *Modernidad e independencias*, 146–47, sees this as a defining moment: "the moral unity of the Hispanic world is now broken ... "

In the open for the first time was the question of the structure and *legal basis* of the Hispanic Monarchy. These issues, already pressing in the Americas, broke through the surface at a time when European Spain was in danger of political obliteration. Discussion of sovereignty soon became the focal issue in *both* segments of the Monarchy, as Guerra has been correct to stress. Removal of unchallengeable central authority in the form of the hereditary monarchy in Madrid left open the unresolved questions of where sovereignty lay in the absence of the king and the relation of outlying provinces and territories to the metropolitan center in Spain. The result of such discussion could be a rapid descent down the slippery slope of political abstraction and position-taking, with recrimination and violence as a likely consequence. The collapse of the Supreme Central Junta of Seville at the end of January 1810 undermined the façade of unanimity across Spanish America, which had spontaneously appeared during the summer and autumn of 1808.[20]

THE PORTUGUESE ROYAL GOVERNMENT IN BRAZIL

The Prince Regent and his contingent disembarked in Bahia on January 22, 1808. His first action was to issue the decree of February 28, 1808, which opened Brazilian trade to friendly foreign states, a measure welcomed by Brazil's leading political economist, José da Silva Lisboa. The principal beneficiary would be Great Britain. In such a way, Brazil became directly bound to British commercial interests, which were in competition with those of metropolitan Portugal. A complementary decree followed on April 1, which authorized manufacturing in Brazil.[21]

D, João took the precaution of ratifying the existence of the Portuguese juntas on January 2, 1809, since they represented the interests of all corporative bodies in the country, including the Church. They did not, however, claim the right to form a Cortes. Beresford, with the support of the Prince Regent, was anxious, in any case, to centralize authority there. The Prince and Souza Coutinho sought to bring the Lisbon Regency under the control of Rio. Given the dire situation inside Portugal, word spread that the former metropolis was now being treated like a "province of Brazil." The question of how long the Royal Family and government would remain in Brazil soon became an issue in Portugal, where the

[20] Breña, *El primer liberalismo*, 14, 30, 66, 219.
[21] Maxwell, "Generation of the 1790s," 143. Alexandre, *Os Sentidos do Império*, 769–80.

dynasty was in danger of losing prestige. The relationship between Portugal and Brazil preoccupied ministers from 1808 until João VI (as he had become in 1816) finally returned to Lisbon in 1821.[22]

Concentration of the center of power in the Monarchy in Rio also had implications for the rest of Brazil. It meant a growing tendency to centralize authority there as the new capital of the Monarchy. This was bound to have negative repercussions in the provinces, particularly those further away from the capital and with strong regionalist traditions of their own. The Prince Regent and his chief minister struggled to make the government more coherent within Portuguese America without any recourse to representative government. Economic ties within the southeast drew the southern portion of the province of Minas Gerais closer to the capital as the principal food supplier. This brought local power groups into the Rio network. Similar developments were also taking place in the provinces of São Paulo, linking it also with Minas Gerais and, further into the interior, to Mato Grosso and Goiás, and with the south. Tensions grew, however, between the merchants of Rio and those of the north-east and the former metropolis.[23]

The Rio merchants already controlled the traffic between Brazil and Africa. The coastal trade between Rio and the south-east and north-east was more in Brazilian than in Portuguese hands. Over the broader period from the 1790s to the 1830s, Brazilian large-scale merchants consolidated their position, gained access to the *Real Junta de Comércio* under D. João, and increased their weight in government circles under the post-1822 Brazilian Empire. Possibly fewer than thirty individuals stood at the apex of this horizontal and vertical network. Effectively, their principal figures were the Carneiro Leão family, which rose through the slave trade and importing from Portugal to become the owners of urban and rural properties and relatives of other leading merchant families. Great landowners under Dom João, they became members of the Royal Household under his son, the Emperor Pedro I. António da Silva Prado, originally a tax-farmer, made his money though sugar-planting and refining, and became one of the city's principal bankers. The acquisition of former Jesuit properties and the stimulus of growing tobacco, indigo, and sugar

---

[22] Coclet da Silva, *Inventando a Nação*, 188, 195, 202–8, 212–13, 218, 221–23. Souza, *Patria Coroada*, 39–42.

[23] Kirsten Schultz, "Royal Authority, Empire, and the Critique of Colonialism: Political Discourse in Rio de Janeiro, 1808–1821," *Luso-Brazilian Review*, 37, no. 2 (2000), 7–31: pp. 9, 12–25. Coclet da Silva, ibid, 221, 124. Souza, ibid, 48–49.

in the environs of the city increased the concentration of land in fewer hands. These estates increased their number of slaves, but also employed free labor, had fixed resident workers, and rented to tenants.[24]

The royal government in Rio worked to have the Brazilian notables on board through the distribution of honors and titles, the assignment to official duties, and membership of distinguished Orders. Brazilian notables were brought into partnership with a form of enlightened monarchism that continued what had been practiced in Portugal during the previous century. All of this privileged the south-east. Yet, these developments also involved a deepening partnership with the British. The Treaty of Commerce and Navigation of February 19, 1810, however, did not give the British special privileges or a monopoly of trade with Brazil. It did reduce customs duties from 24 percent to 15 percent at a time when British merchants in wartime conditions in Europe were the only major traders likely to benefit, but that reduction was unlikely to wipe out local artisan produce in the interior provinces of Brazil. Much would depend on the capability of distribution and the purchasing power of the inhabitants, large numbers of whom were slaves. It did, however, damage the position of Oporto and Lisbon merchants. Alexandre estimates a 90 percent loss of capital in the Brazil to Portugal re-export trade between 1802–7 and 1825–31.[25]

The interests of the Brazilian commercial and landed élites conflicted with those of the Portuguese merchants. Throughout the 1810s the latter complained of the inundation of the home market by British products – from textiles and shoes to household linens. During that decade, the two principal sections of the Lusitanian Monarchy inexorably drifted apart, a situation made worse, from the Portuguese perspective, by the Royal Family's continued sojourn in Brazil. The issue preoccupied ministers in Rio de Janeiro, who sought to repair the damage through the rhetoric of "One Sole Nation." Furthermore, the ambiguities of the British connection were becoming clearer on both sides of the Atlantic. British pressure on the Rio government to abandon the slave trade aggravated the planters and their spokesmen. On the other hand, Brazil benefited from a direct trade with Britain, which had previously passed through Lisbon and Oporto. The idea of the unity of the Lusitanian Monarchy on the basis of the mutual interests of its component parts might have to give way to

---

[24] Souza, ibid, 45–49.
[25] See Alan K. Manchester, *British Pre-eminence in Brazil: Its Rise and Decline* (Durham, NC 1933). Alexandre, *Os Sentidos do Império*, 771–76.

some other form of organization that no longer presupposed the restoration of the old metropolitan monopoly. Among Brazilian notables, the idea of a "Brazilian Empire" gained currency during the 1810s. This was not regarded as the formula for creation of a separate Brazilian state but as the principal means of keeping the broader Lusitanian Monarchy alive. According to this view, Lisbon would take a back seat in favor of Rio de Janeiro, where the monarch resided. One major problem would arise with this: The outlying provinces of Portuguese America had to be drawn effectively under the control of Rio and diverted from their existing relationship with the peninsula. Several municipal councils viewed such a prospect with consternation. The unity of the Brazilian sector of the Monarchy was by no means assured.[26]

The overriding issue of the relationship of Rio to Lisbon came to a head in 1814–15 with the ending of the war in Europe. Pressure from Portugal for the Royal Family and government to return to Lisbon increased, as did the dissatisfaction when they did not. Into that uneasy situation came the Prince Regent's decree of December 16, 1815, which caused incomprehension and outrage in Portugal. It described the Monarchy as the "United Kingdom of Portugal, Brazil, and the Algarves." This meant that "Brazil" had equal status to the other two components of the Monarchy. The inspiration for this decree came from the Count of Palmela, Portugal's emissary at the Congress of Vienna, which was in the process of attempting to shape a peaceful future for Europe on the basis of the restoration of the old monarchies swept away by the French Revolution and its Napoleonic successor. The intention of the decree was to bind the provinces of the Monarchy closer together by removing any idea that "Brazil" was a colony. In reality, it meant that the government in Rio no longer regarded Portuguese America as an agglomeration of semi-autonomous provinces but as one of the three component kingdoms of equal status within the Monarchy as a whole. The conscious intention was to avoid the fragmentation and warfare then characterizing much of Spanish America. Within Brazil the implication of extended dominance from Rio de Janeiro was also abundantly clear. Deepening resentment in the north-east would lead to outright rebellion, favoring the establishment

[26] Coclet da Silva, ibid, 222–25, 230–40. Maxwell, "Generation of the 1790s," 137. Souza Coutinho, in 1798, had originally suggested the division of Portuguese America into two large provinces, Rio de Janeiro in the south and Pará in the north, since the Monarchy was conceived as composed of provinces of equal status. After 1808, such a solution no longer applied. Had it taken effect in 1798, the possibility existed that two "Brazilian" states might have emerged at Independence.

of a republic, in Pernambuco in 1817. The decree of 1815 also proposed complete equality between the European and American inhabitants of the Monarchy. In retrospect, the decree seems transcendent. At the time, its consequences could not be foreseen. Had the decree established a "Dual Monarchy" of Portugal (with the Algarves) and Brazil? No one knew. That, in any case, would have meant something very different to "One Sole and United Kingdom." Might a Dual Monarchy of Brazil and Portugal have stood a chance of survival? Whatever the case, the Rio de Janeiro government issued no further declarations on the subject and did nothing that might be construed as stemming from its decree.[27]

THE SPANISH AMERICAN JUNTAS

The political thinking that went into the tentative formation of American juntas in 1808–10 derived from varied sources. It looked back in varying parts to neo-scholasticism, Natural Law theories, elements of the Hispanic Enlightenment, and ideas and examples from abroad. Undocumented were the conversations in homes, on estates, in *tertulias* or cafés concerning the state of government under Charles III and IV, the distribution of power within the Monarchy, the nature or degree of representation, and the potentially explosive topic of sovereignty. All juntas, whether peninsular or American, had three objectives in common: their avowed loyalty to the Bourbon dynasty as the legitimate monarchs of Spain and the Indies; the unity of the Hispanic Monarchy with its political center in a Bourbon Madrid; an active struggle against the Bonapartist usurpation.

The historiography has given rise to the idea of "autonomy." This term, however, was not used at the time. It begs the question of whether the juntas of 1808–10 represented a conscious bid by the American élites for home rule, that is to say, for a devolution of power away from the political center of the Monarchy in the peninsula and toward the formation of local administrative bodies (with some form of representation) in the overseas territories. While there is no doubt that American élites did want greater representation within *existing* institutions in their own territories, little evidence suggests that they envisaged in 1808 home-government on a lasting and institutional basis. Their aims were, in any

---

[27] Roderick J. Barman, *Brazil. The Forging of a Nation, 1798–1852* (Stanford 1988), 44–45. Coclet da Silva, ibid, 246, 250–57.

case, to provide a temporary surety in the absence of the Bourbon king against Bonapartist extension to the Indies.

In many respects, American élites were not taking bold initiatives but attempting to use the crisis in order to assure their greater participation in the affairs of the Monarchy as a whole. They were not taking steps away from that whole. All the declarations of summer and autumn 1808 asserted the unity of the Hispanic Monarchy. However, this desire for continued unity in face of extreme danger may have been wishful thinking. In the Indies, a pluralist view of the Monarchy was emerging. From New Granada, the *Outline of Grievances*, written on behalf of the City Council of Santa Fe de Bogotá in November 1809 by Camilo Torres supposedly for dispatch to the Seville Supreme Central Junta, expressed such a position. Torres stressed the American desire for union but also for effective participation within it. Reform of grievances, not separatism, was the aim. From an American perspective, this implied constitutional equality with peninsular Spain for all components of the Monarchy. It also claimed entitlement to form American juntas parallel to those of provincial Spain. In Torres' judgment, only equal representation on the Supreme Central Junta could reconstruct the Monarchy on a basis acceptable to American élites by restoring the balance, which many Americans argued, had been overthrown by the eighteenth-century Bourbon ministers.[28]

The authorities in place in the Americas regarded pressure for juntas as subversive and acted accordingly. They precipitated conflict, deepened suspicion and bred antagonisms. Their actions in 1808–10 contributed in no small way to the escalation of violence across Spanish America in and after 1810. Yet, the crux of the problem was the apparent collapse of metropolitan Spain. This prospect left the royal authorities in the Indies with a sense of complete abandonment; they were left to their own devices in dangerous times. It would require immense political skill, including judicious employment of military force, available policing powers, and skillful propaganda, to remain in power in potentially turbulent American cities. This was, furthermore, the age that was living through the aftermath of the American and French Revolutions.

Argument over the right to form American juntas took place within the context of the colonial *ancien régime*. This meant, in the terms of reference and instinctive attitudes of the Spanish American version of the *sociedad estamental*, the European juridical structure of estates and corporations.

---

[28] Portillo, *Crisis atlántica*. Breña, *El primer liberalismo*.

Although the "estates" were less clearly defined or identifiable in the Indies, corporations, such as the *cabildos* and *consulados*, certainly were, and the juridical exemptions and privileges of the Catholic Church remained abundantly clear. The protagonists of American juntas in 1808–10 had every intention of upholding these structures. Indeed, they identified them as a prime aspect of their perceived notion of legitimacy. This was their interpretation of the peninsular "fundamental laws of the realm." Before we rush to attribute revolutionary intent on the part of the American élites in 1808, we need to remember that it was the *cabildos*, those largely unreformed municipal councils of the old regime, which most vocally promoted the idea of juntas.[29]

The crisis of 1808–10 exposed another level of tensions. This was the rivalry between capital-city élites and their counterparts in the provincial capitals. The assumed hegemony of the former usually provoked serious opposition or outright resistance from the latter. There were several outstanding examples of this in all four viceroyalties and in the captaincies-general as well. Capital-city *cabildos*, when proposing American juntas, could expect to face a two-pronged opposition, first from the *audiencias*, and second from the provincial capitals. This could clearly be seen in the territory of the Audiencia of Quito in 1809 and 1810, when the capital city's bid for supreme power was opposed by the outlying cities, in particular Guayaquil and Cuenca, which became Royalist strongholds.

THE CASE OF MEXICO CITY

On July 19, 1808, the Mexico City Council, viewing itself as the vanguard of dynastic legitimacy and unity, denounced the royal abdications as "null and invalid because they were contrary to the will of the 'Nation,' *which had called* the House of Bourbon to the Throne as descendants of the Kings and Lords of old." This was very old-fashioned thinking, which, however, had an alarming ring to it. The city councilors called for the convocation of a "general junta" as an emergency measure. The *Real Acuerdo* two days later rebuffed the Council's impertinence and rejected its claim to speak on behalf of the "Nation." In the view of the Audiencia, no institutional changes were necessary because all existing bodies had been legitimately constituted by the monarchs. During the months of July to mid-September 1808, Mexico City councilors maintained that the "kingdoms" of the Americas had the same rights as those of the peninsula.

[29] Guerra, *Modernidad e independencias*, 160, and Breña, *El primer liberalismo*, 86.

They ventured to argue, on August 5, that sovereignty had devolved on "the Nation," and that the Mexico City Junta should exercise it on the model of Seville or Valencia. Since Viceroy Iturrigaray concurred, four consultative juntas met on August 9 and 31 and September 1 and 9, and in the final one the subject of convocation of representatives of the realm was discussed. Defenders of the existing system of government feared the consequences of discussing the status of New Spain within the Monarchy and the origin, nature, distribution, and exercise of political power. This provided the key issue behind the coup on the night of September 15, initiated by Consulado merchants and Audiencia magistrates, which removed the viceroy.[30]

The traditionalism of city councilors in the summer of 1808 could be seen in Fray Melchor Talamantes' writings, often regarded as an advanced statement of the American position. Talamantes became one of the central figures in the search for a new legitimacy to counter the usurpation. This Mercenarian friar was of Peruvian origin. His texts reveal that he belonged to the tradition that argued for the continuing legitimacy of the violated "fundamental laws" and for the contractual nature of monarchy. For Talamantes, as for the sixteenth-century thinkers, sovereignty would revert to the "nation" or "people" in the event of a dynastic crisis. His *Congreso Nacional del Reino de Nueva España*, of August 23, 1808, and *Representación Nacional de las Colonias. Discurso Filosófico*, of August 25, 1808, took for granted that the nation in question was the whole Hispanic Monarchy. He regarded Spain as *"la parte principal de nuestra patria"* and France as its particular enemy. Nevertheless, metropolitan Spain, in his view, had lost its sovereignty: for that reason, the Americas had the right to repossess it. This presented for him a specific problem: the four viceroyalties were constitutionally independent of one another. Their source of unity, Spain, was absent from the picture, as he understood it in August 1808. New Spain, the senior viceroyalty,

---

[30] Hernández y Dávalos, *Colección de documentos*, vol. 1, no. 199, 475–85, Ayuntamiento to Iturrigaray, Mexico City 19 July 1808; no. 200, p. 486, Iturrigaray to *Real Acuerdo*, Mexico City 19 July 1808; no. 201, pp. 486–68, *Real Acuerdo* to Iturrigaray, Mexico City 21 July 1808, and no. 211, pp. 509–10, same to same, 6 August 1808. See also Fray Servando Teresa de Mier, *Historia de la revolución de Nueva España, Antiguamente Anáhuac* (André Saint-Lu y Marie-Cécile Bénassy-Berling, coordinadores, París 1990 [1813]), Libros I-VI, 41–187. There were as many as 87 members in the first Mexico City Junta and 81 in the second junta on 9 August. The third junta, on September 1, had seventy-five members, when sharp divisions concerned which (or none) of the Spanish juntas to recognize. The fourth junta, on September 8, discussed the question of convening a "congress" from the cities and towns of New Spain.

henceforth became the focus of continuity and cohesion, as Brazil had in the Lusitanian case, although Talamantes made no mention of that. Mexico City, he argued, now replaced Madrid as the central point of the Monarchy. Accordingly, Talamantes proposed that the Viceroy of New Spain should convoke a "congreso nacional" for the entire Hispanic Monarchy. The clear implication was that representatives from the other territories should convene in Mexico City. At the same time, he gave no indication in the fifteen categories of representation that such a congress would be other than a body reflecting the existing juridical structure, with the full sanction of the Catholic religion. Innovation in the form of equality before the law was not considered.[31]

The principal tasks of this congress would be limited to a declaration "in the presence of God and his saints of the liberty, independence, sovereignty, representation, dignity and integrity of the Spanish Nation," – in opposition to the Bonaparte usurpation. The congress would then confirm the positions of all existing authorities, not removing them from office, and uphold and restore "all the fundamental laws of the realm, not innovating in any way on this matter."[32]

The implication that a subordinate territory such as New Spain should take upon itself the task of reconstituting the Monarchy must have appeared deeply subversive at the time. Talamantes even contemplated the dispatch of an ambassador to the Congress of the United States, evidently regarded at that time as a naturally friendly power, and another to London, in order to coordinate among the three countries a general opposition to Napoleonic France. The radical implications of this proposal could not have been lost on defenders of peninsular hegemony. The recommendation that the Inquisition should be made subordinate to the Archbishop, head of the secular hierarchy, and that it should confine its activities exclusively to ecclesiastical affairs, was not new. The significance of this proposal lay in the fact that Talamantes was not advocating the extinction of the Holy Office. On the contrary, he reserved a place for the most senior Inquisitor in the "congreso nacional." Finally, his recommendation for freedom of manufacturing, commerce, and agriculture looked forward to the Eleven Propositions that would be presented by the American deputies in the Cádiz Cortes in February 1811.

---

[31] Héctor Cuauhtémoc Hernández Silva and Juan Manuel Pérez Zevallos (eds.), *Fray Melchor Talamantes, Escritos Póstumos, 1808* (Mexico City 2009), 68–73.

[32] *Talamantes. Escritos*, 53–88: pp. 68–71, 73, 76, 83. It would also extinguish the "pernicious *Consolidación de Vales Reales*."

This suggests that, among Americans, such issues were already being discussed in the summer of 1808.[33]

The coup that terminated these discussions came three months before the formation of the Supreme Central Junta of Seville. The crushing of the junta movement in Mexico City, the most populous city of the American empire, provided a lesson for other city councils across Spanish America. Sure of support in Spain from the Patriot regime, peninsular authorities and their allies within the Americas were prepared to take measures to curb a repetition of the formation of juntas across Spain. Within New Spain, the repression that followed the coup ensured that no further initiatives would be launched from the capital city, a situation that opened the way for the provinces themselves to attempt their own solutions to the perceived problem of peninsular dominance and peninsular ambiguity toward Bonapartist rule in Spain.

The arrant peninsular nature of the coup of the night of September 15–16, 1808, in which some 300 merchants and employees of the Parián broke into the viceregal palace and arrested Iturrigaray, his wife, and family, was hugely divisive. In the first place, it left American members of the colonial élite in the lurch, hardly able to conceive what had happened and wondering what the political consequence might be for them. Even more serious was that, despite an apparent peninsular success in the capital city, the repercussions of the coup left *peninsulares*, particularly merchants and traders, isolated and dangerously exposed to popular vengeance for all their monopolizing and sharp practices over a long period of time.

New Spain would differ from Spanish South America in two important respects during the next period of crisis in 1810. Creole militias and city councilors did not take control of the capital city, as they would do in Caracas, Buenos Aires, Bogotá, and Santiago de Chile between April and September. Second, in New Spain, religious fervor, combined with popular indignation and desire for revenge against the *peninsulares*, fueled the initial uprisings in 1810 and infused the insurgency that followed.

THE SITUATION IN QUITO

The territory under the jurisdiction of the Audiencia of Quito had been detached from the Viceroyalty of Peru in 1739 and included in the new Viceroyalty of New Granada. In 1803, the Crown detached the

[33] *Talamantes. Escritos*, 73, 77–79.

department of Guayaquil from Quito and placed it directly under the control of the Viceroy in Lima. The coastal perspectives and interests of the port city were in any case distinct from those of the sierra cities, in particular Quito. Furthermore, the close economic and strategic links with Callao and Lima had made Guayaquil part of the Peruvian Pacific coastal economic system. These territorial changes created a sense of entrapment among the creole élite of Quito between Santa Fe and Lima, the two viceregal capitals, and explained demands for the establishment of a distinct Captaincy-General in Quito, as would be the case in Venezuela and Chile. At the same time, the economic circumstances of the latter part of the eighteenth century, into which the Bourbon commercial measures fell, worsened the position of Quito as the center of a trading network, which exchanged the highland area's textiles for silver in the market of Potosí. The decline of production at Potosí late in the century led to a collapse in the demand for textiles and a shortage of capital in the Quito sierra, especially among the hacienda producers and *obraje* operators.[34]

Bourbon attempts to tighten fiscal control of the overseas territories, which affected the Audiencia of Quito during the 1750s and 1760s, had led to the Quito anti-tax demonstration in May 1765. Only the intervention of creole property-owners and the senior clergy averted disaster for the royal administration. Described by Anthony McFarlane as "one of the longest, largest, and most formidable urban insurrections to take place in eighteenth-century Spanish America," this movement did not, however, lead to any alliance between the Indian communities of the sierra, alive with their own particular grievances, and the urban plebeians.[35]

As was the case later in the New Granada rebellion of 1780, and again during the crisis of the Monarchy in 1808–10, élites in New Granada and Quito put forward their vision of a "mixed monarchy," in which the

---

[34] For the economic position of Quito within the Andean network, see Carlos Sempat Assadourian, *El sistema de la economía colonial: Mercado interno, regiones y espacio economico* (Lima 1982); Kenneth J. Andrien, *The Kingdom of Quito, 1690–1830. The State and Regional Development* (Cambridge 1995), 165–204. Silvia Polomeque, "Continuidad y cambio entre la colonia y la República. Estudio de los circuitos mercantiles y de las especializaciones productivas regionales en Cuenca, Ecuador," in Jorge Silva Riquer, Juan Carlos Grosso, Carmen Yuste (compilers), *Circuitos mercantiles y mercados en latinaoamérica. Siglos XVIII y XIX* (Mexico City 1995), 235–90: see pp. 244–50.

[35] Anthony McFarlane, "The Rebellion of the *Barrios*: Urban Insurrection in Bourbon Quito," in Fisher, Kuethe, and McFarlane (eds.), *Reform and Insurrection in Bourbon New Granada and Peru*, 197, 213, 214–17, 241.

exercise of sovereignty was shared between king, nobles, and commons, coming together in a *cortes*. The pluralist vision of the Monarchy came into public view again during the crisis of 1808–10. It formed the background to the call for a distinct Quito Junta. The complaint was that "arbitrary" measures by the metropolitan government had led to the effective lapse of the *cortes*, a situation that suggested that the Monarchy, pushed out of balance, had been set on the road to "despotism."[36]

Americans were preoccupied with political legitimacy. Protagonists of the Junta of 9 August–October 1809 avowed their loyalty to the Bourbon dynasty, the unity of the Monarchy, and the centrality of the metropolis within it. They saw no reason to break the interdependence of the European and American sectors of the Hispanic Monarchy. Their insistence on a Junta derived from their opposition to Santa Fe de Bogotá and Lima as dominant political entities, not from any desire to become independent of Spain. The key figure in this process was Juan Pío de Montúfar (1758–1818), the second Marqués de Selva Alegre, son of a former President of the Audiencia, and the scion of a major sierra landowning and mercantile family. The principal ideologist was the jurist, Manuel Rodríguez Quiroga, who had imbued the political philosophy of consent and the right of resistance to tyranny elaborated by the Spanish Jesuit, Francisco Suárez (1548–1617), the Dutch philosopher of the Law of Nations, Hugo Grotius (1583–1645), and the German Natural Law theorist, Baron Samuel von Pufendorf (1632–94), whose books, among others, he had in his personal library. Rodríguez argued that a "constitution" existed in which king, nobles, and people together formulated laws and, he added, consented to taxation. It applied equally to the American territories of the Monarchy as to the metropolis. The Natural Law theories could be seen clearly in the idea of the retrocession of sovereignty, as a result of the illegal abdications of 1808. They encouraged the belief in the Americas that sovereignty was not indivisible but shared or plural.[37]

The outlying cities, led by Cuenca and Guayaquil, did not support the Quito Junta's attempt to assert jurisdiction over the entire jurisdiction of

---

[36] Federica Morelli, *Territorio o nación. Reforma y disolución del espacio imperial en Ecuador, 1765–1830* (Madrid 2005), 27–32.

[37] Christian Büschges, *Familia, honor y poder. La nobleza en la ciudad de Quito en la época colonial tardía (1765–1822)* (Quito 2007 [Stuttgart 1996]). Morelli, *Territorio o nación*, 35–46.

the Presidency. The latter's Governor appealed to the Viceroy of Peru to send in troops to extinguish the junta. Arrests and sentences followed, raising further tension in the city. In the meantime, the authorities in Quito swore to recognize the Supreme Central Junta of Seville.[38]

THE SITUATION IN UPPER PERU (CHARCAS)

Upper Peru's principal city, Chuquisaca (present-day Sucre), had been the seat of an *audiencia* since the mid-sixteenth century. Its university, which attracted students from a wide geographical radius, became a center of Enlightenment in the reigns of Charles III and Charles IV, educating such later paragons of the Independence era as Manuel Belgrano, Mariano Moreno, and Bernardo Monteagudo. Like so many other Spanish American colleges, seminaries, and universities, it upheld the teaching of Natural Law. Charcas, however, was situated at the nodal point of what became after 1776–78 the two political and economic rival poles of Buenos Aires and Lima. The educated élite of Chuquisaca were reluctant to see their region subordinated to either pole. Accordingly, they used the opportunity provided by the metropolitan crisis to strike out for separate development. This did not entail separation from the Hispanic Monarchy or repudiation of the Bourbon dynasty but certainly did imply a readjusting of the political balance within the recently created Viceroyalty of the Río de la Plata. The Audiencia disliked Goyeneche's threatening insistence that it should unequivocally recognize the Seville Supreme Junta. A further problem entered the arena when the Princess of Brazil, Carlota Joaquina, sister of Ferdinand VII, proposed herself as regent in the Viceroyalty. The prospect of subordination to the interests of Portuguese Brazil, the traditional enemy, compounded the insult of French usurpation in the peninsula. The junta movement in Spain provided the model for the Audiencia of Charcas to assert its claim to be the principal, legitimate authority in Upper Peru.[39]

In conjunction with the city council and the university, the Audiencia convened an open meeting of all the principal authorities with the object of removing its president and the archbishop, branded as partisans of

---

[38] Morelli, *Territorio o nación*, 48.
[39] For the background, see John Lynch, *Spanish Colonial Administration. The Intendant System in the Viceroyalty of the Río de la Plata, 1782–1810* (London 1959), 267–73. See Clément Thibaud, *La Academia Carolina y la independencia de América. Los abogados de Chuquisaca (1776–1809)* (Sucre 2010).

Carlota Joaquina, and forming a distinct Upper-Peruvian junta. The Audiencia envisaged the creation of a network of subordinate juntas in the capitals of the other three intendancies established in Upper Peru in 1782, and sent out emissaries, for instance, to La Paz. This movement came from within the judicial, municipal, and intellectual élite of the principal city of Charcas. It was not a revolutionary attempt from below and took the form of loyalism not separatism. Within the specifically Upper-Peruvian context, the Audiencia sought to asset its own supremacy as legitimate delegate of the king's judicial authority, entitled thereby to exercise sovereignty in his absence. Its objective was to maintain a centralized, unitary power within the area. From the perspective of Chuquisaca, broad issues explained this move, not least of which was the fact that Viceroy Baltasar Hidalgo de Cisneros of Buenos Aires had not been directly appointed by the king but by the Seville Central Junta on February 11, 1809. The Audiencia's stance, however, bypassed the viceregal office and what remained of the metropolitan government. It amounted to a politically perilous, unilateral attempt to reconstitute the structure of authority in one segment of the River Plate Viceroyalty.[40]

The movement in La Paz began on July 16, 1809 when the Governor-Intendant and the Bishop were both removed by a city council-led junta on the same grounds as the authorities in Chuquisaca. Again the model was the Spanish juntas for the defense of the rights of Ferdinand VII. La Paz reported its actions to the Chuquisaca Junta two days later. Subsequently, it sent emissaries to the Peruvian cities of Puno, Cuzco, and Arequipa to follow suit, a departure regarded with alarm in Lima. La Paz, remote from Lima and after 1776 in another viceroyalty, still formed part of a business and cultural triangle that included Arequipa and Cuzco. La Paz also lay at the heart of a complex commercial hinterland of its own, which the social composition of its city council reflected. Groups of local hacienda-owners and merchants dominated the council. The latter were generally Spanish shopkeepers and warehouse-owners, who had become permanent residents in the territory. The *hacendados* of the *altiplano* and the valley area of the *yungas* were interlocked through commercial and matrimonial connections and constituted the richest and most important creole families in Upper Peru. Coca-leaf was their principal product, 95 percent

---

[40] Marta Irurozqui Victoriano, "Soberanía y castigo en Charcas. La represión militar y judicial de las juntas de La Plata y La Paz, 1808–1810," *Revista Complutense de Historia de América*, vol. 37 (2011), 49–72: see pp. 54–56, 67–68, examining why junta protagonists in Chuquisaca and La Paz were subjected to different punishments.

of which went to the mining population of Potosí to alleviate sickness and hunger.[41]

The élite *golpistas* in La Paz evidently did not fear stirring up a groundswell of lower-class discontent, even though the district was heavily indigenous in composition. *Hacendado* indebtedness, resulting from the decline of the Potosí mines after 1790 and the collapse of coca prices from a preceding peak, seemed to have provided the mainspring for their action. It raised the question of debt and credit, especially since Spanish-peninsular merchants supplied the latter. The city council, moreover, criticized the impact of increased import of European goods, possibly from the establishment of the *Cinco Gremios Mayores de Madrid* in Arequipa. At the same time, local élites resented the drain of revenue down to Buenos Aires. The top levels of society divided over these issues, and the crisis of 1808 provided an opportunity for the estate-owners of La Paz, already economically weakened, to attempt a home solution by taking power themselves.[42] The city council spearheaded the junta movement in La Paz, in contrast to that of Chuquisaca, which was led by the Audiencia. For that reason, it looked more radical than its predecessor.[43]

The wider dimension soon became clear, since both juntas directly challenged the viceroys in Buenos Aires and Lima, who accordingly planned concerted action to stamp them out. As in Peru in 1780–81, and later in Cuzco in 1814–15, the only way the *juntistas* could have salvaged their position would have been by extending the scope of their movement to other social groups. They were not given time to do so. Abascal instructed the Intendant of Huarochirí, Juan Ramírez, a hardened peninsular army officer, to recruit soldiers for a strike against La Paz, which would be led by Goyeneche. With recruits from southern Peru as well, Goyeneche stationed 2500 men above the city and marched in at the head of a further 800 men on October 15, dissolving the junta and arresting its leading partisans. Although Abascal had acted in concert with

---

[41] Rossana Barragán, "Españoles patricios y españoles europeos: Conflictos intra-elites e identidades en la ciudad de La Paz en vísperas de la Independencia, 1770–1809," in Charles Walker (compiler), *Entre la retórica y la insurgencia: las ideas y los movimientos sociales en los Andes. Siglo XVIII* (Cuzco 1996), 113–71: pp. 114, 116–17, 120, 135–42. Irurozqui Victoriano, "Soberanía y castigo," pp. 60, 63.

[42] Barragán, "Españoles patricios," 117–18, 120.

[43] Luis Miguel Glave, "Una perspectiva histórico-cultural de la revolución del Cuzco en 1814," *Revista de las Américas. Historia y Presente*, no. 1 (Spring 2003), 11–38: pp. 35–36, argues that events in La Paz in 1809 and Cuzco in 1814 formed part of a common process and that the movement in La Paz differed from that in Chuquisaca. Irurozqui Victoriano, "Soberanía y castigo," 65, 68–69.

Viceroy Cisneros, who was preparing the campaign to reduce Chuquisaca, his actions against La Paz extended *de facto* Peruvian control across the Desaguadero border between the two viceroyalties. The decisive action taken by Peru's viceroy indicated the urgency with which he felt that the junta movement in La Paz should be suppressed and severely castigated, since he faced a parallel junta movement from Quito after August. The success of both would have placed the viceregal government in Lima in serious difficulty. Between November 13, 1809 and January 26, 1810, treason trials were conducted in La Paz. As a result, the two principal leaders, one of whom was Pedro Domingo Murillo, were hanged and seven others garroted. Ramírez took over the Governorship-Intendancy of La Paz, and banished the remaining participants on March 3.[44]

Mariscal del Campo Vicente Nieto put down the Chuquisaca movement on December 24, 1809. He removed the offending magistrates from office, stripped others of their status, confiscated properties and papers, and banished other protagonists of the junta from the city. There were, however, no treason trials and executions. The guilty parties were not arraigned for treason but were corrected for overstepping the mark. Nieto became the new president of the Audiencia. Among those temporarily imprisoned were two *oidores* and the clerk of the Audiencia, and Monteagudo. Irurozqui argues persuasively that the explanation for the discrepancy of sentencing between the two cities lay in the fact that the Audiencia had promoted the movement in Chuquisaca, rather than the *cabildo*. The magistrates and the junta had attributed sovereign rights to themselves, which they had no business to do, since they transgressed the established hierarchy of authority in the viceroyalty. This was not treason but an unwise action.[45]

THE CARIBBEAN COAST, THE "FIRST INDEPENDENCE," AND PROVINCIAL RIVALRIES

In northern Spanish America, reception of the news of the collapse of the Supreme Central Junta, the beginning of the siege of Cádiz, and the hasty appointment of a Regency Council, claiming to inherit the right to

---

[44] Irurozqui Victoriano, "Soberanía y castigo," 53, 60, 62 note 41, 64. Ramírez was the same commander who crushed the Cuzco Rebellion in 1815. Judges from the Lima Audiencia participated in the trials in La Paz.

[45] Irurozqui Victoriano, "Soberanía y castigo," 53–55, 59–60.

exercise sovereignty, were greeted with a mixture of horror, despair, and incomprehension. An imminent disintegration of metropolitan Spain seemed to leave Spanish America to its own devices – an empire without a metropolis. On April 19, the city council of Caracas, representing the leading planter families, transformed itself into a *de facto* government of Venezuela, backed by the militia of the Aragua Valley, most of whom were *pardos*. Deposing the Captain General with his governing administration and dissolving the *audiencia*, the twenty-three members of the Supreme Junta of Venezuela asserted Ferdinand VII's sovereign rights against the French usurper, but also the people's right to act in such a way. Further complicating this revolutionary assumption of power, the Junta then requested, on April 20, all the provinces to recognize its provisional sovereignty. In short, the Venezuelan Junta assumed the authority vacated by the former Supreme Central Junta of Seville. Only Coro and Maracaibo refused to concur. A communication on May 3 explained to the Regency Council that Venezuela did not recognize the sovereign authority that it claimed. The Junta also opened direct communications with the non-Spanish Caribbean islands and sent commissioners to London.[46]

The news from Spain and Caracas arrived at a time of heightened tension between the port-city of Cartagena and the viceregal authorities in Santa Fe de Bogotá. The city élite of merchants, *hacendados*, lawyers, militia, and Army commanders represented the perspective of the Caribbean coast, which differed strikingly from that of the eastern-Andean cordillera, where Santa Fe was located. At the heart of the tension between Cartagena and Santa Fe lay the prevalence of contraband along the Caribbean coast. All social groups in the city depended for their livelihood on contraband through Jamaica and Curaçao; even provincial governors participated in it. By the later eighteenth century, the prime issue had become food supply for the expanding city. The wheat-producing estates of the eastern cordillera proved incapable of supplying the coast with sufficient, good-quality flour. Accordingly, cheaper and better flour was imported illegally by shippers from Baltimore in exchange, as elsewhere in the Caribbean, for tropical produce. Santa Fe regarded the Caribbean coastal zone as a troublesome frontier, operating largely beyond its control. Cartagena, at the head of an overwhelmingly rural province of some 150,000 inhabitants, functioned as the center of

---

[46] Guillermo Morón, *A History of Venezuela* (translated from the Spanish by John Street) (London 1964), 98–102.

wide-ranging commerce, legal with Spain and illegal beyond the empire, linking the gold-producing zones deep in the New Granada interior to the external market. In contrast to the Veracruz and Lima merchants, those of Cartagena were not primarily linked to the merchants of Cádiz, but, in effect, operated outside the Cádiz network.[47]

The two zones, the eastern cordillera and the Caribbean coast, were culturally different. The majority of Cartagena's population consisted of negroid mixtures – *mulatos, pardos,* and *zambos,* free blacks, and a relatively small number of slaves.[48] Distinctive leaders, such as Pedro Romero, had already emerged before the events of 1809–11 thrust them into the political center. Most of the mixed groups were artisans and a good number of them were militiamen for defense against British or French attack. As in the case of Cuba from the 1760s, the refortification of the city required craftsmen as well as soldiers, who with their families increased the port-city population. A small white élite of merchants and hacienda-owners prevailed in the administrative organs of the city, notably the fifteen-member municipality (eight of whom were creoles) and the *consulado,* incorporated in 1795. The former had nine merchants, two of them creoles and seven *peninsulares,* with three sons of merchants and three sons of soldiers. Some fifty merchants operated in the city, the principal of which, from the 1780s, were José Ignacio Pombo, Juan de Dios Amador, and Matías Rodríguez Torices, the two latter *peninsulares.* The senior military commander in the city, Mariscal del Campo Antonio Narváez, was a creole. The leading families, as elsewhere in Spanish America, were interrelated and involved in business partnerships. Their principal bugbear was Santa Fe.[49]

Pombo, married to Amador's daughter, held many of the offices in both the *cabildo* and *consulado,* and was a critic of the restrictions imposed by

---

[47] Alfonso Múnera, *El fracaso de la nación. Región, clase y raza en el Caribe colombiano* (1717–1810) (Bogotá 1998), 48, 54, 68, 72–74, 82, 85–88, 102, 120–27, 145. Gold represented 85 percent of the exports through Cartagena by the end of the eighteenth century.

[48] Aline Helg, "The Limits of Equality: Free Peoples of Color and Slaves during the First Independence of Cartagena, Colombia (1810–1815)," *Slavery and Abolition,* 20, no. 2 (August 1999), 1–30, argues that socio-economic divisions, class, and ethnic complexities prevented the attainment of a common racial consciousness among free, slave, and all- or part-black groups.

[49] Múnera, *El fracaso de la nación,* 23–27, 89, 104–5, 107–8, 117–18, 143. Pombo originated from Popayán, the son of a Spanish nobleman, but had been active in Cartagena from 1784 and operated the city's most important mercantile house. The majority of the lawyers had been educated at Santa Fe's celebrated Colegio del Rosario.

the colonial system. He saw in open trading with friendly foreign states the principal means of releasing the economy of New Granada from stagnation. Although the legal trade had doubled in value between 1784–93 and 1765–78, it still remained small in comparison to other Spanish American territories. Furthermore, transatlantic warfare after 1795 virtually closed it altogether, making Cartagena even more dependent on the extra-colonial (or contraband) trade. By 1807, imported wheat covered 60 - percent of the market in Cartagena. For such reasons, the Cartagena authorities took the decision on April 12, 1809 to defy the prohibitions continually imposed by the viceregal government in Santa Fe, and unilaterally opened the port to foreign goods. Principally, this meant to US wheat, flour, rice, and other foodstuffs. In this way, they reduced viceregal authority to a nullity and marginalized the Patriot regime in Seville. Peninsular and creole merchants in Cartagena were in agreement, counting, as they did, on the support of the mixed population in the city.[50]

The decision of August 1809 signified that Cartagena no longer recognized the political system centered on Santa Fe. Actions by the *cabildo* and *consulado* were opposed in Santa Fe, especially from the chief accounting body, the *Tribunal de Cuentas*, which held the port-city responsible for the backwardness of agriculture in the interior. Its Chief Accountant, Manuel Bernardo Álvarez, a creole and chief businessman in the capital, defended the political supremacy of Santa Fe, along with his two nephews, Antonio Nariño (1765–1823) and Jorge Tadeo Lozano, one of the cordillera wheat-producers. Into this situation came the news of the Caracas Junta's disavowal of the Regency Council.[51]

Having received news from Andalusia and Caracas, Cartagena's decision whether to recognize the Regency or not proved hard to make. The city council's *síndico procurador* (elected councilor), Dr. Antonio José de Ayos, recommended, on May 15, the formation of a Junta of eighteen members, representing heads of households (*vecinos*) in all city *barrios*, to share in the running of the province with the governor on the model of the Spanish juntas. Ayos referred to the provisions of the Laws of the Indies for the intervention of the people in the political processes, which "the three centuries of bad government" had distorted. On June 14, 1810, the *cabildo* removed the Governor and sent him back to Spain. Armed men from the *barrios*, under Romero's leadership, supported the *cabildo*'s action. Narváez and Pombo played the front role in the

---

[50] Múnera, *El fracaso de la nación*, 65, 86, 102, 107, 110, 128–43, 147, 174–75.
[51] Múnera, *El fracaso de la nación*, 152–54, 157–69.

transition, along with the law-graduate José María García de Toledo, another son of a Spanish merchant, who would shortly become the principal political figure. Like Pombo, García de Toledo, has been regarded as a representative of enlightened views. He had married into hacienda wealth in sugar and livestock, and was a slave-owner. Unlike Caracas, the authorities in Cartagena recognized the Regency Council. The latter, however, denounced their action and dispatched another Governor. In effect, the Regency regarded the authorities in the city to be in a state of rebellion.[52]

In the capital, the viceroy and *audiencia* hesitated to recognize the Regency until June 2. Finally, on July 20, the Cabildo of Santa Fe took the decision to remove them and form a *Junta Suprema de Santa Fe del Nuevo Reino de Granada*. Santa Fe declared its continued loyalty to the king but declined to recognize the Regency Council as the legitimate authority in the Monarchy. It asserted the right of Santa Fe to exercise the full jurisdiction that the *audiencia* had exercised. A similar range of provincial dissent, particularly where juntas had already been formed in advance of Santa Fe, arose in response. The new regime in Santa Fe proved incapable of persuading four of New Granada's main provinces – Cartagena, Tunja, Antioquia, and Popayán – to cooperate with it in the formation of a constitutional system. The authorities in Patriot Spain denounced these actions in New Granada as rebellion.[53]

When the congress opened on December 22, 1810, it represented the interests of little more than the eastern-Andean cordillera. Under the presidency of Álvarez and with Nariño, who had arrived back in Santa Fe on December 8, as secretary, this congress also declared its sovereignty over the entire territory of New Granada. Lozano became the first president on April 1, 1811. The Santa Fe regime was dominated from September 19, 1811 by a Nariño opposed to all centrifugal tendencies. On November 27, 1811, in response, deputies from Cartagena, Antioquia, Tunja, Pamplona, and Neiva formed a rival confederation known as the *Provincias Unidas de la Nueva Granada* with a constitution providing for autonomous provinces. The Santa Fe regime established the "Republic of Cundinamarca" on April 17, 1812, thereby abandoning earlier loyalty to the king. This "Republic," however, only

[52] Daniel Gutiérrez Ardila, *Las vacilaciones de Cartagena, Polémicas neogranadinas en torno a la creación del Cionsejo de Regencia* (Bogotá 2012), 17–24, 41–63. Múnera, *El fracaso de la nación*, 157, 159, 176, 200.
[53] Gutiérrez Ardila, *Las vacilaciones*, 24–25.

controlled part of the eastern cordillera. Nariño thereupon used force to subdue the provinces of Socorro and Tunja, causing the president of the rival Tunja congress, Francisco José de Caldas, to flee to Antioquia, and obliged them to join Cundinamarca. Only in July 1813 did the "Republic of Cundinamarca" break entirely with the Hispanic Monarchy as a separate state.[54]

The other provinces began to take their own initiatives. In Cali, the *cabildo* rejected the legitimacy of the Regency Council but defended the rights of Ferdinand VII. This was confirmed when the Governor of Cali, Dr. Joaquín Caicedo y Cuero, a scion of the famous local family, summoned an open meeting (*cabildo abierto*) of all the constituted bodies, which agreed on condition that the province's "usos y costumbres" – its perceived traditional practices – were observed. In Socorro, center of the *comunero* rebellion of 1781, the verdict was outright rejection of the Regency Council. In Antioquia, recognition was given though uncertainty reigned.[55]

The practice of *cabildo abierto* proved crucial in all this discussion, as in Buenos Aires, Santiago, and elsewhere in South America. The "opening" of the largely unelected *cabildos*, dominated in any case by local families, did not signify a sudden conversion to "democracy" but a gathering together of all the existing authorities and persons of substance in their respective cities to decide together on an exceptional matter. The initiative was being taken in the provincial city councils without waiting for a lead from Bogotá.[56]

THE DIS-UNITED PROVINCES OF THE RÍO DE LA PLATA

In Buenos Aires, the Revolutionary Junta, which took power on May 25, 1810, equally rejected the Regency Council but opted for a watch-and-wait strategy, refraining from participating in the Cortes. Although regarded as rebels in Cádiz, the Buenos Aires Patriots still made no open breach with metropolitan Spain.

Instead, the capital city set about imposing its authority over the other component provinces of the former viceroyalty. In effect, the first major decision of the revolutionary regime was to send troops to assert its

---

[54] Margarita Garrido, *Antonio Nariño* (Bogotá 1999), 65–70. Múnera, *El fracaso de la nación*, 168–70.

[55] Gutiérrez Ardila, *Las vacilaciones*, 11–35.

[56] Gutiérrez Ardila, *Las vacilaciones*, 35–36.

authority in Paraguay and Upper Peru. The adhesion of the interior
provinces in the sub-Andean zones, similarly, could not be counted
upon automatically. There, as elsewhere, local families divided over current issues struggled with one another for supremacy within their localities, as they had done to a lesser degree before the revolutionary era
began. Local resistance in Córdoba meant that Buenos Aires' troops had
to impose the authority of the capital-city Junta there. Ambrosio Funes,
brother of the celebrated Dean Gregorio Funes of the Córdoba cathedral
chapter, from one of the city's leading families, held the office of
Intendant-Governor in 1815–16. The long-lasting struggle with the
Peruvian Royalist Army for control of Upper Peru meant that the far-
northern provinces of Tucumán, Cuyo, and Salta assumed strategic
importance. Three military failures in Upper Peru between 1810 and
1815 would leave this zone as the future borderland of the new Platine
state. Exposure to the vacillating advances and retreats of the Royal army
sharpened political divisions during that period.[57]

Government by two Triumvirates between September 1811
and January 1814, modeled on the Roman Republic, still did not lead to
outright proclamation of republican government. Furthermore, the
Constituent Assembly, which opened on January 31, 1813, singularly
failed to produce a constitution for the new state. Not until after the
king's closure of the Cortes in May 1814 did the Buenos Aires Patriots
begin to move in the direction of independence from Spain and republicanism. In the meantime, the provinces of Santa Fe and Córdoba
proclaimed their independence from the city of Buenos Aires in 1815.

Provincial resentment of the port-capital was not assuaged, with the
result that capital-city centralists faced demands for a federal system.
The Constitution of 1819, nevertheless, established a centralist structure,
thereby ensuring that the federal–central conflict would plague the new
republic until the 1860s. The provinces of Tucumán with Catamarca and
Santiago del Estero, and Entre Ríos, joined with Corrientes, formed separate republics in 1819–20, followed by the provinces of Córdoba and La
Rioja. Impromptu pacts and private understandings between rival provincial chieftains enabled the United Provinces to survive the 1820s.[58]

---

[57] Tulio Halperín Donghi, *Politics, Economics and Society in Argentina in the
Revolutionary Period* (translated by Richard Southern) (Cambridge 1975), 120–21,
239–46, 264–65.
[58] Nicholas Shumway, *The Invention of Argentina* (Berkeley, Los Angeles and London
1991), 43–45, 49–52, 63–66.

As in New Granada, the Platine revolutionary movement represented political not social transformation – at least in intent, rather than unintended consequences of actions taken. It envisaged the replacement of the governing scale of Spanish officials by representatives of the local families – at least, it did in the eyes of the latter. In reality, the cause of much resentment was the superimposition of new authorities sent from the city of Buenos Aires entrusted with the imposition of the revolutionary system. In the colonial era, local authorities had usually survived by blending in with the local interest groups. The new authorities soon discovered that this was the best way to stay in office. Alongside them, the customary inter-family rivalries continued as the wider struggles to provide some form of stable government to ensure the survival of the revolutionary system took place within and around them. The new regime's lack of financial resources to pay for an impartial civil service and policing agencies to enforce the will of central government meant that, in reality, power would be delegated to the local interest groups or would be taken by strong men who rose to power and wealth through the course of the fighting. One such figure was the La Rioja provincial chieftain, Juan Facundo Quiroga, militia captain from 1816, in succession to his father, whose cattle estates, prospering from supplying the armies on the military frontier, he inherited. The rise of such *caudillos*, sustained by and sustaining their local landed élites, would set the tone for the following half-century of Argentine political life.[59]

As revolutionary activity spread across Spanish America from the spring of 1810, the Court and government in Rio began to cast an eye over the turmoil, especially in the River Plate zone. Opposed to the Buenos Aires Junta's claims were the Royalist governor and garrison in Montevideo, across the river. Conflict opened the possibly of a Luso-Brazilian intervention in the Banda Oriental, ostensibly designed to assist the Spanish Royalists, but, in reality, to reverse the Treaty of San Ildefonso of 1777 and recover control of Colônia do Sacramento on the northern bank of the river. The British Minister Plenipotentiary in Rio, Lord Strangford, Ambassador in Lisbon from 1806, and the London government opposed such designs. Strangford managed to secure a truce, providing for the departure of Portuguese forces from the Banda Oriental. Much confusion has arisen surrounding Strangford's objectives in Brazil; he was the only British diplomat in Ibero-America at that time. It seems clear, though, that he followed Foreign Secretary George Canning's

[59] Halperín Donghi, *Politics, Economy and Society*, 253, 261, 263.

indications on November 26, 1808 that the loyalty of the Spanish American territories to Bourbon Spain should above all be preserved, since Spain and Britain were fighting together against Napoleon. At the same time, he should further Britain's strategic and commercial interests. This left him in an ambiguous position with regard to the Buenos Aires Junta. Above all, he was determined to halt Luso-Brazilian expansion southwards.[60]

Yet, D. João's virtually estranged wife, Carlota Joaquina, sought to assert her claim to exercise the regency over all the Spanish American territories. Strangford, however, was determined to block her meddling. Carlota Joaquina, for her part, continued correspondence with potential supporters in Buenos Aires and other cities in South America. After the restoration of peace in Europe, furthermore, Strangford pressed D. João to return to Lisbon. D. João, thereupon, intrigued with his Prince Regent counterpart in London to secure Strangford's removal, which was accomplished on April 8, 1815, when the former finally left Rio.[61]

THE SITUATION IN CHILE

A similar display of divided and nuanced upper-class sentiment to that appearing in New Granada and Quito also occurred in Chile in a different cultural context. As in the case of Quito, a principal motive for action during the crisis years lay in further assertion of the small territory's distinctness from the Viceroyalty of Peru. The Spanish Crown's policy of diminishing the position of Peru within South America had already led to the establishment of a distinct Captaincy-General of Chile and Consulado in 1795.

Basque immigration to Chile during the eighteenth century, stimulated by the establishment of registered shipping by the Cape Horn route after 1740, considerably reinforced the social composition of the Chilean oligarchy, which had its political base in the City Council of Santiago and its material wealth in the Central Valley. The Basques, from a variety of commercial and industrial backgrounds, inherited the tradition of the *fueros* still enjoyed by their four home provinces. They came less as solitary individuals but as educated groups with experience and skills to offer. Very soon the younger men married into Chilean landed families,

---

[60] John Street, "Lord Strangford and the Río de la Plata, 1808–1815," *HAHR*, vol. 30 (1953), 477–510: see pp. 479–85, 491.

[61] Macaulay, *D. Pedro*, 30–31, 39–40.

thereby increasing their spread of activities through agriculture, commerce, and mining, to municipal and ecclesiastical offices. They contributed to the foundation of dynasties bearing a range of Basque surnames – Eyzaguirre, Errázuriz, Larraín, Arístegui, Undurraga, and so on. Domingo de Eyzaguirre, for instance, left his native Vizcaya at the age of twenty-three, working at the Royal Mint first in Mexico City and shortly afterwards in Lima, before moving definitely to Chile in 1757, where he married the niece of the Bishop of Santiago in 1765, who was herself the daughter of a prominent Basque resident of Concepción. Eyzaguirre became a Santiago City Councilor in 1768 and died in 1800, the owner of the Hacienda de San Agustín de Tango outside the city. The political activities of such families ranged throughout the crisis of the Monarchy, the process of Independence, and well into the nineteenth century.[62]

The Basque families played a leading role in the junta movement in Chile. Santiago de Chile followed the example of Buenos Aires.[63] The *Junta de Gobierno* formed on September 18, 1810 asserted the principle that Chileans enjoyed the same rights as inhabitants of the Spanish peninsula in accordance with the Castilian legal tradition. It saw Chile as a component of the Monarchy but not a dependency of Spain. Yet, the "Nation" they defended against Bonapartist usurpation was clearly the whole Monarchy, not any particular part of it. The Santiago municipality played a decisive role in this process, opening the political process to some 400 members of the urban articulate classes though a "*cabildo abierto,*" on the lines of the Buenos Aires' Revolution of May. The Santiago Junta, playing for caution, recognized the Regency Council and duly informed both it and the Viceroy of Peru of this fact. The Chilean Patriots were anxious to avoid intervention from Lima, even though the conflict in Upper Peru made this unlikely for most of the period 1810–13. Unlike Buenos Aires, the Chilean colonial militias were weak and lacked any experience of real combat. Agustín de Eyzaguirre, one of its leading councilors and son of Domingo, led the "creole party," which itself divided into factions formed by rival family groupings. Allied with Eyzaguirre were Fernando Errázuriz, Diego Larraín, and Juan Manuel Infante. This Eyzaguirre graduated from the University of San Felipe,

---

[62] Salvador Méndez Reyes, *Las Élites criollas de México y Chile ante la Independencia* (Mexico City 2004), 274–86.

[63] Simon Collier, *Ideas and Politics of Chilean Independence, 1808–1833* (Cambridge 1967), 12–15, 120. Lynch, *The Spanish American Revolutions* (1986), 44–58, 132–36, 195–97, 239–41.

traded with Spain, Peru, and Mendoza, and had commercial contacts in Rio de Janeiro and Buenos Aires, extending to Cádiz and London.[64]

In general, separatist sentiment remained a minority persuasion throughout Spanish America during the period 1808–12. In the Captaincy-General of Chile, monarchist sentiment still remained strong into the middle of the 1810s, even though several Chilean Patriot leaders, such as Bernardo O'Higgins, were separatists. The separatist persuasion gained ground in response to the restoration of absolutism in Chile by the Peruvian Royalist army, which extinguished the experiment in home rule after its victory at Rancagua in October 1814. Eyzaguirre and other participants were dispatched into a grim exile on the Pacific islands of Juan Fernández.[65]

As in all the other cases, the city council of Santiago also played the decisive role in the formation of a congress, which opened on July 4, 1811. It represented the moderate views of the Santiago-educated élite, who still considered their country to be part of the Hispanic Monarchy. Before devising a constitution, this congress issued a Regulation providing for the separation of powers and a three-member Executive, a reaction to the concentration of power under absolutism. When the more radical Army officer, José Miguel Carrera, dissolved Congress and issued the Provisional Constitutional Regulation in October 1812, it became clear that Chile, on a more revolutionary course than before, would not be implementing the Cádiz Constitution.[66]

The radical tendency of Carrera's regime provided the reason for Viceroy Abascal's decision to send Peruvian troops under Mariano Osorio into Chile *in order to enforce implementation of the Spanish Constitution of 1812*. The first of three Peruvian interventions in Chile began in March 1813, and after the arrest of Carrera the governing senate imposed the 1812 Constitution at the time that it was being abolished in Spain by the king, news of which reached Chile from Buenos Aires on August 26, 1814. The Battle of Rancagua on October 1–2, 1814 extinguished the remnants of the Chilean Patriot regime that had been in power in one form or another since September 18, 1810. Osorio, a veteran of the war against the French Revolutionaries, governed

[64] Méndez Reyes, *La Élite criolla*, 286–310.

[65] Juan Luis Ossa Santa Cruz, *Armies, Politics and Revolution. Chile, 1808–1826* (Liverpool 2014), 51–55.

[66] I am indebted to Dr. Juan Luis Ossa Santa Cruz for allowing me to consult his manuscript, "De Cádiz a la América del Sur: el viaje de una ilusión constitucional," [2013], 8–9, 13–14.

a restored Royalist Chile from October 1814 until December 1815, re-establishing the Audiencia of Santiago in March 1815.[67]

AMERICAN CONSTITUTIONS

The South American movement for the rejection of the legitimacy of the Regency Council began in Caracas six months before the Extraordinary Cortes would actually open in Spain. In Caracas, and in Buenos Aires in the following month, the subjects of representation and equality of rights assumed immense proportions. The climax came when both cities removed peninsular authorities and established juntas of their own to manage their affairs. Santa Fe de Bogotá followed the example of Caracas in July, although in a completely different political context. These three movements were not initially separatist but asserted local determination to control the workings of political life. In Quito, the second round of the junta movement began on August 2, 1810, directed chiefly against the repressive regime installed in the city by Peruvian Royalist forces, beginning with an assault on the prison. The President of the Audiencia authorized a *cabildo abierto* of all leading authorities in the city and released the prisoners. When the Regency Council's representative, Carlos de Montúfar (1780–1816), son of the president of the earlier Junta, arrived in Quito on September 12, the question of recognizing the Regency divided the new junta. A reconstituted Junta on September 19, including Montúfar, recognized the Regency Council.[68]

In contrast to New Spain and Peru, the top-level colonial political structure collapsed between April and September 1810 in both Caracas and Santa Fe, where the Regency Council and Cortes in Spain were rejected. In Buenos Aires and Chile, the Juntas were more ambivalent. In all four instances, the move from colonial authorities to local juntas took different forms. Royalist allegiance remained vital in outlying Venezuelan cities, in coastal and southern New Granada, and in southern Chile.

Although a political transformation, regarded in Patriot Spain as rebellion, had taken place, the social and juridical structures were left untouched. These latter were not regarded as part of any specific problem.

---

[67] Ossa Santa Cruz, *Armies, Politics and Revolution*, 55–81.
[68] Guadalupe Soasti Toscano, *El Comisionado regio. Carlos Montúfar y Larrea. Sedicioso, insurgente y rebelde* (Quito 2009). Morelli, *Territorio o nación*, 49–50.

The key to understanding the motives and justifications lay in the Natural Law tradition. The concept of the "community of the people," which, in effect, meant the sum of the juridically constituted corporations of the realm, was brought forward to give moral credence to the political transition. The seventeenth-century elaboration of this idea resulted in the application of "the rights of peoples" in specific political instances – the absence of a monarch or the right to oppose tyranny.[69]

The example of the United States was more clearly observed in Caracas than, for instance, in Mexico City, which at that time was a good deal further away in terms of political distance. Regular maritime connections across the Caribbean brought news of political innovations as well as slave rebellions in French Saint-Domingue.[70] Republicanism, however, still remained a minority persuasion in Spanish America. Outstanding Patriots, such as Miranda and Nariño, were republicans.[71] Patriot Venezuela declared independence from the Hispanic Monarchy on July 5, 1811 as a republic. Its first constitution owed a great deal to the United States' Constitution of 1787, which was federal and preserved slavery. In striking contrast to the subsequent Constitution of Cádiz, both the first constitutions of Venezuela and New Granada were bicameral.[72] On November 11, 1811, Cartagena declared independence from Spain, as well as from Santa Fe. The Cartagena Constitution of 1812 was republican, representative, and liberal. Nariño, who admired George Washington and Benjamin Franklin, presided over the Republic of Cundinamarca from September 1811. The Province of Antioquia issued its own Constitution on May 3, 1812, proclaiming that sovereignty resides "originally and essentially in the people," while remaining a part of the United Provinces and under the General Congress of New Granada. Santa Fe de Bogotá did not declare independence from the Hispanic Monarchy until July 18, 1813. The two principles of federalism and republicanism predominated in this first phase of the New Granada independence movement. Pombo's Preliminary Discourse in 1811, for instance, drew from Natural Law in the Spanish American tradition but

[69] María Teresa Calderón and Clément Thibaud, *La Majestad de los pueblos en la Nueva Granada y Venezuela, 1780–1832* (2010), 175–200: see pp. 182–91.
[70] Alejandro E. Gómez, "La caribeanidad revolucionaria de la 'Costa de Caracas': una visión prospectiva (1793–1815)," in, Hébrard and Verdo, *Las Independencias*, 35–48.
[71] Anthony McFarlane, "Identity, Enlightenment and Political Dissent in Late Colonial Spanish America," *Transactions of the Royal Historical Society*, Sixth Series, VIII (1998), 309–35: p. 324.
[72] Lynch, *Spanish American Revolutions*, 195–98.

also outlined the principles of federalism and their application to the US Constitution.[73]

The General Congress of Venezuela, which proclaimed itself to be "constituent," lasted from February 2 until December 21, 1811. Its deputies came from the provincial juntas. Together they established a "confederation," although the two terms, confederation and federation, were often used indistinguishably. Its central government in Caracas was conceived with ample faculties. In other words, the new political system was not intended to be weak and divided but unified under a clearly defined central government. The component parts were provinces and were not envisaged as autonomous states with their own constitutions. Bolívar's subsequent criticism of the First Venezuelan Republic, blaming federalism for political failure, obscured the original intention. In Santa Fe, by contrast, the intention was different. Fearing recurrence of tyranny, the Santa Fe Junta in its Instruction of October 26, 1810 provided for the division of powers and a three-man rotating Executive. The forty-two members of the Constituent College issued an Act of Federation of the United Provinces of New Granada on November 27, 1811. In order to take effect, however, this Act had to be ratified by each one of the component provinces (*gobiernos*), some of which, such as Cartagena on November 11, had already proclaimed themselves autonomous, sovereign states and, in some cases, adopted their own constitutions. This concept of "federalism" was looser than in Venezuela, since these "states" participated in the wider body of their own volition. The Union, furthermore, did not renounce the authority of the Spanish Crown or declare independence at that point. In fact, initiatives on this sensitive issue would be taken within the "states," rather than by the Union.[74]

Most American constitutions synthesized perceived local traditions, commonly understood Hispanic traditions, and contemporary thinking. As such, they were not derivative of US or French models but *sui generis*. Bicameralism differentiated them from the Cádiz Constitution's unicameralism. In Spanish America, bicameralism did not have the stigma that it had in the France of 1791 and the Spain of 1812, because there was no formal nobiliar estate. In Spanish America, the prime concern was the

---

[73] Daniel Gutiérrez Ardila, *Las asambleas constituyentes de la Independencia. Actas de Cundinamarca y Antioquia (1811–1812)* (Bogotá 2010), 258, 261. Calderón and Thibaud, *La majestad de los pueblos*, 91–96.

[74] Daniel Gutiérrez Ardila, *Asambleas constituyentes*, 18–28. See also Calderón and Thibaud, *La soberanía de los pueblos*, 185.

assertion of the local élites' right to participate in the government of their own provinces and in their own capital cities. For the most part, the revolution ended there: ended, that is, in the institutionalization of control by the predominant families.

In Spanish America in these years, the unyielding problem remained one of how to legitimize these actions. The Santa Fe Junta invoked the "law of peoples" in its Declaration of September 28, 1810.[75] We should not be surprised to find the rights of states or the Rights of Man intertwined with the upholding of traditional corporate structures, declarations of the unique veracity of the Catholic religion, and the determination of new governments to protect it as their moral duty. No such constitutional experiments took place in either Brazil or Portugal at this time. On the contrary, João VI continued to govern without recourse to representative institutions of any description.

[75] Thibaud in Calderón and Thibaud, *La soberanía de los pueblos*, 183.

5

Hispanic America – Violence Unleashed

What factors made the situation in Spanish America so incandescent? Recent focus on the Cortes of Cádiz has lately come to obscure – or even brush out – the impact of violence in shaping the nature of the incipient sovereign-states that emerged from the disintegration of the Hispanic Monarchy on the American continent.[1] Was the outbreak of violence during the 1810s a sideshow, when the real focus should be on the "silent revolution" of constitutional forms and ideas?[2] Concepts such as the expansion of the "public sphere" in the work of Guerra have obscured the necessity of explaining what people thought they were fighting and dying for in this period.[3]

---

[1] There is a broad literature: see, for instance, Anthony McFarlane and Marianne Wiesebron (coordinators), *Violencia social y conflicto civil: América latina, siglo XVIII–XIX*, in Cuadernos de Historia Latinoamericana, AHILA, no. 6 (Ridderkerk 1998); Christon I. Archer, "The Cutting Edge: The Historical Relationship between Insurgency, Counterinsurgency and Terrorism during Mexican Independence, 1810–1821," in Lawrence Howard (ed.), *Terrorism: Roots, Impact, Responses* (Westport, CT 1992), 29–46; Eric A. Johnson, Ricardo D. Salvatore, and Pieter Spierenburg (eds.), *Murder and Violence in Modern Latin America* (Oxford 2013), with attention to the chapter by Alan Knight.

[2] Antonio Annino, "Cádiz y la revolución territorial de los pueblos mexicanos, 1812–1821," in Antonio Annino (compiler), *Historia de las elecciones en Iberoamérica, siglo XIX* (Mexico City 1995), 177–226: see pp. 12, 177, 215. For a contrasting view, Miguel Angel Centeno, "The Centre did not Hold: War in Latin America and the Monopoly of Violence," in James Dunkerley (ed.), *Studies in the Formation of the Nation State in Latin America* (London 2004), 54–76: p. 66.

[3] See the discussion in William H. Sewell, "Collective Violence and Collective Loyalties in France: Why the French Revolution made a Difference," *Politics and History*, 18, no. 4 (December 1990), 527–52, concerning attempts to identify different categories of violence, their objectives and consequences.

I propose to examine the question of violence *before* discussion of the strengths and weaknesses of the Cádiz experiment initiated in the Spanish peninsula. Royalist intervention to extinguish the Junta of Quito and La Paz had already occurred before the Cortes had met. The outbreak of insurrection in New Spain occurred in the week before the Cortes began its sessions. Armed conflict in Venezuela accompanied the Cortes deputies' discussion of the shape of the future Constitution of the Monarchy, which was to be the panacea. Declarations of juridical equality between Americans and Europeans arrived in the Americas in the midst of tensions already bursting into outright conflict. The Constitution of Cádiz represented less a new dawn for Spain and the Americas than a last ditch attempt to hold together the Monarchy already breaking apart. In that sense, the declarations of principle made in the Constitution amounted to abstractions thrown against the wind.

CATEGORIES OF VIOLENCE

Patrice Gueniffey's examination of Terror during the French Revolution provides a guideline into the study of violence. A distinction is made between crowd violence or bread and tax riots, on the one hand, and revolutionary violence. Conversely, a distinction has also to be made between exemplary punishments, imposed as deterrents, and Terror employed systematically by government as a political weapon designed to extirpate opposition and instill conformity. There were, then, differing categories and degrees of violence during the French Revolution from 1789 through the 1790s. The September prison massacres, for example, did not result from government initiative. Violence and Terror were not identical. Not all the violence in the Revolution occurred during the Terror, usually dated from the Convention's Order of September 5, 1793 until the fall of Robespierre on July 27, 1794. Similarly, not all acts of Terror occurred within those months. In the selection of victims by the state, acts of Terror occurred from the time of the National Assembly in 1789–91 and after July 1794. The institutions put in place by revolutionary governments for such actions antedated the Terror proper and also enabled their continuation afterwards. The concentration of arrests and executions in the months of 1793–94, however, marked them out as a special category. In the Terror, the objective was defined by government and the intended victims identified as "enemies of the people," a categorization open to many interpretations. This was a political strategy – deliberate, rational, and calculating, with the inducement of fear regarded as necessary in order to attain specific political objectives. The objective was to push the revolution forward as a new form of human existence, forestall dilution, and prevent its overthrow. In that sense, Terror was outside or above the law, which was seen by its enactors as inadequate to deal with the emergency identified.[4]

The Tupac Amaru rebellion in southern Peru in 1780–81 and the Tupac Katari rebellion in Upper Peru, the New Granada *comunero* rebellion, the Quito riots of 1765, and the Mexican riots of 1766–67 differed in dimension, duration, and impact from the many smaller rebellions, demonstrations, and protests across American territories during the colonial era. These latter also reflected a consciousness of traditions, customs, and ethnic or corporate identities, which seemed at the specific time of conflict to be threatened or violated. When rural and small-town dwellers used violence to halt transformations that threatened village life and local traditions, rather than to create a new social and moral order, this could not be described as revolutionary action, despite its insurrectionary form. To these causal factors we can add responses to ill-treatment of labor, violation of village rights, and conflicts over land or water usage or boundaries. At the same time, frequent popular recourse to litigation challenged abuses and violations by the propertied classes.[5] This is not to imply that colonial life amounted to a constant ferment, but it is to state that the propertied, moneyed, educated, and articulate had always to take note that those socially beneath them were unlikely to remain passive if provoked beyond endurance. The violence in Spanish America between 1809 and 1826 did not occur in a vacuum. Nevertheless, its scale and impact were unanticipated and unprecedented. Wide discrepancies in the forms and uses of violence appeared across the sub-continent at this time. Most Spanish American revolutionary movements did not employ systematic terror.

---

[4] Patrice Gueniffey, *La politique de la Terreur* (Paris 2000), 12–17, 21–27, 31, 40–41.

[5] See for instance: Segundo E. Moreno Yánez, *Sublevaciones indígenas en la Audiencia de Quito desde comienzos del siglo XVIII hasta finales de la colonia* (Quito 1978); William B. Taylor, *Drinking, Homicide and Rebellion in Colonial Mexican Villages* (Stanford 1979); Eugene D. Genovese, *From Rebellion to Revolution. Afro-American Slave Revolts in the Making of the Modern World* (New York 1981 [1979]; Craig T. Jenkins, "Why Do Peasants Rebel? Structural and Historical Theories of Modern Peasant Rebellions," *American Journal of Sociology*, 88, no. 3 (1983), 487–514; Friedrich Katz (ed.), *Riot, Rebellion, and Revolution. Rural Social Conflict in Mexico* (Princeton 1988); Susan Schroder (ed.), *Native Resistance and the Pax Colonial in New Spain* (Lincoln and London 1998).

The Spanish American concept of revolution differed strikingly from the French experience of the 1790s. In Spanish America, there was, on the whole, little intention on the part of revolutionary leaders to overturning established modes of belief and social organization. By contrast, the element of restitution rather than social revolution often remained predominant. While it can certainly be argued that Spanish Liberals sought to transform the political and juridical order in the peninsula, there is little sense that Spanish American autonomists or even separatists exhibited a similar intention in their territories. Even Morelos, whose political thought entailed the nullification of colonial racial categories, intended to uphold the juridical privileges of the Church inherited from the colonial era. Few, if any, Spanish American revolutionaries intended to subvert the traditional religion and the ecclesiastical order, as French Jacobins had done in 1793–94.

Beyond the violence of contending armies in the battlefield across Spanish America, there were many other categories of violence: large-scale insurrections, such as the Hidalgo Rebellion in New Spain in 1810–11 and its long aftermath under Morelos' military leadership from 1811–14; the Venezuelan Royalist insurrections of 1812 and 1814, and the Cuzco Rebellion of 1814–15; insurgencies like those in Mexico and Upper Peru throughout the decade and in southern Peru in the aftermath of the Cuzco Rebellion's defeat and across the central Andes during the early 1820s; provincial and local revolts along the Cauca Valley between 1810 and 1815; counter-revolutionary violence by the Royalist authorities holding on to power in New Spain and Peru in 1810–15, and the repression conducted by the Royal Expeditionary Force under Pablo Morillo in Venezuela and New Granada in 1815–17. To these categories we can add forced recruitment into Royalist or Revolutionary armies, into insurgent bands and into Royalist defense forces on haciendas and in organized villages.[6]

Insurgencies also have a growing literature of their own. A recent interpretation, focusing on contemporary Colombia, South Sudan, and the struggle for Kurdistan, describes insurgents as "non-state armed actors that use violence to reformulate or destroy the foundations of politics in an existing country." The reformulation of legitimacy

---

[6] Guillermo Hernández de Alba Lesmes, *Recuerdos de la reconquista. El Consejo de Purificación* (Bogotá 1935), 4–10. Stephen K. Stoan, *Pablo Morillo and Venezuela, 1815–1820* (Columbus, OH 1974).

accompanies this process of upheaval.[7] Insurgencies, generally adopting guerrilla tactics, conduct lower level operations, which depend upon opportunities rather than skilled planning, whenever an overall direction is absent. Too weak to challenge entrenched positions outright or to engage with armies in the open field, they rely on stealth. They require support from the countryside for foodstuffs and from the towns for information. Control of the countryside's resources becomes vital to counterinsurgency strategy and involves sporadic demonstrations of violence designed to counter collaboration with insurgents or to punish captured and identified rebels. The latter respond in kind.

The Mexican Insurgency and the Cuzco Rebellion of 1814–15 certainly fell into the above categories, and both sought to establish alternative legitimacies to their respective viceregal administrations. The difference between them, other than duration, was that the latter had an alternative capital city in Cuzco with all its historical traditions and symbolic significance. The Mexican insurgents, in eleven years of struggle, never had anything comparable. Furthermore, the Cuzco rebels had contact with other revolutionary forces beyond the borders of their own viceroyalty, namely the official armed forces of the Revolutionary Junta of Buenos Aires, commanded by Belgrano, and the various rebel bands across Upper Peru (Charcas). Bolívar, for his part, could move from Venezuela to New Granada and back again, re-igniting different theatres of war. Despite attempts to make contact with the government of the United States and occasional cooperation with privateers operating out of New Orleans, Mexican insurgents remained overwhelmingly confined to their own territories.[8]

The social history of the Independence era still offers us little in the way of understanding the cultural, moral, and psychological impact of these varied forms of the exercise of violence, although Van Young's *The Other Rebellion* does go a long way in this direction. Despite historians' frequent encounters with archival documents dealing with disputes, Iberian America had not been accustomed to widespread violence. Federica Morelli contrasts the relatively peaceful conditions in colonial Ibero-America to conditions in Europe from the sixteenth to the nineteenth centuries. The upheavals of the 1810s and early 1820s altered this state

---

[7] Claire Metelits, *Inside Insurgency. Violence, Civilians, and Revolutionary Group Behaviours. On the Front Lines with the FARC, SPLA, and PKK* (New York 2010), 3.

[8] On trans-border operations and influences, see Idean Salehyan, *Rebels without Borders. Transnational Insurgencies in World Politics* (Ithaca and London 2009), 20–26.

of affairs considerably. Morelli attributes much of the Republic of Ecuador's nineteenth-century instability to the preceding legacy of violence. One result of armed conflict in the Wars of Independence was that arms fell into the possession of groups of people other than the official power.[9]

The continued fighting brought the lower sectors of the population into the forefront of the action.[10] Many communities found themselves caught between both sides; many wanted just to stay out of the conflict and try to preserve their existing way of life. Villages divided or changed loyalties by choice or by force. Insurgents increasingly took to fortified positions, hillsites of difficult access, or island redoubts. Conflict destabilized rural life, cut towns off from their countryside, and interrupted communications and trade routes, mine-production and investment, and the dispatch of revenue from the silver mines. Foraging armies and irregular bands destroyed the legal structures and practices upon which the colonial system had been based. Frequently, the insurgent movement broke into autonomous bands or was only loosely or nominally held together.[11]

Once unleashed, violence rapidly went out of control and no one could put a stop to it. Many sought to extend it further. Informal leadership, often unaware of the consequences of its actions, lost control completely. Improvised soldiers, who in their pre-revolutionary lives may have been clerics or lawyers, rapidly lost control of the forces they purported to command. Local chieftains, accustomed to the leadership of armed men, emerged with their own bands and agendas. Professional soldiers strove to discipline their forces, prevent desertions, and control associated guerrilla units reluctant to recognize any other authority.[12]

INSURRECTION IN NEW SPAIN

Historians continue to wrestle with the problem of what caused the conflagration in New Spain after September 1810. Contemporaries had also struggled to find an explanation. The initial focus of the insurrection

---

[9] Eric Van Young, *The Other Rebellion. Popular Violence, Ideology, and the Mexican Struggle for Independence, 1810–1821* (Stanford 2001). Morelli, *Territorio o nación*, 131.

[10] Juan Ortiz Escamilla, *Guerra y Gobierno. Los pueblos en la Independencia de México* (Mexico City/ Seville 1997), 101, 113–18.

[11] Ortiz Escamilla, *Guerra y Gobierno*, 107–13, 118–41. Moisés Guzmán Pérez, "Lecturas militares. Libros, Escritos y Manuales de Guerra en la Independencia," *Relaciones*, 110, vol. xxviii (primavera 2007), p. 136.

[12] McFarlane, *War and Independence*, 410.

lay in the center-northern Bajío in areas already affected by economic changes and at a time of subsistence crisis.[13] The subsistence crisis did not cause the rebellion. The roots lay further back and went deeper in the social and economic life of New Spain, particularly its most dynamic regions, and in the popular culture and religious perspectives of its ordinary inhabitants. Even those contributory factors would have been insufficient to generate such a long-lasting and violent upheaval. The political crisis throughout the Monarchy, penetrating most levels of society, provided the mainspring. At the same time, in several strategically located provincial capital cities – San Luis Potosí, Zacatecas, Guadalajara, and Valladolid de Michoacán – royal authorities and the groups around them were either divided, in conflict, or already losing control by the outbreak of rebellion in mid-September 1810.[14]

Starvation, migration into the cities, and the sense of doom pervading the most badly hit areas enabled rebel groups to exploit these extreme conditions of social disruption and despair. The major areas of insurrection and insurgency tended to be those in which the impact of both long- and short-term economic change had been most disruptive of working-peoples' lives. As is well-known, economic growth in late colonial New Spain had been uneven and regionally differentiated. At its greatest impact, it tended to depress living standards in a context of population growth, market pressures, and sporadic subsistence crises. The correlation between the impact of economic change and the potential for insurrection, or between subsistence crisis and conflict, is never easy to determine. The center-northwest continued to be the scene of repeated conflict between Royalist forces and insurgent bands through the 1810s.[15]

---

[13] AGN [Mexico City] Intendentes 73, exp. 4, Riaño to Archbishop-Viceroy Francisco Lizana y Beaumont, no. 15 reservada, Guanajuato 25 August 1809: exp. 7, ff.9–11, Domínguez to Lizana, Querétaro 19 September 1809, ff. 69–70 obv, Domínguez to Lizana, Querétaro 2 September 1809. Lizana was viceroy from July 16, 1809 until April 25, 1810. John Tutino, *From Insurrection to Revolution in Mexico. Social Bases of Agrarian Violence, 1750–1940* (Princeton 1986), 164–78, 247–48, 254–57, 260.

[14] Hermés Tovar Pinzón, "Insolencia, tumulto e invasiones de los naturales de Zacoalco (México) a fines del siglo XVIII," *Cuadernos de Historia Social y Económica*, 10 (1985), 1–18. Tutino, *From Insurrection to Revolution*, 109–19, 151–78. Hamnett, *Roots of Insurgency*, 125–77.

[15] Brian R. Hamnett, "Royalist Counterinsurgency and the Continuity of Rebellion: Guanajuato and Michoacán, 1813–20," *Hispanic American Historical Review*, 62, no. 1 (1982), 19–48.

The rebellion led by the priest Miguel Hidalgo and the militia Captain Ignacio Allende was rooted in the localities of the central and southern Bajío. Provincial origin derived from the impossibility of rebellion in the capital city, and from failure to subvert the colonial militia on a scale significant enough to transform it into the instrument of revolutionary political change. This ensured that the Mexican road would be long, bloody, and concentrated in the provinces, in contrast to the swift overthrow of the Spanish authorities in South America beyond Peru. The Mexican insurrections from 1810–11 drew on existing grievances but they also represented something new. They developed a moral justification for the challenge to the existing structures of power. They drew together different peoples across localities and provinces, and across social and ethnic groups; as a result, broader leadership cadres emerged. New legitimacies produced new loyalties and identities, many as disparate as the localities that gave rise to them. They had a lasting impact on popular consciousness, and conversely, on the minds of the owners of property and capital, which would resound through Mexican history in the nineteenth century.[16]

The initial focus of rebellion was directed against the *gachupines*: it became immediately clear that the rebellion intended to exclude them totally from the life of New Spain. This term of abuse applied indiscriminately to all persons of Spanish-peninsular birth, regardless of their duration in New Spain, their intermarriages and American-born families, or the American foundation of their material interests. When Hidalgo raised the cry, "Death to the *Bad Government*!" as one of his four declarations in the *Grito de Dolores* during the night of September 15–16, 1810, it rapidly became clear that this, intentionally or not, became an invitation to assault all *gachupines*.[17] In no other Spanish American territory was the hostility so explicit, until Bolívar's proclamation of "War to the Death" on Europeans and their collaborators in Venezuela in 1813. Viceroy Francisco Venegas (1810–13), wrote to the Cádiz government that the prime explanation for the violence in New Spain was hatred of the *gachupines*.[18] Rebel propaganda sought to encourage creoles to align with the uprising, despite the

---

[16] Brian R. Hamnett, *Roots of Insurgency. Mexican Regions, 1750–1824* (Cambridge 1986, and the second updated Spanish edition, Mexico City 2010), 136–75. Ortiz Escamilla, *Guerra y Gobierno*, 178.

[17] Hamill, The *Hidalgo Revolt*, 118–26. Marco Antonio Landavazo, "Para una historia social de la violencia insurgente: el odio al 'Gachupín,'" *Historia Mexicana*, 233, vol. LIX, no. 1 (July-September 2009), 195–255: see pp. 195–202.

[18] Venegas to the Minister of Grace and Justice (confidential), Mexico City 22 January 1812, in Ferrer Muñoz, "Guerra civil en Nueva España," *AEA*, 391–434: p. 396.

horror among the propertied classes at the pillage and killings. As Hugh Hamill observed, "Those who responded to Hidalgo's call to arms during the first weeks of the campaign were chiefly Indians and castes." A force of 25,000 had appeared before Guanajuato, and by the time of Valladolid's surrender on October 16, this had increased to some 60,000 men, women, and children. Most were armed with farm implements or whatever weapon they themselves could find or make.[19] The questions still remain: where had they all come from, who were they, and why were they there?

The scale of hatred against the Spanish in New Spain was far greater than in New Granada or Peru. The explanation lies in the greater amount of money to be made during the eighteenth century in the expanding mining economy of New Spain. In response to this, commercial and financial networks spread outward from the capital city through the provinces and localities, as not only smaller merchants but also district administrators sought to take advantage of these connections. Santa Fe de Bogotá, by comparison, had nothing like the degree of central dominance in the political and economic sense enjoyed by Mexico City, where power was concentrated.[20]

The Mexican insurrection of September 1810 took the viceregal administration, army commanders and European inhabitants by surprise. It began with the pillage of Celaya and the slaughter of the defenders of the Guanajuato Granary on September 28 and the two-day sack of the city, one of the wealthiest in New Spain and center of silver-mining. At least 400 Europeans were put to death during the Hidalgo phase of the insurrection, although the number differs upward. While in Guadalajara, Hidalgo issued a proclamation warning Europeans and sympathetic Americans of an impending death penalty should they oppose the insurrection with arms or speak openly against it. Informers would receive a reward of 500 pesos.[21]

---

[19] Hamill, *The Hidalgo Revolt*, 127–31, 135. The term "Indians" may well refer less to the tribute-paying, community-based Indians of colonial terminology than to a general branding of lower-class rural folk as "Indians," which has passed into the historiography. "Indians" was a term applying to a broad range of social groups, with distinct ethnic and linguistic origins. I recall many conversations with the late Paul Vanderwood, concerning the difficulty of applying acceptable definitions to Mexican population components in the eighteenth and nineteenth centuries.

[20] This comparison originates from a conversation with the Colombian historian, Daniel Gutiérrez Ardila, at the Canterbury Colloquium on the Independence Movements held on March 15–16, 2013.

[21] Hamill, *Hidalgo Revolt*, 193–94. Moisés Guzmán Pérez, *Miguel Hidalgo y el gobierno insurgente en Valladolid* (Morelia 2011), 23, 138, 141, 154–55, 159, 165, 169–71, 191. Landavazo, "Para una historia de la violencia," 206–8.

Initial clerical leadership by parish priests gave the insurrection a degree of legitimacy in the view of potential participants, which challenged that claimed by the viceregal authorities.[22] The movement's religious character differentiated it from those elsewhere in Spanish America. This outstanding feature still needs explanation. Why, in the name of religion, did so many country-people and small-townsmen take the decision to leave their homes, often with their immediate family, and follow the priest, Hidalgo, into armed rebellion? This issue becomes particularly serious, since the Mexican bishops unanimously condemned the uprising. Was a rebellion also taking place within the Church as the body of Christian believers, as well as in the secular dimension – if, that is, the two could be separated in the New Spain of 1810? Both sides unleashed violence in defense of the same religion.

The principal leaders of the Mexican insurrection – Hidalgo, Allende, Aldama, Abasolo, Morelos, the brothers Rayón, Cos, Matamoros, the Galeana family from the Pacific coastal zone of present-day Guerrero, the Bravo family from the Pacific coastal hinterland, and Guerrero from Tixtla on their borderlands with Puebla – were lower secular clerics, junior militia officers, and provincial landowners or lessees. Ignacio López Rayón, in the hope of drawing together the strands of insurgency, established what he described as the *Suprema Junta Nacional* in Zitácuaro, in north-eastern Michoacán, on August 21, 1811. This, however, lasted only four and a half months, until brought down by Calleja's military intervention on January 2, 1812. López Rayón's attempt to claim leadership of the revolution thereby disintegrated.[23]

Royalist Spanish America had to save itself in the years 1811–13 before any substantial peninsular forces could be dispatched. The strength and duration of Royalist sentiment still requires fuller investigation.[24]

---

[22] Christon I. Archer, "Bite of the Hydra: The Rebellion of the Cura Miguel Hidalgo, 1810–1811," in Jaime E. Rodríguez O. (ed.), *Patterns of Contention in Mexican History* (Wilmington, DE 1992), 69–93: see pp. 78–80.

[23] Ernesto de la Torre Villar, La *Constitución de Apatzingán y los creadores del estado mexicano* (Mexico City 1964), 37–41.

[24] Edmundo A. Heredia, *Los vencidos. Estudio sobre los realistas en la guerra de independencia* (Córdoba [Argentina] 1997) points to (p. 149) the growing disillusionment among loyalists at the short-sightedness of metropolitan-government policies, although not necessarily resulting in defection to the revolutionary camp. Rebecca A. Earle, *Spain and the Independence of Colombia, 1810–1825* (Exeter 2000), 15, comments "the origins of Spanish American royalism need exploration as much as the origins of republicanism." See also Steiner Saether, "Independence and the Redefinition of Indians around Santa Marta, Colombia, 1750–1850," *JLAS*, 37 (2005), pp. 55–80, for Royalist allegiance among the Indians of the Caribbean coast. Marcela Echeverri,

Royalist forces in New Spain eventually recovered the tactical initiative. Rebels found little support among the peasant communities of central New Spain, where conditions and perceptions remained significantly different from those in the core zone of the insurrection, as Van Young extensively examined.[25] Gueniffey's distinctions could apply to counter-revolutionary regimes as well as to revolutionary systems. Counter-revolutionary measures, or "White Terror," were severe right from the beginning: Brigadier José de la Cruz, Captain General of Guadalajara, imposed martial law and a range of drastic penalties in the villages for collaboration with insurgents.[26]

Royalist Armies, furthermore, faced the problem of the changing face of insurgencies throughout the decade of fighting. At first, with Calleja's Regulation of 1811, and then more systematically from 1813, commanders of the official forces began to work out what they hoped would be effective counterinsurgency strategies in coordination with the political authorities in Mexico City. As Viceroy from March 1813, Calleja transferred the focus of counterinsurgency operations to the provinces. His Civil and Military Regulation of March 5 concentrated the army in strategic localities and proposed the formation of self-defense forces in the cities, towns, and haciendas. These Regulations represented the core of Calleja's "organization policy," fortifying estates, ranchos, and villages, providing them with garrisons, and raising urban forces paid for by the local notables, and sending out "mobile bands" (*destacamentos volantes*) to chase off raiders or root them out. This overall strategy required effective government control of local sources of food and revenue.[27] The crucial years were 1815–16, when the full extent of the strain on the official armed forces became apparent. They could not deliver the long

---

Indian and Slave Royalism in the Age of Revolution: Reform, Revolution, and Royalism in the Northern Andes, 1780–1825 (Cambridge 2016), with its prime focus on the Popayán zone, will undoubtedly shed further light on this neglected subject.

[25] Hugh M. Hamill, *The Hidalgo Revolt. Prelude to Mexican Independence* (Gainesville 1966), 175–79, drew attention to this, concluding that "within six weeks of the Grito de Dolores, most of the Kingdom had decided against the Revolt." Tutino, *From Insurrection to Revolution*, 139–51. Van Young, *The Other Rebellion*, 433–42, 463–66, 496–516.

[26] See, for instance, Gwynne Lewis, "The White Terror of 1815 in the Department of the Gard," *Past and Present*, 58 (1973), 108–35. Guzmán Pérez, "Lecturas militares," 103.

[27] See Christon I. Archer, " 'La Buena Causa:' The Counterinsurgency Army of New Spain and the Ten Years' War," in Jaime Rodríguez (ed.), *The Independence of Mexico and the Creation of the New Nation* (Los Angeles 1989), 85–108, and "Politicization of the Army in New Spain during the War of Independence," in Jaime Rodríguez (ed.), *The Evolution of the Mexican Political System* (Wilmington, DE 1993), 17–43.

hoped-for "final blow." This became the bitter realization of Calleja's viceregency of 1813–16, despite innovative counterinsurgency techniques. Royalist authorities began to fear that the official armed forces might collapse under the strain, especially since large swathes of territory in New Spain still remained under the control of insurgents or local chieftains.[28]

THE IMPLOSION OF VENEZUELA

Very different circumstances and alignments applied in Venezuela to those in New Spain. The focus of popular anger there was the coastal, planter-oligarchy, representatives of which had seized power in Caracas in April 1810. In Venezuela, memories of the repression of the protests of 1749 remained strong, especially since it had fallen heaviest on the newer and lesser planters of the Tuy Valley zone south and east of Caracas. Paradoxically, resentment of the planter élite (*mantuanos*), concentrated in the Caracas municipality, pushed the hard-pressed, smaller growers, many of them immigrants from the Canaries, into the Royalist camp.[29]

Conflicts between the *mantuanos* and rural workers of the coastal zone in 1810–12 and with *pardos llaneros* of the Orinoco interior, who rose in 1814, dominated the first five years of Venezuelan attempts at self-government. Into that relentless violence came the Republican Executive Power's decree of April 16, 1812, threatening all enemies of the Republic by word or deed with death. It was used against anyone resisting conscription under the decree of June 19. Subsequently, Patriots in Cartagena, on January 16, 1813, determined that all European Spaniards, whether guilty of resistance or not, should automatically be shot. Then came the decree issued by Bolívar declaring "War to the Death" in 1813 on Spaniards. These measures sought to intensify and extend the violence across the province, not to diminish it. The intention was to compromise fatally all those opposed to the revolutionary movement that he led. He had been a separatist and republican since at least 1805 and that was what he meant by "revolution." Bolívar, although significant from the

---

[28] Archer, "Years of Decision," 125–49.
[29] See McFarlane, *War and Independence*, 85–143, for Venezuela and New Granada. Manuel Lucena Salmoral, "El colapso económico de la Primera República Venezolana," in Antonio Annino, Marcello Carmagnani et al. (eds.), *América Latina: Dallo stato coloniale allo stato nazionale*, 2 vols. (Milan 1978), vol. 1, 163–86. Inés Quintero, "Representación y Ciudadanía: Venezuela, 1808–1814," in Ortiz and Frasquet (eds.), *Jaque a la Corona*, 103–22. Ferry, *Colonial Elite*, 174–76.

beginning and demonstrating military skill in 1813–14, only became the principal figure in the Independence movement in northern South America after 1817 and saw his authority decline after 1824.[30]

The decree on "War to the Death" was signed by Bolívar, as Commander-in-chief of the so-called Army of the North, at his Trujillo base on June 15, 1813. As such it formed part of his campaign from New Granada, where there was already a Patriot Congress, to liberate Venezuela from the Royalists. As in New Spain, the focus was on the peninsular Spaniards, who were to be shot as traitors and their properties confiscated if they did not collaborate in the liberation campaign. In Mérida, on June 21, he reaffirmed this policy of implacable hatred toward the Spanish, who had no place in Venezuela. In accordance with this decree, Bolívar, on February 14–16, 1814, had 800 Royalist Spanish and Canariot prisoners executed in La Guaira, despite appeals for clemency from the Archbishop of Caracas. The Patriots sought to justify this treatment by pointing to Royalist atrocities during the rebellion of Monteverde against the First Venezuelan Republic. The Trujillo decree exposed the undeveloped sense of national identity in the province and pointed to the long, hard road to Independence. It sought to give Americans a consciousness of their distinction from Europeans (and Canariots). That objective ran counter to the idea propagated by the Cádiz constitutionalists that Spain and the Empire constituted "One Nation." Bolívar intended to blow this concept apart. Instead, America was to be a separate Republic without the Spanish connection and colonialists. All Americans were to recognize this as their only loyalty on pain of punishment. As much as anything, the virtual legitimizing of property seizures was designed to boost the material resources of the Patriot cause. With regard to the decree, "the greatest outrage was ... its application to non-combattants." It went out of control in 1817 when twenty Capuchin priests, caught in the middle of the fighting, were done to death in Guayana province, accused of helping the Royalists, and no one in the Patriot camp was punished for the outrage.[31]

---

[30] John V. Lombardi, *Venezuela. The Search for Order. The Dream of Progress* (New York and Oxford 1982), 138–39. Thibaud, *Repúblicas en armas*, 91–105. John Lynch, *Simón Bolívar. A Life* (New Haven and London 2006), 26–27. Ferry, *Colonial Elite*, 205–13: the Bolívar family had remained apart from the 1749 protests.

[31] *Decretos del Libertador, 1813–1825*, 3 tomes (Los Teques 1983), Tome 1, 5–9. Lombardi, *Venezuela*, 139–40. Thibaud, *Repúblicas en armas*, 130–34. Lynch, *Simón Bolívar*, 79–80, 282.

The policy of "War to the Death" generated a violent Royalist response, which combined with other factors to shape the Boves Insurrection of 1814. This destroyed the Second Venezuelan Republic. Clément Thibaud puts forward a strong case for the non-white population aspiring to juridical and political equality with whites, rather than for their wholesale elimination in some form of revolutionary race war. Insurrection was the principal means available to force the leading authorities of the two Republican governments to do this. The Orinoco plainsmen (*llaneros*), furthermore, strongly reacted against coastal proprietors' attempts to extend control over land and livestock and curb their freedom of movement. A series of Ordinances to this effect, starting in 1773, were repeated in those of 1811 issued by the First Venezuelan Republic. Popular resistance demonstrated that they would be as unenforceable as the colonial laws. The cattle barons were among the principal figures of Caracas, a clear indication that the *llanos* were not isolated but formed part of a network of interests linked to the coastal oligarchy. A large number of small farmers, not dependent on haciendas, and livestock-owners, many of them without land titles, made their livelihood on these plains. Forced recruitment into Republican armies further incensed the rural population of the interior. Desertions were frequent.[32]

The insurrection of the *llanos* in 1813 and 1814 greatly extended and deepened the savage violence across the country. The *llaneros* came from many races and mixtures of races; their principal characteristic was not their class or their race but their style of life, which adapted easily to mobile warfare. Their principal leader, Tomás Boves, was a white Asturian who had been a pilot on the voyages from Spain to the Indies. He was in the *llanos* in exile, after involvement in the contraband trade with the Dutch island of Curaçao, off the Venezuelan coast. José Yáñez came from San Fernando de Apure at the center of the *llanos*. These leaders raised bands that were personally loyal to them: virtual private armies but rooted in their localities. Both sides lacked the financial resources necessary to sustain armed forces for long periods. As a result they lived off the land, which had terrible and lasting consequences for the country's productive wealth. The habit of pillage by both armies, furthermore, led to the proliferation of banditry, which continued after

---

[32] Juan Uslar Pietri, *Historia de la rebelión popular de 1814* (Paris 1954). Germán Carrera Damas, *Boves. Aspectos socioeconómicos de la Guerra de Independencia* (Caracas, third edition, Caracas 1972 [1968]), 158. Thibaud, *Repúblicas en armas*, 149–214: see pp. 160, 163–171, 194–96, 198.

Independence in 1821. Boves and the other leaders exploited religious sentiment, hostility to Caracas, and hatred of the Republican armies' white officers, but these were wars within wars rather than invitations to slaughter. The Republicans exploited fears of race war and slave insurrection stirred up by Royalists.[33]

A large section of the *llanero* population consisted of those who would be described as "castas" in the Cádiz Cortes. During the debates on the constitution and the representative system in process of construction, these "castes" of African descent were to be excluded from exercise of any of the new rights of citizenship. This treatment ran counter to the aspirations of the non-white population to juridical equality with whites. The defeat of Bolívar's army by Boves' forces at La Puerta on June 14 opened the way to Caracas and brought down the Second Venezuelan Republic. Boves and his second-in-command, Morales, finished off the Republican army in eastern Venezuela on December 5.[34]

The Cortes' exclusion of the African-derived "castes" in 1811–12 from the exercise of political rights became public at a time of heightened tension in Venezuela, where the First Republic was brought down in a Royalist-led rebellion of varied ethnic groups. In 1813–14, the Second Republic would succumb before the Royalist uprising originated across the Orinoco Plains. These risings in Venezuela were Royalist in the sense that they opposed the monopoly of power by the creole élite; they were not Royalist in the sense that they defended either Spanish-colonial institutions or the policies of the Cádiz Cortes. Alignments responded to purely Venezuelan circumstances and did not reflect a wider conflict between metropolitan Spain and its American dependency. For this reason, we can understand the facility with which the *pardos llaneros* "changed sides," once Bolívar after 1816 brought the principle of racial equality into the Patriot cause.[35]

Bolívar's forces were by no means united or homogenous. Given the variegated ethnic composition of Royalist forces as well, this further modifies the traditional portrayal of a race war and a war between coast and interior. Within the Republican camp there were also commanders from non-white groups. The emergence of Manuel Piar, later to be regarded by Bolívar as a rival, was a leading example. Piar, a negro or

---

[33] Carrera Damas, *Aspectos socioeconómicos*, 140–66. Thibaud, *Repúblicas en armas*, 183, 186, 197, 201.
[34] Thibaud, *Repúblicas en armas*, 199, 202–4, 212.
[35] Thibaud, *Repúblicas en armas*, 194–200.

mulatto from Curaçao, had taken part in the Haitian Revolution against the white planter class. Operating initially under the direction of Santiago Mariño, commander of virtually autonomous forces in the Eastern provinces and another rival of Bolívar, Piar became the dominant figure in Guayana by the mid-1810s. None of these leaders, Republican or Royalists, could ever have risen to positions of command and influence without the particular conditions of warfare. If they survived the conflict and the political in-fighting, the possibility existed that they would continue to exercise influence in the country, once the outcome of the struggle had become clear. Their presence ensured that the earlier idea of an oligarchs' republic would be finished forever.[36]

In Venezuela, political projects remained unrealized and racial complexities unresolved, when Morillo, commander of the Spanish Expeditionary Force, landed on the island of Margarita, off the Venezuelan coast, on April 9, 1815. The metropolitan government had dispatched this force with the intention of reducing Venezuela and New Granada to obedience. Morillo, like Calleja in New Spain, and Ramírez in Peru, was a product of the Castilian military tradition. He originated from the province of Zamora, and had served in the peninsula against French forces, rising to the rank of Field Marshall. Wounded at Vitoria in 1813, Morillo formed part of the military that rallied to the king in May 1814 and helped sustain the restoration of absolutism, when Ferdinand VII abolished the Constitution of 1812 and nullified the work of the Cortes throughout the Monarchy. The success of the Expeditionary Force would mean similar nullification of all the other constitutions brought into existence since 1810. As in the peninsula, those suspected of complicity in the "conspiracy to strip the king of his sovereignty" would be punished.[37]

Morillo entered Caracas on May 11, and established courts martial to try the accused, a process that lasted until August 1817. He imposed a forced loan on the city and confiscated the properties of identified separatists. Such actions escalated tensions and further polarized opinion among the leading American families, already threatened by the upsurge

---

[36] Thibaud, *Repúblicas en armas*, 136, 176, 202–3. Thibaud makes an interesting comparison between the *llaneros* and the Cossacks.

[37] For his defense against allegations of harsh conduct, see Pablo Morillo, *Mémoires du Général Morillo, Comte de Carthagène, Marquis de la Puerta, Rélatifs aux principaux évenements de ses campagnes en Amérique de 1815 à 1821* (Paris 1826). After Independence, Morillo returned to Spain to become Ferdinand VII's Captain General of New Castile and Madrid. He died in exile in France in 1837.

of violence against them in 1812 and 1813–14. The long-term result was to undermine the legitimacy claimed by the Royal government and keep alive separatist sentiment. In many respects, Morillo's actions, combined with the memory of the Boves insurrection, made Independence rather than Union a more acceptable prospect.[38]

RIVAL INSURRECTIONS IN NEW GRANADA AND THEIR OPPOSITION

The intensity of conflict along the coastal zone of New Granada and up the Magdalena River led to division within Patriot ranks between moderate reformers, radical revolutionaries, white élites, mulatto or free-black artisans, and militiamen, and between all of them and the Royalists, still in control in Panama, Santa Marta, and Maracaibo. Each side oscillated between attempts to recruit popular support and fear of popular participation. For the white minorities, the greatest fear of all was that non-white groups would act of their own accord, pursuing their own grievances, becoming, as it were, "out of control." Marixa Lasso argues persuasively that legal and political equality for the non-white population became the key issue, and that democratic forms of government were for the first time associated with racial equality.[39]

As we have seen, Cartagena separated from Santa Fe in order to promote its own economic interests by managing foreign relations and thereby to feed its population. The *cabildo* and *consulado*, the main protagonists of this decision, were able to count on majority support from the mulatto and other racially mixed groups. This support, however, was not passive. The Cartagena cabildo authorized the formation of a multi-racial militia force, the Patriot Voluntary Battalion, to protect the new regime. This latter consisted of members of the already predominant élite minus the peninsular political authorities. Pedro Romero, the mulatto leader, became a colonel in the Getsemaní Lancers, drawn from this mainly black and mulatto *barrio*. Cartagena's independent action meant the outbreak of armed conflict with the Royalist-held city of

---

[38] Morillo, *Mémoires*, 32–47.
[39] See Marixa Lasso, "Los grupos afro-descendientes y la independencia: ¿un nuevo paradigma historiográfico?" in Clément Thibaud, Gabriel Entin, Alejandro Gómez, and Federica Morelli (comps.), *L'Atlantique révolutionnaire: une perspective ibéro-américanine* (Paris 2013), 359–78.

Santa Marta, and also with Mompox at the Magdalena riverhead, which proclaimed its separation from Cartagena in August.[40]

The Cartagena Junta in December 1810 provided for the political equality of all racial groups, providing they were in work, male heads of families, or house-dwellers. This would include large numbers of artisans. The alliance of 1810 in the city broke down early in February 1811, when a group of dissident Spanish merchants and military commanders attempted a *coup d'état* in the port-city with the object of overthrowing the Junta and deporting its members to Spain. The spontaneous action of the mulatto *barrios* led to the seizure of Spanish merchants thought to be involved during the period from 4 to 10 February. Such actions filled the Junta leaders, hoping to keep to a moderate line, with terror, and they allowed any Spaniards who had not been seized to escape to Royalist Santa Marta. Popular reaction to the attempted coup forced a radicalization of the Cartagena revolution. On February 11, 1811, mulattoes and blacks from Getsemaní obliged the Junta to declare absolute independence from Spain. Although leaders from the élite were left in place, power slipped from their grasp. Mulatto leaders, such as Romero and Pedro Medrano, with their armed support, became major figures in the period from 1811 to 1815, especially so after the death of Pombo in 1812. Secession from the Hispanic Monarchy transformed Cartagena into an independent Republic. The Constitution of the State of Cartagena, on June 15, 1812, published three months before the Spanish Constitution of Cádiz, established equal rights for all free men, rejecting thereby the Cortes' refusal in the debates of August and September 1811 to grant political rights to "castes." The Cartagena Constitution prohibited the slave trade but it did not abolish slavery outright, preferring, instead, a process of gradual manumission. During the period from June 1812 until August 1814, the Presidency of the new Republic fell to the young radical lawyer Manuel Rodríguez Torices, another *ilustrado* son of a Spanish merchant of considerable wealth, and co-editor of the newspaper *El Argos Americano*, which closely followed political events in Cádiz.[41]

Armed conflict tore apart the Caribbean coastal zone and its Magdalena hinterland from 1811 to 1816. The collapse of the First Venezuelan Republic strengthened the Royalist position, enabling

[40] Múnera, *El fracaso de la nación*, 164–66, 176–80.
[41] Múnera, *El fracaso de la nación*, 182–87, 192–94, 197–203, 207–8. Masso, "Los grupos afro-descendientes," 363, 375.

Viceroy Montalvo to transfer his temporary seat from Panama to Santa Marta by June 1813. Rival maritime blockades of Cartagena and Santa Marta accompanied campaigns across the hinterland to eliminate each other's positions. The collapse of the second Venezuelan Republic and the outbreak of civil war within the Cartagena Patriot regime drastically weakened the revolutionary cause. The revolution in Cartagena degenerated from September 1814 into an ongoing power struggle between radicals and moderates, which resulted in the definitive defeat of what Alfonso Múnera has described as the "popular party of the mulattoes and blacks" early in 1815. This was a particularly dangerous time for the port-city, given the advance of local Royalist forces from Santa Marta, the continued hostility of Santa Fe, and the restoration of absolutism in Spain by a Ferdinand VII determined to re-establish full peninsular control over the Indies. This situation was made worse by the intervention of Bolívar, leading an army against Cartagena in support of the Confederation of New Granada. Bolívar's army besieged Cartagena from March 26 to May 9, 1815, with deleterious results. The Royalists swept along the coast and hinterland, seizing Barranquilla and then Mompox on April 29, 1815, to control thereby the main access to the interior, which was by river. At the news of the arrival in Venezuela of Morillo's Expeditionary Army from Spain, Bolívar took refuge in Haiti.[42]

Morillo landed in Santa Marta on July 6 with 6000 men. The process of destroying the New Granada revolutionary movements now began in earnest. When he arrived in Santa Marta on July 23, Morillo re-established the Inquisition, abolished in November 1812 during the revolution, in accordance with Ferdinand VII's decree of March 31, 1815 stating that the Holy Office should be re-established wherever it had existed before 1808. This was a political measure, designed to facilitate investigation of conduct during the revolutionary years and prevent further dissent. Morillo took his lodgings in the Inquisition building. The Inquisitor became the interim governor of the vacant diocese of Cartagena. On September 5 and October 31, he appealed to the local clergy to remain loyal to the Spanish monarch and encourage their parishioners to do likewise. After a 116-day siege, Morillo took Cartagena on December 6, as scenes of horror at the sight of the starved and diseased city presented themselves. Six to seven thousand people died during the siege. A further 2000 sailed out of the city the day before the surrender on the ships of the corsairs operating in the Caribbean. Many of them

---

[42] Múnera, *El fracaso de la nación*, 208–11.

perished before they reached Haiti or Jamaica. Romero did reach Haiti but died there in obscurity. Morillo had the nine leaders in the Junta executed and their property confiscated, which left their families destitute. A further thirty-five persons from the non-élite sectors of the revolutionary movement were also executed.[43]

Morillo's Manifesto to the inhabitants of New Granada, on January 22, 1816, warned them that the king of Spain would tolerate no dissidence among the clergy, since the stability of the Throne rested upon the foundation of religion. He described the association of members of the clergy with the revolutionary movements as sacrilege. A further instruction from the Inquisitor, on June 18, 1816, reminded all subjects that they were required to denounce suspected heresy and sacrilege to the Holy Office. Measures were taken to seize all incriminating books and punish their readers. In the Inquisitor's view, the majority of Cartagena's inhabitants were scandalously irreligious: He appealed to them to observe the precepts of Christian morality and behavior.[44]

The two sieges of Cartagena by Bolívar and Morillo crippled the revolutionary movement in the city and its surrounding region and enabled the latter's advance into the interior. As creole separatists, including Bolívar, would learn, racial equality had to be bound into territorial patriotism if the cause of Independence were to succeed. There was early evidence of this realization in the Mexican rebels' abolition of Indian Tribute, racial hierarchies, and slavery in 1810–11. The experience of revolution in New Granada and Venezuela threw this issue into the foreground.

Further intense and prolonged conflict took place along the Cauca Valley. Sugar-plantations, connected to the gold-producing province of the Chocó, covered part of this area, the properties of a slave-owning élite mainly resident in Popayán, which together with the province of Pasto fell under the jurisdiction of the Audiencia of Quito.[45] The city of Popayán, whose leading citizens had difficulty deciding whether they were for the royal cause or for independence, changed hands several times during the struggles between the Royalists of Quito, the separatists of Santa Fe, and

---

[43] Morillo, *Mémoires*, 60–61. Múnera, *El fracaso de la nación*, 211–15.

[44] AGI Santa Fe 668 includes the king's approval of the executions on August 12, 1816. José Toribio Medina, *Historia del Tribunal del Santo Oficio de Cartagena* (Santiago, Chile 1899), 391–98, 407–15. The Inquisitor, Dr. Juan José Oderiz (b. 1772), was a *peninsular*, who departed for Spain in February 1819. Morillo, *Mémoires*, 68, 72.

[45] José Escorcía, "Haciendas y estructura agraria del valle del Cauca, 1810–1815," *Anuario Colombiano de Historia social y de la cultura*, X (1982), 119–38.

local Cauca-Valley insurgents (in 1811–12), with deleterious results for the local economy and the personal wealth of the élite.[46] Within the Cauca region, the city of Cali represented the principal rival to Popayán, and joined a chain of lesser cities to form the Confederation of the Cauca Valley in 1811. The risings in the Cauca Valley from that year onward resulted less from Santa Fe's example than from local conditions and, accordingly, involved both the creole élite and the various mulatto and negroid groups below them.[47]

Morillo entered Santa Fe on May 6, 1816. This marked the termination of the first republican period. The trial of suspects followed, leading to the execution of 125 persons, including one of the principal leaders, Camilo Torres, President of the United Provinces of New Granada from November 15, 1815. Both he and Vice-President Rodríguez Torices, former President of Cartagena, were caught in Popayán, after a failed attempt to flee the country, taken to Santa Fe and tried by court martial. They were shot in the back as traitors in the main square on October 4, 1816, and their heads then cut off and displayed for a time in cages in the city. Francisco José de Caldas, a leading figure in the New Granada Enlightenment and editor of two Santa Fe newspapers in the early revolutionary period, was shot on October 29. As in Caracas, the repression involved property confiscations and fines. The first President of Cundinamarca (from April 1 to September 19, 1811), Jorge Tadeo Lozano, who had left politics after his overthrow by Nariño, had been seized, kept in confinement for two months, and then put before a firing squad on July 6. The Quito Junta leader, Carlos Montúfar, was apprehended in Popayán and executed on September 3. Dissident clergy, principally Francisco Caicedo, Vice-President of the Congress of Cundinamarca in 1811, were deported to Spain.[48] Measures such as these, which struck at the social and intellectual élite, permanently undermined the legitimacy of Spanish rule in New Granada and revived the

---

[46] For the conflicts in the Cauca Valley, and the position of the Popayán élites, see Archivo Nacional de Historia del Ecuador, Presidencia de Quito, vols. 468 (1811), 483 and 484 (1813), 512–16 (1815–16), 531–32 (1816).

[47] See Hamnett, "Popular Insurrection," 303–13.

[48] José Manuel Restrepo, *Historia de la revolución de la república de Colombia en la América meridional*, 4 vols. (Besançon 1858), vol. 1, 422–48. Hernández de Alba Lesmes, *Recuerdos de la reconquista*, 4–10. Brian R. Hamnett, "The Counter-Revolution of Morillo and the Insurgent Clerics of New Granada, 1815–1820," *The Americas*, xxxii, no. 4 (April 1976), 597–617. Helg, "Limits of Equality," 9–10. Morillo, *Mémoires*, 79–83.

separatist cause as the only remaining recourse.[49] Morillo removed Viceroy Montalvo, unenthusiastic at the scale of repression, and replaced him in August 1817 with the hardline Colonel Juan Sámano, who had supervised the repression in the capital.[50]

ROYAL-GOVERNMENT LOSS OF POLITICAL CONTROL IN CUZCO, 1810–1815

Viceroy Abascal's response to the events first in Quito and Upper Peru in 1809, and later in Chile in 1813, involved the direct intervention of Peru into the affairs of other territories. This policy, in the case of Upper Peru, led to re-annexation to the Viceroyalty of Peru in July 1810, in response to the May Revolution in Buenos Aires, thereby reversing the Bourbon division of the two Perus in 1776. The Regency Council in Spain does not appear to have initiated these policies. In fact, Abascal had been left to his own devices during the French advance through Andalusia at the turn of 1809–10. The instrument of Abascal's policy of combating the Platine revolutionaries was the Army of Upper Peru, formed on July 13, 1810, under the command of Goyeneche and funded by the Consulado of Lima. Goyeneche's appointment meant his departure from the crucial political position of Cuzco, where he had been appointed governor in 1808.[51]

In Upper Peru, intercity rivalries combined with racial and ethnic conflicts to broaden the field of tension and the propensity for violence. The presence of the Platine Army under Juan José Castelli, the nominee of the Revolutionary Junta presided over by Cornelio Saavedra, further inflamed this state of affairs. That proved to be the case with the prosperous and strategically situated city of Cochabamba, where an uprising removed the Intendant and recognized the Revolutionary Junta of Buenos Aires on September 23, 1810. This action posed a great danger for Royalist forces, since it cut off those in Chuquisaca and Potosí from Goyeneche's Army on the Desaguadero and enabled the Platine victory at Suipacha on November 7 and La Paz' declaration for the revolutionary

---

[49] Earle, *Spain and the Independence of Colombia*, 75–90, compounded as it later would be by the failure of Spanish Liberals, in power from 1820 to 1823, to understand the impact of ten years of warfare in the country (p. 45.)

[50] Blanco-Fombona (ed.), *Ultimos virreyes de Nueva Granada*, 141–58. "Informe secreto rendido por el virrey don Juan Sámano," in Sergio Elías Ortiz (comp.), *Colección de documentos para la historia de Colombia (Época de la Independencia)*, third series (Bogotá 1966), 241–45.

[51] For the Goyeneche family, see Part I, Chapter 2.

cause on November 16. As a result, a creole faction in Potosí placed the Intendant, Francisco de Paula Sanz, under arrest. After Castelli occupied the city on November 25, he had Sanz and Vicente Nieto, President of Charcas, executed in the principal square on December 15. This disaster provided Castelli's Buenos Aires forces with a forward base of operation inside Upper Peru, from which to advance toward the Desaguadero and thence take the war into Peru proper. The two decisive political factors, however, would be the willingness of the urban élite to sustain the presence of Platine forces in their cities, and the attitude of the Indian majority of the population, which had its own interests and objectives to pursue.[52]

Goyeneche, in command from 1810 to 1813, proved to be an effective combatant not only in holding the Desaguadero line but also in advancing across Upper Peru with several victories to his credit, notably at Guaqui against the Platine army, on the southern shore of Lake Titicaca, on June 20, 1811. The Army of Upper Peru's principal source of recruitment was among the Indian communities of southern Peru. The support and participation of Pumacahua and Choquehuanca proved vital. A major war followed for control of Upper Peru, a territory with a long history of insurrection and internal divisions, which were given a new lease of life and transformed by the generalized conflict across Spanish South America.[53]

The political problem in Cuzco, in the rear of the fighting, was that with the departure of Goyeneche a series of interim governors lost control of the city. One of these was Pumacahua, President of the Audiencia from September 1812, who feared that the new Spanish Constitution would undermine his authority. The arrival of the Constitution of Cádiz in the city on December 10, 1812 divided the urban élite over the timing and practice of its implementation, with the Cabildo struggling to displace the Audiencia from the dominant political position it had held since its foundation in 1787. Most of the

---

[52] *CDIP*, XXII, no. 1 (1972), 207–9, Abascal to Secretary of War, Lima 22 October 1810; pp. 212–13, ibid to ibid, Lima 14 November 1810. McFarlane, *War and Independence*, 147–64. Lynch, *Intendant System*, 276–78, 294, 298.

[53] *CDIP*, XXII, no. 1, 202–5, Abascal to Secretary of War, Lima 23, July 1810; 206–7, ibid to ibid, Lima 8 September 1810; 215–16, ibid to ibid, 17 November 1810. Cristóbal Aljovín de Losada, *Caudillos y constituciones. Perú, 1821–1845* (Lima 2000), 195, note 52, the Cabildo of Cuzco's complaint that the Royal Army recruited 18,540 of the department's Indians between 1808 and 1820; complaints also came from Puno. Peralta, *La Independencia y la cultura política*, 114.

magistrates of the Audiencia of Cuzco, led by the *Regente*, Manuel Pardo, a native of Galicia who had been in Peru since 1794, opposed the prompt application of the Constitution, which they saw as compromising their position as the link between Abascal's government in Lima and the Army of Upper Peru.[54]

In the *cabildo*, the partisans of the Constitution were already accusing the Audiencia of deliberately withholding funds for the elected deputy of Cuzco to proceed to the peninsula and take his seat in the Extraordinary Cortes, which had opened in September 1810. Elections on February 7, 1813 resulted in the formation of a Constitutional City Council, which henceforth became a pole of opposition to the Audiencia. The constitutionalists intended to modify the composition and practice of government in Cuzco in accordance with the form of indirect representation established by the Cádiz Cortes. In reality, this meant the substitution of one group of lawyers – creole in origin – for the dispossessed group of peninsular lawyers.[55] Tensions deepened within the city during the year 1813, when Brigadier Martín Concha y Xara was interim Governor, replacing Pumacahua in April.[56]

The struggle between these two institutions and the various factions ranged within them created the conditions that enabled the seizure of power on August 3–4, 1814 by another group not bound to either of the other two. By that time, domination of the city by an interrelated oligarchy had become a political issue, which bypassed the earlier issue of Cabildo–Audiencia rivalry. The urban political struggles since 1810–11 destabilized not only oligarchic control but also the hold of the viceregal government over the city. When the new group seized power in August, the Cuzco oligarchy and the viceregal authorities lost political control for the first time.[57] In this sense, these events in the city indicated that

---

[54] Felipe A. Barreda, *Manuel Pardo Ribadeneira, regente de la Real Audiencia del Cuzco* (Lima 1954), 12–15, 21. The senior magistrate (*oidor decano*), Pedro Antonio Cernadas, another *gallego* with long residence in Peru, had family connections with the Concha y Xara family, which was among the élite. The Spanish constitutional experiment is the subject of the following chapter.

[55] Heraclio Bonilla, *Metáfora de la Independencia en el Perú* (Fondo Editorial del Pedagógico San Marcos, quinta edición, Lima 2010 [primera edición, 1972]), 158–60.

[56] Luis Miguel Glave, "Antecedentes y naturaleza de la revolución del Cuzco en 1814 y el primer proceso electoral," in Scarlett O'Phelan Godoy (compiladora), *La Independencia en el Perú. De los Borbones a Bolívar* (Lima 2001), 77–97.

[57] Victor Peralta, "Elecciones, constitucionalismo y revolución en el Cuzco, 1809–1815," in Carlos Malamud (ed.), *Partidos políticos y elecciones en América Latina y la península ibérica, 1830–1930*, 2 vols. (Madrid 1995), vol. 1, 83–112.

a political revolution had taken place, which had a significant social dimension.

This rival group was led by the Angulo brothers, who were creoles with business interests and professional status, including several clerics. They were not among the top families. They and their immediate associates, like Gabriel Béjar and the Spanish-born priest, Francisco Carrascón, prebendary of the cathedral in Cuzco from 1800, formed the Revolutionary Junta of Cuzco.[58] Glave describes this group as "part of a large body of small proprietors and agricultural traders of *mestizo* or creole origin." José Angulo, from Apurímac, was a hacienda-owner from Abancay who traded in Cuzco and had transferred a sugar-producing estate to his brother, Vicente, who rented a mill in Quispicanchis. Juan Angulo was parish priest of Lares with a Theology doctorate from the University of San Antonio Abad. Another brother, Mariano, who had some military experience, owned a small estate in Chinchero, which was within Pumacahua's *cacicazgo*. Vicente and Mariano were products of the Colegio de San Bernardo. José took the military leadership of the rebellion. The rebels arrested the magistrates of the Audiencia and the acting-Governor, Concha.[59]

Even so, support for this coup d'état within the city could not be guaranteed. The position of the Angulo *golopistas* in 1814 remained precarious. Once installed in power, the new group desperately needed allies to counter an impending reaction from the Lima authorities and the Army of Upper Peru. In such a way, the longstanding rural discontent became subsumed into what had been originally an urban revolution. José Angulo's appeal to alienated Indian noblemen, like Pumacahua, both of whose wives came from the Loaysa family, and Marcos Garcés Chillitupa, *cacique* of Oropesa, a descendant of the Inca Huayna Cápac and at that time Lieutenant-Colonel of Militias in Quispicanchis, and to the Indian communities beneath the caciques, resembled the first appeal of the Mexican conspirators in 1809 for popular support. As a result, it transformed an originally creole-led movement into a popular insurrection comparable to Hidalgo's in 1810–11.[60]

---

[58] Hamnett, *Revolución y contrarrevolución en México y el Perú* (second edition, 2011), pp. 182–93.

[59] Luis Miguel Glave, "Un héroe fragmentado. El cura Muñecas y la historiografía andina," *Andes*, no. 13 (2002), p. 5. Glave, "Antecedentes," 86, 95. San Bernardo had been founded in 1619 by the Jesuits (expelled in 1767).

[60] Luis Miguel Glave, "Una perspectiva histórico-cultural de la revolución del Cuzco de 1814," *Revista de la América. Historia y Presente*, no. 1 (Spring 2003), 11–38. Cornejo

The municipality, which on principle remained *fidelista*, did not participate in the Cuzco Rebellion of August 1814, still retaining belief in the 1812 Constitution as the panacea.[61] The Cuzco Governing Junta on September 17 denounced the viceroy as an "inhuman monster" and Spanish rule as "three centuries of misery and pillage." The city councilors criticized inobservance of the Constitution by the Lima administration and idealized the Inca era.[62] The rebellion in the city did not bring unity but deepened existing rifts and left the constitutionalists marginalized.

Although the Cuzco Rebellion of 1814–15 should be understood on one level within the general context of Andean rebellion already discussed, political conditions had drastically changed across mainland Spanish America by the middle of the 1810s. The two decisive external factors operative were the interregnum in Spain and the capture of power by revolutionaries in Buenos Aires in May 1810.

In 1814 the political situation inside the city of Cuzco was considerably different from that which had been the case in 1780 at the time of the outbreak of the Tupac Amaru Rebellion. By contrast to the latter, the rebellion of 1814 began *inside* the city. José Angulo and Carrascón provided the ideological direction of the movement, which sought to align with the Buenos Aires revolutionaries. This pan-revolutionary dimension had not existed in 1780–81. Furthermore, the position of the bishop, Pérez Armendáriz, remained ambiguous.[63]

The rebel leadership argued that the policies of the Cádiz Cortes continued those of the Bourbons, rejected unitarism, and called for the formation of an entirely new political unit outside the Hispanic Monarchy to be based in Cuzco but encompassing Lima, Buenos Aires, and Montevideo. This, Carrascón described as *"nuestro vasto Imperio Peruano,"* consciously appealing as Tupac Amaru and Juan Santos

---

Bouroncle, *Pumacahua*, 264–68. David Cahill, "Una vision andina: el levantamiento de Ocongate de 1815, *Histórica*, XII, no. 2 (December 1988), 133–59: see p. 144.

[61] AGI, Cuzco 8, Vidaurre a Fernando VII, Lima, 16 de abril de 1816. Garrett, *Shadows of Empire*, 249–50. Peralta, *La Independencia y la cultura política*, 149–50, 166–75.

[62] *CDIP*, tomo III, vol. 6, 216–20, Mensaje de la Ciudad del Cuzco al virrey de Lima, Cuzco 17 de septiembre de 1814.

[63] At the request of the Cuzco Junta, Bishop Armendáriz commissioned Carrascón and Dr. Juan Gualberto Mendieta, parish priest of Yaurisque, to negotiate with the military commanders of the government of Buenos Aires, on October 20, 1814, "treaties of peace and union." *CDIP*, tomo III, vol. 7, 347–49. Vicente Angulo, from Ayaviri on February 28, 1815, expressed to Ramírez his joy at the successes of Platine force, stressing general support among Americans for "the system of independence." *CDIP*, tomo III, vol. 6, *Diario de la Expedición de Ramírez*, 242.

Atahualpa had done, to an idealised and Christianised Inca past. A large part of the city clergy went along with this. In contrast to the 1780–81 movement, the Cuzco rebels no longer thought in terms of the colonial old regime but, by appealing to support from the Buenos Aires revolutionaries, envisaged a new departure. Rejecting Cádiz constitutionalism, Carrascón declared that America was capable of formulating its own constitutional system with a Cortes based in Cuzco. Belgrano, commander of the Platine forces in Upper Peru, told Angulo on October 30 that theirs was "our common cause."[64]

When Pumacahua joined the rebellion, he brought into it his large number of adherents, and a strong political base in Sicuani. Perhaps he saw a last chance of bidding for independent power in the highland zone under cover of the war in Upper Peru, with the prospect of salvaging the authority of the Indian nobility.[65] This altered the nature and course of the original urban rebellion, reviving the span of grievances that had fired previous Andean insurrections. The 1814 movement spread across the central Andes and into Upper Peru, taking control of crucial cities like Huacavelica and Huamanga, and then Puno and Arequipa in the south. The rebels held La Paz from late September into November, where they executed the creole loyalist, the Marqués de Vallehoyos, a former Intendant, sixteen other creoles and fifty-six Europeans, and sacked houses and warehouses in the city. The Intendant of Arequipa (since 1811), José Gabriel Moscoso, nephew of the former bishop of Cuzco, was taken to Cuzco and executed there on January 19, 1815.[66]

Indigenous participation extended to zones where the southern caciques like Pumacahua had no influence. It frequently went well beyond cacique-led uprisings and had its own agenda in the defense of community against outside pressures from state, Army recruitment, hacienda,

---

[64] *CDIP*, tomo III, vol. 6 *La revolución del Cuzco de 1814*, Recopilación y prólogo por Horacio Villanueva Urteaga (1971), 212, Angulo, *Manifesto to the Inhabitants of Cuzco*, Cuzco 16 August 1814; 216–20, Angulo (*Message from the City of Cuzco*) to Abascal, Cuzco 17 September 1814; Carrascón, *Sermon*, Cuzco 5 September 1814; III, 7 (1974), 547–56, Carrascón, *Proclamation*, Cuzco 16 August 1814; 360, Belgrano to Angulo, General Headquarters at Bartolo, 30 October 1814. Glave, "Una perspectiva histórico-cultural," 11–38. Jorge Cornejo Bouroncle, *Pumacahua. La revolución del Cuzco de 1814. Estudio documentado* (Cuzco 1956), 264–68, 295–98. D. P. Cahill, "New Viceroyalty, New Empire, New Nation. A Transnational Imaginary for Peruvian Independence," *HAHR*, 91, ii (May 2011), 203–35: p. 229, for vision of a mega-state to supersede colonial rule.
[65] Aljovín de Losada, *Caudillos y Constituciones*, 194–95.
[66] Glave, *Vida, símbolos y batallas*, 176, and "Una perspectiva histórico-cultural," 11–38. Aljovín de Losada, *Caudillos y Constituciones*, 194–95.

merchant, and mine-operator, and from the burdens of Tribute and forced *repartos*, price-fixing and trade-monopolies. Many *yanaconas* refused to work on the haciendas to which they were bound. In Andahuaylas and Huamanga, spontaneous uprisings by indigenous communities broke out in response to the spread of the rebellion. In the latter city, commercial houses and the home of the Intendant were sacked. In Huancavelica, the Intendant was seized but managed to escape to Lima. Most such local insurrections were directed against the symbols of private wealth and government authority. Even when local Royalists managed to regroup in Huanta around a local hacienda-owner and militia officer, awaiting relief from Lima, Royalist forces only managed to recover the cities and the lines of communication but made no headway in the countryside, where the rebellion continued to spread. Indigenous rebels on occasions formed guerrilla bands known as *montoneras*, which raided haciendas and mines, attacked strategic points, and singled out loyalist Indian *alcaldes* and any other defenders of colonial rule.[67]

At Umachiri (in the Lampa district), on March 10, 1815, Ramírez' army of veterans, with accompanying artillery pieces, smashed a rebel force of some 30,000, mainly community Indians, only 800 of whom had rifles – and those were mostly deserters from the Army of Upper Peru. Ramírez shot one in every five of his captives and set the rest free. The Lima forces' commander, Lieut-Col. Vicente González, did the same in his repression of the rebellion in Huamanga and Huancavelica. Pumacahua was executed in Sicuani on March 17, and José and Vicente Angulo, Béjar, and Chillitupa in Cuzco's central square on March 29. As in the cases of the defeat of Tupac Amaru in 1781 and Hidalgo in 1811, rebellion did not end with this but persisted in a fragmented form, in southern Peru into the year 1816. The rebel priest, Ildefonso Muñecas, who originated from Tucumán, the son of a Basque merchant, led several *montonera* raids from his base in Larecaja, which he controlled as a *republiqueta* with some 3500 rebels. A large area of the Titicaca shore remained under rebel control for a long time; all rebel areas had their own local chieftains. Abascal put González in control of the Intendancy of Puno to carry out Ramírez' instructions for the repression of rebel villages

---

[67] Sala y Vila, *Y se armó el tole tole*, 227–45. The rebels in the vicinity of Cuzco did not envisage the abolition of Tribute, which they collected in Tinta, Paucartambo, Calca, and Quispicanchis in order to pay for their army. This was not the case, however, in Andahuaylas or Aymaraes (pp. 238–39). Aljovín, *Caudillos y Constituciones*, 206, points out that Pumacahua supported his forces by raising tribute in 1814.

from mid-April. In Azángaro in June, rebel leaders and one in every five participants were executed.[68]

Another rebellion broke out in Ocongate (Quispicanchis), led by Jaime Layme, an Indian farmer, from February 1815 with possibly some 3000 men from local *ayllus*, acting at first in concert with José Angulo in Cuzco. Even so, the Ocongate uprising, east of the city, was *sui generis* and not a subordinate to the urban movement. Angulo, in fact, ordered Layme's arrest but he was able to flee from the city to the Collao, where he encountered Muñecas, though without joining his band. Instead, he joined up with the rebels in Marcapata, who had risen against their parish priest for seizing control of the *cacicazgo*. He was able thereby to return to Ocongate, where a new struggle opened, with considerable indigenous support, against the creoles and mestizos who had appropriated Indian lands.[69]

This might be viewed as a parallel movement to those in the Titicaca districts and in Larecaja and Pacajes across the Upper Peruvian shore under Muñecas until his defeat by the then Royalist commander, Agustín Gamarra, in February 1816. In all these outbreaks, the white population were the victims of murder and pillage.[70] The viceregal government's attempts to collect Tribute, restored on March 1, 1815 by Ferdinand VII, met with sullen opposition, with rumors of further uprisings in Puno and Aymaraes in 1818.[71]

The southern-Peruvian rebellion threatened to inflict huge damage on the viceregal government in Lima because it interrupted communication with the Army of Upper Peru, still fighting to push back the Buenos Aires revolutionary army. The Cuzco rebels' contacts with Belgrano exposed the full extent of such a threat. This attempt to connect the two movements explained, in part, the severity of Ramírez' repression. It also demonstrated that the Cuzco Rebellion was not primarily a regionalist movement, especially since, within Peru, it extended as far as Huamanga and captured both La Paz and Arequipa. This is not to deny regional elements within it, the hostility to Lima, for instance, but they lay beneath a much deeper and broader cultural and social response to Spanish colonial rule and the abuses that accompanied it – or, even, shaped it in the Andean zones.

---

[68] Sala i Vila, *Y se armó*, 239–43. Glave, "Un héroe fragmentado," 11–13.

[69] Cahill, "Ocongate," 143, 149, 151–53.

[70] Glave, "Un héroe fragmentado," 5–11. Muñecas (b. 1776 or 1778) was murdered on May 16, 1816, while a prisoner of the Royalists.

[71] Sala i Vila, *Y se armó*, 250–57. Cahill, "Ocongate," 133–59.

Although little is still known about the social consequences of the Cuzco Rebellion, the deepening weakness of the colonial state in Lima and the continuing struggles within Upper Peru contributed to the loss of control of the indigenous workforce by the traditional powers in the localities. In the aftermath of Independence, relations would have to be conducted more by negotiation than by outright compulsion – at least, until a future re-establishment of state power in the Perus. Although nothing came of the eighteenth-century Andean visions of an alternative political society, finished off definitively at Umachiri in 1815, tension between Lima and the southern Andean provinces never ceased. It would form part of a generalized resentment from the provinces at the pretensions of the Lima élite as the sole organizer of the Peruvian Republic from 1826 onwards. The war waged by the Army of Upper Peru ensured by 1815 that the authorities in Buenos Aires permanently lost control there. The final defeat of the Royalist Army at Junín and Ayacucho in 1824 promptly ensured, whether Bolívar liked it or not, the formation of the separate state of Bolivia in 1825. All subsequent attempts at reunion in the 1830s and 1840s failed, in part due to the hostility of Chile and Buenos Aires. The Republics of Peru and Bolivia inherited the unresolved problems of their colonial predecessors and accumulated further problems, deriving, first, from the consequences of violent struggles during the 1810s and early 1820s, and, second, from their new international position as sovereign states.[72]

Military defeat and repression of massed bands of peasants, rural workers, and small-town folk, often with their women and children in tow, represented an entirely different type of warfare to the engagement of opposing, trained and equipped, armies. Insurgent defeats at Puente de Calderón and Umachiri differed in nature from the defeats inflicted by armies on other armies, as at Boyacá, Junín, or Ayacucho. Rifle-power and artillery frequently decimated badly led and ill-equipped rebel forces. The treatment of rebel leaders differed markedly from the social graces accorded to the defeated commanders of opposing armies. The former could expect the noose or the firing squad; the latter might enjoy conversation tinged with regret but refreshed by cups of tea, as was the case after Ayacucho.

During the wars, popular groups discovered their strengths but also their weaknesses. The experience of the wars revealed a capacity for mobilization, which did not necessarily have to be precipitated or

[72] See Thomson, *We Alone Will Rule*, 227, 267–68, 270.

controlled from outside the villages and localities in question. Social tensions within the cities reflected the scale of conflict beyond them and the disputed nature of the post-Independence political structures and alignments. Destabilization of village life and the destruction of men and resources in the fighting during the 1810s contributed to the bitter social conflicts of the following fifty years. The availability of lower- and middle-level leadership became apparent. The motives for participation varied greatly, at times determined by ongoing conflicts with landowners or merchants. Collapse of broader conflict did not necessarily mean the abandonment of localized struggles.

The Caribbean coast, a major yellow fever zone, could not have been a worse destination for Morillo's Expeditionary Army. It is difficult to ascertain why Ferdinand VII decided to send it there rather than the more salubrious River Plate zone. In all, Morillo's vast force, many of them Peninsular War veterans, arrived in a Venezuela where one-sixth of the population had already fallen victim to civil war since 1810. In the siege of Cartagena, disease rapidly ate away at these European newcomers to the tropics. When Morillo returned to Venezuela in the summer of 1816, the threat of fever prevented operations on the Orinoco plains, enabling Bolívar's local forces to regroup around Angostura, which henceforth became their operating base.[73]

---

[73] J. R. McNeill, *Mosquito Empires. Ecology and War in the Greater Caribbean, 1620–1914* (Cambridge 2010), 267–281.

6

The First Spanish Constitutional Experiment: The "One Sole Nation," and Its Opponents (1810–1814)

In this chapter, I view the Spanish constitutional experiment of 1810–1814 not as the solution to the problem of how to preserve the unity of the Hispanic Monarchy but as part of the problem. As historians, we need to find out what was wrong with the Cádiz Cortes' policies and why the Constitution of 1812 and accompanying legislation failed to result in a viable constitutional process. This is a major problem, which has not been given the attention it deserves in recent historical literature on the first Hispanic constitutionalism. It is major because it failed not once, in 1814, but twice, in 1823. This failure exposed metropolitan Spain and its surviving overseas territories to two periods of restored absolutism, 1814–20 and 1823–33, both of which began with allegation, calumny, denunciation, and persecution. That experience scarred Spanish political life well into the twentieth century.

The historical importance of the Cádiz Constitution for Spanish America has been recognized in the historiography at least since the beginning of the twentieth century.[1] We should still remember, however, that it was widely rejected across Spanish America. Constitutional alternatives were put forward in Venezuela, New Granada, Mexico, Chile, and the River Plate between 1811 and 1816. Several were republican and some federal. These alternatives clearly emphasized two points: first, that in Spanish American perspectives, there already existed constitutional

---

[1] See, for instance, James Q. Dealey, "The Spanish Sources of the Mexican Constitution of 1824," *The Quarterly of the Texas State Historical Association*, III, no. 3 (January 1900), pp. 161–69, and Nettie Lee Benson, *Mexico and the Spanish Cortes, 1810–1822: Eight Essays* (Austin and London 1966), pp. 7–9.

traditions in the Hispanic world on which to draw and that not everything depended on Cádiz; second, that many Spanish Americans believed that if the Hispanic Monarchy were to become constitutionalized, no reason existed why there should be one constitution for the entire Monarchy. That is to say that they rejected the idea, persisting among peninsular constitutionalists in the 1810s and early 1820s, that the Monarchy consisted of "One Sole Nation." The issue between 1810 and 1815 was whether there should be individual constitutions within these territories rather than a centrally imposed one.[2]

CRITICS OF THE LIBERAL PROJECT

All was not a stark contrast between well-intentioned reforming liberals and rabid reactionaries. The Natural Law tradition, the Law of Nations (*Ius Gentium*), the medieval inheritance of the Hispanic kingdoms, and the contractual theories of sixteenth-century Spanish thinkers, Vitoria, Soto, Mariana, and Suárez, suggested constitutional alternatives to the liberal constitutionalism introduced in the Cádiz Cortes. Their proponents were not absolutists; they had strong criticisms of the way the monarchy had developed under the Bourbons and Habsburgs. Critics of Liberalism, such as Francisco Javier Borrull, Felipe Aner, Jaime Creus, Lázaro del Dou, and Pedro Inguanzo, were also, as deputies in the Cortes, critics of eighteenth-century absolutism. They viewed with skepticism, however, the Liberal attempt to remove the corporate bodies inherited from the Middle Ages and the *ancien régime*, because they viewed this as endangering the safeguards protecting the subject from a powerful state.[3]

Critics of measures adopted by the Liberal group could also be found within the reforming camp. The most cogent among them was Blanco White. Born in Seville in 1775, the son of an Irish merchant, he had become, after ordination in 1800, professor at the *Sociedad Económica de los Amigos del País*, college rector and then, at the age of twenty-six, Principal Cleric in the city's Royal Chapel of San Fernando. He knew

---

[2] Calderón and Thibaud, *La magestad de los pueblos*, 91–124. Daniel Gutiérrez Ardila (compilador), *Las Asambleas constituyentes de la Independencia: Actas de Cundinamarca y Antioquia (1811–1812)* (Bogotá 2010), pp. 17–30, 169–86. Jean-Pierre Dedieu, Michel Bertrand, Lucretia Enríquez, Elizabeth Hernández, "Abriendo la conciencia del reino: Cádiz y las independencias americanas," *Boletín de la Academia Chilena de la Historia*, Año LXXVIII, no. 121 (2012), pp. 61–96.

[3] See Bernice Hamilton, *Political Thought in Sixteenth Century Spain* (Oxford 1963). Hamnett, *La política española*, 103–6.

French, Italian, and English, became a leading figure in intellectual life, associated with Alberto Lista, and grew increasingly critical of the Church, frequenting Quintana's literary and political *tertulia*. Blanco abhorred the religious fervor in the uprisings of 1808. He took the decision to leave Spain when the French Army occupied Andalusia early in 1810. Once the critical tone of "El Español," published from London, became known in Cádiz, the Regency Council banned it throughout the Monarchy on November 15, 1810.[4] Blanco, influenced by observation of British practice, believed that the Cortes was wasting its time formulating a Constitution based upon theory rather than experience, and that its foremost mistake had been in not reorganizing the judicial power right at the beginning. Instead, there had been too much discussion of balancing the respective powers.[5]

UNICAMERALISM OR BICAMERALISM? – A KEY ISSUE

Blanco's were not the only reservations among the reformers. The issue of unicameralism became a source of division within the Liberal camp, dividing it between "moderates" and "radicals" during the second constitutional period of 1820–23. When Liberals finally recovered power after 1834, Francisco Martínez de la Rosa (1787–1862), the leader of the "moderates," sponsored the *Estatuto Real*, which adopted a bicameral solution with the establishment of a Senate.[6]

Writing retrospectively, Martínez de la Rosa would express the opinion that with the 1812 Constitution "it was virtually impossible to govern a vast and historic Monarchy" such as Spain's.[7] This was not an uncommon view at the time and thereafter. It conditioned retrospective analysis of the failure of the second constitutional period of 1820–23 and laid the foundations for the long, almost uninterrupted, hold on power in Spain by the "moderates" between 1834 and 1868. It is worth looking at this issue in perspective.

---

[4] Diego Martínez Torrón, *Ideología y literatura en Alberto Lista* (Seville 1993). Fernando Durán López, *José María Blanco White o la conciencia errante* (Seville 2005), 48–67, 76, 80–83.

[5] José María Blanco White, "El Español," 8 vols. (London 1810–1814), no. XVI, 30 July 1811.

[6] See Joaquín Torres Villarroya, *El sistema político del Estatuto Real (1834–1836)* (Madrid 1968).

[7] Francisco Martínez de la Rosa, *Bosquejo histórico de la política de España*, in *Obras de . . .*, edited by Carlos Seco Serrano, 8 vols. (Madrid 1962), VIII, 336.

A leading figure in the debate on Spanish affairs both in Spain and in London was Lord Holland, the celebrated Whig reformer and nephew of Charles James Fox, the principal Whig figure of the 1800s. Holland House would become in the 1810s and 1820s the prime political meeting-place for the Whig opposition to Tory rule and a pole of attraction for Spanish Liberal and reformist exiles. It attracted British figures such as Scott, Byron, and Macaulay. Holland, who first visited Spain in 1793, aged 20, and his wife both knew Spain well, and were attracted by its history, literature, and contemporary political figures, many of whom they knew personally. He had first met Jovellanos and Agustín Argüelles in Asturias in 1793 and remained in touch thereafter.[8] The Hollands resided in Madrid from 1802 to 1805: They were received at Court by Charles IV and María Luisa; they knew the Condesa de Montijo and were familiar with the *ilustrados* and reformers among the nobility. They returned to Spain in October 1808, after the uprisings against the French Intervention and remained in the country until August 1809, mostly in Seville, which, as we have seen, became the seat of the *Junta Suprema Central* and capital of "Free Spain" between December 1808 and January 1810. This time they brought the politically astute Dr. John Allen and the youthful Lord John Russell, future Prime Minister, with them. While the Supreme Junta functioned from the Royal Alcázar, the Hollands took up residence in the Palace of the Dueñas, which for a time became a surrogate Holland House. They knew most of the political and literary figures in Seville at that time – Saavedra, Quintana, Lista, Capmany, Antonio Valdés, Blanco White, and Martín de Garay, for instance. Holland's views were closest to those of Jovellanos, the experienced senior figure. Chastened by cruel experience of the twists and turns of politics, Jovellanos remained determined to turn the younger generation away from what he believed to be impracticable and perilous radical projects.[9]

---

[8] Argüelles, from Asturias, had worked his way up through the civil service from entry in 1800, first with Moratín in the Foreign-Language Translation Office, and later with Manuel Sixto Espinosa at the Royal Bond-Amortization Treasury, though he was despatched to London 1806 and thereby avoided the fall of the regime in 1808. In Seville, he attached himself to the Quintana group.

[9] See Henry Richard Vassall, Lord Holland, *Further Memoirs of the Whig Party (1807–1821) with some Miscellaneous Reminiscences* (London 1905) and Elizabeth, Lady Holland, *The Spanish Journals of ...* (London 1910). Lloyd Charles Sanders, *The Holland House Circle* (London 1908). *Cartas de Jovellanos y Lord Vassall Holland sobre la Guerra de Independencia (1808–1811)*, 2 vols. (Madrid 1911). Manuel Moreno Alonso, *La forja del liberalismo en España. Los amigos españoles de Lord Holland, 1798–1808* (Madrid 1997).

Both Jovellanos and Holland strongly argued for the direct participation of the Nobility and Prelates in the reconstituted political processes following the collapse of absolutism. They favored a model not dissimilar to the British House of Lords, which combined the first and second estates of continental European *ancien régime* systems. Both opposed unicameralism. Holland's views were also close to those of Blanco White, who, in self-exile, would become part of the Holland House circle. Holland, in Seville, became alarmed at the delay in convoking the Cortes. This situation seemed to reach a climax during May 1809, when Holland pressed the matter to Jovellanos, while Quintana wrote to Holland, blaming Jovellanos for the delay. The Junta's decree of May 22, calling for a Cortes with an upper chamber, seemed to break the deadlock, except that the decree was then unaccountably lost. Holland, however, had a copy of it and, when back in London, handed it over to Blanco White, who published it in "El Español" on September 30, 1810. With the loss of the decree in Seville, the Liberal group around Quintana pressed their case for a one-chamber Cortes. Even so, Holland complained to Jovellanos, upon return to London, that still no Cortes had assembled. This made the Junta as a supposedly reforming body seem puny compared to Napoleonic Spain.[10]

Jovellanos continued to argue for an upper chamber of Grandees and Prelates to act as a moderating influence on the 300 or so representatives in a lower house. He was worried that without the two chambers, the democratic ideas held by members of the younger generation might prevail. Jovellanos, furthermore, disliked the idea of the Supreme Central Junta leaving the future structure of representation to the forthcoming Cortes once it had assembled. The Supreme Central Junta collapsed before any convocation of the Cortes had actually taken place.[11]

In despair, Jovellanos wrote to Holland from the Isla de León on February 2, 1810 that to his dismay "a party of pig-headed mischief-makers, giving no thought that they were working for their ruin" had excluded moderates such as Garay, the Marqués de Campo Sagrado, and Valdés from the constitutional commission. He described himself as cast into outer darkness, despite forty-three years of service to the country. The Regency, from which all members of the Junta had been excluded, appeared to fear the convocation of the Cortes. By the summer of 1810, he was writing to Holland telling him that he was aware of the rebellion in Caracas. Out of the picture altogether in the west Galician fishing village

[10] Moreno Alonso, *La forja del liberalismo*, 115, 129–31, 137–39, 220–21, 225, 244–45.
[11] Moreno Alonso, *La forja del liberalismo*, 173–77, 182–84, 221, 227–30.

of Muros, Jovellanos saw no need for a declaration on sovereignty and expressed his despair at the unicameral nature of the Cortes, which, as he saw it, could only result in instability, especially since the legislature had effectively subordinated the executive. There would be no second chamber. Instead, the "traditional constitution," in his view, had been destroyed in favor of the ideas of Locke and Rousseau.[12]

When the Constitution was published in Cádiz, Holland, who saw how much the Cortes had departed from the British model, strongly disliked it. In this he was joined by Blanco White and the young Martínez de la Rosa, then assisting him with "El Español." Holland found another ally in the Duque del Infantado (1773–1841), whom he had first met in 1804 and again in Seville in 1808–9, but of whom Jovellanos held a low opinion. For a time, Holland appeared to think that Infantado might be the man of the moment to save Patriot Spain from itself. The Duke, in April 1813, had declared himself to be an opponent of the group that he described as the "Liberal party, composed mainly of demagogues of both hemispheres." In late June, Holland confided to Infantado his disappointment with several of the Cortes' measures – the prohibition of deputies from holding public office, indirect elections, no re-election – and the urgency of keeping the "liberals" out. Again expressing the importance of an upper chamber, Holland appealed for the formation of a "moderate party" to uphold good reforms, such as the abolition of seigneurial jurisdiction and the Holy Office, but mold the Constitution to respond to current needs. The members of this "moderate party" would be the great landed proprietors and the men of experience. Unlike the City of London, neither the great commercial oligarchs nor a mercantile bourgeoisie seemed to be available in Spain at that time, or else he might have mentioned them as another potential stabilizing element in the political processes.[13]

THE "NATION" ACQUIRES THE ATTRIBUTE OF SOVEREIGNTY

What the Extraordinary Cortes actually intended to do, when it declared on September 24, 1810 that Sovereignty resided in the "Nation" is not easy to determine. In the first place, it did not say that it resided in the "People," since there had been no revolution attributing power to such an entity. Second, it was clear that the Cortes intended to preserve the Monarchy deriving from the early medieval kingdoms. Yet, it had not

---

[12] Moreno Alonso, *La forja del liberalismo*, 229–32, 234–38, 256–68.
[13] Moreno Alonso, *La forja del liberalismo*, 262–63, 268, 275, 278, 282–83.

been summoned by the king, and its form differed from the type of Cortes that had last met in 1789. In order to fend off the charge of illegitimacy, the Extraordinary Cortes proclaimed itself to be the only body within the Hispanic Monarchy that had the right to exercise sovereignty. Since the Spanish Patriots were fighting a war of survival against a Napoleonic Empire that owed its existence to the French Revolution, the Cortes had no intention of copying the institutions and practices of the enemy. The Decree of Sovereignty, the work of Muñoz Torrero, should be seen also in that context: as a declaration of the illegality of the Bayonne abdications and the accession of Joseph Bonaparte to the Spanish Throne. It was, then, in the context of the time first and foremost an anti-Bonapartist act. However, that act had perilous implications: It nullified the actions of Bourbon monarchs, responsible only to God, and subjected the morality of them to the judgement of the Cortes. The purpose of the Cortes was to preserve the rights of the dynasty, while its political objective was to reform the system of government.[14]

The term "Nation" had no necessarily revolutionary implications and explicitly rejected any notion of the European metropolis and the overseas territories as distinct nations of their own. The term "Nation" was something that everyone, except convinced separatists, could agree on. In that sense, it had some pedigree. Yet, nothing was simple. Bourbon ministers were no longer in power; the monarchy of Charles III had long passed; absolutism had fallen, and the present king was a prisoner in France. The Cortes' use of the term "Nation," then, would have serious implications for the immediate future – especially since, when the Cortes opened on September 24, 1810, much of Spanish America was already in crisis. The matter became one of how the Cortes intended to define the "Nation" and how institutions would reflect this new understanding. The core of the matter was the application of the principle of representation and the distribution of political power. On October 15, 1810, the Cortes reiterated the decrees of the Supreme Central Junta and the Regency Council that all territories of the Monarchy were of equal juridical status, "composing one sole Monarchy, one sole Nation, and one sole Family." The political center of this Monarchy and Nation would continue to be in the Spanish metropolis. The Cortes would thereupon proceed to

---

[14] Manuel Chust, "Las Cortes de Cádiz, la constitución de 1812 y el autonomismo americano, 1808–1837," *Bicentenario. Revista de Historia de Chile y América*, vol. 5, núm. 1 (2006), 63–84: p. 66.

determine the number of representatives to be elected from each of these territories.[15]

Much would depend on the categorization of those eligible or ineligible for the status of citizen with the right to vote and the right to be represented. The Cortes took the decision to exclude the "castes," as we discussed in the previous chapter, from the exercise of citizenship. Large numbers of people were thereby deprived of political rights. Whether this was a cynical maneuver on the part of peninsular deputies, designed to reduce significantly the representation accorded to the American sectors of the Monarchy, or whether it was a serious misreading of the political and social aspiration of mixed-race groups is difficult to ascertain. The Constitution of 1812 repeated this position, while making provision for a future possibility of access to citizenship through personal qualities and achievements for those who were legitimate and the sons of married parents.[16]

The idea of the Nation also excluded the regions, former kingdoms, and principalities. The Cortes rejected both a reversion to the pre-1715 status of the peninsular realms, with their distinct parliaments, and the devolution of power to the capitals of the American territories. The Liberal group's rejection of any resurrection of the regional *fueros* of the pre-Bourbon era should be seen in conjunction with their intention to demolish as much as they could of the corporate inheritance of the pre-1808 era. Opposition to the Liberals' proposals came at the time largely from jurists (lay or clerical) in the Cortes, and focused principally on the restoration of lost *fueros* in specific regions such as Catalonia or Valencia, rather than on a general broadening of the range of representation. There does not seem to have been any mass movement behind them.[17] The Cortes also inherited the Supreme Central Junta's objective of subordinating the provincial juntas to a central authority. Portillo puts forward the view that from the start, on September 24, 1810, the Cortes

---

[15] Breña, *El primer liberalismo*, 142–45. José Álvarez Junco, *Mater Dolorosa. La idea de España en el siglo XIX* (Madrid, tenth edition, Madrid 2007 [2001]), 82–83, points out that Jovellanos had rejected the idea of separate privileges for provinces and spoke of "unity" and "uniformity" of political institutions.

[16] *Constitución Política*, arts. 18 and 22. James F. King, "The Coloured Castes and American Representation in the Cortes of Cádiz," *HAHR*, XXXIII, i (February 1953), 33–64.

[17] *Diario de las discusiones y actas de las Cortes*, 23 vols. (Cádiz 1811–1813), VIII, 12–13 September 1811, 254–95: Borrull, Aner, and Dou were the principal exponents of such a view.

remained intent upon substituting a "revolution of the Nation" for what had been a "revolution of the provinces."[18]

Similarly, the Cortes rejected any form of devolution of power to the American territories. The Liberal leadership, with Toreno in the vanguard, utterly rejected any suggestion of federalism within the Monarchy, regarded as identical to fragmentation. On August 25, 1811, José Miguel Guridi y Alcocer, deputy for the Mexican province of Tlaxcala, argued for recognition of a plurality of nations. Antonio Oliveros, opposing this on September 2, stressed that the idea of a "Spanish Nation" was designed to include Americans within it. Quintana equally stressed this point, rejecting the idea that "Catalans," "Valencians," "Basques" should take precedence over "Spaniards." Muñoz Torrero argued for "one, indissoluble kingdom" and no subdivision into separate realms or nations. Liberal unitarists feared that a sovereignty divided might lead to its legitimate exercise by representative institutions within the American territories. Toreno made a point of stressing this on January 10, 1812: All representation was to be concentrated in the "*National* Congress" in the metropolitan capital. It does not appear that any of them envisaged a middle way between unitarism and disaggregation.[19] As Roberto Breña has argued, it was in Cádiz that the great opportunity to preserve the unity of the Monarchy was available but also lost.[20]

Unitarism proved to be another of the major criticisms in the first and second constitutional periods. Again, it was never resolved. In this sense, the Liberal administration and its supporters in the Cortes continued the unitarist policies of the Bourbon ministers by other means. This latter consisted of placing the Constitution as the focal point of unity within the Monarchy. The Liberal group, with Argüelles in the lead, argued that with the Constitution there were now no longer any just sources of grievance within the Monarchy, since arbitrary government had been permanently superseded.[21]

Liberal centralism or unitarism fell into place comfortably with anticorporatism. The nobility and the clergy would not be reconstituted in an upper chamber on the British model, and there would be no Cortes of the

---

[18] Portillo, *Crisis atlántica*, 101.
[19] Álvarez Junco, *Mater Dolorosa*, 82–88. Chust, "Las Cortes de Cádiz," 69–74, 76–77.
[20] Breña, *El primer liberalismo*, 119–20.
[21] *Actas de las sesiones secretas de las Cortes Generales Extraordinarias de la Nación española* (Madrid 1874), 15, 19.

three estates or *brazos*. Individual noblemen or clerics, however, would certainly be able to sit as deputies in the one-chamber Cortes, although the basis of election would henceforth be representation according to population not juridical status. The "Nation," then, would consist of citizens, equal before the law. Here were the three classic principals of Liberalism – sovereignty of the nation, equality before the law, representation according to population. In this respect, the momentary victory of noble factions in March 1808 in securing the overthrow of Godoy was snatched from them by the unicameral structuring of the Cortes in 1810 and the implementation of the principle of juridical equality.[22] Noblemen in Spain were not overthrown, driven into exile, or executed, as they had been in Revolutionary France, but continued to find places in administration and the representative body. Yet, the social reality beneath the new parliamentary system continued to be that wide swathes of peninsular territory still lay within the bounds of seigneurial jurisdiction – lay or ecclesiastical. The Cortes would attempt to deal with this issue in 1811 and 1813.[23]

THE RELIGIOUS DIMENSION

Although rarely omitted in historical discussion of the two constitutional periods, the religious dimension frequently takes second or third place in terms of focus. Positioning the Cortes, an elective body with a changing number of deputies, at the center of the political processes in the absence of the monarch threw to the forefront the issue of the status of the Catholic Church. Episcopalism, Jansenism, and Regalism, together with *ilustrado* attitudes on major issues, characterized the responses of the Cortes of 1810–13 to issues involving the position of the Catholic Church in the Monarchy. All such positions sought to reduce the powers of the Papacy and Roman Curia in the affairs of the Spanish Church. During the first constitutional period, episcopalism was shared across the political

---

[22] Álvarez Junco, *Mater Dolorosa*, 88–93, comments on the Spanish nobility's lack of coordination and leadership, differentiating it from the British nobility, which fully participated in the parliamentary system in both Houses, and from the service-nobility of the Russian and Prussian Monarchies. It could never provide any form of aristocratic constitutionalism to counterbalance the liberal form.

[23] *Diario de las sesiones*, VII, 448: On August 11, 1811, the Cortes voted to open positions in naval and military academies to all respectable citizens, thus removing nobiliar exclusivity.

spectrum: The Bishop of Calahorra, for instance, a leading opponent of the Liberals, was also an episcopalist.[24]

Reform of the Church had been in the air throughout the Bourbon eighteenth-century. Monarchs aimed to bring the Spanish Church more tightly under royal supervision. Charles III, who would never have allowed the Church to be weakened, supported reformers in these endeavors. Reforming clerics, however, concentrated more on renovation of the spiritual life and the forms of outward practice than on issues of royal power. The impact of events outside Spain, however, provided fuel for their enemies. The ideas of reforming clerics in Spain became associated with heterodoxy in the eyes of their increasingly virulent traditionalist opponents. This conflict within the clerical body and among Catholics deepened during the first constitutional period.[25]

It might be possible to argue that the Cortes sought to replace the idea of a Catholic Monarchy, subsisting from Habsburg times, with one of a "Catholic Nation." Article 12 of the Constitution, upholding the exclusive Catholic establishment, may be understood in that sense.[26] The Cortes as a whole was neither anticlerical nor committed to any program of secularization, despite the allegations of the opponents of reform. The objective seems to have been transformation of the Hispanic Monarchy into a form of Liberal-Catholic state.[27]

In 1810–14, the issue became: would it be possible to reform the Church in Spain through the medium of the elected constitutional assembly, the Cortes? Reform of political institutions heightened the question of reform within the Church in Spain, especially since clerics accounted for one-third of the members of the Extraordinary Cortes. The debate on the status of the Catholic Church in Spanish society began on September 2, 1811. Leading Liberals – Argüelles, Toreno, José María Calatrava, Manuel García Herreros – allied with clerical reformers – Villanueva, José Espiga, Diego Muñoz Torrero, Ruiz Padrón, Oliveros, Juan Nicasio Gallego, Francisco Serra – in these debates. The Cortes' aim was to

---

[24] Emilio La Parra López, *El primer liberalismo español y la Iglesia. Las Cortes de Cádiz* (Alicante 1985), 17–21.

[25] William J. Callahan, *Church, Politics, and Society in Spain, 1750–1874* (Cambridge, MA 1984). Sánchez-Blanco, *El Absolutismo y las Luces*, pp. 252–56.

[26] Carlos Garriga Acosta, "Cabeza moderna, cuerpo gótico: la Constitución y el orden jurídico," *Anuario de Historia de Derecho Español*, 81 (2011), 99–162: see p. 100.

[27] La Parra, *El primer liberalismo*, 49–58, 65, 106–7. Argüelles criticized article 12 in retrospect in his *Examen* of 1837, and Toreno, *Historia*, saw it as a "grave error"; Calatrava regarded Catholic establishment as the equivalent of persecution.

emancipate the Church in Spain from integration within the institutions of the *ancien régime*. Two problems complicated this – the question of seigneurial jurisdiction, a large proportion of which was exercised by ecclesiastical bodies, and the future of the Holy Office of the Inquisition.[28]

Defenders of the Inquisition argued that liberty of the press, established in October 1810, opened the way to antireligious pamphleteering. They did not believe that the Press-Boards set up by the Cortes in October 1810 would be effective or that episcopal censorship would be adequate. They did not like the idea of an elected body, which had attributed to itself the exercise of sovereignty, as the guardian of the faith. They were not convinced by the provision that "the Nation" would uphold the Catholic religion, without any specific protecting body being mentioned or "protection" defined. Pedro Inguanzo, for instance, never ceased to regard Liberalism as a secularizing ideology, and opposed both Muñoz Torrero and Villanueva on that issue. In Parra's view, the Liberals of 1810–13 did not declare with sufficient emphasis that they regarded Liberalism and Catholicism as perfectly compatible, and, when positions hardened in 1813–14, they became the object of a violent pro-clerical reaction that looked to the return of the king to remove the Liberals from power.[29]

The 1812 Constitution did not refer specifically to the Inquisition. According to Article 371,

All Spaniards had the freedom to write, print and publish their political ideas without need of license, review or approval before publication, in accordance with the restrictions and responsibility which the laws establish.[30]

What this meant when religion was broached remained unclear. Several leading traditionalists, such as Angel Lera and Simón López, campaigned on April 12, 1812 for preserving the Inquisition. On July 1, eight bishops exiled in Majorca followed them, warning of the spread of dangerous literature. The Bishop of Tuy, in southern Galicia, warned that only the Holy Office could suppress scurrilous newspapers. The decree abolishing the Holy Office on February 22, 1813 provided for the bishops' approval

---

[28] La Parra, *El primer liberalismo*, 22, 27–28, 31–32, 38–39, 50–51. Muñoz Torrero had been Rector of the University of Salamanca in 1787–89: Serra came from the University of Valencia; Oliveros was a canon of the Colegiata de San Isidro, stronghold of Jansenism in the Godoy era.

[29] La Parra, *El primer liberalismo*, 38–39, 41–46, 65.

[30] *Constitución política de la Monarquía Española* [Cádiz 1812] (Barcelona edition of 1836), art. 371.

of any material dealing with religion. In other words, episcopal censorship still existed, along with the censorship committees established under the Law on Freedom of the Press. The Papal Nuncio, Gravina, opposed the 1813 decree, along with several bishops and sixty-eight deputies and the newspaper, *Censor General*. For encouraging the Bishop of Jaén and the Cathedral Chapters of Granada and Málaga to oppose the decree, the Cortes expelled the Nuncio on July 9. If the Pope had not been in virtual captivity in France, this action would have created a serious breach between the Holy See and the Spanish State. It inflamed opinion within Spain and deepened the polarization within both the Cortes and the country. The Bishop of Tuy returned to the fray in August and November 1813, warning this time that incendiary papers were undermining article 12 of the Constitution. The clergy were active across liberated Spain in the elections to the Ordinary Cortes, which saw four bishops chosen as deputies, including Fray Veremundo Arias, OSB, Bishop of Pamplona, a vehement opponent of Liberalism, to represent Navarra, and Jerónimo Castrillón, a priest from Huesca, to represent Aragon.[31]

LEGISLATIVE OR EXECUTIVE SUPREMACY?

Where did the decision-taking actually lie? Was it with the Regency Council or the ministers? There does not seem to have been a cabinet or a form of collective ministerial responsibility. Ministers were not chosen from the Cortes but appointed separately by the Regency Council, as in presidential rather than parliamentary systems, but there was neither a President of the Republic nor a resident king. The Regency had to inform the Cortes before the names of prospective ministers were published.[32] Once the Cortes had convened, it immediately became clear that the Regency Council would simply be its tool, rather than an effective Executive Power. Given the profound reaction against absolute monarchy, coupled as it had been under Charles IV with the supremacy of the favorite, Godoy, the Cortes had no intention that any other authority but itself should prevail in the political processes.

In a closed session of the Cortes on August 23, 1811, the deputies heard a reading of the Representation presented by thirty-three of their

[31] Hamnett, *La política española*, 166–73.
[32] Roberto Blanco-Valdés, *Rey, Cortes y fuerza armada en los orígenes de la España liberal, 1808–1823* (Madrid 1988), 82–83.

colleagues on August 1. They complained that the American territories had not been consulted before the establishment of either the Supreme Central Junta or the Regency Council. Since they were, along with peninsular territories, engaged in a common struggle against Bonapartist usurpation of the Crown, they explained that American juntas had been formed for the same purpose as those in Spain. They had no confidence in any peninsular juntas and maintained that American juntas were a temporary measure until the king returned to reclaim his sovereignty. The deputies said that their political objective was to put an end to colonial abuses and restrictions. They appealed to the Cortes, claiming that their persistence was the cause of American dissent. They made it clear to the rest of the Cortes that they saw no moral obligation to recognize the Regency Council, which had acted between February and September 1810 as though it had the sole right to be the governing body of the Monarchy. While this Representation, in effect, rejected separatism, it left open the question of what the American territories would, in fact, recognize.[33]

The Regency Council held its sessions in the customs house of Cádiz. The first Regency met from 3 January 31 until October 8, 1810: It consisted of five members, one of whom (from February 5) was American. The only figure of proven substance was Saavedra. General Castaños, victor of Bailén, was not a politician, nor was his colleague, Naval Lieutenant-General Antonio de Escaño. The Bishop of Orense was an aged traditionalist out of sympathy with the form and purpose of the Cortes. His refusal to take the oath required by the Decree on Sovereignty provoked the first crisis of the constitutional era. Lardizábal similarly regarded the Cortes with suspicion. He would provoke the second crisis. As we have seen, the legitimacy of the Regency was immediately questioned in Spanish South America. Five ministers took office after appointment by the Regency, none of them of any distinction. The convocation of the Cortes was entrusted to the Regency, in accordance with the Supreme Central Junta's decree of May 22, 1809. Once the Cortes had convened, the Regency immediately resigned, although the Cortes declined to accept this. Instead, it commissioned the Regency to act as the Executive Power, thereby making clear the Regency's subordination to the Cortes. By October, relations between the Regency and the Cortes had become tense.[34]

---

[33] Breña, *El primer liberalismo*, 153–55.
[34] Rafael Flaquer Montegui, "El ejecutivo en la revolución liberal," in Miguel Artola (ed.), *Las Cortes de Cádiz* (Madrid 2003), 37–65: pp. 42, 46–47.

The second Regency lasted from October 28, 1810 until January 11, 1812. This was a Regency of three largely non-political figures, one of whom was General Blake. In the ministry the only major figure was José Canga Argüelles, Finance Minister from January 14, 1811 until February 6, 1812, when he joined the Council of War. The Cortes, in the meantime, debated the provincial regulations for the Executive Power, which came into force on January 16. They provided for a three-man Regency chosen by secret ballot in the Cortes and removable by the deputies at any time. Its task was the publication and enforcement of laws passed by the Cortes, filling civil and military offices, and presenting prelates after informing the Cortes beforehand. The Cortes held its last sessions on the Isla de León on February 20, 1811 and moved to the Church of San Felipe Neri in Cádiz, where sessions began on February 24. By March 1811, relations between the Regency and Cortes had once more deteriorated, reaching crisis point by July. Lardizábal's arrest on October 14 further heightened tensions in Cádiz.[35]

The third Regency lasted from January 21, 1812 until March 8, 1813. The central figure among the now five Regents was Infantado, a close friend of the king but not a skillful politician. Among the five was Lieutenant-General Enrique O'Donnell, Conde de La Bisbal, whose resignation on August 18, 1812 would provoke a severe crisis over the conduct of the war. On January 26, a "Regulation of the Regency Council" was published, outlining the functions and responsibilities of this body, which included the allocation of the armed forces and the minting of coinage. The Regents were to work with the Ministers of State and also with the newly established Constitutional Council of State. There were now three bodies spread across the Executive Power, not just two. This Council of State was to act as an assessor of the conduct of the Regency, which was to hear its views before enacting the decrees of the Cortes, acting in foreign affairs, and proposing laws to the Cortes. It would also present to ecclesiastical positions, thereby depriving the Regency of this faculty, and nominate magistrates. This Regulation specified that ministers, their total increased to seven on February 6, were responsible to the Regency Council, but a second Regulation on April 8, 1813 made them responsible to the Cortes, as were also the Regents.

---

[35] Gabriel Lovett, *Napoleon and the Birth of Modern Spain*, 2 vols. (New York 1965), vol. 1, 378. Flaquer Montegui, "El Ejecutivo," 48–51. The Minister of the Navy was José Vázquez Figueroa, who would become a minister in Ferdinand VII's first absolutist regime.

Ministers were required to appear before the Cortes, when summoned. Dispute over conduct of the war opened the breach between this Regency and the Cortes in July 1812, but its fall came in March 1813, following refusal to order the reading in pulpits of the Cortes' decree of February 22, 1813, which abolished the Inquisition.[36]

It was the Third Regency that had authorized, on March 19, 1812, the publication of the Constitution of 1812 after its signature by the deputies. Thereupon, the Minister of Grace and Justice, Ignacio de la Pezuela, sanctioned its distribution throughout the Hispanic Monarchy – or rather, those territories under Patriot control in Spain and still under Royalist control in the Americas. The Constitution passed to the principal authorities of the Indies, the viceroys and captains general, for distribution to the *audiencias*, Intendants, and city councils in their territories. Once these authorities had decided on the date of publication and on what (under the prevailing circumstances) was to be published or withheld, they would determine the appropriate moment when elections could take place for proprietary deputies to the Cortes. We should remember at this point that in Royalist Spanish America, the system of government prevailing before 1808 was still in place. According to the instructions given by the Regency and Cortes, all civil, ecclesiastical, and military authorities were to obey the Constitution and take an oath of loyalty to observe it.[37]

The fourth and last Regency lasted from March 8, 1813 until the collapse of the Liberal regime on May 4, 1814. As the seven ministries began to expand their powers, the Regency diminished in stature in relation to them. There was still no ministerial coordination, however, and considerable changes of personnel. General Juan de O'Donojú became Minister of State from October 10 until December 2, 1813, moving to War, only to resign in protest at the appointment of the Duke of Wellington as Supreme Commander of the Allied Armies in the peninsula. This Regency collapsed in the face of the king's clamorous procedure down the Levantine coast to Valencia.[38]

---

[36] Flaquer Montegui, "El Ejecutivo," 52–58. Vázquez Figueroa left office on April 22, 1812; José García de León y Pizarro, another future minister of Ferdinand VII, became Minister of State on February 6, 1812 until January 14, 1813. Juan Pérez Villamil replaced La Bisbal on September 25, 1812. He, too, became a minister of Ferdinand VII.

[37] *Constitución política*, 5–18: Cortes to Regency, Cádiz 18 March 1812, that the laity and clergy were to take the oath of observance; Regency to De la Pezuela, Cádiz 23 May 1812. Pezuela acted as Minister of State from May 12, to September 27, 1812.

[38] Flaquer Montegui, "El Ejecutivo," 58–65.

THE CONTROVERSIAL NATURE OF THE CÁDIZ LOCATION

The historical literature points unequivocally to the influence exercised by the Cádiz merchant community on the deputies of the Cortes and the Liberal administration. In Timothy Anna's view, for instance, "peninsular policies toward questions of American trade necessarily became dominated by the interests and wishes of Cádiz." These went in direct opposition to the aspirations of Americans for freer access to trade. With the collapse of the Supreme Central Junta of Seville and the reconstitution of the Patriot regime at the Bay of Cádiz "the Regency would be for the next four years a kind of hostage to the business and political interests of Cádiz." The port's leading citizens elected a city government, the *Junta Superior de Cádiz*, which supplied funds for the Regency from taxes and from sums sent from the American territories. Some twenty leading merchants and officers of the armed forces composed this committee, which met under the presidency of General Francisco Javier Venegas. On February 28, 1810, the Junta of Cádiz published a statement of its views on the subject of the empire. The merchants drew attention to the omnipresence of their agents and dependents through a commercial system in which they, despite the Bourbon reforms, still controlled 80 percent of Spain's trade with the Americas. In effect, the Junta provided the other side of the coin to the Regency's declaration two weeks previously that Americans were free men in control of their own destinies. The decision taken by the Venezuelan planter élite to form its own provincial junta on April 19 was a direct response to the Cádiz merchants' reassertion of the colonial monopoly and their influence over the Regency Council. The Cádiz merchants stamped immediately on a Regency decree of May 17 appearing to allow freedom of trade between all American ports and those of foreign colonies and European states. The Regency withdrew it on June 27. In the meantime, Buenos Aires had formed its own junta on May 25.[39]

The role of Cádiz is also central to Michael Costeloe's analysis of how Spain lost control over continental America. Demands grew in Cádiz during 1811 for the dispatch of military forces from the peninsula to subdue American territories refusing to recognize the Regency and Cortes. For the British ally, this was an alarming prospect, since it

---

[39] Timothy E. Anna, *Spain and the Loss of America* (Lincoln and London 1983), 55, 60–62, 81–82. Venegas became Viceroy of New Spain shortly afterwards. Breña, *El primer liberalismo*, 111–12, 116–17.

would mean diverting troops from the peninsula, the principal theatre of war. Henry Wellesley, British Minister in Cádiz, sought to contain such demands by offering in June British mediation between Spain and its dissident territories. When it became clear that the British would view sympathetically the cause of American free trade and seek commercial concessions for themselves, the Cádiz mercantile community roundly opposed mediation and pressed the Cortes accordingly. On August 11, the Cortes rejected the idea of British mediation. Shortly afterwards, Cádiz merchants met the Navy Minister to discuss financing an expeditionary force to put down the dissident movements in America.[40]

Proposals by the Consulado of Cádiz for the establishment of a contingency fund from fresh taxation of the American trade were approved by the Cortes and implemented by the Regency Council in September 1811. Recruitment of troops began in unoccupied provinces through October. The Reinforcements Committee (*comisión de reemplazos*) sent two small expeditions to New Spain and Montevideo in the following month to reinforce Royalist forces in those regions. The mercantile community of Cádiz, already hit by changes in commercial patterns and the diminution of its Atlantic trade, financed the first armed attempt from the metropolis to fight back against autonomy and insurgent movements in the Americas. This action, however, compromised the position of the American deputies in the Cortes, most of whom opposed the use of force. The Cortes rejected a second offer of British mediation in July 1812, and a third in May 1813.[41]

The British Government did not wish to see the separation of the American territories from Spain in the middle of a war in the peninsula, when American resources would be cut off from Spain. Ministers in London believed that Spain's refusal to negotiate threatened to drive the American territories into outright separatism. They had no intention of supplying the Spanish government with further subsidies if it refused to discuss commercial concessions. Representatives of the Revolutionary Juntas of Caracas and Buenos Aires were already in London, requesting support. The British government firmly rejected any suggestion that, as an ally of Spain, Britain had a duty to support Spain in the repression of dissidence in the Americas.[42]

---

[40] Michael P. Costeloe, *Response to Revolution. Imperial Spain and the Spanish American revolutions, 1810–1840* (Cambridge 1986), 55. Breña, *El primer liberalismo*, 152.

[41] Costeloe, *Response to Revolution*, 56–57.

[42] C. K. Webster, *Britain and the Independence of Latin America, 1812–1830*, 2 vols. (London 1938), vol. II, 309–31.

In January 1814, the Ordinary Cortes, with the French in retreat across northern Spain, transferred its location to Madrid. Although this removed the government and deputies from the immediate influence of the Cádiz mercantile community, two other problems arose. Madrid had been the controlling center of the old Monarchy and inherited the traditional view of Castilian supremacy within the peninsula and empire. Second, and more serious in the short term, was the inclusion of large areas of Spanish territory, which had little or no sympathy with or comprehension of the Liberal project, within the new constitutional system. This would present the Liberal administration with the problem of how to remain in office in face of growing opposition within the country and the Cortes.

THE CORTES AND THE AMERICAS

The two unresolved issues of equality of representation and liberation of commerce remained the principle sources of division between European deputies and their sixty-three American counterparts. Beyond articulating these demands, however, neither American deputies in the Cortes nor the makers of opinion in the overseas territories showed much radicalism in their thinking. Morales Duárez (Peru), for example, successfully opposed the extension of political rights to the castes of African origin on October 15, 1810. The range of opinion among Americans in Cádiz from the absolutist stance of Lardizábal y Uribe to the federalism of Miguel Ramos Arizpe (Coahuila) and Ramón Feliú (Peruvian but deputy for Ceuta) concealed a basic conservative stance among the majority of them. Thirty-eight deputies, among them Mariano Mendiola Velarde (Querétaro), opposed the absence of wealth and property qualifications for deputies during the discussions on the project for article 91 of the Constitution.[43] The Cortes, while undermining the corporate structure of the old regime in the peninsula, left intact "the hierarchical and segregated colonial order." Lineage, then, remained a defining element in status in Spanish America.[44] The Cuban planter interest blocked the abolition of

---

[43] *Diario de las discusiones*, IX, 27 September 1811, 18, 38–52. *Actas de las sesiones secretas de las Cortes Generales y Extraordinarias de la Nación Española* (Madrid 1874), 15: 10 October 1810. There would be some 250 deputies representing peninsular constituencies. Peru was assigned twenty-two deputies to the Cortes, although only eight actually arrived in Cádiz, where they joined the five existing substitute deputies (*suplentes*) already chosen among Peruvian residents in the city.

[44] Christopher Schmidt-Nowara, *Slavery, Freedom, and Abolition in Latin America and the Atlantic World* (Albuquerque 2011), 78, 110, 129. In Cuba, free blacks (114,000 in

slavery in the Cortes of Cádiz. The subject was not mentioned in the Constitution of 1812. The expansion of the sugar economy and the import of slave labor explained this reluctance. The growth of sugar helped to explain the rising importance of Havana within the Spanish colonial system at a time of crisis in colonial relationships on the American continent.[45]

The viceroys in New Spain and Peru, the two territories in which Royal governments in their capital cities would face the strongest armed opposition, saw their authority reduced by the Liberal ministry's administrative and jurisdictional changes. Nettie Lee Benson's study of the considerable impact that the first constitutionalism had in New Spain makes this point early on. For the three viceroys of 1810–21 in New Spain, the change caused consternation.

> It placed each of them in turn in a peculiar situation. Each had been named viceroy of a colonial kingdom with full regal power, but under the new government's Constitution and the laws passed by the Cortes the position of viceroy did not and could not exist, for it was replaced by the much more limited position of political chief. The question each 'viceroy' had to face in the midst of a rebellion was: What, then, is my position? ... Not even the Regency, or for that matter the Cortes, foresaw what the Constitution would mean to administrators in the New World.[46]

Venegas authorized publication of the Constitution in Mexico City on September 19, 1812. He was a less confident and skillful politician than Abascal in Peru. The latter had first arrived in the Americas as a young man and subsequently became President of the Audiencia of New Galicia from 1799 to 1806. Venegas arrived for the first time at the moment of the outbreak of the Hidalgo insurrection. He panicked at the prospect of American victories in the elections for the constitutional municipality of Mexico City under the terms of the Constitution and suspended them on November 29, 1812, along with those for the deputies to the Cortes and for the formation of the *Diputación Provincial* of the Province of Mexico. He did not, thereby, suspend the implementation of the provisions of the Constitution for the entire area of his immediate jurisdiction but only on those three points. A few days later, on December 5, Venegas also suspended article 371 of the Constitution, which provided for liberty of the press, on the grounds that it threatened

---

1800) and whites (274,000) always outnumbered slaves (212,000, rising to 320,000 by 1842).

[45] Schmidt-Nowara, *Slavery, Freedom, and Abolition*, 4, 83.

[46] Benson, *Mexico and the Spanish Cortes*, 8–9. See article 324 of the Constitution.

the security of the state. He had proclaimed it in his *Bando* of October 5, which meant that freedom of the press in New Spain existed for only sixty-one days during the Venegas viceregency.[47]

In Royalist Spanish America, the Cádiz constitutional system offered educated Americans the prospect of political advancement and enabled them to challenge the absolutist tendencies of the remaining viceroys. This was not, however, the same as Home Rule. In Peru, once the Constitution had been published on October 1, 1812, Abascal attempted to control as much as he could of the electoral processes and the elected institutions. He authorized the establishment of liberty of the press in Lima on April 18, 1811 and with it the *junta de censura*. Even though a critical press resulted – in the form, for instance, of *El Peruano Liberal* – Abascal did not feel the need to suppress it. In contrast to Mexico City, elections to the Constitutional City Council of Lima, the *diputación provincial*, and for deputies to the Cortes in the nine eligible cities were successfully held in Peru. The viceroy exercised the positions of president of the Constitutional City Council and the *diputación provincial* in Lima, in order to supervise their workings. Neither Venegas nor Calleja did this in Mexico City. Abascal intervened in the electoral processes and distribution of appointments wherever he believed he might get away with it. In the long run, however, Abascal failed to control either of the city councils of Lima and Cuzco, as the electoral success of the pro-Home Rule faction in Lima around the Chilean-born *oidor* Miguel de Eyzaguirre (1747–1854), brother of Agustín, one of the leaders of the Chilean Junta, testified. Peruvian deputies in the Cortes, with Morales Duárez in the vanguard, repeatedly but unsuccessfully pressed the Regency Council for his removal. In these attempts, they coordinated their actions with the principal proponents of autonomy, Eyzaguirre, who in May 1812 advocated the opening of Peruvian ports to foreign traders, and the Conde de la Vega del Ren.[48]

---

[47] AGI México 1882, Venegas to Minister of War, Mexico City 14 December 1812. Benson, *Mexico and the Spanish Cortes*, 22–24, 72–74.

[48] Víctor Peralta Ruiz, *La Independencia y la cultural política peruana (1808–1821)* (Lima 2010), 105–6, 112, 118–20, 122–24, 130–37, 179, 182, and the same author's "El impacto de las Cortes de Cádiz en el Perú. Un balance historiográfico," *RI*, LXVIII, no. 242 (2008), pp. 67–96. Morales Duárez died on April 2, 1812. Eyzaguirre had been *alcalde del crimen* since 1806. He had spent the three years from 1803 in Madrid, where he had seen the decay of metropolitan government under Charles IV. In his capacity as *Protector de Indios*, he had denounced in August 1807 the subdelegates' *repartos* to the indigenous communities.

The debate in Peru, as it appeared in the press, in the city councils, and undoubtedly in private salons and *tertulias*, concerned the nature and scope of the constitutional system introduced from Cádiz; how members of the Peruvian élites and articulate groups might advance their positions through it; how it might neutralize Indian grievances through incorporation through the exercise of the vote; and how the existing structure of society might be preserved whether because of it or in spite of it. Much would depend on the definition of "citizen" within the specific local Peruvian contexts. That, in turn, pointed back to the perennial issue of the Indian tribute as the major source of government revenue. The Cortes abolished Indian tribute on March 13, 1811, thereby plunging the royal administrations across the Spanish American territories, already beset by fiscal problems of the gravest order, into further difficulties. Abascal, throughout the duration of the constitutional system, sought unsuccessfully to have this measure reversed, faced as his government was by a full-scale war across Upper Peru and by the threat of uprisings in Lower Peru.[49]

In Quito, under the control of Peruvian Royalist forces from May 1812 acting in concert with opposition provincial cities, the royal authorities took the decision to suspend article 310 of the Constitution. This had provided for the transformation of the closed municipalities into representative institutions through election and the extension of councils to all population centers above 1000 inhabitants, which did not already have them. While welcoming the publication of the Constitution with jubilation on July 18, 1813, the existing city council of Quito requested the temporary suspension of popular elections owing to the unsettled situation in the territory of the Audiencia of Quito.[50]

In Quito, Peru, New Spain, and across the remaining territories under Royalist control, the fundamental problem was the different perspective that the Liberal administration in Cádiz and the Americans in the overseas capitals and provinces had of the Constitution's electoral provisions and purposes. The former regarded them as aspects of central control, binding the latter into the united Nation through the medium of representative institutions. The metropolitan government regarded the

---

[49] Peralta, "El impacto," 72, 76.
[50] AGI Lima 799, President and City Council to Regency Council, Quito 21 July 1813. Morelli, *Territorio o Nación*, 53, 78–79, 84, 123, 172–73, 233. In effect, this meant that existing *repúblicas de indios* would also continue in Quito.

Diputaciones Provinciales, for example, as branches of the central executive. Argüelles argued that they had no representative character. The Americans regarded Constitutional Councils and Provincial Deputations as bodies through which local interests could finally gain a voice within the imperial system. That is, they saw them as the means of promoting their own interests. Ramos Arizpe welcomed them for their potential as embryonic provincial legislatures. This was exactly what the peninsular Liberals intended them not to become. Even American autonomists did not regard the Cádiz system as a potential threat, once brought under their control in the local contexts, but as a useful means of consolidating their positions in relation to both the royal administration in their capitals and to the rest of the population below them. Such a position had nothing whatever to do with the unitarist goals of the Cádiz or Madrid Liberals.[51]

In Quito, for instance, the apparent innovations of the Liberal project concealed traditional aspects. Although article 11 of the Constitution provided for the future administrative divisions of the Nation, elections were to be based on the existing structure of parishes, districts, and provinces, thereby enabling not only members of the clergy (who presided over ceremonies of oath-taking) but other traditional interest groups to exercise a decisive influence over the three stages of the electoral process. Furthermore, the status of *vecino*, so fundamental in the colonial period in determining social status and influence, was retained for the exercise of the rights of citizenship. Without any definition of wealth or property qualification for the right to vote and stand for election, *vecindad* became crucial as the deciding factor in an individual's exercise of these rights. This status required residence in a recognized community, property-ownership, and the position of male head of the family. The selection of who should be regarded as a *vecino*

---

[51] Manuel Ferrer Muñoz, *La Constitución de Cádiz y su aplicación en la Nueva España (Pugna entre Antiguo y Nuevo Régimen en el virreinato, 1810–1821)* (Mexico City 1993), 225–32. There were to be forty-five *diputaciones provincials* – thirty in the peninsula but only nineteen in the Americas, of which there were to be six in the former Viceroyalty of New Spain (Mexico City for New Spain, Guadalajara for New Galicia, San Luis Potosí for that province plus Michoacán and Guanajuato, Durango for the *Provincias Internas de Occidente*, and Monterrey for the *Provincias Internas del Oriente*; two were assigned to Peru. Articles 324–337 of the Constitution dealt with these bodies. Only three actually functioned in the full Viceroyalty of New Spain. Peralta, *Independencia*, 117–19.

depended on local contexts, as decided by the appropriate electoral committee. Morelli convincingly argues that such practices resulted in an "oligarchization of the political processes," which had little to do with sentiments of attachment to a wider "Nation."[52]

When Calleja took office in March 1813, he began the implementation of the Constitution in New Spain, with the exception of article 371 on freedom of the press, regarded as too risky while the insurgency continued. In the following month, he allowed the elections to the Constitutional Council to resume in the capital. On July 13, elections took place for deputies to the forthcoming Ordinary Cortes of 1813–14. The viceroy was peeved to discover that in the result several identified members of the American group known as "the Guadalupes," who were in touch with insurgent leaders, had been elected. He thereupon cut off their funds for travel to Spain. New Spain was assigned six Provincial Deputations, four of which actually convened, beginning with Mérida (Yucatán) on April 23, 1813. They consisted of seven elected members and three substitutes in each of them. In all, five different elections for deputies to the Cortes would take place in New Spain: some 160 Mexicans were elected between 1810–14 and 1820–22, of whom over seventy (not including substitute deputies) actively participated in debates.[53]

VIEWS OF THE ROOT CAUSES OF THE ESCALATION OF CONFLICT

Always concerned with the American problem in *El Español*, Blanco White was highly critical of the opportunities missed by the Regency Council and the Extraordinary Cortes to resolve the issue of American dissidence through a constructive policy of conciliation. He opposed the appointment of controversial military figures to key positions in the Americas, such as Venegas to New Spain and Elío to Montevideo, and the dispatch of peninsular troops in the Americas from 1811. Blanco saw the roots of American disillusionment with continued participation within the Hispanic Monarchy as a result of the denial of equal representation to the American territories and the unwillingness to sanction commercial concessions desired by the Americans. He attributed both to the hold over the administration by the Junta of Cádiz, mouthpiece of the Cádiz

---

[52] Morelli, *Territorio o Nación*, 92–104, 109, 112. A good many of those who had participated in the autonomy movements of 1809–12 secured election under the Cádiz system.

[53] Benson, *Mexico and the Spanish Cortes*, p. 6.

merchants.[54] Blanco condemned the armed conflict in the Americas as the "worst catastrophe which could befall Spain." America was, in any case, too vast to be put down by force. He recognized that what had broken out was a civil war, which the Cortes had the duty to extinguish, but was failing to do. Devastating war in the Americas deprived Spain of revenues needed to wage war in Europe to defend its own sovereignty against the French intervention. Along with the issue of American representation in peninsular bodies, Blanco identified the denial of the right of Americans to form their own juntas as another major source of grievance, and one which led to unilateral action in the cases of Quito, Caracas, and Buenos Aires. Instead, the Cortes should have allowed this on an interim basis until representatives from the American territories had arrived in the Cortes and an American Plan of Government had been jointly formulated. Instead, the Cortes' measures served only to fortify those Americans who wanted separation from the Monarchy.[55]

For the expression of criticisms such as these, Blanco was denounced in the Cortes and execrated in Cádiz and regarded as *persona non grata* in Liberal Spain. Although a defendant of the continued unity of the Hispanic Monarchy, his writings exercised a strong influence in the Americas during and after the Independence struggles.

The Mexican former Dominican, Fray Servando Teresa de Mier (1763–1827), witnessed the early sessions of the Extraordinary Cortes on the Isla de León from September 1810 until October 1811. Although not selected as an American *suplente*, he knew the American deputies and listened to debates from the public gallery. Mier's *History of the Revolution in New Spain*, was written in order to rebut the claims of the architects of the peninsular coup of September 1808 by appealing to the "traditional constitution" of the Monarchy. He justified the formation of American juntas in 1808–10 on that basis. Mier would play a major role in discussing the issues arising from the conflict between the ideas of Empire or Independence, examining, like Blanco, whether some form of

[54] Blanco White, "El Español," volume I (London 1810–11), no. 1, 30 April 1810; no. VIII, 30 November 1810; no. IX, 30 December 1810; no. XI, 28 February 1811; no. XIV, 30 May 1811. Several American newspapers, among them the Chilean, *El Monitor Araucano*, re-published sections from *El Español*.

[55] Blanco White, "El Español," no. X, 30 January 1811; no. XIV, 30 May 1811; no. XVII, 30 August 1811; no. XIX, 30 October 1811.

middle way would be possible. Mier's was the first work to offer an interpretation of what was happening in the Americas.[56]

Although a native of Nuevo Leon, who spend the crucial years from 1794 to 1816 outside New Spain, Mier was a well-connected and acute political observer with a skillful writing style. Mier spend the period from October 1811 until May 1816 in London, where he became an associate of Blanco White. During the first year in London, Mier and Blanco argued over the degree of autonomy or independence that the American territories should have, and specifically over the Venezuelan revolution of 1810–11, which Mier supported. He also sympathized with Ignacio López Rayón's attempts to coordinate the Mexican resistance under the Junta de Zitácuaro in 1811–12. Originally Mier had favored outright independence, but, under Blanco's influence, he modified his view, favoring, by 1813, a distinct *cortes* for each of the Americas within the Hispanic Monarchy. Mier attacked the idea that Spain and the Empire formed "one, sole Nation and family." He regarded the Cádiz Cortes as no less colonialist than the absolute monarchy had been. He criticized it as illegitimate and inapplicable, because the Cortes had failed to address American grievances and for removing the Laws of the Indies and undermining the "traditional constitution" of Spanish American jurisprudence, violated by the absolute monarchs. Mier disliked the Hidalgo Rebellion in New Spain and regarded it as a dangerous distraction. In effect, he placed the origins of the revolution not in the *Grito de Dolores* but in Mexican reaction to the *gachupín* coup of September 15, 1808. He compared Calleja to the Duke of Alba in the Netherlands in the 1570s and the counterinsurgency to the Conquest by Hernán Cortés.[57]

Mier shared with Blanco and with the peninsular Liberals the desire to transform the Monarchy into a constitutional system, but he did not share

---

[56] Saint-Lu and Bénassy-Berling (eds.), *Fray Servando Teresa de Mier: Historia de la Revolución*, Book VIII, 219. This work was dedicated to the French-Revolutionary Constitutional Bishop, Henri Grégoire. Mier possessed a copy of Flórez Estrada's *Examen imparcial de las disensiones de América con España* (London 1811), in which he justified establishment of American juntas. Mier returned to New Spain with the unfortunate Mina Expedition of 1817, was imprisoned until 1821, spent eight months in Philadelphia in 1821–22 on his way home, and did not play a part in Mexican affairs until 1822, when elected deputy for his home province of Nuevo León in the First Mexican Constituent Congress. By this time a republican, he bitterly opposed the First Mexican Empire and was imprisoned again from August 1822 until March 1823. Elected to the more federalist, Second Mexican Constituent Congress, he opposed the idea of sovereignty of the states.

[57] Mier, *Historia*, Books 1, 45; II, 65, 90; III. 118–19; V, 129–59; VII, 189–214; XI, 343–46; X, 362; and lxxii.

the unitarism argued by Argüelles, Toreno, and Muñoz Torrero. For Mier, the breaking point was the denial of American parliaments and the concentration of all representation in the metropolitan capital. One of Mier's most enthusiastic readers was Bolívar during his exile in Jamaica in 1815.[58]

Blanco's remarks hit many nails on the head. While he believed that it was better to have some constitution rather than none at all, the Cádiz Constitution left a lot to be desired. He criticized the requirement for future deputies to take an oath to observe the Constitution, when no provision was made for its reform within an eight-year period. An even bigger problem, in his judgment, was the Cortes' decree of May 16, 1812, which prevented existing deputies from seeking election in what would be the forthcoming Ordinary Cortes, thereby excluding men of experience. Then there was the imbalance between the three Powers under the principle of separation of Powers. The restriction of royal faculties would make the Constitution, as it stood, inimical to any monarch. Furthermore, the adoption of the French model of indirect election, taken from the Constitution of 1791, undermined the direct relationship between the electorate and the elected deputies. Finally, Blanco disliked the religious intolerance of article 12. By 1814, Blanco was convinced that the Cádiz constitutional system was heading for disaster.[59]

THE LIBERAL RÉGIME'S TAX REFORM

The impact of the Cortes' tax reform of September 1813 created a climate of hostility to the new regime. Spain's tax system was already, in the eighteenth century, inadequate for the imperial government's requirements. All significant efforts for reform had come to nothing during the reign of Charles III, leaving confusion and inhibiting the increase of revenue within Spain. That, in turn, led to increased dependence on American remittances. Since Charles III's governments contributed only 9 percent of total public expenditure to servicing debt – considerably less than in Great Britain, they proved incapable of mobilizing sufficient resources to sustain a concerted war effort. The traditional revenues of state, largely founded on indirect taxation, were unable to cope with intervention in the North-American War in 1779. Instead of raising new taxes, Cabarrús had introduced the

---

[58] Mier, *Historia de la Revolución*, Book XIV, 659–703; see also xcix.
[59] Blanco White, "El Español," V (London 1812), *Breves reflexiones sobre algunos artículos de la Constitución española que preceden*, 76–80; VIII (London 1814), *Reflexiones sobre los asuntos de España*, 82–96, 295–98.

wartime *vales reales* in 1780, as a means of servicing debt. The collapse in value, however, prompted loss of confidence in the government and explained its resort to disamortization in 1798.[60]

The deepening financial crisis of the reign of Charles IV pointed to the necessity of creating new revenues, but in the circumstances of 1805–13, no possibility existed of so doing. The collapse of the financial system of the old regime between 1795 and 1808 was compounded by the difficulties in the American mining sector, the financial pressures on the viceroyalties, and the wartime disruption of transatlantic commerce. Accordingly, the Liberal administration in 1813 revived earlier attempts at reform as an urgent means of raising revenue when faced with the consequences of war in the peninsula and rebellion in the Indies. The glaring reality was that there could be no going back to the financial system of the old regime. Ferdinand VII's first restored absolutism of 1814–20 would learn this fact the hard way and be forced into an attempted financial reform of its own in 1817. Canga Argüelles, as Liberal Finance Minister in 1813, focused on the issue of direct taxation, with a view to raising 516,864,322 reales as a result. The British introduction of a direct income tax on January 9, 1799, appears to have been an example to follow. The British measure was essentially a war tax in a country under huge military pressure, which would greatly increase during the following decade. It was a striking innovation, since no government had imposed direct taxation due to the risk of losing revenue from existing taxes and taking on new administrative expenditures. A political consensus obtained in Great Britain through parliamentary government to sustain the public debt as the major means of financing the war effort. This was possible because of the strength of the economy as a whole. No such option had been available for Caroline Spain.[61]

In September 1811, the Liberal administration, asserting its claim to be a legitimate and responsible government, had recognized the debt inherited from the absolutist regime. This meant that the institutions created for

---

[60] Richard Bonney, "The Eighteenth Century: II. The Struggle for Great Power Status and the End of the old Fiscal Régime," in Richard Bonney (ed.), *Economic Systems and State Finances* (Oxford 1995), 315–90. Saiz Pastor and Vidal Olivares, *El fin del antiguo régimen*, 197–98. Hernández Abreu, "Evolución histórica de la contribución directa," *Revista de Economía Política*, no. 61 (1972), 31–90. Torres Sánchez, "'Las prioridades de un monarca ilustrado'," 407–36.

[61] José Canga Argüelles, *Diccionario de Hacienda con aplicación a España*, vol. 1 (Madrid 1833–34), 355–61. Hernández Abreu, "Evolución," 90. Torres Sánchez, "'Las prioridades'," 425–28, 435.

the purpose of servicing the debt had to be in effective order. The government moved toward the idea of establishing a British-style National Debt, when, in November 1813, it transformed the *Caja de Consolidación* into a *Junta Nacional de Crédito Público*. This committee would have to determine how great the debt was, how it should be serviced, with what priority, and what could eventually be paid off. The government recognized the debt incurred by the wartime issue of *vales reales* but also the property transfers since 1798 from ecclesiastical bodies to the Spanish state as a means of restoring the value of these government bonds. These properties became "national," a term that recalled the French Revolution's nationalized ecclesiastical properties, thereby further incensing an already suspicious clergy. Suspicions were confirmed when the Liberal administration proposed to put these confiscated properties up for sale, thereby extending the policy of 1798, which had aroused so much hostility then. A further disamortization appeared imminent. Canga, we should remember, had worked under Godoy for five years in the *Caja de Consolidación*. In that sense, he was continuing in the early 1810s the financial policies of Cabarrús, Saavedra, and Gardoqui in the 1780s and 1790s. For the time being, at least, there could be no expectation of significant supplementary remissions from continental America. In effect, what Canga had to do was remove the obstacles to raising taxes that had prevented eighteenth-century ministers from doing do. This produced in Spain the Tocquevillian situation of the Liberal regime fulfilling the tasks that absolutist ministers would like to have done.[62]

The government's fiscal reform plan of September 13, 1813 provided that the new "contribución directa" would become the basis for superseding the fiscal system of the old regime. It would come into force in January 1814. Sales and consumption taxes like the *alcabala*, the *cientos*, the *millones*, and the Aragonese *equivalentes*, imposed by Philip V, would disappear. Both the nobility and the clergy would be eligible for payment of the direct tax, fixed by the civil authorities, the Intendants, Provincial Deputations, and Municipal Councils. The Liberal administration abolished all government monopolies and internal customs duties, in order to stimulate trade by releasing private enterprise. In many respects,

---

[62] Saiz Pastor and Vidal Olivares, *El fin del antiguo régimen*, 198–200. Hamnett, *Política española*, 159–63. Abreu, *"Evolución,"* 72. Between 1808 and 1814, the debt increased from 7,000 million to 12,000 million reales. Between 1785 and 1808 and 1814 and 20, government income fell from an annual average of 1,200 million to 700 million reales. Cabarrús, in the meantime, had become Joseph Bonaparte's Minister of Finance in the government in Madrid.

this reform represented the culmination of the policies associated with the *ilustrados* but impossible to put into practice within the context of the old regime.[63]

Outdated statistics combined with local obduracy to frustrate the working of the reform. Indignation came from impoverished rural communities when they received notice of the quotas assigned to them for payment. The Ordinary Cortes listened on April 12, 1814, for instance, to the complaint from the Provincial Deputation of Segovia a month earlier that the devastated province could not possibly pay the quota assigned and requested a downgrading to the level assigned to the provinces of Ávila, Valladolid, and Madrid. Ultimately, the pressure of the new tax on rural society and the hostility this generated provided the groundwork for the collapse of the first constitutional regime.[64]

Fiscal opposition, particularly across the war-devastated central areas of Spain, combined with discontent over early privatizing measures in rural and small-town communities. Not everywhere, however, opposed Liberal measures. In rural Valencia, for instance, where peasant communities subjected to seigneurial jurisdiction and noble-landlords demanding rental payments at difficult times were already taking matters into their own hands, independently of the Liberal administration in Cádiz and later Madrid, the administration in 1813–14 found itself beleaguered, caught between anti-seigneurial strife that it could not control, on the one hand, and violent hostility on the other, which sought to bring down the regime and undo all its works.

THE LIBERALS PERMANENTLY IN POWER?

The second major issue, which equally put the Liberal group in a bad light, was its determination to hold on to power, despite the changing political composition of the deputies. On September 23, 1813, the Liberal administration established a *Junta Preparatoria* to examine the entitlement of deputies elected to the Ordinary Cortes to take their seats. Although it consisted of both Americans and Europeans, only two members, Creus and Dou, were recognizably traditionalists. Well-known Liberals, such as

---

[63] A major problem was that the population figures and quotas assigned were to be based on the census of 1799, republished in 1803, that is, before the subsistence crisis of 1803–5 and before the impact of the peninsular war of 1808–13.

[64] *Actas de las sesiones de la Legislativa Ordinaria de 1814 (1 March to 10 May)* (Madrid 1874), 329–43.

Villanueva, Antillón, Canga Argüelles, Martínez de la Rosa, and Istúriz, and their American allies, Ramos Arizpe, Larrazábal, Feliú, and Maniau, dominated this committee.[65]

The Ordinary Cortes had two phases. The first of these took place in Cádiz from October to December 1813, and the final session in Madrid from January to May 1814. The last seven months of the constitutional system are less clear than in the previous years. The striking feature is the increasing number of traditionalist deputies, opponents of the Liberals, elected from the provinces of Spain liberated from French occupation. The moderate Liberal Marqués de Miraflores put it this way,

This Cortes, whether through the influence of enemies of the reforms, or some other reason, was composed of a great number of those already commonly called 'serviles,' whereas those who wished to continue the reforms of the Extraordinary Cortes were called 'liberals' ..."[66]

These newer deputies do not appear to have been endowed with political skills and were unable to displace the Liberals from power.[67] Several of them, however, focused on the destruction of Liberal ideology and sought to undermine the legitimacy of the administrations that had taken power since September 1810.

The *serviles* of 1813–14, opposing the Declaration of Sovereignty in October 1810, argued that sovereignty lay with the king. Much of the propaganda against Liberalism was the work of Churchmen. One of these was Fray Simón López, elected deputy for Murcia, who already in 1809 had denounced the influence of "philosopher-freemasons."[68] Arias, Bishop of Pamplona, who had defended the Inquisition in 1812–13, supported them.[69] The newspapers *El Procurador General* and *El Atalaya de la Mancha* strove to discredit the reforms of the Extraordinary Cortes by denouncing them as "Bonapartist." *El*

---

[65] *Actas de la sesiones de la Legislatura Ordinaria de 1813 (1 October – 19 February 1814)* (Madrid 1876), 2–3.

[66] Marqués de Miraflores, *Apuntes histórico-críticos para escribir la historia de la revolución de España desde el año de 1820 hasta 1823* (London 1833–34), 13.

[67] National Archives (Great Britain), Foreign Office 72, volume 159: Henry Wellesley to Foreign Secretary Castlereagh, no. 10, Madrid 21 January 1814.

[68] Álvarez Junco, *Mater Dolorosa*, 345, 349. López would become Ferdinand VII's Archbishop of Valencia.

[69] José Goñi Gaztambide, "Un Obispo de Pamplona, víctima de la Revolución. Fray Veremundo Arias, de Teixeiro, OSB (1804–1815)," *Hispania Sacra*, 19, no. 37 (January–June 1966), 6–43.

Procurador, taking into account the number of traditionalists in the Cortes, called on January 30, 1814, for an end to the "revolution."[70]

This was the Spanish Liberals' prime dilemma: Were they to surrender power to an anti-Liberal majority, and what would happen to the reform program and the Constitution of 1812 if they did? An identical dilemma was faced by most such regimes across Europe and Ibero-America in the course of the nineteenth century. Most Liberals in Europe and Latin America believed that their reforms had a moral dimension and a progressive intent. They could not allow power to fall into the hands of those who would destroy the new structures and block further changes. In order to forestall such attempts by those they regarded as obscurantists and reactionaries, they faced the unpleasant decision of whether to undermine the representative nature of the system they had created so that they would be in a position to protect their reforms from subversion or termination and themselves from possible recrimination or even arrest. This issue first came into the light of day in Spain during the first half of 1814. It would recur in 1822–23 and 1834–40.

By the spring of 1814, seventy-seven deputies represented the Spanish interior and the province of Galicia. Little is known about these deputies but it is likely that they were confused, indifferent, or opposing when it came to the new structures put in place by the Liberals. The latter sought to hold on to power through control of the Election Scrutiny Committee. This body verified the credentials of those elected. It became notorious for blocking the entry of deputies suspected of being ill-disposed toward the Liberal reforms.[71]

The action of a segment of the military enabled Ferdinand VII to close down the Cortes and begin the arrest of deputies to be charged with the crime of attempting to strip the king of his sovereignty. The two principal army commanders behind this royal coup d'état were Eguía, who became Minister of War, and Francisco Javier de Elío (1767–1822), whom Ferdinand made Captain General of Valencia. They were assisted by Montijo and the two well-known absolutists Juan Pérez Villamil and Lardizábal. Violating the instructions of the Cortes, Elío in April 1814 handed over his military command to the king, who had not yet sworn to observe the Constitution. Elío came from a Navarrese military and nobiliar background. He had trained at the Puerto de Santa María Military Academy from 1783 and then joined the Seville Regiment as a lieutenant.

---

[70] Miguel Artola, *Orígenes de la España contemporánea*, 2 vols. (Madrid 1959), vol. 1, 619.
[71] Hamnett, *La política española*, 170–73, 179–80.

After action in North Africa, he had fought in the Spanish Roussillon campaign of 1793–95 against French Revolutionary forces. By 1805 he was a colonel and stationed in the Indies, where he remained until 1811 after four years as Governor of Montevideo and Captain General of the Banda Oriental.[72]

The Cádiz Cortes and the Constitution of 1812 were last-minute attempts to salvage by different principles a Monarchy already in the process of disintegration. The Cádiz proposal was only one of several available at the time in response to the breakdown of the Spanish metropolis during the 1800s. Within the Americas, other methods of "recomposing the body politic" were put forward.[73] Venezuela and New Granada, for instance, both published their own constitutions before the Cádiz Constitution appeared in print. Events were already passing on when the Cádiz Liberals attempted to draw the unravelling threads of the Monarchy back together again.

Although the Constitution of 1812 replaced an absolutists system of government, it did not resolve the problem of the concentration of power at the metropolitan center. This had already become an issue in the Americas from at least the 1770s, when the metropolitan government sought to tighten central control by removing local figures from administrative and judicial positions in the Indies.[74] A principal explanation of the disaggregation of the Monarchy between c. 1770 and the 1820s lay in the mistaken belief in Madrid, and later Cádiz, that its disparate territories should be governed by one, sole body of laws and by identical institutions all bound to the center. The desire for homogeneity had been at the core of Gálvez' policies for the empire in the period from 1765 to 1787. This was also the purpose of the 1812 Constitution, as many Liberal leaders were at pains to explain.

---

[72] The Liberal regime had him garroted on September 4, 1822.

[73] Portillo, *Crisis atlántica*, 22.

[74] Given the upsurge of violence after 1809–10, Rodríguez' statement in *The Independence of Spanish America* (Cambridge 1998), 94, that "The Spanish Cortes provided the American autonomists with a peaceful means to obtain home rule," is misleading. The Cádiz Liberals had no intention whatever of granting home rule to the American territories.

7

The Counter-Revolution and Its Opponents
(1814–1820)

The opportunity to launch a concerted attack on Liberalism and its perceived antecedents arose from the contradictions in Liberal policy. The Spanish Liberals of 1810–14 found themselves faced with the dilemma of creating a one-party state with the object of defending the reforms they had set in motion. These reforms included a series of measures affecting the Church, the exercise of jurisdiction, the basis of taxation, and the nature of property-ownership. The Liberals, through fear that their reforms would be abandoned or reversed, believed that they could not afford to take the risk of allowing their opponents to take power. This determination to hold on to control of the ministry in the early months of 1814 threw their traditionalist opponents into the arms of the king, who was committed to no form of constitutionalism.

Viewed from within the peninsula, Spanish Liberalism was already in crisis during the time of the Ordinary Cortes of 1813–14. Viewed from the American perspective, the Royalist position had begun to appear stronger than during the earlier crises of 1808 and 1810. In short, the prospects for insurrection did not look promising when Ferdinand VII returned to the throne in May 1814.

Looking back from the beleaguered Liberalism of the mid-1830s, Miraflores argued that the "State sank to a new low" in the first restored absolutism. In two and a half years, there were seven Ministers of Finance, a situation that spoke for itself. The regime was plagued by a series of conspiracies. The desired return to the world as it was before 1808 was more easily decreed than done. Setting the regime of 1814–20 in context, Miraflores wrote that all governments between 1808 and 1832 "had possessed the deplorable art of committing suicide as a result of miscalculations."[1] The king's reputation has never been successfully rescued from the negative historical verdict on it, despite some attempts during the Franco period. Miguel Artola, the leading historian of the early nineteenth century during the second half of the twentieth century, pointed to Ferdinand VII's "lack of political talent, his incomprehension of the real problems and his total unconcern for how any solution might be found."[2] Perhaps the most devastating criticism of Ferdinand's regime was that it had failed to address any of the problems that had given rise to the American or Spanish peninsular grievances during the interregnum of 1808 to 1814 or before.

THE DEMONIZATION OF LIBERAL CONSTITUTIONALISM
IN SPAIN AND SPANISH AMERICA

Ferdinand VII was determined above all to restore the Crown to the position it had enjoyed during the reigns of his father and grandfather, neither of whom had depended on government through the mediation of a Cortes of any form. Royal favorites behind the scenes and an unstable group of mediocrities replaced Liberal ministers. The experience of the first period of restored absolutism between 1814 and 1820 not only deepened the divisions within Spain but also accelerated the disaggregation of the Hispanic Monarchy on the American continent.[3]

The years 1814–20 were crucial for the relationship between the Spanish metropolis and its continental American territories. They might even be regarded as the time that Spain lost. Ferdinand VII, returning from captivity in France, brought an end, with the support of a group of traditionalists and a section of the military, to the Hispanic Monarchy's first experience of representative government, the first attempt to constitutionalize an imperial state. The king and his supporters accused the Cortes of attempting to usurp royal sovereignty and initiate a revolution in Spain on the model of the French Revolution. This position received

---

[1] Miraflores, *Apuntes histórico-críticos*, xxi, 23–29: the only mitigating fact was that Don Carlos, Ferdinand's younger brother, had not succeeded to the throne on the king's death in 1833 (p. xviii).

[2] Miguel Artola (ed.), *Memorias de tiempos de Fernando VII*, Biblioteca de Autores Españoles, tome 98, vol. 11 (Madrid 1957): Estudio preliminar, v-lvi, see p. lv.

[3] For differing interpretations, see: José Luis Comellas, *Los primeros pronunciamientos en España, 1814–1820* (Madrid 1958); María de Carmen Pintos Vieites, *La política de Fernando VII entre 1814–1820* (Pamplona 1958); Josep Fontana Lázaro, *La quiebra de la monarquía absoluta, 1814–1820. La crisis del antiguo régimen en España* (Barcelona 1971); Hamnett, *La política española*, 198–219.

support from the highest levels, when Pope Pius VII's Encyclical *Etsi longissimo*, on January 30, 1816, identified the Spanish American movements with the French Revolution and exhorted rebels to make their peace with Ferdinand VII. The king, on April 6, sent copies of this Encyclical to the American bishops.

Following the royal coup d'état of May 10–11, the arrest of some thirty-eight deputies as ringleaders of Liberalism, henceforth regarded as a reprehensible ideology, brought in a period of calumny, denunciation, and fear.[4] The Mexican deputy, Canon Antonio Joaquín Pérez, a signatory of the 1812 Constitution and former President of the Cortes, played a key role in these denunciations. The king's order of May 14 instructed him to report confidentially on the nature of events in New Spain, the Cortes' response to them, and the actions of the Regency Council. Pérez wrote to the Duque de San Carlos, four days later, saying that American deputies had abused their positions in order to further the separatist cause. He confided to San Carlos that he distrusted Calleja, who was married to an American, as viceroy, in spite of his military successes against the rebels. These were calumnies of the highest order. In Pérez' view the Cortes had exacerbated the political uncertainty in the American territories of the Monarchy by publishing decrees of sovereignty of the nation and liberty of the press. As a reward for this partisanship, Pérez was promoted to the Bishopric of Puebla, his home city, in mid-December.[5]

A wide-ranging investigation of political conduct in Spain and America lumped constitutionalists and separatists together in the same nefarious category of "disciples of the Encyclopaedists," conspirators and traitors. An *ad hoc* extraordinary tribunal called the Commission of State Crimes was set up to manage these trials as best it could, given the nebulous nature of the allegations. Such measures cast out of government some of Spain's most talented figures and experienced legislators. Legitimism in the Hispanic world soon came to symbolize a series of illegitimate activities on the part of the absolutist state.[6]

Ferdinand VII betrayed his erstwhile traditionalist supporters from the Ordinary Cortes. No corporative Cortes of estates, as advocated by several Catalan and Valencian deputies between 1810 and 1812, and by

---

[4] Ignacio Lasa Iraola, "El primer proceso de los liberales," *Hispania*, XXX, no. 113 (1970), 327–83.

[5] AGI Estado 40, Pérez to San Carlos, Madrid 18 May 1814. See also José Antonio Serrano Ortega (coordinator), *El sexenio absolutista. Los últimos años insurgentes: Nueva España (1814–1820)* (Zamora 2014), 55–76, 191–227.

[6] Biblioteca Nacional [Madrid], MSS 12,463, no. 4, ff. 13–20, Madrid 24 May 1814.

the so-called Persas of 1814, resulted from the king's restoration with their moral assistance. Ferdinand picked off their leaders one by one, rewarding them with ecclesiastical preferment. The generals, like Eguía and Elío, who had made the swift coup possible in the first weeks of May 1814, became Captains General in Valencia and Montevideo, respectively. No evidence has yet come to light that the "serviles" remained a politically identifiable factor during the first absolutism, despite the implicit denial of what they seem to have been declaring as their political objective. Certainly, their repudiations of absolute monarchy during the six years after 1808 were not repeated under Ferdinand VII.

RESTORED ABSOLUTISM AND AMERICAN LOYALISM

The restoration of absolutism struck at the heart of American loyalism by depriving Americans of representation. Ferdinand VII extended the Valencia Decree of May 5 to the Indies on May 24. On June 15, the King suppressed the Provincial Deputations and the Constitutional City Councils. Ferdinand on July 2 re-established the Council of the Indies on the pre-1808 basis. These actions deprived the participating groups, who were not separatists, of any further possibility of taking advantage of the electoral provisions in order to consolidate their local positions.[7] Calleja published the news in Mexico City on August 14 that the king had closed the Cortes, abolished the Constitution, and finished with the constitutional system on the grounds that they had diminished his rights and prerogatives. The same news was received in Lima on October 14. The unelected or Perpetual Councilors regained the positions they had lost in 1812.[8]

Although Abascal welcomed the restoration of absolutism, it took place at a time when the Army of Upper Peru had pushed the Buenos Aires revolutionaries from the *altiplano*, and other Peruvian forces had established control in Quito after 1812 and in Chile in 1814. The royal coup against the Cortes did considerable damage to Abascal's carefully nurtured policy of Concord and to the legitimacy of the royal government in Peru.[9]

---

[7] *Decretos del Rey Nuestro Señor D. Fernando VII,* 17 vols. (Madrid 1815–1833), vol. 1, 32–36, 74–75, 102, 145–53.

[8] AGI Lima 794, Juan Andrés Ballesteros to Pedro Macanaz, Lima 17 October 1814.

[9] AGI Lima 796, Abascal to Secretary of the Indies, no. 37, Lima 14 June 1815. Jorge Basadre, *El azar en la historia y sus límites* (Lima 1973), 129–34. Peralta Ruiz, *En defensa de la autoridad,* 183.

In Spain, the Veracruz deputy, Joaquín de Maniau, was sentenced to eight years in confinement. The king, however, decided to pardon him on May 29, 1815, although he was to be restricted to Granada and kept under surveillance.[10] Ramos Arizpe, who had also been arrested, was confined to a convent of strict observance in Valencia on December 15, 1815 and remained there until his release in the Liberal Revolution of 1820.[11] Early in 1815, the Junta of Security in Mexico City arrested Lic. J. B. Raz y Guzmán, the leading figure among the "Guadalupes," after the capture by Royalist troops of confidential insurgent documents at Tlacotepec on February 19, 1814. Capital-city lawyers were prominent among the more than twenty other names involved.[12]

On July 21, 1814, the king re-established the Inquisition throughout the Monarchy. In New Spain, the restored Holy Office prepared the case against Morelos in November 1815. Its attention was directed not only against insurgents but also against constitutionalists, branded as disciples of the French Revolution by the Inquisitor General. Like his counterpart in New Spain, Abascal was skeptical of the urgency of restoring the Inquisition throughout the Monarchy. It appears that he obstructed the restoration of the Holy Office through delay, incurring the hostility of the Inquisitors-in-waiting, who appealed against him to the king. Ferdinand removed him from office in 1816.[13]

One striking feature of these years was the fact that leading Royalists were denouncing each other, to the extent that little trust could have been possible among them. This state of affairs at the core of the first absolutist regime was a destabilizing factor that has passed unremarked. The two most poisonous pens or tongues belonged to the two Mexicans, Bishop Pérez and former-Minister Lardizábal. Calumny and suspicion brought down Viceroy Calleja, who had achieved more than anyone in holding back the insurgencies in New Spain, in 1816. Like Abascal, Calleja was a veteran American official with a strong military background, having arrived in New Spain with Viceroy Revillagigedo the Younger in 1789. Calleja's matrimonial connections in New Spain opened him to allegations that he favored creole interests and even a separate government in

---

[10] AHN Consejos 6297, leg. 1, no. 110: Joaquín de Maniau.
[11] AHN Consejos 6298, Miguel Ramos Arizpe, ff. 2–31.
[12] Virginia Guedea, *En busca de un gobierno alterno: Los Guadalupes de México* (Mexico City 1992), 338–42.
[13] Víctor Peralta, *En defensa de la autoridad: política y cultura bajo el gobierno del virrey Abascal, Perú, 1806–1816* (Madrid 2003), 94–99. Serrano Ortega, *El sexenio absolutista*, 77–105.

Mexico City. His chief opponent in Madrid was Lardizábal. From Puebla, Bishop Pérez launched a vindictive personal campaign against Calleja, designed to undermine his position in the eyes of an impressionable king, who rarely knew who to trust.[14]

The new viceroy, Juan de Apodaca, had been a naval officer and an envoy of the Patriot Government to London. He was, however, new to the Americas, and, as such, had no previous experience of the ongoing insurgencies and rebellions there. In an attempt to bring an end to the insurgency and costly repression, Apodaca systematically developed earlier policies of granting amnesties for rebels tired of the struggle. This was a risky strategy, since it opened the way for amnestied rebels to return to the fray, should the conditions prove favorable. Furthermore, old pockets of resistance continued and new theatres opened, although on a smaller scale than in the first half of the decade. Insurgent contact with New Orleans-based privateers among the lesser ports and landing on the northern Veracruz coast also continued unabated.[15]

Across South America the restoration of absolutism opened the way for a revival of the waning separatist cause. The metropolitan government never understood the depth of colonial grievances against the commercial regulations. Given that the Regency Council and Cortes in 1810 had declared Spanish America to be an equal part of the Monarchy, Americans did not see why the restrictions should not be removed. Although Abascal opposed the ending of the monopoly, the faction within the Consulado of Lima linked to the Royal Philippine Company, the Pacific coastal trade, and the landowner-exporters of the coastal valleys argued for the opening of Callao to foreign merchants. Colonial administrations, however, depended on taxation of trade: Peru especially needed to increase revenue to cover military expenditure. In both the Viceroyalties of New Spain and Peru, the need for revenue remained desperate during the 1810s. Taxation of direct trade with foreigners might have been a possibility, but that was still prohibited. Viceroy Pezuela (1816–21), however, found it necessary to ignore the restrictions in 1818–20, in order to raise revenue to sustain his government in Peru. The irony of violating the trade monopoly in order to preserve the empire was lost on no one.[16]

[14] Hamnett, *Revolución y contrarrevolución en México y el Perú*, 246–51.
[15] Hamnett, *Roots of Insurgency*, 187–88.
[16] Marks, *Deconstructing Legitimacy*, 147–48, 151–52, 156, 159–60, 168, 175–79, 186–88.

DECLARATION OF INDEPENDENCE
IN THE RIVER PLATE, 1816

The collapse of two triumvirates and the continued inability of the new order to provide working institutions for the new state compromised the survival of the Platine Revolution. Until 1815, reconciliation with metropolitan Spain was still regarded as a possibility on both sides of the Atlantic. However, the implications of Ferdinand VII's restoration of absolution concentrated minds in the Americas: There would be no home rule permitted anywhere. Political power in Buenos Aires became concentrated in the hands of a Supreme Director of State in the person of the army officer Juan Manuel de Pueyrredón between 1815 and 1819. Pueyrredón had considerable experience of civil government both in Spain as representative of the Buenos Aires City Council and in the Viceroyalty as Intendant of Córdoba and Charcas before taking supreme command of the Revolutionary Army of the North.

After nearly six years of prevarication over the issue of outright separation from the Hispanic Monarchy, the dissident provinces of the Río de la Plata finally proclaimed their separation from it. When the entire revolution seemed on the point of collapse, the Buenos Aires government convened a fresh congress in Tucumán for March 1816, in the hope of conciliating the dissident interior provinces, but the advance of the Peruvian Royalist Army in the north obliged congress to regroup in Buenos Aires. This congress declared the independence of the United Provinces from Spain as a republic on July 9, 1816. Halperín Donghi has made clear what this implied for ordinary citizens: It ended a long period in which an ambiguous stance toward the Revolution had still been possible.

Independence meant the identification of the Revolutionary cause with that of the nation, which had been born out of a course of events which might be celebrated or deplored (more often the latter than the former) but which was, nevertheless, irreversible.

No nation, however, existed in the River Plate Provinces at that time. There was no sense of it from below, where local and provincial loyalties predominated. What might at some time in the future eventually be regarded as a nation still remained nothing but the territory dominated by the government.[17]

---

[17] Tulio Halperín Donghi, *Politics, Economics and Society in Argentina in the Revolutionary Period* (Cambridge 1975), 204, 206–7.

The declaration should be seen in relation both to political maneuverings in Buenos Aires and to the international situation. The principal danger to Buenos Aires within the immediate River Plate area was removed when Gaspar Vigodet, Captain General of the Banda Oriental (from 1811) and Governor of the city, surrendered Montevideo to Platine forces on June 23, 1814. This proved to be a catastrophic blow to the Royalist cause in South America, since it removed one side of the pincer that was to have crushed the Buenos Aires Revolution. The other side was the advance of the Army of Upper Peru from the *altiplano* toward Tucumán. Montevideo, if it had held out, might have been the destination of Morillo's army of 10,000, which was subsequently sent to Venezuela.

Montevideo had become the principal local opponent of the Buenos Aires Junta from May 1810. After September 1810, Captain General Elío had appealed in vain to the Buenos Aires Junta to send deputies to the Cádiz Cortes and conform to the constitutional system. Elío's plan to strike against Buenos Aires from the Banda Oriental, however, was frustrated in 1811 by the rising of the Montevideo hinterland under José Artigas in support of the Revolutionary Junta. The rebel siege of Montevideo had obliged Elío, well aware of the possibly fatal consequences of doing so, to appeal to assistance from the Luso-Brazilian government in Rio de Janeiro, which had always aspired to incorporate the territory into Brazil. Portuguese intervention forced a truce on Artigas and the siege ended. When the Luso-Brazilian forces withdrew in 1812, Artigas renewed the siege, this time with a view to creating a new political unit out of the Banda Oriental and the Platine provinces of Entre Ríos, Santa Fe, Corrientes, and Córdoba. This threat to the Junta's position obliged the Buenos Aires regime to capture Montevideo in order to prevent this. *Porteño* control of the city did not last long, since, in 1815, Artigas pushed Buenos Aires forces out of both Montevideo and the rest of the Banda Oriental. That turn of events provided the opportunity for a Luso-Brazilian force of 10,000 men to invade the territory in the following year, allegedly in the name of the restored Spanish monarch as a joint monarchist response to the Tucumán declaration. This force took Montevideo in January 1817. As a result, the Rio de Janeiro government annexed the Banda Oriental, incorporating it into Brazilian as the "Provincia Cisplatina."[18]

---

[18] Webster, *Britain and the Independence of Latin America*, I, 66–71. John Street, *Artigas and the Emancipation of Uruguay* (Cambridge 1959).

WAS THERE A COUNTER-REVOLUTION
IN THE LUSO-BRAZILIAN MONARCHY?

Both Portugal and Portuguese America remained beyond the sphere of the continental-European Congress Powers and the Counter-Revolution after 1814–15. The metropolis lay under the effective control of Beresford until his expulsion in 1820, and was thereby isolated from the pressures emanating from the other Powers. Portugal took a different course to that of Spain under Ferdinand VII. Brazil, the political center of the Monarchy since 1808, remained under the Regency of Dom João, who continued the policies associated with Souza Coutinho when he became João VI in 1816. Brazil also took a different course from Royalist Spanish Americas. Besides, there had never been an Inquisition in Brazil, and hence, not one to restore. Brazil, more so than Portugal, maintained continuity with the policies of eighteenth-century ministers and those of the period before 1808, while still upholding the inheritance of absolute monarchy. There were different strains of opinion among the groups in the Luso-Brazilian Monarchy most clearly influenced by the Enlightenment. Several of these strains moved into opposition to the Court in Rio de Janeiro, presenting a more radical aspect that encompassed an egalitarian form of constitutionalism and the renewed idea of a republic in Brazil.[19]

The apparent promotion of the status of Brazil as a Kingdom in its own right, although conceived purely as a tactical maneuver by the Rio government, generated a shocked response in Portugal. The former metropolis saw itself demoted, if not superseded, as the focal point of the Monarchy. Pressure was renewed in Lisbon for the king to return. As the situation in Portugal deteriorated in response to the Court's apparent preference for Rio, the British Government also lent its support to the idea of return. In the Brazilian provinces, the question of whether this declaration stimulated *national* sentiment has to be understood within a context of prevailing provincial identities. "Pátria" and "nação" had in no sense become interchangeable at this stage.[20]

Examination of internal and regional politics in Brazil reveals a picture of deepening differences and unresolved tensions. Although the rebellion of March to May 1817 in Pernambuco spread over a wide area to Paraíba, Alagoas, Ceará, and Rio Grande do Norte, its leaders

---

[19] Newitt and Robson, *Lord Beresford and British Intervention*.

[20] Márcia Berbel, "Pátria e patriotas em Pernambuco (1817–1822): Nação, Identidade e Vocabulário político," in István Jancsó (org.), *Independência: História e Historiografía* (São Paulo 2003), 345–63.

soon found themselves unable hold on to power in Recife. The rebels rejected monarchy and the reigning Braganza dynasty, proclaiming a republic in Pernambuco on March 7. Furthermore, the rebellion was focused on the north-east and appealed to the tradition of the uprising against Dutch rule in 1654. This regional patriotism in 1817, which generated a degree of support across the social spectrum, was directed against the political dominance of the south-east. A major issue arising in the historical interpretation of the 1817 rebellion is whether the rebels envisaged the creation of an independent Brazilian republic, rather than aiming to detach the north-east from the Rio de Janeiro royal government. If the former, then the rebellion might be described as proto-nationalist. Amaro Quintas, for instance, writing during the Presidency of Getúlio Vargas, saw it as a potentially nationalist movement, which found some support in the south-east and Bahia, as well as in Pernambuco's neighboring provinces. Quintas and De Mello see the rebellion as revolutionary, libertarian, and republican, while at the same time drawing from Pernambuco's historical roots as a semi-autonomous captaincy, which had single-handedly driven out the Dutch and voluntarily renewed its allegiance to the Bragança dynasty. This voluntarism had never been recognized by the monarchs. Accordingly, the Dean of Olinda (in *sede vacante*) pointed to the contractual nature in the formation of the Portuguese Monarchy and nation, and that the constitutional tradition established in the Middle Ages extended to the entire territory of the Luso-Brazilian Monarchy. The contractual idea helps to explain the province's attitude toward outside impositions.[21]

The appearance of republican sentiment in the Brazilian provinces was no new phenomenon. Court corruption, office-seeking, and peninsular disdain for Brazilians all played their part in this. The tax burden fell heavily on the north–east, where sugar and sugar-derived liquors were already declining. The focal points of the revolution were not, however, in the humid south but in the drier northern zone beyond Recife in the direction of Paraíba. There the control of Portuguese merchants over external trade was weaker and the population considerably less bound to the great sugar landlords. This was the zone of expanding settlement,

---

[21] Amaro Quintas, *A revolução de 1817* (Rio de Janeiro 1985 [1939]), 46–47, 54–55. Evaldo Cabral de Mello, *A outra Independência. O federalismo pernambucano de 1817 a 1824* (São Paulo 2004), 20–21, 45–46.

freer labor, artisan textiles, and cotton cultivation, expanding from the 1780s, oriented to the industrial markets of France and Great Britain.[22] The leading figure in the 1817 Rebellion, Father João Ribeiro, was a Pernambuco mulatto born in 1766, who became a locally well-known Natural Scientist and Botanist and one of the professors at the Olinda Seminary.[23] Members of the clergy were the most educated and articulate members in local society, partisans in the main of imperial unity through the adoption of some form of liberal constitutionalism.[24] The rebel leadership was torn between libertarian instincts and respect for property rights, which extended to slaves. It attempted to gain support among the free-blacks and mulattoes, of which there were many in the north-east. The leadership believed that Brazil's future lay in full and equal integration of the non-white population. The failure of the rebellion, despite initial extension beyond Pernambuco, lay largely in the absence of widespread popular support. Even though this rebellion lasted only seventy-five days, its impact was considerable, since it exposed the depth of division within the Kingdom of Brazil. Its potential capacity for recruitment among lower-class sectors of the population sufficiently alarmed the government in Rio for it to impose exemplary punishments.[25]

The three Royal officers established special military commissions to try to sentence those captured or arrested. Leading clerics were defrocked and then executed. Executions ceased by royal order on August 6 but the investigations carried on into 1818. Those still not tried were finally amnestied in 1821, including Frei Caneca (b. Recife, 1779), who would be the leading figure in the subsequent rising of 1824. This repression left bitter memories in the region and prepared the way for the political upheavals of 1821–23 and for a second rebellion in 1824. Ribeiro, however, had already committed suicide in despair at the disaster.[26]

---

[22] Gilberto Vilar de Carvalho, *A liderança do clero nas revoluções republicanas, 1817–1824* (Petrópolis 1979), 21–23. Quintas, *A revolução*, 80–85, 95. De Mello, *A outra Independência*, 30, 57–62.

[23] Vilar de Carvalho, *A liderança do clero*, 19, 66–69, 150. Quintas, *A revolução*, 74–75.

[24] Quintas, *A revolução*, 92–96, 141, Vilar de Carvalho, *A liderança*, 66, 72. De Mello, *A outra Independência*, 36–37.

[25] Barman, *Brazil. The Forging of a Nation*, 59–61, argues that it "shook the existing system to its foundations" in a way that the previous rebellions of 1789 and 1798 had not done. Quintas, *A revolução*, 102–5, 118, 129. Vilar de Carvalho, *A liderança*, 28–30, 32–33, 68–59. De Mello, *A outra Independência*, 29, 47–48, points to maritime contact with the United States and instinctive support in the north-east for a US-type federalism, though more on the lines of the Articles of Confederation of 1776 than the Constitution of 1787.

[26] Vilar de Carvalho, *A liderança*, 32–38, 42–43, 75–78.

Whether we regard the 1817 Rebellion as an isolated incident, an abortive revolution in a largely uncomprehending society, or part of a broader undercurrent of constitutionalist opposition to the Bragança absolute monarchy is a difficult question to answer. Much has depended on the historiographical perspective – nationalist, regional, social, or traditionalist – of the authors interpreting it. Even so, the links between 1817 and 1824 and the later Praiera Rebellion of 1848–49 in the north-east, let alone the recurrent rebellions from the 1830s into the 1850s do point to widespread and repeated opposition to the concentration of power in the three main provinces of the south-east, Minas Gerais, São Paulo, and Rio de Janeiro, first under the Portuguese Court from 1808 to 1821 and subsequently under the First Empire of 1822–31, the Regency of 1831–41, and through the Second Empire of 1841–89.

Metropolitan Portugal also escaped the atmosphere of recrimination and suspicion that characterized Restoration Spain. Portugal, in fact, could hardly be said to have passed at all through the rigors that characterized so much of the European Restoration. Under Beresford's control, the political life of the former metropolis appeared to have been frozen, once the French had been beaten back after Salamanca in 1812.

An abortive uprising to be led by Field Marshal Gomes Freire de Andrade, an experienced soldier who had served with the Portuguese Legion and the French Army in Germany, was put down in 1817. It seems to have been directed against the absent king, the Regency Council, and Beresford's role as Commander-in-chief. Betrayed on May 25 by another officer, a court martial followed, after which its leader, who happened to have been Grand Master of the Lisbon Masonic Lodge since 1815, was hanged with eleven others on October 18. Three more were transported to Angola or Mozambique for periods of five or ten years. Beresford most probably overreacted and the sentences caused consternation. Yet, the conspiracy is difficult to fathom, not least because of the curious career of Freire. Most of his life and career had been spent out of Portugal and he had served with the army of the enemy. Freire, however, came from a distinguished family. Born in 1757 the son of the Portuguese Ambassador in Vienna and an Austro-Bohemian wife who was a relative of Pombal, he had only arrived in Portugal in 1781 and began service in its armed forces in the following year. In 1788–89, we find him in the service of Catherine II, fighting in the Russian Army in the Crimea against the Turks, as a result of which he became a Colonel, a rank subsequently recognized by the Portuguese Army. Later he fought with Portuguese forces in alliance with the Spanish against Revolutionary

France in the Roussillon campaign of 1793–95. He appears to have become a freemason in Vienna earlier in the 1780s and affiliated to the Grand Orient of Lisbon in 1802. Closely associated with Napoleon, he was Governor of Dresden during the French occupation of Saxony.[27]

This attempted coup resembled, though not in the personality of its leader, the conspiracies brewing in Spain around Masonic lodges after 1817, as we have discussed. It may have been an anticipation of the outbreaks in Oporto and other cities in 1820, which brought the Liberals to power. Yet, it seemed like a shot in the dark; unless further evidence comes to light, it does not appear to have had the preparation of the Spanish conspiracies of 1817–20.

FERDINANDINE SPAIN WITH THE CONTEXT OF THE EUROPEAN RESTORATION

At the Congress of Aix-la-Chapelle in October–November 1818, a working arrangement was formed between Castlereagh and Metternich to divide the principal issues of the day between them, making Spain and Spanish America a British concern, while leaving Italian affairs to Austria. In this way, each sought to marginalize France, and prevent a combination of Bourbon France and Imperial Russia. Metternich also wished to have a free hand in German affairs, while both he and Castlereagh agreed to exclude Spain from the Congress, especially since the Russian Ambassadors in Paris and Madrid were pressing for its attendance.[28]

British policy seems to have been the isolation of Ferdinandine Spain. Although part of the Congress System, Great Britain did not join the Holy Alliance proposed by Tsar Alexander I in 1815 in an attempt to provide a new moral order for the conduct of international affairs. The British Government's overriding aim was to keep Bourbon France out of Spain, and, by continuation, out of Spanish America. Although not opposed on

---

[27] See online, *O Portal da Historia: Dicionário: Biography of Gomes Freire de Andrade* (1757–1817). As a senior Army officer, Freire requested to be executed by firing squad, since hanging was for common criminals, but the request was ignored, a further cause of dismay in Portugal. A Royal pardon, given Freire's status, was not requested, though it could have been. Paquette, *Imperial Portugal*, 106, states that the conspirators favored a convocation of the Cortes, although no particular type is specified, "with a view toward declaring a constitutional monarchy."

[28] C. M. Woodhouse, *Capodistrias. The Founder of Greek Independence* (Oxford 1972), 177–83.

principle to Congress intervention in the affairs of other states, Britain remained strongly opposed to any suggestion of European intervention against the Spanish American revolutionaries. The regime in Buenos Aires remained tacitly under British naval protection, despite a parallel support for the Portuguese government in Brazil.

Attempted isolation of Spain between 1814 and 1820 threw Ferdinand's ministers into the arms of the Tsar. Imperial Russia in 1814 had reached the pinnacle of its prestige in Europe, as a result of the advance of the Russian Army from Borodino in 1812 to Paris in 1814.[29] The Tsar, who had begun his reign in 1801 as a successor to Catherine the Great's reform policies, had in 1818–19 turned over in his mind the idea of granting the Empire a constitution on the model of the Constitutional Charter granted to the Kingdom of Poland in November 1815, but nothing came of it.[30]

In a similar vein, the Russian Imperial Government oscillated between notions of conciliation toward the Spanish American Patriots and repression in support of the Spanish metropolis. Ferdinand's Minister in St. Petersburg, Francisco Cea Bermúdez, sought the Tsar's diplomatic support in 1816–17 against Luso-Brazilian designs on the Banda Oriental. The five Powers met in Paris in February 1817 to warn the Court in Rio de Janeiro of their disapproval of the invasion. The Russian role in bringing about this meeting aroused the suspicions of the other Powers. The Spanish and Luso-Brazilian Governments, however, showed little interest in conciliation of rebels, but, on the other hand, the British Government opposed repression, especially if it were to mean continental-European joint intervention on behalf of the Iberian monarchs. Castlereagh explicitly stated this in August 1817. British and Russian policies began to move in opposite directions. Accordingly, the Tsar sought to bring Spain and France into closer harmony with Russia through his Ministers in Paris and Madrid. The association between Spain and Russia culminated in the convention of August 11, 1817, originally suggested by Ferdinand in March. This was the result of the diplomacy of Dmitri Pavlovich Tatishchev, the Tsar's Minister Plenipotentiary in Madrid from 1815 to 1821. The *camarilla*, rather than the ministry, were involved in this, although Eguía, Minister of War and a confidant of the king's, was party to it. The Navy Minister, Vázquez Figueroa, who

[29] Dominic Lieven, *Russia against Napoleon. The Battle for Europe, 1807–1814* (London 2009), 465–520.

[30] Hugh Seton-Watson, *The Russian Empire, 1801–1917* (Oxford 1967), 157–58, 172.

had no access to the *camarilla*, was not. The ships would transport another Spanish expeditionary army to follow Morillo's and complete the "pacification of the dissident American territories." Russian policy toward the Iberian Monarchies followed the principles of legitimism but, at the same time, moved in relation to events in Ibero-America. Commercial interests remained slight, but it should not be forgotten that Imperial Russia at this time possessed American territories with interests down the northern California coast. Although Russia had few direct concerns with Spanish America, the Imperial Government looked to Brazil, the seat of the Portuguese monarch during the 1810s, as its most favorable geopolitical point of contact.[31]

The Tsar began to work on improving relations with the Luso-Brazilian Court during 1817 after the arrival of the Russian Ambassador extraordinary. The Pernambuco rising of March to May considerably influenced the direction of Russian policy toward Brazil, which was perceived by Russian diplomats, especially Pozzo di Borgo and Tatishchev, as heading in the same direction as the Spanish American colonies. When news came of the River Plate Provinces' declaration of Independence from Spain and then of San Martin's crossing of the Andes into Chile, the St. Petersburg Government rallied to the support of Spain's request in the summer of 1817 for Allied intervention. At the same time, Pozzo di Borgo drew the Tsar's attention to the inability of the Iberian Powers to control their American-continental territories, especially in view of their resistance to reforms. In other words, force alone could not guarantee the survival of their empires. The Russian Government's Memorandum of November 1817 specified that pacification should accompany liberalization of the Iberian colonial systems.[32]

Five Russian ships of the line and three frigates arrived in Cádiz in February 1818 amid widespread rumors concerning their ulterior purpose, which the Tsar couched as an instrument for combating piracy. A scandal followed when it was discovered that most of the ships were in a poor condition after the four-month sail from Estonia to Cádiz. However, nothing was done to refurbish them, as though the Navy Minister preferred to ignore their existence. Accordingly, the Tsar sent

[31] Russell H. Bartley, *Imperial Russia and the Struggle for Latin American Independence, 1808–1828* (Austin 1978), 104–18, 122–23.
[32] Bartley, *Imperial Russia*, 118–20.

three more frigates from Kronstadt, which arrived in Cádiz in November.[33]

The Tsar supported the admission of Spain to the Congress of Aix-la-Chapelle, which met on September 30, 1818, but Austria, Prussia, and Great Britain blocked it. Alexander found no support for joint intervention in Spanish America, and Spain, for its part, presented no proposals for reform. Even so, Ferdinand VII addressed a second appeal to the Powers that they should unite against republicanism in the New World. The French representative, the Duc de Richelieu, suggested recognition of the independence of the River Plate, providing a European prince (presumably French) as constitutional monarch. Castlereagh, supported by Austria and Prussia, insisted that Spain should grant concessions to the Americans, whether in revolt or not. Spain declined to reply to the Duke of Wellington's offer of mediation and, in effect, terminated any further possibility of Allied mediation. At the same time, Metternich reassured Pedro Cevallos, Spanish Minister in Vienna, that the Congress had no intention of admitting any representative of the rebel Spanish American colonies. Russia, finding no support, dropped its call for allied intervention as impracticable, as the Tsar informed Ferdinand VII in December. In this way, any final attempts on the part of Legitimist Powers to assist Spain on the matter of its American territories came to an end.[34]

THE RETURN OF THE LIBERATORS

Although the Venezuelan popular Royalism of 1812–14 had been disastrous for the separatists, the king's restoration in 1814 provided Bolívar with the opportunity to revive the dying separatist cause. Royalist repression in New Granada offered him widespread support among a shocked and aggrieved élite. Even though the experience of the "patria boba" had destroyed the credibility of the Independence cause, and the risings on the Caribbean coast and along the Cauca had exposed its social exclusivity, the impact of restored Royalism deprived the monarchy of its legitimacy. This happened in New Granada well before the élite of New Spain or Peru took the decision to abandon the royal cause in 1820–22.

---

[33] Bartley, *Imperial Russia*, 124–27.
[34] Webster, *Britain and the Independence*, I, 14–15. William Spence Robertson, "Russia and the Emancipation of Spanish America, 1816–1826," *HAHR*, 21, ii (May 1941), 196–221, and by the same author, "Metternich's Attitude towards Revolutions in Latin America," *HAHR*, 21, no. 4 (November 1941), 538–58. Bartley, *Imperial Russia*, 129–30.

Exile in Jamaica and Haiti following the disastrous collapse of the Second Venezuela Republic encouraged Bolívar to reflect on the causes of revolutionary failure. Two conclusions emerged: First, federalism exaggerated provincial centrifugal tendencies; second, the social base of the separatist cause had to be broadened. This latter explained his tactical alliance with Páez, who by 1816 had become the principal leader of the *pardos llaneros*. In the years of defeat and exile, Bolívar learned the need for racial equality, if the revolution in tropical South America were ever to succeed. That influenced his decision to establish the base of the next revolutionary attempt in the *llanos* of the Orinoco. At the same time, however, Bolívar, coastal landowner from the Aragua Valley and scion of a leading creole family, constantly warned of what he called "pardocracy," and took exemplary measures to prevent it. Bolívar's Angostura Address of 1819 clearly differentiated Venezuelan conditions from those existing in the British Thirteen Colonies at the time of their independence, and he, therefore, rejected the US Constitution of 1787 as a model for Spanish America. This pointed to a significant and major parting of the ways between the two Americas. In his view, federalism played into the hands of provincial interests and thwarted the construction of a strong central government. The Venezuelan Constitution's division of the Executive Power into a triumvirate made things worse. Bolívar drew upon Montesquieu's, *De l'Esprit des Lois*, to affirm that political systems should follow natural conditions and habits.[35]

Bolívar was well aware of the wide differences in origin and culture between the inhabitants of his potential new state, and the enduring legacy of the centuries of colonial rule. The new system would rest on the basis of sovereignty of the people, the division of powers (another principle derived from Montesquieu), equality before the law, and civil liberty. This would entail, at least in principle, the proscription of slavery. At the same time, he appealed to the legislators to keep their eyes fixed above all on the "British constitution," in which he saw an ideal balance between the stability provided by monarchy and the best of liberal and republican principles. He recommended a bicameral assembly with a senate as the upper chamber, though not elected as in the United States but appointed for the purpose of achieving the political equilibrium

---

[35] Simón Bolívar, *Address to the Venezuelan Congress at Angostura, February 15, 1819* (Cambridge 1923 [Spanish text]), 9–12, 26.

lacking, as he saw it, in the Cádiz system. This Senate was designed to become the fulcrum of the constitution.[36]

San Martín's agents operated in Counter-Revolutionary Chile in 1815, giving details of troop movements. His Army of the Andes left Mendoza in late January 1817. After the occupation of Santiago, his agents were in contact with separatist groups in Lima during the years 1817–20. One of their aims was to bring about the defection of segments of the armed forces in Peru, once this Army had landed on the Peruvian coast.[37] San Martín's crossing of the Andes outflanked the Army of Upper Peru, made its continued advanced perilous, and threatened to strike eventually at the heart of Royalist resistance in Lima.[38]

Vigodet, back in Madrid after the fall of Montevideo, sent a long Memorandum to Ferdinand on June 23, 1817, advising what might be done to save the situation. He pointed to the surprise in Lima that San Martín had appeared in force in central Chile at a time when the Army of Upper Peru was advancing from the *altiplano* down toward Tucumán. Vigodet was aware that the Buenos Aires rebels were arming a fleet, with the intention of landing San Martín's army on the Peruvian coast. He warned that, unless the king took urgent action, all of South America would be lost. The problem, he conceded, was the deplorable condition of Spanish-government finances and the parlous state of the Navy. Insurgent corsairs were operating with impunity against Spanish trade in the Atlantic, and the Luso-Brazilian occupation of the Banda Oriental further hindered matters. However, he trusted that the attempted revolution in Pernambuco might have taught the Rio government a lesson by exposing its own precarious position. However, he recommended an appeal to the Luso-Brazilians to assist Spain in the capture of Buenos Aires and the extinction of revolution at its source, though it would take an army of 10,000 men to accomplish this. Vigodet put the focus on the Expeditionary Force currently being prepared in southern Spain, in the hope of coordination with a renewed advance by the Army of Upper Peru through Tucumán to Córdoba, with a side-expedition from Entre Ríos to bring Paraguay back into the empire. The Viceroy of Peru should be in overall command of the campaign for the reconquest of Chile.

---

[36] Bolívar, ibid., 14–22.   [37] Basadre, *El azar*, 154.

[38] For the counter-revolution in Chile, 1814–17, and the impact of the Army of the Andes, Ossa Santa Cruz, *Armies, Politics and Revolution*, 50–81, 82–110, 191. Bernardo O'Higgins, who would become Supreme Director of Chile until January 1823, commanded one-third of this Army during the crossing of the Andes.

No mention was made of any possible reaction in Chile to this. Vigodet said that he had no knowledge of whether the Lima government had managed to establish a naval blockade of the Chilean coast in order to prevent the dispatch of San Martín's army. The two bottom lines, however, were the cost, which, including the ships would be 70 million reales, and the need for secrecy. This latter proviso suggested that the Spanish government and Court were porous.[39]

We do not have any record of the king's response to this Memorandum. In reality, the financial situation would determine everything. In effect, the peninsular government had no direction in which to turn. The agreement of August 1817 for the purchase of the Russian ships fell into this context. Once they had arrived in Cádiz, much would depend on the swift response of the Navy Secretary. He, however, seemed uninterested in the dispatch of the Expeditionary Force against Buenos Aires, complaining on August 11, 1818 that insufficient funds had been allocated to the Navy for such a purpose. Mismanagement led to the removal of the minister in September.[40]

Vigodet, however, kept his eyes on the situation in Peru, pressing in April 1819, nearly two years after the original Memorandum, for urgent aid to the viceroy. The position of the Royalist government in Lima was desperate in every sense by the years 1817–19, and Pezuela could find no way out it.[41]

OPPOSITION, FAILURE, AND THE COLLAPSE OF SPANISH ABSOLUTISM

The metropolitan government's failure to resolve the outstanding financial question undermined effective government in the peninsula and efforts to raise and transport sufficient forces across the Atlantic. Despite Ferdinand's nullification of the preceding Liberal administration's measures, none of the outstanding problems of metropolitan Spain, which had given rise to them in the first place, had gone away. Abolition of the Fiscal Reform of 1813 and the restoration of the tax system prior to 1808 left the government bereft of revenue and without the possibility of increasing income from new sources. It could not even pay the interest on credit received. As a result, after a few years in office, the absolutist

---

[39] ARPO, PR FVII, tomo 16, ff. 159–173 *vta.*, Vigodet to the King, Madrid 23 June 1817.
[40] Fontana, *La quiebra*, 224–27.
[41] ARPO, PR FVII, tomo 22, ff. 1–5 *vta.*, Vigodet to the King, Madrid 7 April 1819.

regime was obliged to embark upon some kind of financial reform of its own. This became the principal task of Finance Minister Martín de Garay, who took office in December 1816. Garay had been a younger associate of Jovellanos in the days of the Seville Central Junta, and has been described as a "*sub-ilustrado.*"[42]

Garay's solution was to abolish the traditional *rentas provinciales* and *equivalentes*, restored by Ferdinand after May 1814, and replace them with a modified form of the Cortes' *contribución general* proportionate to capacity to pay. Provincial capitals and port-cities permitted to trade received special rates, but the tariffs were not published until the middle of 1818. The Garay reform still planned to take two-thirds of revenue from traditional sources and only one-third from the "direct contribution." The basic problem, however, continued to be the absence of up-to-date statistics. Although the financial reform of 1817 did come into effect, technical difficulties frustrated its effectiveness, with the result that chaos ensued. Garay was removed from office as part of a ministerial renovation in September 1818.[43]

From its inception, Ferdinandine absolutism was contested by subterranean movements, which usually came to nothing. They were symptomatic of the loss of the constitutionalist leadership through proscription and exile. At first they stemmed mainly from within the armed forces, but after 1817 the presence of a civilian opposition could be seen. This grew in the cities of the strongest Liberal support, usually port-cities and provincial capitals, from Cádiz to La Coruña, Bilbao, and San Sebastián and then down from Barcelona and Zaragoza to Valencia, Alicante, Murcia, Cartagena, and Granada. These two tendencies came together principally through the Masonic lodges, clandestine meeting places for the regime's opponents. By this time, two earlier supporters of Ferdinand had moved into opposition, the Conde de Montijo and the Conde de La Bisbal, both of them army officers. The restored Inquisition became the main governmental instrument for penetrating and rooting out these groups, and thereby frustrating conspiratorial attempts. It worked in collaboration with Minister of War Eguía. In that sense, the post-1815 Inquisition had lost its earlier religious function. The "Confidential Papers of Ferdinand VII," preserved in the Royal Palace Archive in Madrid, reveal a great deal about these operations. The officers of the Inquisition were almost on the point of unmasking the most serious conspiracy of them all, when they

---

[42] Saiz Pastor, *El fin del antiguo régimen*, 201.
[43] Fontana, *Quiebra*, 349–55. Saiz Pastor, *El fin del antiguo régimen*, 201.

were overtaken by the military revolt of January 1820, which would in due course bring down the first absolutist regime.[44]

Only a section of the Army had been instrumental in closing down the Cortes and assisting the re-establishment of absolutism. Other sections had taken part in Wellington's advance into France during 1814. Furthermore, the royal government, hard-pressed financially and worried about the proliferation of armed men in the country in the aftermath of war, set about reducing their number or preparing part of the remainder for dispatch to the Indies. This latter policy aroused considerable opposition among those who suspected that they would never return. Costeloe has suggested that the total number in active service in Spain came to 148,643 men. Of these, 17,139 were sent to America during 1815, including the 10,000 who sailed under Morillo's command to Venezuela. Three further expeditions, totaling 4344 men, went to various positions in the Indies in 1816. The royal government, however, had still not found how to pay the forty-four-month arrears in soldiers' and sailors' pay.[45]

The first of these conspiracies was led by the Navarrese, Francisco Espoz y Mina, in September 1814, and the second by Juan Díaz Porlier in La Coruña in September 1815. The third, the republican "Triangle Conspiracy" of February 1816 similarly collapsed, as did those of Colonels Lacy and Miláns del Bosch in Catalonia and Vidal in Valencia, both in 1817. Vidal planned to kill Captain General Elío as he left the theatre, and proclaim the Constitution of 1812. Such failures demonstrated the need for planning and organization; spontaneous uprisings under the expectation of support among soldiers or civilians were useless. This is where the role of Montijo and La Bisbal was necessary. The organization provided by the lodges proved to be so crucial. The old dissidents of the pre-1808 era, the junior army officers of the war years, and businessmen, merchants, lawyers, purchasers of appropriated Church properties, and Liberal intellectuals came together in such cells. Before 1816, masonry had little significance in Spain. The Vidal conspiracy, however, had originated among masons and secured the support of the merchant house of Bertrán de Lis, a junior member of which was among twelve conspirators shot in the back as traitors when Vidal was hanged. By the end of March 1817, Elío's wave of repression had put

---

[44] Brian R. Hamnett, "Liberal Politics and Spanish Freemasonry, 1814–1820," *History*, 69, no. 226 (1984), 222–37. Comellas, *Primeros pronunciamientos*, still remains the main text.

[45] Costeloe, *Response to Revolution*, 60–66, 72.

another forty-four persons in jail in Valencia. Mariano Bertrán de Lis escaped to Cádiz in the company of a co-conspirator, the future Liberal Finance Minister of the mid-1830s, Juan Álvarez Mendizábal.[46]

Montijo, who had expected political reward in Madrid for his role in the royal coup of May 1814, was, instead, consigned to Granada, a city remote from decision-making, as Captain General. There, he founded the *Gran Oriente de Granada* in 1816. The Montijo family had always opposed reactionary clericalism in Spain before 1808, and tended to think of themselves as in the tradition of Aranda. Association with identified Liberals through the masonic lodges would not have seemed too radical a departure for the Count. The logical consequence of such an action, however, would mean the imposition of the 1812 Constitution on the king. Montijo, in the latter years of the decade, does not appear to have been averse to that. The Archbishop of Granada denounced him as a Liberal and an inveterate enemy of Throne and Altar. Investigations followed his removal in June. His close associate was Colonel Juan van Halen, the Spanish-born son of a naval officer of Flemish origin who had served Joseph Bonaparte until his defection to the Patriot cause early in 1814 and conversion to Liberalism through the influence of Villanueva and O'Donojú. Van Halen, with three of his associates, founded the Murcia, Cartagena, and Alicante lodges in 1817. In June 1819, Eguía took over the Captaincy-General of Granada. The arrest of Van Halen led to the uncovering of the network of lodges in the south-east and east, with army officers in the leadership.[47]

When La Bisbal became Captain General in Cádiz once again in 1818, the Expeditionary Force destined to suppress the revolutionary government in Buenos Aires was stationed in the vicinity of the port. The task of La Bisbal was to subvert it and transform it, thereby, into the instrument for the restoration of the Liberal system in Spain. The Cádiz masons met in the house of Francisco Javier Istúriz, one of the wealthiest of the city's merchants. They were in close contact with junior army officers Rafael Riego, Antonio Quiroga, Felipe Argo Agüero, and Evaristo San Miguel across the Bay, with Antonio Alcalá Galiano acting as the liaison between them. When this conspiracy was discovered in 1819, La Bisbal arrested all the leaders but Riego, thereby allowing the conspiracy to regroup. This it did through the activities of Bertrán de Lis, Mendizábal, and Alcalá Galiano, but the outbreak of yellow fever in the city in September

---

[46] Hamnett "Liberal Politics," 227–28, 231.   [47] Hamnett, "Liberal Politics," 227–31.

frustrated any further action. It also prevented the Inquisition from completing its exposure of the conspirators. On January 1, 1820, Riego launched the uprising, proclaiming the 1812 Constitution in Las Cabezas de San Juan, thereby initiating the revolution that by March had brought down Ferdinand VII's first absolutist regime.[48]

---

[48] Hamnett, "Liberal Politics," 231–36.

PART III

SHATTERING THE GREATER NATION:
FRAGMENTATION, SEPARATE SOVEREIGN
STATES, AND THE SEARCH FOR LEGITIMACY

8

Metropolitan Iberia – Focus of Disunion
(1820–1830)

The Spanish Revolution of January to March 1820 spread alarm through the governments of Counter-Revolutionary Europe. It exposed the vulnerability of the system constructed in 1814–15, with the object of preventing any further revolutionary movements. Liberal Spain instantly became perceived as a source of contagion. The worst fears of the Congress Powers seemed justified when revolutions broke out across the Italian peninsula and in Oporto, Portugal, on August 24, 1820. The problem then became one of how they were to be contained. The Great Powers of Western, Central, and Eastern Europe henceforth faced upheaval across southern Europe, compounded after 1821 by the insurrection of the peninsular Greeks against Ottoman rule. The capture of power in Madrid by radical Liberals in 1822 awakened in Bourbon France fears of a repetition of 1792–93, when power had fallen into the hands of the Jacobins.

A DIFFERENT RESTORATION – THE CÁDIZ CONSTITUTION REINSTATED

The restored Liberalism of 1820–23 reinstated the Constitution of 1812 in Spain and Royalist America. The Viceroys of New Spain and Peru published the Constitution in Mexico City on May 31, 1820 and in Lima on September 9. The Constitution applied once more in the Kingdom of Guatemala, the Spanish Caribbean islands, and the Philippines. Elections were accordingly scheduled for the three representative organs – the Ordinary Cortes, the *diputaciones provinciales*, and the *ayuntamientos constitucionales*. In the Royalist zones of Venezuela and Quito, the Cádiz

Constitution once again came into force. The southern New Granada province of Pasto swore to the Constitution on September 24, and new elections for the *ayuntamiento constitucional* began on January 21, 1821. The rest of New Granada and Venezuela would be governed in accordance with the Constitution of Cúcuta for the Republic of Colombia.[1]

A new generation of Liberals came into the center of affairs in Spain alongside the remnants of the generation of 1810–14. Although the divisions within Liberalism in Spain were not necessarily generational, the "Trienio Liberal" of 1820–23 exposed once again and exacerbated the divisions between "moderates" and "radicals."[2]

The older generation of *doceañistas*, men such as Argüelles, initially secured control of government in Liberal Spain from March 1820. García Herreros held the Ministry of Grace and Justice from February 1821, to be succeeded in October by Vicente Cano Manuel. The Aragonese nobleman, Eusebio Bardají y Azara (1776–1842), nephew of the diplomat, Nicolás de Azara, had been in the diplomatic service in Vienna, Lisbon, and St. Petersburg in the 1800s, Foreign Minister in 1811, and an advocate of British mediation. He also returned to government as Foreign Minister. Bardají's weak ministry fell from office early in January 1822. The new Cortes began its sessions on July 9, 1820. Ministers found themselves squeezed between the king and the clubs. The former sullenly refused support and did his utmost to hinder them.[3]

Teniente General Pedro Agustín Girón, the Marqués de las Amarillas, a grandee with a distinguished record of service in the Peninsular War and in exile after 1814, became the new Minister of War from March 16, 1820. Along with other moderates, he favored a bicameral chamber. The French *chargé d'affaires* commented on his talent for organization, badly needed in the circumstances of 1820. Amarillas was the nephew of both Alejandro O'Reilly and General Castaños, victor of Bailén. He

---

[1] Jairo Gutiérrez Ramos, "La Constitución de Cádiz en la Provincia de Pasto, Virreinato de la Nueva Granada, 1812–1822," *RI*, 68, no. 242 (January – April 2008), 207–24.

[2] Agustín Argüelles, *De 1820 a 1824. Reseña histórica* (Madrid 1864). Encarna García Monerris and Carman García Monerris, "Tiempo de liberalismo y Revolución: España en la primera mitad del siglo XIX," in Ivana Frasquet and Andréa Slemian (eds.), *De las Independencias iberoamericanas a los estados nacionales (1810–1850)* (Madrid and Frankfurt 2009), 263–93. Breña, *El primer liberalismo*, 32.

[3] Anna, *Spain and the Loss of America*, 23, 105, 128, 233. Costeloe, *Response to Revolution*, 36, 57, 195–96. Jesús Cruz, *Gentlemen, Bourgeois, and Revolutionaries. Political Change and Cultural Persistence among the Spanish Dominant Groups, 1750–1850* (Cambridge 1996), 152, 160. The Bardají family held a *mayorazgo* in their home location in the province of Huesca.

opposed the radical wing of the Liberal movement, and especially the type of junior officer, such as Riego and Quiroga, who had initiated the revolt in January 1820. Once power had been won, men like Amarillas sought to hold back the revolutionary tide. Along with other members of this first government, he was associated with the Society of the *Anillo del Oro* (the Golden Ring), which favored the return of the nobility to the center of power through the establishment of a French-style Chamber of Peers. This earned them the virulent hatred of the secret societies and clubs, which strove to bring the ministry down.[4]

In this Liberal Revolution, one-third of the Cortes of 1820 consisted of clergymen and one-quarter of intellectuals and men of the professions. Another 15 percent came from the military and civil service or were politicians by career. Merchants and manufacturers comprised only 4 percent of the membership, the same proportion as members of the nobility.[5] These, then, were the architects of a revolution – but what kind of revolution? Although the Liberal regime came to power after the armed overthrown of the absolutist system, this had not involved any mass, popular movement. In that sense, a political revolution had taken place, though not a social revolution.

For the first time, King and Cortes existed together in the political system: that had not been the case in 1810–14. Conflicts of rival legitimacies would ensue. The king's oath, sworn on March 9, to observe the Constitution of 1812 legitimized the constitutional process. Accordingly, the Spanish bishops swore to uphold the Constitution, although the bishops of Zamora and Santiago refused to do so at first. The king's decree on March 10 reinstated liberty of the press under the terms practiced during the first constitutional period. This meant the re-establishment of the Press-Censorship Boards. Some bishops, however, raised questions concerning the efficacy of this form of censorship in protecting orthodoxy; others declared that the Constitution guaranteed the exclusive position of the Catholic Church. The Cardinal-Archbishop of Toledo, Inguanzo, a leading opponent of Liberalism in the Extraordinary Cortes

---

[4] Archives des Affaires Étrangères, Correspondance Politique: Espagne 729, ff. 325–28, no. 67, M. de Boislecomte to Baron Damas (French Foreign Minister), El Escorial 9 November 1824: enclosure, ff. 341–44v, *notes biographiques*, no. 1. Ramón Mesonero Romanos, *Memorias de un setentón, natural y vecino de Madrid*, [Madrid 1880] in *Obras de Ramón Mesonero Romanos*, 5 vols. (Madrid 1967), Tomes 199–203: Tome V, 100–3. Albert Dérozier, *L'histoire de la Sociedad del Anillo de Oro pendant le triennant constitutionnel, 1820–1823: la faillité du systèm liberal* (Paris 1965).

[5] Álvarez Junco, *Mater Dolorosa*, 272.

subsequently promoted to the episcopate under Ferdinand VII, argued on April 20 in a Pastoral Letter that the Holy Office was no longer needed, since the Inquisition's faculties had once again reverted to the bishops, whose duty was to ensure the purity of doctrine and morals.[6]

On the other hand, the policies adopted by the new administrations sought to complete the task begun in 1810–14 of demolishing the rest of the *ancien régime* in Spain. Given the profound integration of the Church in the institutional and juridical foundations of the old regime, this objective was bound to stir up further resentment among those sections among the clergy. Opposition would focus around the Papal Nuncio, Giustiniani, who exercised considerable influence on the bishops.[7]

Legislation in 1820–21 continued from the previous Liberal regime's policies of 1813 and 1814. Measures taken at its inception by the Liberal administration against the religious orders dated from the Enlightenment's criticism of useless occupations and preference for secular education. In the tradition of eighteenth-century episcopalism, the Cortes in October 1820 subordinated the religious orders to the diocesan bishops. Ferdinand initially refused to sign the document restricting the number of religious orders but was subsequently obliged to do so. That issue marked the end of any possible cooperation between the king and the constitutional ministry.[8]

RADICAL-LIBERALS, MASONIC LODGES AND REVOLUTIONARY CLUBS

The restoration of constitutionalism in 1820 enabled the Masonic lodges to come out into the open, and for clubs, political cafés, and societies to thrive. The principal Masonic centers appear to have been in Andalusia, Valencia, and Catalonia, with eighteen such lodges in the latter. They were not of uniform political orientation but divided between those supporting the moderates and the ministry and in favor of a bicameral Cortes, and their opponents, the radicals, known as "comuneros," who adhered to the original unicameralism of 1812. These latter formed the majority in the Cortes of 1822–23, and supported the younger military

---

[6] Luis Alonso Tejada, *Ocaso de la Inquisición en los últimos años de Fernando VII. Junta de Fe, Juntas Apostólicos, Conspiraciones Realistas* (Madrid 1969), 28–30, 32–37. Monerris and Monerris, "Tiempo de liberalismo," 275.

[7] J. M. Cuenca Toribio, *D. Pedro de Inguanzo y Rivero (1764–1836), último primado del antiguo régimen* (Pamplona 1965).

[8] Anna, *Spain and the Loss of America*, 232–33.

who had made the Revolution of 1820. Each position was represented by a block of deputies in the Cortes: Twenty-one for the moderate masons and fifty-two for the "comuneros."[9] Several historians have drawn attention to the secret societies, which had much greater impact on political life in the principal cities than it had during the first constitutional period. In fact, it was perhaps the *Trienio*'s most characteristic feature.[10]

For Miraflores, another of the Liberal Grandees, the central problem for the regime lay in the destabilizing tendency of the radicals, who stirred up "the crowd." For him, "demagogues" and "anarchists," their strength in the Masonic lodges and Patriotic Societies, undermined the second Liberal experience right from the start. To that should be added the subversive attitude of the clergy, particularly in Burgos, Cáceres, and Seville, and the intrigues of the king, all designed to destroy the constitutional system. A supporter of the moderate position developing under the auspices of Martínez de la Rosa, Miraflores, like Amarillas, detested Riego, Arco Agüero, and the other younger Liberal military, and opposed their appointment as Captains General in Aragon, Málaga, Navarra, and Extremadura in November 1820. Arco Agüero, Riego, and López Baños arrived triumphally in Madrid in April 1820. Quiroga arrived in June as a deputy for Galicia.[11]

According to Comellas' sources, there were several thousand identified masons and members of other political association (*comuneros*) in Spain during this period, most of them from the professional classes, including army officers, clergymen, businessmen, civil servants, and members of the legal profession. It seems, however, that none of the ministers in the first administration of the *Trienio*, such as Argüelles, were masons. The leading radicals, Col. Evaristo San Miguel and Antonio Alcalá Galiano, were, or became, masons. There appear to have been some twenty-three lodges in Madrid alone, a further three in Seville, and others in Zaragoza, Jaén, Santiago de Compostela, and in the Galician port-towns of Ferrol, Vigo, and La Coruña.[12] The *costumbrista* writer, Ramón

---

[9] ARPO PR FVII, vol. 67, expediente ix, ff. 214–21, which contains a Notice of the Secret Societies organized in Spain up to 1823: see ff. 216–16v.

[10] Alberto Gil Novales, *Las sociedades patrióticas: las libertades de expresión y de reunión en el origen de los partidos políticos, 1820–1823*, 2 vols. (Madrid 1975).

[11] Miraflores, *Apuntes histórico-críticos*, 43–46, 50–57, 60, 62–65, 77–78. Mesonero Romanos, *Memorias*, 102–3.

[12] José Luis Comellas, *El Trienio constitucional* (Madrid 1963), 67–82. Alcalá Galiano was elected deputy to the Cortes in 1822 but in the following decade affiliated to the moderate wing of Liberalism.

Mesonero Romanos, drew attention to the Café Lorencini on the Puerta del Sol in Madrid from March 1820 onward, and "La Fontana de Oro" on the Carrera de San Jerónimo, where the "Amigos del Orden," with Alcalá Galiano at their head, used to meet.[13] One of Amarillas' close political allies, Brigadier José de San Martín, whom the War Minister raised to Division Commander, closed down the "Fontana de Oro" in his capacity as Civil Governor (*jefe político*) of Madrid in 1821. For this action he was denounced in the Cortes by radical deputies.[14]

The *exaltados* were ardent defenders of an unreformed Constitution of 1812, opposing the addition of an upper chamber or the restriction of the electorate. Their strength lay in the Army and the clubs in the main cities and the provinces. A radical press argued their case. They gathered support from popular hostility to the administration's tax policy. They were virulent anti-clericals and deeply suspicious of moderate Liberals' attempts to reach a *modus vivendi* with the Church. Although the radicals had a majority in the Cortes as a result of the elections early in 1822, in part due to the prohibition of re-election, the Constitution prevented the appointment of ministers from the sitting legislature. As a result, the king had brought in the leading moderate, Martínez de la Rosa, to form a ministry on February 28. The latter's ultimate intention was to suppress the radical clubs and then reform the Constitution through the addition of the missing upper chamber, strengthen the executive power, and impose a restrictive franchise. That, then, was the program of the Liberal "moderates," and it corresponded to the ideas of Jovellanos, Blanco White, and Lord Holland. Martínez de la Rosa faced persistent hostility from the radical wing of the Liberal camp. Radical pressure and the presence of San Miguel in the government as Minister of State (August 1822–March 1823) provided a powerful motive for the Counter-Revolutionary Powers' intervention in Spain. The British Foreign Secretary, George Canning, hoped to stave off a French Royalist march into Spain by persuading the Madrid government to reform the Constitution. This, the radicals were unwilling to do. French Royalists saw in the Spain of 1822 a re-enactment of the Revolutionary France of 1793.[15]

When knowledge of the king's opposition to the constitutional system became incontrovertible and opposition juntas and uprisings recurred across northern Spain, the position of moderate Liberals became

---

[13] Mesonero Romanos, *Memorias*, 100–1.
[14] AAE CP Espagne 729, ff. 341–4v, *notes biographiques*.
[15] Comellas, *El Trienio constitucional*, 237–95.

untenable. Power slipped out of their grasp into the hands of the radicals. The foundations of Liberal radicalism lay not in Madrid but in the provinces. In that sense, the centralism of orthodox Liberalism now faced a bitter challenge, this time not from reactionaries in the rural redoubts of the far north but in mercantile cities such as Cádiz, Seville, Cartagena, Murcia, Valencia, Barcelona, Zaragoza, Bilbao, and La Coruña, where masonry had grown in the later 1810s. The *sociedades patrióticas* and recurrent news-sheets represented the mouthpiece of radical Liberalism.[16]

THE INHERITED FINANCIAL PROBLEM

Since eighteenth-century ministers had failed to resolve the problem of monetary disunity and territorial privilege in Spain, the first constitutional period's administrative reforms of 1813 had gone hand in hand with the projected fiscal reform. This was resumed after 1820. Only a part of Garay's projected fiscal reform of 1817 was in place when the absolutist regime was overthrown in 1820. Once they had recovered power, the Liberals resumed the financial policy of 1813, levying the *contribución directa* on urban and rural properties, which included those of the nobility. This had been poorly received in the municipalities when it became clear that it replaced the two traditional local taxes. Furthermore, inadequate statistics frustrated proper collection. This and other Liberal measures reflected the administration's desire to create a uniform fiscal and commercial system within Spain, allowing no internal customs barriers, not even the separate customs duties for the Basque Provinces.[17]

The French *chargé d'affaires* provided a detailed summary of the drastic condition of Spanish-government finance as it stood in the early 1820s. At the back of his mind, however, was the perennial problem of how it was that Spain, which had controlled such rich mining resources in Spanish America, still remained a poor country. He attributed this to Spain's weak industrial base and the drain of funds abroad to pay for imported manufactures. In any case, the empire had given Spain a false sense of strength. His analysis was accurate. Attempted financial reforms by Ensenada, Esquilache, and Cabarrús between the 1740s and 1780s had been blocked within the ministry, and Garay's *contribución única* of 1817

---

[16] Raymond Carr, *Spain, 1808–1936* (Oxford 1966), 134–38.
[17] Concepción de Castro, *La revolución liberal y los municipios españoles (1812–1868)* (Madrid 1979), 89. Saiz Pastor and Vidal Olivares, *El fin del antiguo régimen*, 201–2.

had been set at a lower level than Canga Argüelles had set the *contribución directa* of 1813. The Cortes in 1820 had reduced the former by half, since it could not be paid at the level set, and the latter in 1821 also by half, exempting the clergy, though it imposed a contribution of 30 million reales on it. Hardly any revenues came from customs duties on the American trade, which in 1786 had yielded 32 million reales. In his view, Spanish governments had consistently opposed any commercial treaties that might have successfully transformed Spain into the revenue-earning intermediary between Spanish America and the rest of Europe. In the meantime, long-standing taxes such as the *rentas provinciales* had killed Spanish commerce, agriculture, and industry. Boislecomte's pessimism concluded with the statement that maladministration of finance had produced the current misfortunes of the metropolis.[18]

The Liberal administration also returned to the policies adopted on the debt question in 1813. In May 1820, Canga Argüelles, once more Minister of Finance, recognized an internal debt of 6815 million reales, to which he added the debt in unpaid interest of 7206 million reales. The total government debt, therefore, came to 14,021 million reales, double the total it had reached in 1808.[19] The question then became one of how this debt was to be serviced. In government circles, the connection between debt and disamortization, anticipated in Charles IV's measures in 1798 and 1804, was quickly made. Attention would focus on monastic properties during the *Trienio*. Even so, the problem of how to create new revenues still remained, as it had during the first constitutional period, during the first absolutist period, and, later, as it would be during the second period of restored absolutism from 1823 to 1833. There could be no return, pure and simple, to the fiscal structures of the *ancien régime*, as the failure of Ferdinand VII's policies in 1814–16 had shown. There would be no immediately available American supplementary revenues.[20]

The Cortes in 1820 renewed the decree of January 4, 1813 providing for the division and sale of all unoccupied, royal, and municipal lands (*terrenos baldíos, realengos, propios y abritrios*). Municipalities had

---

[18] AAE CP Espagne, tome 729 (October and November 1824), no. 38, ff. 47–68v., Boislecomte to Damas, El Escorial 10 October 1824: ff. 58, 60–66v.

[19] Saiz Pastor and Vidal Olivares, *El fin del antiguo régimen*, 44–45, 214.

[20] Saiz Pastor and Vidal Olivares, *El fin del antiguo régimen*, 221–25. Cuban revenues would restore this imperial contribution, from 1823 until they abruptly stopped in 1866. They became known as the "sobrantes de Ultramar." Cuba, which had until the 1800s depended on the Mexican subsidy (the "situado"), henceforth replaced New Spain as the principal source of supplementary revenue for the Royal Treasury in Madrid.

raised some 70 percent of their income from renting their lands. The only exception was the common pasture lands outside towns (*ejidos*), which on occasions were included in the privatization process, when opportunity for personal gain was perceived. The purpose of the sales to private individuals was to contribute to the amortizing of the public debt. The *Reglamento para la liquidación de la deuda de la nación*, issued on June 7, 1813, had clearly linked the debt question to the sale of "bienes nacionales" on the lines of the French-Revolutionary classification of "National Properties." In Spain, however, these were linked less to appropriated ecclesiastical properties than to lands pertaining to small-town and village communities – one-half of the unoccupied lands (*baldíos*), commons (bienes comunales), municipal lands (*propios*), and the properties of charitable foundations (*obras pías* and *capellanías*). If enforced to the letter, such measures threatened to cause damage and grief across small-town and rural Spain.[21]

The new regime's decree of June 29, 1822 reinforced the policy of 1813. Liberal measures such as these never ceased to be characterized by an intrinsic ambiguity: the urgency of resolving the debt problem, along with the desire to facilitate the emergence of a small- and middle-sized peasantry, in order to resolve the endemic problem of the landless laborer, so prevalent in the south. At the same time, the Liberal administration sought to respond to the proprietary aspirations of the municipal bourgeoisie, which became the main beneficiaries of the sake of the *terrenos baldíos*.[22]

By January 1820, the devaluation rate of the *vales reales*, first created in 1780, had reached 82–83 percent. No interest on the debt had been paid during the first absolutist period. Initially, the return of the Liberals to power raised financial confidence and the devaluation rate declined to 67 percent. Confidence did not remain high, however, since the Liberal administration also failed to pay interest on the debt. Government finances appeared to recover somewhat in the months between August 1821 and June 1822, but collapsed thereafter until the extinction of the Liberal regime in October 1823.[23]

---

[21] Juan Brines Blasco, "Deuda y desamortización durante el Trienio Constitucional (1820–1823)," *Moneda y Crédito*, 124 (March 1973), 51–67: pp. 52–53.

[22] Antonio Miguel Bernal, *La lucha por la tierra en la crisis del antiguo régimen* (Madrid 1979), 81, 129–31, 340, 351. Castro, *La revolución liberal*, 86–88.

[23] Brines Blasco, "Deuda y desamortización," 59–61.

Viewed in the long term, that is from 1798 through to the disamortization of 1855, this policy facilitated a considerable transfer of property from ecclesiastical bodies and civil institutions to existing private landlords or aspirants from the business and professional classes. As a result, disamortization made a major contribution to the final triumph of Liberalism in the Spanish political processes from the mid-1830s. The peasantry, however, did not become the beneficiaries, and their alienation from Liberalism deepened. The implementation of this policy, however, was not systematic; it took place in stages, separated by decades.[24] It was always controversial, whether viewed from the clerical Right or from the radical Left. In the *Trienio*, little was achieved, with the result that the Liberal regime's second tenure in power proved to be erratic and unstable, especially when viewed in conjunction with a fiscal policy that had contributed to the overthrow of the first Liberal regime in 1814.

After the second restoration of absolutism in October 1823, French patience with the Spanish king and his shambolic regime evaporated rapidly. Chateaubriand, the French Foreign Minister who had presided over the military intervention that removed the Liberals from power, observed in March 1824 that Spanish finances were null, that the clergy opposed any attempt at amelioration, and that there was virtually no Army. For his part, the Marquis de Talaru, the French Ambassador, commented that "nothing equals the confusion of the old system of finance in Spain." Talaru was skeptical of the capacity of the Finance Minister, Luis López Ballesteros, to deal with the problem.[25]

THE PORTUGUESE REVOLUTION
AND THE LISBON CORTES

The transformation of political structures within the Lusitanian Monarchy began as a result of the military revolution in Oporto on August 24, 1820. In the first place, the Portuguese Liberals (*"vintistas"*) sought to break the stranglehold over national political life traditionally held by the titled nobility. The transformation of political institutions, and the attack on seigneurial privilege, mortmain, and the religious orders represented the revolutionary content of this early Portuguese Liberalism. Part of this thrust had its origins in the Enlightenment, notably the discussion of privilege, the

---

[24] Artola, Estudio preliminar, v–lvi, see p. xlvi.
[25] AAE CP Espagne 727, ff. 169–70v, Chateaubriand to Talaru, Paris 26 March 1824; ff. 154–61v, Talaru to Chateaubriand, no. 74, Aranjuez 9 June 1824.

financial limitations of the State, and the nature of property-ownership during the later eighteenth century. The extreme circumstances of the 1810s and 1820s made this attempted reform a necessity. Accordingly, Liberalism became the ideology of attack with which to assail an Old Order, itself in difficulty, but surrounded by its juridical protection. The connection between the attack on seigneurial privilege and the urgency of reconstructing metropolitan finance clearly emerged in the early 1820s, as it already had in Spain during the first constitutional period of 1810–14. Aborted in Portugal in 1823, as we shall see later, the reforms were resumed after 1832–34.[26]

The Liberal hold on power in Lisbon and Oporto never ceased to be precarious in the years 1820–23. Opposition came from all sides. The senior nobility – with the exception of the small group supporting the reform project – prepared to oppose policies that stripped them of more than half their incomes, as in the case of the Marquês de Abrantes, further undermining their social and political position. Liberal measures, however, often adversely affected rural communities grouped around their parish priests. Such villages and small towns, particularly in the north and center, had seen their incomes and prospects reduced both by war and depression. These issues fueled opposition, helping to make possible D. Miguel's bid for power as absolute monarch between 1828 and 1834.

The Lisbon Cortes of 1821–23 viewed the Monarchy in a similar light to the preceding absolutist ministers, regarding the whole as the "Portuguese Nation," a unitary state with its political center in Lisbon. José Honório Rodrigues has argued that the Liberals' seizure of power should not be regarded as a revolution in any social sense but as a movement stimulated by prominent peninsular merchants and organized in Masonic lodges. As such, it contained a large residue of resentment toward the continued residence of the Royal Family and government in Rio de Janeiro and at Portuguese loss of control of the trade with Brazil. In his view, the constitutional element was secondary to commercial grievance. Paquette, however, sets the constitutional movement within the context of earlier Portuguese history, namely the search for a way out from absolutism, and influenced by the Spanish and Spanish American examples. The idea of convening the Cortes, in one form or

---

[26] The discussion in Nuno G. F. Monteiro, *Elites e Poder. Entre o Antigo Regime e o Liberalismo* (Lisbon 2003), 152–53, 173–75, 179–80, 191–92, is particularly illuminating.

another, had been vented in intellectual circles in Portugal during the 1790s and 1800s, but the French invasion, war, and devastation in the peninsula, and the transfer of the political authorities and leading merchants to Brazil had frustrated any action. As in Spain before 1808, not even the deterioration of government finances had persuaded the absolute monarchy to summon the Cortes.[27]

The parliament that opened in Lisbon on January 26, 1821, while the king was still in Brazil, described itself as the *"Cortes Gerais e Estraordinárias da Nação Portuguesa."* This resembled the view of the Spanish Liberals, who saw the Hispanic Monarchy of 1810, or what still remained of it in 1820, as the "Spanish Nation."[28] As in the Spanish context, there would be no concessions to autonomy within the overseas territories. Nevertheless, the Portuguese constitutional movement, like its earlier Spanish counterpart of 1810–14 and its contemporaneous second attempt in 1820–23, represented a concerted effort to find a viable way out of the combined inheritance of absolutism. Each provoked traditionalist oppositions, which did not necessarily advocate a return to absolutism but to the "fundamental laws." The reformers sought, through constitutional means, to give new life to their trans-continental Monarchies.[29]

In many respects, the Portuguese Liberals saw themselves as heirs of ministers identified with the Enlightenment in Portugal during the 1790s and 1800s. Similarly, they affirmed their continuing belief in the "One, Sole Monarchy; One, Sole Nation." The Liberals of the early 1820s sought to initiate a further series of reforms designed to bind the "Nation" together more effectively. They regarded the introduction of centralizing administrative measures in Rio de Janeiro after 1808 as a temporary aberration. With the king once more re-established in the metropolitan capital, they saw no further need for such institutions.

This time, the Portuguese Cortes met in a different form to the last old regime Cortes of 1697–98, without a summons by the Crown and without the presence of the king. It meant that, in strict constitutional terms, the legitimacy of the Lisbon Cortes was as much in question as that of the

---

[27] José Honório Rodrigues, *Independência: Revolução e contra-revolução*, 5 vols. (Rio de Janeiro 1975), vol. I, 33, 69–71, 137. Paquette, *Imperial Portugal*, 107, 110, 117–33.

[28] Paquette, *Imperial Portugal*, 140–55.

[29] See A. J. R. Russell-Wood (ed.), *From Colony to Nation. Essays on the Independence of Brazil* (Baltimore 1975) and Leslie Bethell, "The Independence of Brazil," in Leslie Bethell (ed.), *The Cambridge History of Latin America*, vol. III, *From Independence to c. 1870* (Cambridge 1985), 157–96.

Cortes in the Bay of Cádiz had been in 1810. For such a reason, the constitutionalists of 1820 stressed that their movement was fundamentally different from the French Revolution of 1789, seeking not to remove the dynasty but to regenerate the Monarchy as a whole through the benefit of renovated institutions and practices. Their "Manifesto from the Portuguese Nation to the Sovereigns and peoples of Europe" on December 15, 1820 referred only to "the recovery of legitimate liberty." Such a position reflected eighteenth-century discussion of how former liberties lost to "despotism" were to be recovered. By this moderate tone, they hoped to stave off intervention by the Congress Powers. It struck a harmonious chord as well with the Rio élite, fearful of social upheaval. The difference between the old and the new would be the application of the liberal principles of equality before the law and representation according to population rather than by estate or corporation. Yet, the matter of a Cortes without prior royal assent raised the question of the status of the monarch in the abandoned European metropolis. The king's persistence in Rio after 1814–15, when peace had been restored in Europe, significantly undermined his prestige and marginalized him from the political processes.[30]

Like the Spanish revolution earlier in the year, the Portuguese revolution originated in the military, though not from an Expeditionary Army destined for transportation across the Atlantic to put down the independence movement in Buenos Aires. It spread from garrison to garrison, first across the north, and then to the center and south. In response, the Regency Council, appointed by the sovereign still in Brazil, issued a decree convening the Cortes. On September 15, the Lisbon garrison removed the Regents as representative of the absolute monarchy and established a form of provisional government. The Lisbon regime sent Beresford and the British officers of the Portuguese Army back to Britain, freeing themselves thereby from another potential restraint. No king was in residence in Lisbon, as Ferdinand VII had been in Madrid, and so no strong persuasion was needed at that time. The capital-city garrison then obliged the Provisional Government to state that the Spanish Constitution of 1812 would be in force throughout the Monarchy until the Cortes should convene with the purpose of forming a constitution for the whole Lusitanian Monarchy.[31] This declaration made it clear that the new forces

---

[30] Pereira das Neves, *Corundas e Constitucionais*, 167, 170–75, 226. Paquette, *Portugal*, 128–29, 138.
[31] Barman, *Brazil. The Forging of a Nation*, 64.

in power intended to convoke the type of Cortes that had recently been restored in Spain. It would be unicameral and elected on the same tier-system basis as Spain's deputies in 1810–14 and 1820. The Electoral Law of November 22, 1820, which provided for these indirect elections to the General Cortes, failed to mention either Brazil or the other overseas provinces.[32]

These changes, unexpected by the royal administration in Brazil, which initially did not know how to react, had profound implications for the future structure of the Monarchy, for the distribution of power at the top level and in the provinces, and in the relationship between European Portugal and the overseas territories. The overriding sentiment in Portugal and Brazil continued to support the unity of the Lusitanian Monarchy. Portuguese Liberals shared that view as much as the Brazilian élites, though with a different perspective. In Rio de Janeiro, the king's principal minister, Vilanova Portugal, speculated that the Holy Alliance might possibly intervene in the metropolis to stamp out the revolution. British opposition, however, would be likely to frustrate any such idea.[33]

Portuguese Liberals, with radicals, mostly lawyers, in the leadership from November 1820, temporarily adopted the Cádiz Constitution, although they expressed the intention of writing their own. Their leading figure was Manuel Fernandes Thomaz (1771–1822), a former *desembargador*.[34] The Cortes convened in Lisbon on January 25, 1821. Matters turned complicated for the Rio administration when the garrison in Salvador declared its adherence to the constitutional system in Portugal on February 10, and sponsored the formation of a Governing Junta for the province of Bahia. The Rio garrison adhered on February 26. These developments impelled the king finally to take the decision to return to Portugal, with the intention of taking control of the situation. He sailed from Rio with the Court, the royal administration, some 4000 Portuguese, and the Treasury funds, on April 26. João VI took the precaution of leaving D. Pedro in Brazil with the title of Regent. While these preparations were under way, the Rio administration, in the decree of March 13, authorized the election of Brazilian deputies to the Lisbon Cortes in accordance with the Cádiz tier system. Accordingly, the first elections to a representative assembly took place in Brazil, eleven years after the first had taken place in Spanish America.[35]

---

[32] Barman, *Brazil, The Forging of a Nation*, 73, 90–91.   [33] Barman, *Brazil*, 68.
[34] This High-Court judge founded a secret-society in Oporto.
[35] Rodrigues, *Independência*, I, 33. Barman, *Brazil*, 68–72.

Elections began in Rio de Janeiro, for instance, on April 8. The first deputies to arrive in Lisbon were the seven Pernambuco deputies, among them Muniz Tavares, who had been involved in the rebellion of 1817. They arrived on August 29, followed by those from Rio in September and October, and the Maranhão deputies in November. Bahia sent eight deputies, all Brazilian merchants and planters, one of them Cipriano Barata, another conspirator of 1817, who arrived in mid-December. The group that would have the most significant impact among the Americans in the Cortes, the six São Paulo deputies, finally arrived between February and May 1822. As in the Mexican case, several of these deputies also would later become political figures in the independent state.[36]

When the Project for the Portuguese Constitution was published on June 30, 1821, it stated, following the Spanish principle, that the "Portuguese Nation consisted of all Portuguese of both hemispheres," and that "the Nation" exercised sovereignty.[37] The objective of the Cortes was to relocate Lisbon at the center of the Monarchy, in order to counteract the position of the powerful south-eastern élites in Brazil. The Cortes, in September, abolished all the High Courts and administrative bodies established in Rio de Janeiro since 1808, reducing its province to the same status as the other nine captaincies of Portuguese America. This was received in Rio as an assault on the parallel status that the American sector of the Monarchy had acquired after its king's proclamation of the "Kingdom of Brazil" in 1815. It explained the opposition to the Cortes' Order of September 29 for the Prince Regent, D. Pedro, to return to Lisbon. Furthermore, the decree of December 9 separated the civil and military government in Rio, making each individually dependent on Lisbon.[38]

As we shall see, the indignant response in Rio de Janeiro polarized opinion across social groups and political alignments in opposition to the unitary tendencies of the Lisbon Cortes.

RURAL BANDS

Inside Spain, the situation deterioragted fast. The Spanish provincial uprisings from the 1820s onward were not isolated or peculiar instances

---

[36] Hendrik Kray, *Race, State, and Armed Forces in Independence-Era Brazil* (Stanford 2001), 109. Pereira das Neves, *Corundas e Constitucionais*, 175–76, 180–82. Bethell, "Independence of Brazil," 182. The deputies from Minas Gerais never arrived.

[37] Rodrigues, *Independência*, vol. I, 306, 308, 313.   [38] Barman, *Brazil*, 82.

of ignorant and obscurantist reaction, but a shared opposition to measures emanating from an alien central government, which threatened
a way of life and common beliefs. In Torras Elías' view, peasant bands
responded to issues running through the longer period from 1808 to 1840,
placing, thereby, the later Carlism of the 1830s in the tradition of the
uprisings of 1808. He sees the peasant bands not as the tools of the clergy
but as communities caught up in the disintegration of the old regime as
much as were the Liberals themselves. Torras Elías' central point is that
the peasant bands of the 1820s were not rising in defense of the *ancien
régime* but against central power as such, whenever it was exercised at
their expense – as under eighteenth-century absolutism or Bonapartism or
early nineteenth-century Liberalism. To village-dwellers, Liberalism was
nothing more than old *étatisme* in newer form.[39]

Liberalism began to seem a political persuasion characterized by
instinctive fragmentation over virtually every major issue of the day.
The fissure between moderate and radical Liberals in the Spain of the
Trienio is a clear illustration. For the latter, the ultimate hope for long-
term survival as a political force and, in fact, for any lasting capture of
power at the center, lay in the capacity to move beyond discontented
urban artisans to encompass the land-aspiring peasantry, the landless
laborer, and the rural poor generally.

Opposition to the Liberal system showed itself early in the *Trienio*.
There were already an estimated fourteen uprisings in 1820, thirty-five in
1821, fifty-four in 1822, and a further nineteen in the first three months of
1823. On April 17, 1821, the administration issued a law against conspirators. During the course of 1822, the situation considerably worsened,
as the peninsular dissolved into virtual civil war between the official Army
and the rebel forces of provincial juntas of resistance to the government in
Madrid. Villanueva warned the Cortes on March 2, 1822 of the grave
threat presented by widespread rebellion across the country. On June 19,
the Cortes, with the support of the radical wing of Liberalism, urged that
the National Army should treat rebel towns as enemy territories to be
placed under martial law. Martínez de la Rosa, leader of the moderates,
criticized this measure on the grounds that the law of April 1821 was
sufficient.[40]

[39] Jaime Torras Elías, *Liberalismo y rebeldía campesina, 1820–1823* (Barcelona 1976),
147–48.
[40] Blanco Valdés, *Rey, cortes y fuerza armada*, 510–17.

Early in September 1822, the moderates were forced out of government and the radicals, led by Col. Evaristo San Miguel, one of the military revolutionaries of 1820 and commander of the militia forces that had frustrated the king's botched attempt at a coup in July, formed a new ministry.[41] This government henceforth had to find ways of dealing with the insurrections. In August, it declared a state of war to exist in the Fifth Military District, which included Pamplona, Logroño, Vitoria, San Sebastián, and Bilbao. An increasingly isolated government, on October 12, blamed the troubles on ignorance, poverty, and the machinations of a vengeful clergy, and belatedly called for the formation of National Militias at the local level. On November 1, came the decree for the repression of the "popular counter-revolution." All such measures pointed to the Liberals' failure to create a broad base of support in the country, which could enable the survival of the regime. The rebel bands' operations in the remoter countryside, especially in the north, reflected recognition among local royalists that the desired counter-revolution could not be expected from the king or from Madrid.[42]

Most uprisings occurred between active agricultural seasons, an indication of their rural composition. Catalonia and Navarra became centers of rebellion. On December 11, 1821, a Royalist Junta of Navarra, consisting of clerics and noblemen, was collecting border customs revenues. During the second half of 1822, rebellion became generalized through large areas of those two provinces and in Aragon and the Basque Provinces, with rebel zones also in Valencia, Castile, Extremadura, and Galicia. Government loss of control over the mountainous area of northwestern Catalonia and widespread rebel activity in the Principality seriously threatened communications between Barcelona and Madrid. Guerrilla bands, in which clerics played an organizing role, operated against the Army, in which the majority of the officers seem to have been Liberal in affiliation.[43]

The Royalist opposition attempted to set up a provisional government in the form of the Regency of Seo de Urgel on August 14, 1822. The Regency appealed directly to Ferdinand VII to restore the *antiguas leyes y costumbres* and *fueros*, omitting to remind the king that he had not

---

[41] AAE CP Espagne 720 (September to December 1822), ff. 4–6v.
[42] John F. Coverdale, *The Basque Phase of Spain's First Carlist War* (Princeton 1984), 76, 79.
[43] José Luis Comellas, *Los realistas en el Trienio Constitucional* (Pamplona 1958), 62. Coverdale, *Basque Phase*, 76–80.

done so in 1814–20. On September 12, these Regents, under the presidency of the Marqués de Mataflorida and including Jaime Creus (Archbishop of Tarragona) and the Barón de Eroles, sent a copy of their Exposition to the European sovereigns assembled at the Congress of Verona, with the intention of soliciting a joint intervention against the Liberal regime in Spain.[44] Mataflorida complained to Tsar Alexander I that the French Government was not assisting the Regency. Worse, he denounced what he believed to be a French plan to impose on Spain a version of the *Charte Constitutionelle*. Mataflorida regarded the Charter as nothing but a compromise with revolution and Liberalism, which he believed would be intolerable in Spain.[45]

The Regency was swept away by the advance of the Liberal Army under Francisco Espoz y Mina in mid-September 1822, and its members sought refuge in France in December. Over the border in exile, the Regents gave vent to their suspicions of French intentions. They told the Tsar of their regret that the Congress of Verona had entrusted the liberation of Spain to the French, who had never recognized the legitimacy of the Regency of Seo de Urgel.[46]

Clashes between the National Militia formations, always short of men despite the government decree of November 11, 1822, and Royalist bands took place in many localities, often limited but persistent. The hinterlands of Bilbao and Santander showed an example of this during the second half of 1822 and into 1823. In August, the constitutional council of Laredo warned the provincial governor that the situation in the countryside beyond Bilbao was deplorable and the number of militiamen very low, since the town's men were sailors exempt from militia service. Pro-government volunteers from Santander and Reynosa assisted small units from the Regular Army, working with the Civil Governor of Santander, to drive them off in late October 1822. Rebel bands impeded recruitment and removed the Constitution plaque in several villages. Such bands

[44] Archivo del Palacio de Oriente [ARPO], Papeles Reservados de Fernando VII, vol. 22, ff. 246–47, *Exposición dirigida a S. M. el Rey D. Fernando VII por la Regencia que ha de governar a España durante el cautiverio de S. M.* Mataflorida was one of the "Persas" of 1814. Ferdinand had made him Secretary of Grace and Justice in November 1819, a post that he held until March 20, 1820, when swept out of office by the Liberal accession to power. Creus had been one of the leading *serviles* in the Extraordinary Cortes. Eroles had led guerrilla bands in Catalonia against the French from 1808. Ferdinand would appoint him Captain General of Catalonia in 1823–25.

[45] ARPO PR FVII, vol. 22, f. 275, Mataflorida to Tsar, Seo de Urgel 20 October 1822.

[46] ARPO PR FVII, vol. 22, ff. 309–15, Regents to Tsar, Perpignan 18 February 1823.

sought refuge in the mountains, shrouded in mist. The constitutional authorities could not rely on the cooperation of local village officials.[47] The rural and inland character of these rebellions was clear, and they were a northern rather than a southern phenomenon. The disconnection between northern and southern rural political action still requires examination. It is conceivable that the moment of the south had not yet come. That would follow after the results of disamortization became clear during the second half of the century and into the first part of the twentieth century, when the landless laborer and small peasant communities would become politicized through the penetration of Anarchism beyond the reach of conventional political parties. During the *Trienio*, the port cities remained, as in 1810–14, centers of Liberal support. The political authorities in Cádiz, for example, namely the Constitutional Municipality and the Provincial Deputation, on which sat the prominent Liberal merchant, Javier de Istúriz, denounced the Royalist uprisings on May 1, 1821. They also condemned the Austrian intervention to suppress the parallel Liberal revolutions in Italy, and declared their intention to defend the Liberal system in Spain.[48]

Fears among the Liberal moderates, protagonists of the politics of order, encouraged a subtle realignment with sectors of the old nobility for the defense of incomes and property. This concern overrode, on both sides, differences of opinion concerning the degree to which privilege should be expunged from the legal and political system. Mutual dislike of the Patriotic Societies and the National Militia, dear to radical Liberals, further encouraged cooperation. Such accommodation, the elaboration and details of which would have been enshrouded in private exchanges rather than in letters subsequently lodged in archives, opened the way for discussion, at some later stage, of reforming the 1812 Constitution, introducing a bicameral system, and even reconsidering the doctrine of sovereignty as outlined in the decree of September 1810. By contrast, radicals wished to push forward a Liberal revolution, sustained by an armed citizenry in the National Militia, expanding the sphere of press freedom, and providing for a broader expression of public opinion.[49]

---

[47] Biblioteca de Meléndez Pelayo (Santander), Sección de Fondos Modernos, MSS 395 (8.2.39), *Papeles varios referentes a sucesos ocurridos entre los facciosos y los milicianos nacionales de Santander y su provincia en los años de 1822 y 1823*, ff. 18–21v, 104–7, 110–14v.

[48] ARPO PR FVII, vol. 21, ff. 68–69.

[49] Monerris and Monerris, "Tiempo de Liberalismo," 276, 280

AN AMICABLE SEPARATION? PORTUGAL AND BRAZIL, 1820–1824

A prevailing sense of provincial identity still characterized Portuguese America in the early 1820s:

even in 1821, one year before the proclamation of independence, Brazilian representatives to the Portuguese Cortes still made a point of presenting themselves as delegates from their provinces rather than from the colony. Because of these centrifugal tendencies, many leaders of the 1822 movement feared that Brazil would follow the example of the Spanish colonies and split into several states after independence.[50]

It took some time for the Lisbon Cortes to come significantly to the question of Brazil's status within the Monarchy. The Liberal regime intended to reverse the semi-autonomous status of Brazil that the declaration of a Kingdom of Brazil appeared to concede in 1815, in order to integrate the Portuguese American territories more completely into their perception of the Monarchy. The objective was to concentrate authority, representation, and the exercise of power in the Portuguese capital once again, re-converting what unity had actually been constructed since 1808 into provinces directly dependent on Lisbon. Such a policy was regarded by the growing political factions in Rio de Janeiro as an affront. The predominance of Rio, as we have seen, had several times been openly challenged from the Brazilian provinces, in particular Bahia and Pernambuco. In this sense, the Portuguese American provinces had their own objectives, apart from those of the Cortes. With integration in mind, the Lisbon Cortes welcomed the adhesion of Pará and Bahia, through their respective *Juntas de governo* on March 27 and April 16, to the new constitutional system. Such a move seemed divisive in Rio. Two weeks after João VI finally arrived in Lisbon on June 30, the Cortes issued a Proclamation to the People of Brazil, reaffirming the unity of the Monarchy under the constitutional system.[51]

Roderick Barman argues against any proto-nationalist sentiment on the part of the Portuguese American provinces. By June 1821:

the 'Kingdom of Brazil' had dissolved into its constituent parts, not because of the machinations of the Lisbon Cortes but because of the desire of the local notables to recover provincial autonomy and to escape dominance by both Rio de Janeiro and Lisbon. Had this trend persisted, movements for total independence would

---

[50] Emilia Viotti da Costa, *The Brazilian Empire. Myths and Histories* (Chicago 1985), 9.
[51] Barman, *Brazil. The Forging of a Nation*, 73, 90–91.

probably have followed the precedent of 1817 rather than that of 1815, resulting in the creation of regional republics rather than a single state.[52]

Brazil in no sense constituted a unified entity ready to be transformed at Independence into a viable nation. On the contrary, its territories had become accustomed to view themselves as distinct entities, interconnected by loose links of economic necessity, though with little common perception or experience. Each regarded its own "pátria" as the principal reference. The term was not used in a *political* sense in the conspiracies of 1789, 1794, or 1798, and only appeared for the first time in the Pernambuco Rebellion of 1817. That was also when the term, "revolution," was applied in the French-Revolutionary sense. Accordingly, it would be erroneous to refer to one, single independence movement in Brazil: instead, there were a variety of *pátrias*, multiple issues, and differing perspectives. While it is true that the Minas Gerais gold boom of the 1690s to 1750s led to considerable integration of the south-eastern provinces, the northern provinces remained distinct. As Hendrik Kray points out, for the years 1820–25, "the Brazils were a series of Portuguese captaincies … that during these years stood between the competing governments in Lisbon and Rio de Janeiro." Support for the continued unity of the Lusitanian Monarchy in Bahia led the Lisbon Cortes, on May 23, 1822, to recommend dispatch of Portuguese troops to Salvador.[53]

After the king's departure for Lisbon, the Rio élite filled the political vacuum in the south-east. In reality, the intention was to subvert the liberal aspects of the constitutional system, most of all its strengthening of municipal and provincial governments, and to preserve as much of the old system as it could. Such an objective did not come from Rio de Janeiro alone, but from within the social and economic élites in the south-east. Accordingly, growing suspicion of the Lisbon Cortes' intentions implied no desire to return to the royal absolutism of pre-1820. The ideal would be a limited and bicameral form of constitutional government without provincial autonomy but with equal status for the American sector of the Monarchy under the Crown. This is what the *iturbidistas* also seemed to want in Mexico in 1821–23 and what the Lima élite would have preferred in Peru, but the course of events in Brazil took the opposite direction to those in Mexico, where a federal system based on compromise between

---

[52] Barman, *Brazil*, 66.
[53] Machado, *Formação do Brasil*, 123. Kray, *Race, State and Armed Forces*, 5, 108. Barman, *Brazil*, 92.

center and regions was implemented in 1823–25. The speedy recognition of the Lisbon constitutional system by the northern Juntas of Pará and Bahia, aligning with the Cortes, abandoned thereby the previous form of administration centered on Rio. The Cortes recognized the Bahia Junta on April 16 and authorized the formation of Governing Juntas throughout the remaining provinces, bringing to power their local notables. Their multiplication faced the Rio élite with the prospect of isolation in the American territory that they had previously thought they ruled. The threat to undermine the post-1808 system in Portuguese America seemed to come more from the Brazilian provinces than from the Lisbon Cortes. It began to appear as though Portuguese America was destined to repeat the centrifugalism of the Spanish American territories. The Rio Treasury, furthermore, was empty, plundered by the departing king, and little leeway existed for forcing the provinces into conformity.[54]

Reception of the measures taken by the Lisbon Cortes inflamed and radicalized opinion in the city. José Clemente Pereira, president of the city council, a body generally ignored under the absolute monarchy, lent his support, as *juíz de fora*, to the opposition in mid-December, and proposed that Minas Gerais and São Paulo should be brought into the campaign against the Cortes' measures. Pereira, on January 9, 1822, presented a formal petition with some 8000 signatories to D. Pedro requesting him to remain in Brazil and ignore the Cortes' order to return to Lisbon. This occasioned the Regent's famous declaration, "I am staying." The Rio city council, rather in the fashion of the Spanish American municipalities, became the principal body promoting the separate status of Brazil within the Monarchy. Similar roles were played by the city councils of the other south-eastern and southern provinces, Minas Gerais, São Paulo, Santa Catalina, and Rio Grande do Sul.[55]

The Portuguese Liberals and the south-eastern élites of Brazil had differing perceptions of the nature of constitutionalism and contradictory objectives. Since the Rio administration had already rescinded the earlier proscription of masonic lodges in June 1821 and permitted freedom of the press on August 28, opposing views could be publicly circulated and opinion legally organized. The Rio élite gravitated around D. Pedro and José Bonifácio de Andrada e Silva (1773–1838), vice-president of the São Paulo Junta, whose mentor had been Souza Coutinho. Scion of a wealthy

[54] Barman, *Brazil*, 73–75.
[55] Rodrigues, *Independência*, vol. I, 48, 139, 174, 234. Bethell, "Independence of Brazil," 183–85.

family from Santos on the province's Atlantic coast, he had, like many other upper-class Brazilians, received his higher education at the University of Coimbra, but remained in Portugal as a senior figure in the metropolitan administration. Married there, he had not returned to Brazil until 1819. As a result, he had witnessed at first hand the wartime devastation in Portugal.[56]

The Rio élite had rejected the incipient republicanism in the Pernambuco uprising of 1817 and feared the diffusion of political power implicit in the European liberal constitutional project. Both the movements of 1817 and 1821–24 in Pernambuco enlisted the support of free blacks and mulattoes, and the parallels with the evolving political alignments in Cartagena in 1810–15, for instance, were striking. In 1817, repression had fallen heavily on them. The provincial Junta of 1821–24 formed two battalions of blacks and mulattoes in recognition of the social and political weight of those sectors of the provincial population.[57]

Denis Bernardes has argued that the liberal perspectives of the Portuguese constitutionalists had a profound impact in north-east Brazil and formed the background to a renewed constitutional movement in Pernambuco in 1821–22. This he regards as an alternative to the traditionalist project of Rio and a direct challenge to Dom Pedro and José Bonifácio's vision of a monarchical Brazil outside the structures offered by the Lisbon Cortes.

The assertion of Brazilian independence, still maintaining union with Portugal, was intended to convey to the outside world the continued affirmation of monarquical legitimacy and dynastic continuity, while establishing a line of demarcation from the liberalism of the Cortes, which was denounced as the work of factious and destabilising elements.[58]

In this respect, provincial opposition to the Rio project saw in the Lisbon Cortes not so much the attempt to subordinate a divided Portuguese America to Lisbon once again, as a liberation from the south-eastern group, which would still preserve the hegemony of the Pernambuco property-owning élite through liberal-constitutionalist forms.

---

[56] Barman, *Brazil*, 82–85, 92.
[57] Denis Antônio de Mendonça Bernardes, *O patriotismo constitucional: Pernambuco, 1820–1822* (São Paulo and Recife 2001), 618–19, referring also to repeated tension between Portuguese Army officers and mulatto and free black militias in the colonial era.
[58] Rodrigues, *Independência*, I, 234, 261, 322–23. Barman, *Brazil*, 93–96. Bernardes, *O patriotismo constitucional*, 352.

The issue of balance within the Monarchy arose in the Lisbon Cortes just as it did in the two Spanish constitutional periods. In both cases, this issue involved not just relations between executive, legislature, and judiciary at the center of power but also the intensely contested matter of the distribution of power within the constitutional state – both territorial and social. Here the paths differed. Brazilian deputies, conscious of the large and growing free-black and mulatto population sought to have them included in the political processes. In contrast to the Cádiz Cortes, which had excluded African mixed-bloods ("castes") from political rights, the Brazilian deputies secured their inclusion in the Lisbon Cortes. This position was also maintained after Brazilian Independence in 1822, when free-blacks and mulattoes were included as part of the enfranchised component of the population. However, Emperor Pedro I's Constitution of 1824 barred freedmen from participating in the second tier of the election process. The south-eastern élites had in no sense weakened their commitment to slavery and the slave trade, the abolition of which they continued to resist. The rapid expansion of coffee cultivation in Rio de Janeiro's Paraíba Valley and in the province of São Paulo ensured that this would be the case for much of the nineteenth century.[59]

The Rio de Janeiro élite discovered, just as their counterparts in Buenos Aires, Caracas, and Santa Fe de Bogotá had done from 1810, that when they attempted to assert the supremacy of a hegemonic city, strong opposition would form within the outlying provinces. When, by June 1822, it became clear that the possibility of consensus between Lisbon and Rio had collapsed, it became equally clear that the government in Rio, declaring itself separate from the constitutional administration in Lisbon in September, would have to confront the opposition to separation across the north and north-east, where *Juntas de governo* had already replaced the royal-appointed provincial governors. In Pernambuco, for instance, this entailed the removal of the hated General Luís do Rego Barreto, who had led the repression of the 1817 movement. The Junta had selected the Pernambuco deputies to the Cortes. Pernambuco constitutionalists regarded separation from the Portuguese constitutional system by the Rio élite as a threat to the new liberal institutions, and they were determined to resist it. In Maranhão, a Junta Provisória displaced the Governor

[59] Schmidt-Nowara, *Slavery, Freedom, and Abolition*, 144–45. See also Stanley J. Stein, *Vassouras. A Brazilian Coffee County, 1850–1900* (New York 1970); Robert Conrad, *The Destruction of Brazilian Slavery, 1850–1888* (Berkeley, Los Angeles, London 1972). Kray, *Race, State, and Armed Forces*, 19.

and assumed power in 1821–23, reflecting the interests of the provincial landowners and, like Pará, pointing to its direct dependence on Lisbon rather than Rio.[60]

This conflict of interests within Brazil destroyed any prospect of a harmonious autonomy within the Lusitanian Monarchy. Initially, it started as a conflict with Portuguese troops based in America, but, more fundamentally, it became a conflict between the south-eastern elites and the north and north-east, which remained closely oriented to the Portuguese metropolis. These deeply-rooted tensions, anticipated since the 1790s, broke out once more into open warfare, this time over distinct views on the nature of the constitutional system and the distribution of power within it. The city councils of Rio de Janeiro, São Paulo, and in Minas Gerais played the decisive role in promoting separation from Lisbon, and they did so in support of Dom Pedro, who had refused the Cortes' request to return to Portugal. Taking the lead in advocating the south-eastern position was the newspaper *Revérbero Constitucional Fluminense*, which began publishing in September 1821, during the course of 1822. The term "despotism" became applied to the conduct of the Lisbon Cortes rather than to the absolute monarchy, as it was in liberal vocabulary. This paper began to identify the future of "Brazil" in a more radical vein than the élite consensus, as an independent sovereign state like those of Spanish America and the United States. It saw the "pátria" no longer as each of the separate provinces, but as the entire territory of Portuguese America. The Coimbra-educated section of the élite, however, continued to argue for the unity of the Lusitanian Monarchy but they understood this in a different sense to the Cortes Liberals. Their version implied that Brazil, rather than a desperate Portugal, should be the center of this Monarchy. Rio de Janeiro would become again, as in 1808–21, the capital, not Lisbon. José da Silva Lisboa, for example, hoped for continued union under the Braganza dynasty though not under the terms set by the Lisbon Cortes, which, he argued was abusing Portugal's status as the prospective metropolis.[61]

In that sense, Brazilian separatism, imposed from the cities of the south-east, remained monarchical and dynastic. The divergence from the republican models of the Spanish American states in the process of formation in

[60] Matthias Röhrig Assunção, *De Caboclos a Bem-Te-Vis. Formação do campesinato numa sociedade escravista: Maranhão, 1800–1850* (São Paulo 2015), 284–90. Bernades, *O patriotismo constitucional*, 315–54: see pp. 324–31.

[61] Pereira das Neves, *Corundas e Constitucionais*, 173–74, 184, 201, 221–23.

the River Plate, Chile, New Granada, and Venezuela was striking. This Brazilian divergence masked, however, notable similarities with Spanish America. Not least of these was the struggle of the elites to preserve their position within the new polities, whether in relation to the social forces below them or to the rival poles of power in the provinces. Capital-city struggles with the provinces beset virtually all of the former Hispanic-American territories. In Brazil, they characterized the period of the pseudo-republic between the fall of Emperor Pedro I in 1831 and the proclamation of the majority of Pedro II in 1844.

The political transformation in Brazil, realizing in practice in 1822 the potential of the 1815 decree (unexplored at the time by the Court), was designed to preserve the existing social structure and the commercial relationships institutionalized in 1808 and 1810. This readjustment within the Braganza dynasty took place against the background of the Congress System and the Holy Alliance in post-1815 Europe, the Austrian intervention against the Italian Liberal revolutions in 1821, and discussion during the following year of the possibility of intervention by Royalist France in order to remove the Spanish Liberals from power. The Rio de Janeiro elite seized control of the administration in Portuguese America, left over by the departed king, with the intention of controverting the objectives of the Lisbon Cortes and imposing its view on the rest of the country. They portrayed this as a patriotic struggle to prevent the fragmentation of the "Kingdom of Brazil." This meant that the term "union" henceforth acquired a new meaning. In the first place it implied the reversal of the municipal and provincial liberties initiated by the Cortes and the preservation of the pre-1820 system without a return to royal absolutism. Instead, there was to be a limited and bicameral constitutionalism without provincial autonomy.[62]

The architect in the Brazilian process was José Bonifácio, whom D. Pedro appointed Minister of Internal and External Affairs on January 16 1822. President of the Masonic Grand Orient of Rio de Janeiro from late May of that year, he acted as the main barrier to radical pressure for more substantial political change. José Bonifácio, however, still stood for the continued unity of the Monarchy, with Brazil as a self-governing Kingdom inside it. In accordance with that position, he coordinated the convocation of a Brazilian *Constituent* Assembly in Rio de Janeiro on June 3, 1822, after the city council, with radicals led by Joaquim Gonçalves Ledo in the forefront, had petitioned D. Pedro

---

[62] Pereira das Neves, *Corundas e Constitucionais*, 16, 173, 203.

on May 24 to summon such a body. No one within the governing circle in Rio conceived this at that time as other than within the context of the Lusitanian Monarchy. The role of the urban notables, who considered themselves to be "the people," transferred the constitutional principle in modified form to the colony, implicitly limiting royal power, which, until the meeting of the Lisbon Cortes, had been absolute. The existence of a Constituent Assembly implied the exercise of sovereignty and its utilization for the purpose of legitimizing political change.[63]

May and June 1822 represented the turning-point in the relationship between the predominant group in Rio and the Portuguese Cortes in Lisbon. The latter completely rejected the idea of a Brazilian Constituent Assembly as a challenge to and violation of its own exercise of sovereignty. The Rio leadership may have borrowed from Spanish Royalists the idea that the king had been made captive by the Cortes, in order further to legitimize the assumption of power by D. Pedro in his "absence." The intention was to repudiate the authority of the Lisbon Cortes, which, in turn, rejected the idea of an autonomous government in Brazil in mid-August and late in the following month annulled the decree convoking the Brazilian Constituent Assembly.[64]

The protracted arrival of the Brazilian deputies, however, introduced yet another provincial dimension into the controversy over the future structure of the Monarchy. For their part, the São Paulo deputies in the Lisbon Cortes favored the federalization of the Monarchy, much as the Mexican deputies in the Madrid Cortes were proposing to the Spanish Liberal ministry. In accordance with instructions drawn up by José Bonifácio on behalf of the São Paulo Governing Junta early in October 1821 and known as the *Lembranças e Apontamentos*, the deputies continued to take their stand on the unity of the Lusitanian Monarchy, which they viewed as integral and indivisible, but at the same time they argued that the metropolitan government should uphold the special status of the "Kingdom of Brazil" as an equal partner of Portugal within this Monarchy. They presented the Junta's representation to the Cortes on June 17, 1822. The practical objective was the establishment of a separate Cortes for the American sector of the Monarchy. In effect, there would be a Dual Monarchy, each sector with internal

---

[63] Rodrigues, *Independência*, I, 261, 323. Toledo Machado, *Formação do Brasil*, 114–15. Barman, *Brazil*, 93–94. D. Pedro's wife was the daughter of the Austrian Habsburg Emperor.

[64] Barman, *Brazil*, 96. Paquette, *Imperial Portugal*, 153–55.

autonomy. The king would divide his time between the two sectors of the realm. When the king was not in Brazil, the heir to the throne should exercise executive power there. As in the case of the Spanish American deputies in Madrid, they requested equal representation in the Cortes for these sectors. A general Cortes would convene in Lisbon for the purpose of coordinating commercial, fiscal, and defense policy. They shied away from using the term federalism, despite relative familiarity with the United States' system among the Brazilian elites. The *Lembranças* was one of the most important documents of the Portuguese constitutional period. The suggestion of autonomy and a distinct Cortes brought home to the metropolitan government the matter of the still unresolved question of the status of Brazil within the Monarchy. Issues such as these, furthermore, had stunted American support for the Cádiz and Madrid Cortes of 1810–14 and were once more in the course of alienating American deputies in the Madrid Cortes of 1821–22. It is striking that at this apparently late stage the thoughts of the São Paulo deputies were still toward upholding the unity of the Lusitanian Monarchy.[65]

Other Portuguese American provinces pursued their own path, suggesting that the formation of a Brazilian sovereign state might be transformed from imposition by the south-east by merchant and planter notables into either a compromise favorable to the provinces or the result of an armed confrontation. Even if the north-east and north should be defeated, the transition from absolutism to some form of constitutional government in Brazil would mark a significant departure from the political structures and practices of the colonial era. Accordingly, we should not assume that in Brazil the preservation of the Braganza dynasty and slavery indicated that nothing much changed after 1822. On the contrary, the nature and practice of politics changed considerably. Furthermore, the relatively frequent outbreak of armed conflict in the form of provincial rebellions with a profound social content after 1824 pointed to the degree of discontent across the country with the political solution imposed in 1822–23. Many provinces, such as Bahia, were deeply divided. Bahian deputies finally arrived in the Brazilian Constituent Assembly on June 20, 1823. This Assembly considered Brazil as a unity, which, in reality, it was not.[66]

---

[65] Luis Henrique Dias Tavares, *A Independência do Brasil na Bahia* (Rio de Janeiro 1977), 23. Fátima Sá de Melo Ferreira, "Federalismo: Portugal," in Javier Fernández Sebastián (Director), *Diccionario político y social del mundo iberoamericano* (Madrid 2009), 525–35: p. 526. Barman, *Brazil*, pp. 76–77.

[66] Evaldo Cabral de Mello, *A outra Independência. O federalismo pernambucano de 1817 a 1824* (São Paulo 2004), pp. 18–19, views the Brazilian unity posited by Rio de Janeiro as

Dom Pedro's effective declaration of Brazil's sovereign status on September 7, 1822, although rallying Minas Gerais and São Paulo behind him, did not resolve the question of Brazilian Independence: in terms of emancipation it only began it. The provinces, for instance, experienced parallel but distinct processes. Arguing from the perspective of Pernambuco, Evaldo Cabral de Mello points to colonial antecedents, going back to the struggle against the Dutch in this province during the first part of the seventeenth century. The north-east regarded its reunification with Portuguese America and return at that time to Portuguese sovereignty as consensual, a voluntary contract between province and monarch. The crown, the argument went, had violated this contract by imposing new taxes and administrative officials who had not been natives of the province. In Cabral de Mello's view, the struggles of 1817–24 represented local attempts to recover lost rights. Furthermore, new fiscal pressures resulting from the establishment of the Royal government in Rio rekindled regional sentiment and the demand for autonomy.[67]

It is difficult to determine how deeply this thesis of historic precedents permeated provincial society or whether it was an *ex post facto* attempt to legitimize political opposition. Whatever the conclusion, to focus on this loses sight of the uniqueness of both 1817 and 1821–24, which were products less of an unbroken tradition trailing back into a seventeenth-century past, but more about the issues of their time. These, too, were distinct, since the latter movement occurred within the unique context of a constitutionalizing of the entire Luso-Brazilian Monarchy for the first time.

The unsanctioned departure of seven Brazilian deputies, four of them representing São Paulo and the other three Bahia, from the Lisbon Cortes in October 1822 may be regarded as a decisive factor in the division between metropolitan Portugal and Brazil. They fled first to London and thence back to Brazil. The explanation lay in their opposition to the projected Constitution of 1822.[68]

The fracture of the Lisbon Cortes and the rising conservative opposition across Portugal, especially in the northern provinces of Tras-os-Montes and the Minho, exposed the Liberal regime to the prospect of

---

a travesty. Rodrigues, *Independência*, I, 323, 326. Bahia recognized D. Pedro in November 1822. Kray, *Race, State, and Armed Forces*, 3–4, 48–49, 106–8. Röhrig Assunção, *De Caboclos e Bem-Te-Vis*, 290–93.

[67] Cabral de Mello, *A outra Independência*, 20–21, 29–30, 45.

[68] George C. A. Boehrer, "The Flight of the Brazilian Deputies from the Cortes Gerais of Lisbon, 1822," HAHR, 40, iv (November 1960), 497–512.

intervention from the continental Congress Powers. Although the Tory administration in power in London no more sympathized with Portuguese Liberalism than it did with Spanish, Great Britain still remained an informal guardian of Portuguese independence, determined to prevent intervention by other European Powers, especially Bourbon France. The likelihood, however, was that the Portuguese Liberals would be brought down by their own divisions and the strength of domestic opposition.[69]

THE SECOND EXTINCTION OF LIBERALISM IN SPAIN

The failure of moderate Liberals to secure a bicameral system with representation in the Upper House for members of the nobility, and the clear hostility of Spanish Royalists to anything but the restoration of the traditional Cortes of the three estates increased the likelihood of French intervention in Spain. The French government's priority was to extinguish what it believed to be the Spanish equivalent of the Convention of 1793. Austrian intervention in Naples in December 1820 had started the process of extinguishing the revolutionary movements by agreement among the continent-European Powers at the Congress of Verona, which had begun its sessions on October 20, 1822. No official Spanish representatives were present at this Congress. For French Ultra-Royalists, pressing the government of the Comte de Villèle for prompt action, intervention in Spain would take the form of a crusade in defense of Throne and Altar.[70]

French troops were already stationed on the Catalan frontier in November 1822 as a *cordon sanitaire*. The response among radicals in Barcelona was exultant and defiant. The *Diario Constitucional* reported a meeting of the "Patriotic Society of Lacy" on November 22, in which "Citizen" Moreno García declared that the Spanish people had no fear of French forces, since they had fought them tenaciously in 1808–14, a struggle that had given liberty back to Europe and spread fear among tyrants. War with France, he had proclaimed, would provide the opportunity for doing away with "the cowardly moderates," the cause of present-day woes. He had cried, "Long Live the Constitution!" and "Long Live the Sovereign People!" This was taken up by "Citizen" Casas, roundly attacking the moderates and denouncing the clergy: It was time to

---

[69] Alexandre, *Os Sentido do Império*, 596, 609–38, 713–51 refers to "a desagregação do regime."

[70] Comellas, *Trieno constitucional*, 388–93.

seize their immense wealth at a time when the Army and the People lived in misery. Applause greeted his cry that Spain had nothing to fear from foreign powers. Clamorous applause greeted cries of "Death to the *serviles!*" and "Death to the moderates!"[71]

The British Foreign Minister, Canning, vainly hoped that a modification of the 1812 Constitution might be possible in order to forestall a French intervention in Spain, but the Cortes session of January 9, 1823, dominated by the radicals, dashed all possibility of that. In the following month, a mob gathered outside the Royal Palace in Madrid calling for the deposition of the king, who saw in the possibility of foreign intervention a final chance of ridding himself of the constitutionalists. Fearing invasion, the Cortes and government transferred to Seville, taking a protesting king with them. In Seville, Ferdinand VII was deposed on the grounds of moral and physical incapacity under article 187 of the Constitution, and a Regency established, consisting of three generals, Vigodet, Císcar, and Cayetano Valdés. On April 7, the French "Hundred-Thousand Sons of St. Louis," commanded by the Duc d'Angoulême, crossed into Spain, where military commanders, hitherto loyal to the constitutional regime, sought accommodation with their French counterparts. The Cortes and government retreated to Cádiz with the king. From June 23, the French began the blockade of Cádiz. Barcelona remained the only other city in Liberal hands. By September 4, the defenders of Cádiz sought an accord with Angoulême on the basis of a general amnesty. The latter, however, would deal only with a freed king directly. After bombardment of the city, the Liberal regime collapsed and, on September 30, Ferdinand VII was released, under the assumption that a king who had never kept his word on anything, would honor an amnesty.[72]

The Spanish Ultra-Royalists, it turned out, could expect no assistance from either the French Royalists or from their own king. Accordingly, they complained, this time to Metternich, that the French – and Louis XVIII in particular – had never helped the Regency of Urgel when it was in opposition to the Liberal regime. Furthermore, the French Army, when it had crossed the Spanish border, had ordered the disbandment of the "Royalist Army of Spain."[73]

---

[71] AAE CP 720, ff. 189–91, extrait du *Diario Constitucional de Barcelona*, 24–25 November 1822.
[72] Comellas, *Trienio constitucional*, 395–97, 410–22, 430–31.
[73] ARPO PR FVII, vol. 22, ff. 335–40v, Regents to Metternich, Perpignan 2 August 1823.

The extent of Liberal failure to engrain a constitutional form of government in Spain – or to agree among themselves – became abundantly clear. Isolated and finished, Liberal leaders faced no other option but exile or arrest and the death penalty for deposing the king. In their place, a vengeful king and armed royalist bands could not be restrained even by the French government and its military commanders. Ferdinand's first act as a free agent, following the example set by his Valencia Decree of May 4, 1814, was to nullify everything legislated since March 1820. Villanueva and Calatrava went into exile in London, and Flórez Estrada, initially trapped in Granada, eventually followed them. Toreno and Martínez de la Rosa went to Paris. Royalist partisans hunted down Riego, tried him in Madrid and had him publicly hanged on November 7, 1823.[74]

After the Royalist recovery of Madrid on April 23, 1823, a Regency was set up, quite different from the pseudo-Regency of Urgel. The capital-city Regency was presided over by Infantado, the richest nobleman in Spain. Another prominent nobleman with an even more ambiguous political history, Montijo, commented concerning the second collapse of Liberalism, that it had been as impossible in 1822–23 to uphold the Cádiz Constitution of 1812 as it had been to sustain "despotism" before 1808. Writing to La Bisbal, Montijo attributed this impossibility to the "fundamental contradictions and destructive principles" inherent in Liberalism.[75]

Other grandees hoped for a swift return to the pre-1820 or even pre-1810 order of things. As in the recent past, the nobility showed no unity of purpose and no clear political direction. Trusting that the extinction of liberalism would restore their seigneurial rights, they appealed to the Regency on June 22. The Regents, however, simply reissued the king's ambivalent decree of September 15, 1814, demonstrating the latter's lack of interest in siding with senior noblemen in their quest for lost revenues. When, finally, a royal decree was published on August 15, 1825, the king upheld the Cortes' position of 1813 that the presentation of land titles should be the requisite for the right to receive rents.[76]

---

[74] Vicente Llorens, *Liberales y Románticos. Una emigración española en Inglaterra, 1823–34* (Madrid 1968). Manuel Pérez Ledesma and Isabel Burdiel (eds.), *Liberales eminentes* (Madrid 2008), 37–38, 41.

[75] ARPO PR FVII, vol. 21, ff. 44–45, Montijo to La Bisbal, Madrid 11 May 1823.

[76] AHN Consejos 6086, consulta 4 December 1823.

Instead of an amnesty law, Ferdinand issued the decree of October 4, 1823, which swept away all hope of clemency. The king fell into the hands of an ultra-Royalist clique led by canon Víctor Sáez. Liberal leaders fled to Gibraltar, bound for England or France in exile. Many others were put under arrest.[77] The capitulations between constitutionalist forces and the French Army were disregarded by the Spanish royal government and some 80,000 men were left abandoned. The French diplomatic representatives were appalled at the turn of events in Spain. The Ambassador commented that "a total reaction has taken place." Seville was full of refugees whom the decree of October 4 had banished from Madrid. Many persons of birth and wealth were persecuted. The Duque de Frías, for example, had been driven out of Seville by a vindictive Captain General. In Murcia and Valencia, royalist authorities were out of control. In his view, no one took any notice of the ministry, not even in Madrid. The Conde de Ofalia (1775–1847), a moderate royalist, was the leading figure as Minister of Grace and Justice from December 2, 1823 to January 18, 1824 and as Minister of State from then until his fall on July 11, 1824 and internal exile. The Ultra-Royalists despised him. Their paper, "El Restaurador," thundered down on the heads of moderates and Liberals alike. Undisciplined but armed royalist bands created disorders across the country, as though no government existed at all. Most of the clergy opposed the ministry and all French influence, which they saw as a potential threat to their renewed position of strength. While the Catalan littoral remained constitutionalist in sentiment, royalist bands roved the countryside.[78]

The only hope for French diplomacy, the Ambassador believed, was in aligning with the more enlightened segment of the clergy in the hope of placing the highest classes of society in a position of influence. He regarded Ofalia as a key figure in such a process. The exclusion of anyone suspected of being sympathetic to the previous constitutional regime meant that there were very few persons capable of exercising ministerial positions. In the Ambassador's view, the decree of October 4 ought to be revoked.[79]

The question of the system of government in Spain had become an issue among the Great Powers. The center of discontent lay with the French,

---

[77] Josep Fontana, *De en medio del tiempo. La segunda restauración española, 1823–1834* (Barcelona 2006), 70–99.

[78] AAE CP Espagne 726, ff. 129–34, Talaru to Chateaubriand, *Coup d'oeuil sur l'Espagne*, 30 January 1824.

[79] AAE CP Espagne 726, ibid.

who had initiated the intervention in the first place. Government, such as it was, could be described as "organised anarchy," with the multiplicity of councils, each of which considered it had the right to issue official statements, without first informing ministers. "One could say that everything here conspires to prevent proper functioning." Spain, furthermore, continued to insist on its full sovereignty over the American territories. While no one denied that on principle, the Ambassador emphasized that realities were different. Great Britain and the United States wanted free commercial access. The former was threatening to recognize the separated colonies if it did not secure this; the latter spread republican propaganda, supported insurgents, and aspired to head a Pan-American Confederation.[80] Talaru pressed for an amnesty law encompassing both Spain and the Empire. The royalist bands he compared to the counter-revolutionary Vendée rebels of the 1790s, regarding them as a serious threat to the restoration of order in the country. The King opposed any suggestion of amnesty. Talaru urged a Joint Memorandum from the Powers to be presented to the Council of State, although the Spanish government was in such disarray that only inaction and time-wasting would be the likely result. Everyone, he maintained, was aware that Spain had lost her continental-American Empire, and the lack of funds ensured that there would be no hope of ever getting it back.[81]

The French had one strong counter to play: They could threaten the withdrawal of their forces, if the Spanish government continued to oppose an amnesty. Counter-revolutionaries in Spain, however, were calling for the death penalty for all those involved in the aborted revolution. Talaru considered the publication of the Decree of Amnesty of May 12, 1824 to be a triumph of French diplomacy. He had threatened troop withdrawal and warned the king that Spain would become the pariah of Europe otherwise. Talaru complained to Chateaubriand that it had taken six months to persuade the king to agree, and even then he doubted Ferdinand's willingness to comply. Ostensibly, the decree pardoned all but the principal figures of the period from January 1820 to October 1, 1823 – "date of my restitution to the plenitude of rights of my legitimate sovereignty." There were, however, fifteen categories of exclusion from the amnesty, such as Europeans who had collaborated with O'Donojú and

---

[80] AAE CP Espagne 726, ff. 6–12v, Talaru to Chateaubriand, no. 1, Madrid 3 January 1824; ff. 152–59v, Talaru to Chateaubriand, no. 21, Madrid 5 February 1824.
[81] AAE CP Espagne 726, ff. 123–28, Talaru to Chateaubriand, no. 18, Madrid 20 January 1824.

Iturbide in signing the Treaties of Córdoba and supporters of the constitutional system in the Americas. Talaru warned that everything depended on the willingness of the Council of Castile and the Captains General to allow the decree to take effect.[82]

Much to the annoyance of French diplomats, the king decided to issue a new decree on political "purifications," as a complement to the amnesty decree. This appeared in the *Gaceta de Madrid* on August 24. It included all military personnel from the rank of ensign upwards, if they had served under the constitutional system. That meant practically everyone. Boislecomte complained that such a course would provoke a climate of denunciation in the country, where no law existed against calumny.[83]

Although the second extinction of Liberalism may be seen within the context of the European Counter-Revolution, Liberal divisions and the parallel failure to extend their popular base through a wider span of rural areas also provided explanations. Peasant and small-town Royalism did not imply identity or sympathy with seigneurial rights. Opposition to big-city Liberalism, enforced in the localities by the regular army, mobilized widespread support in defense of traditional religion and customs. Liberal privatizing measures, which affected civil and ecclesiastical properties, combined with Liberal definitions of property rights and the intention to defend them, inflamed injured communities when living standards for the rural and urban lower classes remained precarious.[84]

It seems clear also that the breach between the king and D. Carlos, figurehead for the Ultra-Royalists and one of the strongest opponents of amnesty, occurred during the *Trienio*. The king, by October 1824, appeared to be listening increasingly to the more moderate Francisco Cea Bermúdez (1772–1850), his Secretary of State, as well as to the ultras.[85] Ferdinand VII, however, remained for the following ten years of his reign resolutely opposed to the convocation of any type of Cortes, traditional or otherwise, and to any form of Constitution. News in July 1824 that the Portuguese king intended to convoke a *cortes* in

[82] AAE CP Espagne 727, ff. 15–19, Talaru to Chateaubriand, no. 61, Madrid 5 April 1824; ff. 90–94, Talaru to Chateaubriand, no. 68, Madrid 5 May 1824; ff. 192–6v, Talaru to Chateaubriand, no. 78, Aranjuez 9 June 1824.

[83] AAE CP Espagne 728, ff. 27–35v, Boislecomte to Damas, no. 8, Madrid 25 August 1824.

[84] Dérozier, *Quintana*, 650. Torras Elías, *Liberalismo y rebeldía campesina*, 18–19, 22, 26, 30–31.

[85] AAE CP Espagne 729, ff. 76–87, Boislecomte to Damas, no. 41, El Escorial 12 October 1824, f. 78; ff. 119–9v, Boislecomte to Damas, no. 45, El Escorial 19 October 1824. Cea would become a key figure in the transition from absolutism to moderate constitutionalism in the period 1832–34.

Lisbon, although one consisting of the traditional three estates, created alarm in Madrid, especially in view of the support for this from the Diplomatic Corps in Portugal. The news appeared to have made Ferdinand waver in compliance with the amnesty decree.[86]

THE COLLAPSE OF LIBERALISM IN PORTUGAL

This took place in a different way to the Spanish experience. First, the principal opposition to the Cortes came from the queen, Carlota Joaquina, who had refused to swear to the 1822 Constitution, and her younger son, Dom Miguel. Allied to them were the ecclesiastical hierarchy led by the Cardinal-Archbishop of Lisbon, and the senior nobility led by the Duque de Cadaval and the Conde de Amarante, head of the Silveira family of Trás-os-Montes, who had already led a revolt in Chaves in February, with strong support in the provinces of Beira and the Minho. Division within Liberal ranks, the paralysis of government in 1822–23, and opposition from the countryside created the conditions for a military intervention that terminated the Liberal experiment in Portugal. However, this termination took a remarkably different form from its parallel in Spain. In the first place, there was no French-Bourbon military intervention in Portugal. The British, in any case, would never have allowed this. Furthermore, the divisions within the royal family, which came in their gravity to resemble those at the Spanish Court between 1805 and 1808, not only destabilized political life throughout the country but had an international dimension as well.[87]

The coup of May 27, 1823, known in Portuguese history as the "Vilafrancada," which extinguished the Liberal regime, did not lead immediately to denunciation and persecution. João VI, who had sworn to observe the unicameral Liberal Constitution on October 1, 1822, favored a milder form of constitutional rule on the lines of the French Charter of 1814, thereby preferring the French model of the Restoration to the Spanish. The Conde de Palmela (1781–1850), who had opposed the 1822 Constitution as too radical, began to devise a moderated form of constitutionalism in September 1823 and February 1824. The queen and D. Miguel, their eyes on Ferdinand VII's regime in Spain, both opposed even that and sought unsuccessfully to remove the king from the throne with the assistance of the Lisbon garrison. Re-established in control, the

---

[86] AAE CP Espagne727, ff. 283–38, Talaru to Villèle, no. 87, Madrid 21 July 1824.
[87] Paquette, *Imperial Portugal*, 112–14, 179, 184.

king exiled D. Miguel to Vienna, but promised on June 5, 1824 to convene a traditional-style Cortes, in an attempt to sort out the country's political future. Clearly, different concepts of constitutionalism were in the air in Portugal, as in the different context of Brazil, during the first half of the 1820s. The later eighteenth-century idea of a reconstruction of the "traditional constitution" derived from the "fundamental laws of the realm," which also had a certain currency in Spain before and during the first constitutional period, as we have seen, remained one of the options. Domestic fears and international disapproval of the Cádiz Constitution of 1812 and the Portuguese Constitution of 1822, and the example of Emperor Pedro I's dissolution of the Brazilian Constituent Assembly in November 1823, combined to make these constitutional forms seem unacceptably radical during the Restoration era. Pedro, however, granted the Constitutional Charter of 1824 to his Brazilian subjects, as we shall see in the following chapter.[88]

The death of João VI in March 1826 produced a succession crisis with extraordinary dimensions, since the heir was the Emperor Pedro I of Brazil in the form of King Pedro IV of Portugal. Furthermore, Portugal, under British pressure, had recognized the independence of Brazil on April 29, 1825. Rather than presage a reunion of the two separated branches of the Lusitanian monarchy, Pedro handed the Portuguese royal title down to his infant daughter, Maria II, and offered a revised version of the Brazilian Charter of 1824 to Portugal in April 1826. It seemed, at least for a time, that despite independence in 1822 Portugal and Brazil still remained inseparable. Such a view, however, was deceptive, especially since D. Pedro's involvement in Portuguese affairs was criticized in Brazil.[89]

The question of who was to be Regent in Portugal arose. The obvious choice was Maria's uncle, D. Miguel, but he was champion of the absolutist cause. Rebellions in his favor broke out in central and southern Portugal in autumn 1826, with support from Spain. The London Protocol of January 12, 1828 did provide for the Regency of D. Miguel, but on condition that he governed in accordance with the 1826 Charter. Instead, the latter took power for himself as King Miguel I and scrapped the Charter. In order to legitimize his action, he convened a traditional Cortes of the three estates, but began a far-reaching persecution of

---

[88] Paquette, *Imperial Portugal*, 126–30, 134–40, 158–63, 182–85. See the following chapter.

[89] NA FO 63/340, Marquês (formerly Conde) de Palmela (Portuguese Ambassador) to Earl of Dudley (Foreign Secretary), London 23 May 1828. Macaulay, *Dom Pedro*, 229. Paquette, *Imperial Portugal*, 164–65, 170–73, 178–79, 200.

known opponents. The Great Powers opposed D. Miguel's extreme measures, and even the Visconde de Santarém and the Conde de Barbacena, both inside the regime, blanched at that prospect. The consequent polarization between the defenders of the rights of Maria II, mainly the proscribed Liberal Party with its British support, and the proponents of absolutism, Cadaval and the higher nobility, parish priests and peasants across the countryside, principally in the north and center, degenerated into a civil war, which would last until 1834. Government finances languished in disarray.[90]

In due course, the initiative was taken by the Conde de Saldanha (1790–1876), a grandson of Pombal and already a decorated veteran of the Peninsular War. A strong opponent of D. Miguel, he was believed to be in concert with the Liberals, though it is doubtful that he was ideologically one of them. The British minister, unsympathetic to the Liberals, had formed a relatively good opinion of him. The Minister incidentally described himself as a target for hostile criticism from all the Portuguese parties.[91]

Saldanha's career illustrated those earlier imperial careers across the Lusitanian Monarchy. He had fought in the Banda Oriental with Portuguese forces from Brazil against Artigas from 1815 and had been appointed Governor of Rio Grande do Sul in 1821. Upon the secession of Brazil, he returned to the home country, determined to thwart any French Bourbon intervention in Portugal and a restoration of absolutism on the Spanish model. He was briefly Minister of War in 1826, but was then sentenced to death in British exile by D. Miguel in 1828. From the following year, Saldanha, along with Palmela, became the leading émigré opponents of D. Miguel's regime, though from different political perspectives. Palmela, in 1832, became President of the Regency

---

[90] NA, FO 63/340, *Protocol de la Conference tenue á Londres*, 12 January 1828; FO 63/336, J. R. Matthew (British Minister in Lisbon) to Lord Dunglass (Under-Secretary), no. 24, Lisbon 30 August 1828 and no. 78, Lisbon 31 December 1828; FO 63/357, no folio numbers, Mr. Thompson (Lord Mayor) to Lord Aberdeen, Mansion House, London, 29 September 1829, on the plight of British bondholders. FO 63/334, 5 December 1829, on the dire condition of Portuguese finances. AAE CP Portugal 145, ff. 9–12v, M. Meneuil to Comte de la Ferronais (Foreign Minister), no. 18, Lisbon 3 June 1828; ff. 21–215, Meneuil to La Ferronais, no. 20, Lisbon 7 June 1828; ff. 209–10, no. 151, M. Blanchet to Baron de Rayneval (chargé du portefeuille), Lisbon 30 August 1828. AAE CP Portugal 146, ff. 272–3v, Blanchet to Polignac, no. 101, Lisbon 5 September 1829: "the constitutional party is reduced to impotence" – many arrests in Lisbon, Alentejo, and the Algarve.

[91] NA FO 63/332, no. 72, William A'Court to Canning, Lisbon 4 May 1827; no. 83, A'Court to Canning, Lisbon 24 May 1827.

established in the Azores at Terceira in 1829 on behalf of Maria II. By the time D. Miguel was finally forced from power and the Liberals, monarchists led by noblemen and supported by the British, had taken office again, the First Carlist War had already broken out in Spain, in which the partisans of D. Carlos, their strength in the far north and the Valencian interior, sought to remove the Spanish Liberals from power in Madrid. In Portugal, Palmela became Principal Minister under Maria II from September 1834 to May 1835, to be succeeded by his rival, Saldanha, the architect of the military victory over the *miguelistas*, who became President of the Council of Ministers.[92]

[92] Macaulay, *Dom Pedro*, 187–98. Paquette, *Imperial Portugal*, 256–57, 270–76.

9

The Divergence of the American Territories and the Collapse of Their Former Metropoles (1820–1830)

THE BRAZILIAN EMPIRE AS A TRADITIONALIST STATE

On November 12, 1823, D. Pedro, already Emperor of Brazil, dissolved the Constituent Assembly, probably influenced by events in Spain and Portugal. In Brazil, however, absolutism was not restored. Instead, the Emperor, who regarded democracy as demagoguery, granted his own version of a Constitutional Charter on March 25, 1824. It was written within a month by the Council of State and provided for a bicameral legislature, of which the Senate would be appointed for life by the Emperor. As in 1822, deputies would be chosen through a tier system of indirect election, beginning at the parish level and supervised by the town or city councils' presidents. Elections would be held every four years. The deputies would represent the eighteen provinces of José Bonifácio's administrative reorganization in June 1822. A fourth power, the Moderating Power, provided for the Emperor's role as arbiter between the separate powers.[1]

The restrictive, centralist, and monarchist nature of these measures provoked a vehement reaction in the north and north-eastern provinces, linked politically to the earlier movement of 1817. The insurrection led by the cleric, Frei Caneca, in Pernambuco, which began in July 1824, rejected the Court's attempted solution for the Brazilian Empire. Caneca argued

[1] Gilberto Vilar de Carvalho, *A liderança do clero nas revoluções republicanas, 1817–1824* (Petrópolis 1979), 100–2. Macaulay, *Dom Pedro*, 152, 162–65. Toledo Machado, *Formação do Brasil*, 115–18. Rodrigues, *Independência*, I, 4–5. Paquette, *Imperial Portugal*, 155–63, 166–78, where the influence of Benjamin Constant's ideas is also discussed.

that the Emperor's dissolution of the Constituent Assembly signified that the union between the Portuguese American provinces had also been dissolved. He regarded the action as threatening a dynastic autocracy. In Caneca's view, Brazil's separation from Portugal had meant the separation of the provinces from one another and that one province did not depend on any other. Such a view rejected the primacy of Rio de Janeiro. Six northern provinces formed the *Confederação do Equador*, which was republican but not separatist. The Emperor suspended constitutional guarantees in Pernambuco as a prelude to the naval blockade of Recife and military suppression of the rebellion. Fifteen leaders, including Caneca, defrocked by the Bishop of Rio de Janeiro, were executed. The Confederation had taken the United States as a model, though it preferred the Articles of Confederation of 1776 to the Constitution of 1787. Its defeat halted, but did not extinguish, the movement for federalism in Brazil or opposition from the provinces to the system installed in Rio de Janeiro. On the contrary, a series of social and regional rebellions confronted the governing élites throughout the 1830s, 1840s, and into the 1850s.[2]

Bernardes explains the military campaign against the north-east and the ensuing repression in terms of a democratic constitutionalism in the regions opposed to the restrictions imposed from Rio. The Brazilian Empire, with a centralizing intent, faced a major challenge from the idea of a devolved state composed of self-governing provinces.[3] This field of tension had already burst into armed conflict in 1817 and again in 1821–23. It provided a *leitmotiv* throughout the rest of nineteenth-century and early twentieth-century Brazilian history.

The Brazilian Empire was intended to be the structure for preserving south-eastern hegemony. The consequence was the marginalization of the north-east, with its Afro-Brazilian majority population. The defeat of the rebellions of the 1790s to 1850s confirmed this. The expansion of coffee cultivation in the south-east, particularly in São Paulo, reinforced the political predominance of that zone. It also meant that Brazil continued to be a predominantly rural society after Independence, as it was before it.

---

[2] Manuel Correia de Andrade (organizador), *Confederação do Equador* (Recife 1988). Vilar de Carvalho, *A liderança do clero*, 52, 54–58, 60, 136, 140. Cabral de Mello, *A outra Independência*, 44–47. The Confederation also appealed for support to the provinces of São Paulo and Rio de Janeiro. See Jeffrey C. Mosher, *Political Struggle, Ideology and State-Building: Pernambuco and the Construction of Brazil, 1817–1850* (Lincoln and London 2008), 64–76.

[3] Bernardes, *O patriotismo constitucional*, pp. 625–31.

Brazil's trade orientation toward Great Britain did not signify anything new after 1808–22. Brazilian policy-makers, however, had not entirely lost control of the country's political economy. From the 1830s, trade became more diversified, notably in the case of the United States' increased demand for coffee. Brazilian politicians resisted British attempts to force them to terminate the slave trade until 1850. Brazil's late industrialization resulted largely from internal factors. One of them was that government, as in most other Latin American countries, depended hugely on the taxation of the import trade for its regular income. In any case, as Mexican administrations would realize in the 1820s and 1830s, only an extraordinarily high tariff inviting contraband could protect domestic industries, such as cottage cotton-textile production. Even so, Minas Gerais, the main center of textile production, continued to export to other provinces after Independence. The economy had a low technological capacity and did not generate sufficient capital to manage transfer to a nineteenth-century factory system. High transportation costs and low returns on investments further impeded growth until the 1890s, that is, after the final abolition of slavery in 1888.[4]

COMPROMISE OR SECESSION IN SPANISH AMERICA

Even though several continental-American territories of the Hispanic Monarchy participated in the second constitutional period, the political forces gathering within them showed remarkably different tendencies from one another and also from metropolitan Spain. These divergences resulted not only from the impact of civil warfare, but also from issues antedating the dynastic crisis of 1808.

The loss of Chile in 1817–18 was followed by the defection of Guayaquil, where José Joaquín de Olmedo proclaimed independence from the Monarchy on October 7, 1820, thereby depriving Peru of its principal ship-building port and a major link in Lima's Pacific trade. Then, in a night assault on November 5, Admiral Cochrane captured the principal Spanish warship, the frigate *Esmeralda* in the Bay of Callao.[5] When

---

[4] Stephen Haber and Herbert S. Klein, "The Economic Consequences of Brazilian Independence," in Stephen Haber (ed.), *How Latin American Fell Behind. Essays on the Economic Histories of Brazil and Mexico, 1800–1914* (Stanford 1997), 245–46, 248–49, 253–55.

[5] *Documentos para la Historia del Libertador*, tomo XVI, Pezuela to Casa Flores, Lima 10 December 1820, 189–92. John Lynch, *San Martín. Argentine Soldier, American Hero* (New Haven and London 2009), 123–24, 127–28.

the Intendant, the Marqués de Torre Tagle, and the city *cabildo* proclaimed the independence of Peru on December 29 in Trujillo, a chain reaction followed throughout the north. By May of the following year, all northern Peru was under the control of its local élites, disposed to assist the Patriot forces on the coast with men and funds.[6]

Viceroy Pezuela, no partisan of the Cádiz constitutional system, attributed the weakening of the administration in Lima to its re-establishment. Elections to the Constitutional City Council on December 3 resulted in the return of the Condes de la Vega del Ren and San Isidro, former opponents of Abascal, to the center of politics. When the 4500-man Patriot Army of the Andes under San Martín had landed on the coast at Pisco on September 7–8, 1820, the Consulado of Lima could find no funds to defend the capital city. By December 1820, Pezuela was complaining to the Spanish Minister Plenipotentiary in Rio de Janeiro that trade and the money-supply were paralyzed. He was desperate for the arrival of the two ships from Cádiz, promised by Madrid, which, he hoped, could save the Royalist position in Peru.[7]

San Martín, within a few days of disembarkation, sent Col. José Antonio Álvarez de Arenales with 800 men into the central Andes with the task of persuading the districts of Cerro de Pasco and Jauja to support the Patriot cause. The object was discreet harassment of Royalist forces at the flank or rear, in order to undermine their position and provoke defections, while the main Patriot force on the coast built up strength. The model was the guerrilla bands that had obstructed the French in Spain after 1808. Even so, Royalist forces in Peru still totaled 23,000 men. The four southern provinces of Cuzco, Arequipa, Huamanga, and Puno bore most of the cost of the Army of Upper Peru. Arenales formed guerrilla bands in the province of Huarochirí. San Martín instructed him to be mindful of village opinion and avoid abuses. At a time of fluctuating loyalties in the central and southern Andean zones, he stressed the importance of preserving Indian support,

---

[6] AGI Lima 603, Torre Tagle to Council of the Indies, La Paz 28 October 1816; cámara de Indias to Torre Tagle, Madrid 8 March 1817: as *alcalde ordinario* of Lima and a leading nobleman, he had been called upon by Abascal to organize the loyalist Regiment of the Volunteers of "la Concordia del Perú"; he had taken his seat in the Ordinary Cortes of 1813 as a Peruvian elected deputy; the Regency Council appointed him Intendant of La Paz.

[7] *Documentos para la Historia del Libertador General San Martín*, 19 tomes (Buenos Aires 1953–2007), Tome 16 (marzo de 1820 – marzo de 1821), Pezuela to Conde de Casa Flores, Lima 10 December 1820, 192–94.

where available. The organized bands were to operate in conjunction with the Army and not independently. Their task would be coordination of food supplies and the provision of military intelligence.[8]

Unable to finance repression, the Liberal administration in Madrid, on April 11, 1820, authorized Pezuela to negotiate with the Patriots for a compromise solution. The collapse of the Miraflores negotiations in Peru, later in the month, demonstrated the impossibility of reconciliation under the 1812 Constitution. San Martín, despite instinctive monarchist sentiments, insisted on the absolute independence of Peru. In this battle of rival legitimacies, Royalist commanders in Peru took the Constitution as their badge of legitimacy.[9]

In the central Andes, separatists took control in Huancayo, Jauja, and Tarma in November, defeated the Royalists at Cerro de Pasco, the mining town, on December 6, and provoked the defection of both the "Numancia Battalion," which consisted of recruits from northern South America, and several Royalist officers, including Agustín Gamarra, Andrés de Santa Cruz, and Ramón Castilla, who saw no future for the Viceroyalty of Peru.[10]

Led by Pezuela's enemy, La Serna, Royalist officers removed the viceroy from office in the coup d'état of Aznapuquio on January 29, 1821, on the grounds of inactivity. La Serna had fought the French in the siege of Zaragoza in 1808 and been sent to join the Army of Upper Peru under Ramírez. As senior officers, La Serna, Canterac, Valdés, Seoane, and García Cubas favored resistance to Patriot forces and accused Pezuela of weakness. Pezuela maintained that La Serna had disobeyed the instruction to advance on Tucumán in 1816, in order to disperse the separatist

[8] Ella Dunbar Temple, *La acción patriótica del pueblo en la emancipación. Guerrillas y montoneras*. Colección Documental de la independencia del Perú (Lima 1971), 6 tomes: vol. V, no. 1, doc. 159, pp. 186–87, San Martín to Gen. Francisco de Paula Otero (operating under Arenales), cuartel general in Retes 4 January 1821: Otero had been chosen Governor, when the principal residents (*vecindario*) of Tarma separated from the "Nación Española" on November 28, 1820 (doc. 41, pp. 84–85); doc. 170, pp. 196–97, Otero to San Martín, Tarma 11 January 1821; doc. 201, pp. 220–21, San Martín to Chilean Minister, Huaura 29 January 1821; doc. 211, pp. 232–33, Otero to San Martín, Tarma 7 February 1821; doc. 214, p. 235, J. M. Artola (Royalist), *Noticias*, Lima 8 February 1821. Méndez, "La Guerra que no cesa," pp. 390–99. Álvarez was another pro-Independence Spaniard.

[9] José Agustín de la Puente Candamo, *San Martín y el Perú. Planteamiento doctrinario* (Lima 1948), 12. Méndez, "La guerra que no cesa," 400–1.

[10] Natalia Sobrevilla Perea, *The Caudillo of the Andes. Andrés de Santa Cruz* (Cambridge 2012), 50–51, 73. All three were to become Presidents in the republican era. Santa Cruz had fought in the Royalist Army of Upper Peru under Goyeneche and Pezuela in 1811–15.

Congress.[11] This coup marked a serious rupture with the legal order in Royalist Peru, comparable with the removal of Iturrigaray in Mexico in 1808. Its long-term significance was obscured by the prevailing conflict in Peru and the preoccupation of Liberal Spain with conflict in the peninsula.

A second attempt to work out a negotiated solution in the Punchauca talks with representatives of the Cortes failed. As he was preparing to abandon Lima with the Royalist Army, La Serna received news that a commissioner with full powers authorized by the Liberal government in Madrid had arrived in Peru in March 1821. Naval Captain Manuel Abreu had already spoken to San Martín with the object of finding a compromise, beginning with an armistice. At the Hacienda de Punchauca, north of Lima, La Serna and Abreu began talks and a meeting was held between the viceroy and San Martín on June 2. The Lima City Council made a concerted appeal for peace in Peru. As in the case of the Miraflores negotiations, the talks collapsed over Spain's refusal to sanction the independence of Peru. The Royalists, in the meantime, began their strategic withdrawal from the capital on June 25, taking the contents of the Arsenal, Royal Mint, and Treasury with them, while Abreu and San Martín still continued their discussions. This meant continuation of the war.[12] Although withdrawal from Lima was designed to consolidate Royalist positions in the interior, nothing could be guaranteed. On the same day La Serna left Lima, six Indian *principales* and two *alcaldes* of Huarochirí, long a trouble spot for Lima, declared their allegiance to the Patriot cause.[13]

It is difficult to see how the Punchauca negotiations could have succeeded, since Independence and Union were incompatible propositions, despite their conjunction in Iturbide's Plan of Iguala. Although members of the Lima nobility would have supported a monarchy, symbolizing the preservation of the existing social order, their understanding was that it should be in an independent state with possibly a Peruvian version of the *Charte Constitutionnelle*.[14]

---

[11] Biblioteca Municipal Pública, Santander (Spain), MSS de Joaquín de la Pezuela (1761–1830): 2.1, *Manifiesto en que el virrey del Perú … el hecho y circunstancias de la separación de su mando …* (Madrid 1821), 13–14, 20–27, 34–35, 75–82, 114–16, 120–27. This self-defense (129 pp.) was dated April 8, 1821.

[12] Timothy E. Anna, *The Fall of the Royal Government in Peru* (Lincoln and London 1979), 175–79. Lynch, *San Martín*, 129, 154.

[13] Dunbar Temple, *La acción patriótica*, doc. 301, pp. 321–23, Tomás Isidro and Clemente Cajaruaringa to Otero, Huarochirí 25 June 1821.

[14] Puente Candamo, *San Martín y el Perú*, 25, 30–32.

San Martín took up residence in Lima from July 14, 1821 until September 20, 1822. He proclaimed the independence of Peru in Lima on July 28, 1821, even though the Royalist Army was still in the field and occupying the central and southern provinces. As Protector of Peru, from August 3, he abolished the Constitution of 1812 on August 9, opening the way for the formulation of a distinct Peruvian Constitution outside the Hispanic Monarchy. He appointed three ministers to assist in the government, the principal of whom was Bernardo Monteagudo, Minister of War and Navy, as determined as the Protector to destroy the remaining links between Peru and the Hispanic Monarchy. Unanue, a senior figure of the Enlightenment since the 1790s, took the Ministry of Finance, a crucial position in view of the collapse of government finance during the Pezuela era. José de la Riva Agüero, who held the rank of Colonel in the Militia, became President of the Department of Lima, while his future rival, Torre Tagle, now Mariscal del Campo, commanded the militia force of the "Peruvian Legion of the Guard."[15]

The absence of a constitution for Peru did not signify that the country remained without laws. While it was true that the Protector's *Estatuto Provisional* of October 8, 1821 concentrated power in the hands of the Executive in the form of a Council of State of twelve members, all existing laws continued in force. Although the Protector abolished the Audiencia of Lima and the Mining Tribunal on August 4, a Supreme Judicial Chamber (*Alta Cámara de Justicia*) was to replace them. The new regime recognized all *bona fide* debts incurred by its predecessor, with the exception of debts incurred in the counter-revolutionary struggle.[16] Continuities, however, subsisted alongside discontinuities and innovations. The collapse of the viceregal regime on the coast entailed the definition of who constituted the new Peru. The Protectorate declared that the name "*indios*" should be forever abolished and replaced by that of "*peruanos*." What this implied in judicial and institutional terms for the Indian communities, the *repúblicas de indios* of the colonial era, would remain to be defined later in the decade and thereafter. Many of those in the central and southern Andes still fell under Royalist rule and such regulations as those issued from Lima did not apply. What the new regime proposed to do with respect to revenue, following the renewed

---

[15] AGI Lima 800, *Colección de los bandos publicados por el gobierno de Lima independiente*, pp. 25–28, 33–34. Departments replaced the colonial Intendancies.

[16] AGI Lima 800, *Colección*, pp. 25–28, 33–34. Guillermo Lohmann Villena, *Los ministros de la Audiencia de Lima* (1700–1821) (Seville 1974), cxvii–cxix.

abolition of Indian tribute, was also unclear. With regard to the coastal haciendas' slave workforce, only slaves who had actually enlisted in Patriot forces could expect emancipation. The remainder were instructed to return to their estates within fifteen days of publication of the decree of July 23. Severe penalties were prescribed for anyone who disobeyed this instruction. Nevertheless, by the decree of August 12 all children born of slaves after July 28, 1821 were automatically freed.[17]

The collapse of viceregal Lima led to the exodus of *peninsulares* from Patriot Peru. It is difficult to quantify this, since the figures vary. Royalist leaders also discovered that few magistrates remained to administer justice in the Audiencias of Cuzco and Charcas. The Lima émigré, José María Ruybal, suggested that 300 Europeans left for Spain and a further 500 for Chile. Since the *peninsulares* had been among the wealthiest men in Peru through their commercial activities, the new regime attempted in vain to halt the exodus. Ruybal pointed to the erosion of support for San Martín in Lima because of the financial burdens imposed by his regime, and that eminent Peruvians were disillusioned that they had not found another George Washington in the Protector. The fall of Monteagudo in June 1822 pointed to the impending collapse of the San Martín regime in Lima. This appears to have been the work of Riva Agüero in a jockeying for power in Lima.[18]

SEPARATISM, REPUBLICANISM, AND THE REJECTION OF SPAIN

Simón Bolívar, operating from his base in Angostura in the Orinoco Basin, launched a vigorous campaign westward across the *llanos* into New Granada and routed the Royalist Army at Boyacá in 1819. This provoked the final collapse of the Viceroyalty of New Granada and undid the work of Morillo after 1816. Once in control of much of Venezuela and New Granada, Bolívar sought to unite the two territories, despite the separate development of Venezuela since 1777, as a potentially strong northern South-American state on the grounds that it might be capable of

---

[17] AGI Lima 800, *Colección*, pp. 17, 35, 49–41.

[18] AGI Lima 800, Colección, pp. 9–10, 30–31. AGI Lima 798, Ruybal to Antonio Luis Pereira (Spanish Consul), Rio de Janeiro 27 July 1822. AGI Lima 762, La Serna to Minister of Grace and Justice (Madrid), no. 31, Cuzco 15 March 1822 and no. 9, Cuzco 11 September 1822. Jorge Basadre, *Historia de la República del Perú*, vol. 1 (1822–1866) (Lima), 82.

maintaining its position and holding off any European or counter-revolutionary attempt to overthrow it.

After ten years of fighting across northern South America, the news that the Liberal regime was proposing a compromise solution fell on welcoming ears, since both sides were anxious for a respite. On June 6, 1820, the Madrid administration authorized Morillo to come to terms with Bolívar, declaring its intention to send commissioners to Venezuela. Once again, the peninsular Liberals deceived themselves into believing that the Constitution of 1812 would be the panacea. Bolívar and the Venezuelan leaders accepted none of that. Even so, their commissioners agreed at Santa Ana (Trujillo) to a six-month armistice on November 26 and the termination of the "war to the death." The armistice in Venezuela lasted only a few weeks. The deteriorating situation in the city of Maracaibo, culminating in the Patriot General Rafael Urdaneta's removal of the Royalist authorities on January 28, 1821, reopened conflict in mid-April. Morillo, in the meantime, who had already lost more than two-thirds of the original force through disease, handed over command to his subordinate and discreetly returned to Spain.[19]

The Congress of Cúcuta, on the Venezuelan side of the Andean border met between May and October 1821 to give shape to the "Republic of Colombia" on the basis of the Fundamental Law issued at Angostura on December 17, 1819. Nariño, released from incarceration in Spain by the Liberal Revolution, returned to New Granada in 1821 and presided over the Congress. Bolívar's victory over the remaining Spanish forces at Carabobo on June 24, 1821 terminated the possibility of any further Royalist government in the country. Puerto Cabello, the last remaining bastion, fell to Páez on November 8, 1823.

Article 2 of the Constitution stated that sovereignty resided essentially in the "Colombian Nation." This declaration had three implications: first, it implied the total rejection of any idea that the Hispanic Monarchy constituted the Nation; second, that there would be no more monarchies in Spanish South America; and, third, that neither the provinces nor any other component part of the new state possessed as such any share in the possession and political exercise of sovereignty. In this way, Bolívar was determined to put an end to Venezuelan federalism and New Granadan localism. Congress, however, did not adopt his idea of a *hereditary* senate, despite a bicameral structure of representation. In Lynch's assessment, the

---

[19] Anna, *Spain and the Loss of America*, 233–37. McNeill, *Mosquito Empires*, 271, 278, 281.

Cúcuta system "was an elitist project imposed by the few on the many, who were not consulted, and it left the question of national identity unresolved."[20]

The Colombian Constitution of Cúcuta in 1821 began the movement away from the broad franchise of the 1812 Constitution. Restrictions on the franchise by means of property qualifications, an age limit of twenty-one years, proof of regular employment, house-ownership and value of property, marital status, and eventually (from 1849) literacy for the right to vote reflected a concern among the élites at the prospect of lower-class participation in the political processes. Furthermore, the practice of indirect election continued for Congress and the municipal councils, repeated again in the Constituent Congress of 1829 with higher rates of qualification, indicating a preference for the propertied and professional classes. After Quito seceded as the Republic of Ecuador in 1830, the first Ecuadorian Constitution set even higher qualifications, confining the vote to literates in a society in which the overwhelming majority remained illiterate.[21]

Bolívar's decree of May 20, 1820 promised protection for the Indian communities as the social group that had suffered the most under "Spanish despotism." He called for the restoration of lands taken illegally, regardless of who had usurped them. The objective was to promote the distribution of community lands among individual families according to need and capacity. Any remaining lands were to be auctioned, with preference given to existing holders. The product of sales would go toward the payment of Tribute (not yet abolished) and for the annual salary of 120 pesos for school-masters in each of the *pueblos*. The civil justice and the parish priest, acting in accord, were to appoint such teachers. The decree specified that all children between the ages of four and fourteen were to attend school and receive instruction in the basic necessities of reading, arithmetic, religious principles, and the rights and duties of man and the citizen. Indians, it was hoped, would learn thereby that they were free men no different from any others in the Republic.[22] The decree had to be repeated on February 12 the following year, owing to complaints of non-compliance from the *pueblos* of the province of Tunja. Bolívar referred to such abuses as "iniquitous."[23]

---

[20] Lynch, *Bolívar*, 141–46.   [21] Morelli, *Territorio o Nación*, 126–28.
[22] *Decretos del Libertador*, 3 vols. (Los Teques 1983), I, 194–97, Cúcuta 20 May 1820.
[23] *Decretos*, I, 227–29, Santa Rosa 12 February 1821.

Competition for the allegiance of lower social groups appeared in New Granada just as it had in Venezuela and continued in Peru. Different social and ethnic groups negotiated allegiances during the conflict, with the two overriding issues of reduction of Tribute payment and emancipation from slavery paramount. Faced with menacing armies from Santa Fe and the insurrection of the Cauca Valley towns, Royalist Governor Miguel Tacón of Popayán recruited support among the Indian communities and the slaves working in the gold-producing tropical lowlands. Gold had become in the eighteenth century the principal commodity of the Popayán province, which had 15–20,000 black slaves and a hacienda structure linked to the mining sector. The Valencia, Caicedo, Mosquera, and Arboleda families of Popayán rose on gold, slavery, landed property, and livestock. Royalist offers of a one-third reduction in Tribute quotas aimed to recruit Indian commoners. Local dynamics and popular consciousness of the twists and turns of political events at a time of great fluctuation influenced lower social group allegiances. They also affected upper-class allegiances and those middle sectors caught between the others groups.[24]

Treason, desertion, and corruption plagued Bolívar's government in Colombia during 1821 as much as they would later in Peru after 1823. On his way south early in January 1822 for the campaign to finish off royal authority in Quito, Bolívar instructed the municipalities of Cali, an early center of republican support, Buga, Cartago, Toro, and Caloto, all Cauca Valley towns, to recruit men aged between fifteen and forty years, both free and enslaved, for his forces. Should any individual hide from the recruiters, his family was to be arrested and sent to the general barracks. Those who refused to comply with the order would be put before a firing squad in the public square.[25] In Lima, Bolívar established the death penalty for any official convicted of taking more than ten pesos from the public funds.[26] The death penalty was also his response to desertion or conspiracy to desert from the armed forces. Deserters were to be replaced by their next of kin in the villages from which they had been recruited, and their families were to bear the cost of uniforms and armaments so lost – or, in default, by the *pueblo*. Such measures indicated the prevalence of

[24] Echeverri, "Popular Royalism," pp. 241–50, 255–60, 268–69. Hamnett, "Popular Insurrection and Royalist Reaction," 293–326.

[25] *Decretos*, I, 247–48, Cali 2 January 1822.

[26] *Decretos*, I, 283, "Palacio Dictatorial de Lima" 12 January 1824.

desertion among Patriot forces, a phenomenon also experienced by the Royalists.[27]

Sucre's victory over Melchor Aymerich, President of the Audiencia of Quito, at Pichincha on May 22, 1822 extinguished royal authority in the capital but still left Royalist bands in control of the roads. The southernmost province of New Granada, Los Pastos (Pasto, Barbacoas, and Patía), where Indians formed the largest component of the population, had been a Royalist stronghold. The capital, a city of some 8000 inhabitants, had a long tradition of rivalry with the fellow woolen-producing city of Quito further south in the Andean chain. The Pasto municipal council resented subordination to the Audiencia of Quito, calling in 1809 for an *audiencia* in Pasto, a college of higher education, and in 1814 a bishopric as well. On a smaller scale, this resembled Arequipa's struggle to shake of judicial dependence on Cuzco. In 1809, Pasto had rejected the claims of the Supreme Junta of Quito. The Pasto council also made strong efforts to reduce the burden of tribute-payment in the countryside. Like the Royalist position of Santa Marta on the Caribbean, opposed to Cartagena, Pasto had impeded republican control of all of New Granada.[28]

In the early 1820s the issue became one of whether Royalist Pasto could survive the impact of the military successes of Bolívar and Sucre in Venezuela, New Granada, and Quito. Republican forces obliged Pasto Royalists to capitulate on June 8, 1822, and the urban elite appeared to have reconciled themselves to the Republic, although the Indian communities of the countryside remained Royalist in sentiment. A further revolt took place in July, which gave local Royalists control of much of the province, threatening communications between New Granada republicans and Sucre's army in Quito. Like the concertina warfare across Central Peru and in Lima and Callao, in 1821–23, this conflict seemed to be less a miniature version of the wider conflict than a localized struggle with its own issues. An insurrection in Pasto on October 28 enraged Bolívar who, using the extraordinary powers granted him by the Congress of the Republic of Colombia, ordered the confiscation of the rebels' properties. He included in this penalty the properties of all those who had not vacated the city when it was under Royalist control. Bolívar saw the rebellion as the action of the entire city and berated its strong resistance to Sucre's forces before the city finally fell on December 24.

---

[27] *Decretos*, I, 286–88, Trujillo (Peru) 15 March 1824.
[28] Earle, *Spain and the Independence of Colombia*, 47–54, 95–96.

Bolívar, who arrived there in the following month, denounced the city as "furiously hostile to the Republic," and deserving of "severe and exemplary punishment."[29]

NIGHTMARES IN THE BOLIVARIAN DREAM

The political élites of the new Republic of Colombia on June 23, 1824 set about dividing the extensive territory into twelve departments, 36 provinces, and 228 cantons, although they were not homogenous units. The institution of departments clearly reflected a centralist intent and a rejection of federalism. The former Audiencia of Quito, pushed into this union, became known as the "Departamento del Sur," with one municipal district (*municipio*) for each canton, less than under the Cádiz system but more than there had been under colonial absolutism. Since the traditional base of the power of local notables had been in the cities, the Bolivarian structure encountered opposition from them, which would ultimately contribute to the break-up of the Greater Colombian state.[30]

These political elements, when combined, illustrate the continuing importance of the municipalities and the groups dominating them at the provincial and local levels – and in the capital cities. Every attempted reformation of the political system from the highest level downwards had to take this into consideration in whatever part of Spanish America. It pointed to the resilience of local élites and especially to their capacity to subsume reforms from the outside, regardless of their initiators' purposes, into their own scale of interests. The Hispanic-American municipality had a long history and, reformed or unreformed, representing the interests of those who held power and wealth at the local and provincial levels. They were the principal survivors in the complex transition from colonial old regime to separatist, independent, sovereign states. Altered as they were under different constitutional systems, they remained the elements of continuity and stability when central governments crashed. Wherever they could, the municipalities held Hispanic American society together when faced with the prospect of anarchy.

Bolívar saw the Congress of Ocaña, which met to revise the Constitution of Cúcuta, as the last hope for saving Colombia from

[29] AHNE Presidencia de Quito 584 (1821), República de Colombia, vols. 596 and 603 (1822), 607 (1823). *Decretos*, 1, 273–74, Pasto 13 January 1823. *Decretos*, I, 256–58, Bolívar to Antonio Obando, Cuartel General in Tulcán 12 June 1822.

[30] Morelli, *Territorio o Nación*, 240, 250–56.

disintegration. It opened south of Bogotá on April 9, but of the 108 elected delegates, 44 were absent. His ultimate but unfulfilled hope was that Colombia would adopt the Bolivian Constitution of 1826 (which I shall discuss shortly), but the supporters of Francisco de Paula Santander, the principal figure in New Granada, who formed the largest contingent present, remained determined to resist authoritarian tendencies by upholding the existing constitution and rescinding the clause permitting the exercise of extraordinary powers by Bolívar. This marked the defining breach with Santander and the source of Bolívar's determination to adopt extreme measures to defend his creation. Bolívar scrapped the Constitution of Cúcuta on August 27, 1828 and established a Dictatorship in Colombia, abolishing Santander's office of Vice-President. The Dictatorship, designed to last until a new congress convened on January 2, 1830, should be understood in the Roman sense of rule during an emergency: it did not signify arbitrary government but upheld the rule of law and the basic principles for which Bolívar had always stood. It did mean, however, that his preoccupation with strong, central decision-making, seen in the life-presidency of the Bolivian Constitution, became uppermost and subordinated all other considerations. Bolívar's action, though, provoked a group of thirty young conspirators to attempt his assassination on September 25.[31]

Bolívar dead or alive, the fiscal problems of the new state would not go away. Attempts to remove colonial taxes often deprived the exchequer of revenues and led eventually to their reinstitution, sometimes under another name. On October 15, 1828, for instance, Bolívar decreed that Colombian Indians were to pay a *contribución personal de indígenas*. This was the Tribute under another name. Its justification was, according to the preamble, that Indians had requested that they pay only one tax, rather than the range of them paid by other citizens of the Republic. They were, thereby, freed from payment of *alcabalas* on their own produce, from military service (though they could volunteer, if they so chose), from parish dues (since local clerics were to be paid a wage), and national contributions. Personal services would be remunerated. Bolívar reiterated previous legislation on the division of community lands among working families for their needs, although commons for grazing were not to be touched.[32]

---

[31] Lynch, *Bolívar*, 232–43.
[32] Bolívar, *Decretos*, III, 171–78, Palacio de Gobierno, Bogotá 15 October 1828. The tax fell on males between eighteen and fifty years of age capable of earning a living at the rate of 3 pesos 4 reales per year, paid in two installments.

In Venezuela, Bolívar, on March 8, 1827, issued a new *Regulation for Public Finance* in response to the inadequacy of revenues from its Departments and to rectify the inefficiency of tax-collection. In the Departments, the Intendants were in charge of revenue-collection, including the Tobacco Revenue. The Liberator accordingly defined the functions of the principal financial agencies. On the following day, he defined the duties of the Customs Houses and listed the ports authorized for external trade, and on March 19, the regulation for the Tobacco Revenue, described as one of the principal revenues of state. Coordinated in the General Administration in Caracas, the provinces would also have Tobacco Administrations, for example, in Barinas, Cumaná, and Maracaibo. The aim would be to restore its former prosperity, establishing regular visitations by officers and mounted patrols.[33]

It remained to be seen whether this mountain of decrees – regulating, correcting, punishing, founding, defining – would ever have the desired effect within the context of new and untried institutions. Bolívar's presence in a country or province usually entailed a series of reforms of lax practices and entrenched attitudes. It must have seemed to his contemporaries like a deluge, but once the waves had subsided, much that had always survived still remained in place.

MEXICAN CONSTITUTIONALISM AND FEDERALISM

The formation of an autonomous government opened the way for the modification of provisions of the 1812 Constitution, still in force in the country. The *iturbidista* Regency Council, accordingly, proposed to convene a bicameral Mexican Cortes on November 17, 1821, abandoning unicameralism and reviving a form of corporate representation for the upper chamber. This reflected the interests of the propertied and professional classes behind the *iturbidista* project. Its 128 members were to be selected according to position, profession, and status.[34] There was little support for this proposal and when the first Mexican Constituent

---

[33] Bolívar, *Decretos*, II, 98–155, *Reglamento de la Hacienda Pública*, Cuartel General in Caracas 8 March 1827; 166–82, *Reglamento de Aduanas*, Caracas 9 March 1827; 215–61, Arreglo y régimen de la Renta de Tabacos, Caracas 19 June 1827.

[34] Benson, *Mexico and the Spanish Cortes*, 33, including future political figures such as Alamán, Manuel Gómez Pedraza, Michelena, and Lorenzo de Zavala. Frasquet, *Las caras del águila*, 133–35.

Congress met on February 24, 1822, it conformed to the Cádiz principles and not to the neo-corporatism of November 17.[35]

Iturbide had been raised to the position of Emperor by acclaim in July 1822, ratified by vote of Congress, and then crowned by the Bishop of Puebla in the absence (in Spain) of the Archbishop. Conflict between the Emperor and Congress led to the arrest of deputies on August 26. Included in the arrests were Mier, José María Fagoaga and the former insurgent, Bustamante. Emperor Iturbide suspended Congress on October 31. This action raised the questions of the form of government and where sovereignty lay. The *Junta Nacional Instituyente*, which replaced the Congress, proposed on November 22 a *Provisional Political Regulation* designed to strengthen the power of the executive, but opposed by Zavala, recently abandoning the Spanish Cortes, and Bustamante, always a bitter enemy of Iturbide. He warned that sovereignty resided in the *Mexican* Nation and that the suspended deputies were its representatives.[36]

Political stalemate in Mexico City gave the initiative to the provinces. An apparently minor rebellion by a section of the Army in the port of Veracruz under the command of Antonio López de Santa Anna, until that time a collaborator of Iturbide, called on December 2 for the reinstallation of the Constituent Congress and initially for a republic. Gaining the support of Guadalupe Victoria, a former insurgent leader, the Plan of Veracruz disavowed the Empire. Ostensibly, this rebellion, when 600 Spanish soldiers in contact with Royalist Havana still occupied the fortress of San Juan de Ulua, offshore from the port of Veracruz, stalled. It did, however, spark off parallel movements. Bravo and Guerrero reignited the opposition to Iturbide in the area between the Valley of Mexico and the Pacific, and called for the reinstallation of the First Congress, leaving to it to decide the form of government for the country. This rebellion equally stalled. The Emperor sent General José Antonio Echávarri, Captain General of Puebla, Oaxaca, and Veracruz, to extinguish Santa Anna's rebellion in case the situation worsened. Echávarri, however, unwilling to enter into armed conflict, defected with his forces to the rebel side and issued the Plan of Casa Mata on February 1, 1823. That changed the situation dramatically, reanimating constitutionalist hostility and destabilizing the First Mexican Empire. The Plan called for the convocation of a second Constituent Congress through fresh elections on the

---

[35] Frasquet, *Las caras del águila*, 148–49, 246.
[36] Frasquet, *Las caras del águila*, 220–21, 246, 266–69, 295.

same basis as in 1822. As events developed thereafter, the likelihood was that this projected Congress would reflect the composition of forces behind the Casa Mata rebellion.[37]

Although designed to restore constitutional government, the Plan of Casa Mata made no mention of federalism or a republic. It did specify that until the new Congress met the Provincial Deputation of Veracruz was to assume the government of the province, the first in Mexico to be taken over in this way. The precedent was set thereby for other provinces to follow suit. The city council of Veracruz, the army in Jalapa, and the garrison at Perote all adhered to the Plan of Casa Mata. Support also spread through the provinces, where local army commanders and city councils took the initiative in claiming power.[38]

The political consequences of the Plan proved to be radical: movements throughout the provinces undermined central government by creating *de facto* governments. Defections continued among Iturbide's supporters and sections of the army. The Military Commander of Puebla, the Marqués de Vivanco, adhered to the Plan of Casa Mata on February 10, 1823, followed five days later by the Provincial Deputation and the City Council. Two weeks later, the Council selected Patricio Furlong, second *alcalde*, with one of the councilors, to greet the Army of Casa Mata when it arrived at Puebla. The Council listened to a reading of Santa Anna's manifesto sent from Veracruz, and discussed parallel developments in the provinces of San Luis Potosí and Coahuila-Nuevo León.[39]

Having lost control of all the provinces, Iturbide re-established the First Congress on March 4, 1823, in order to restore a semblance of constitutionality to the regime. However, only fifty-eight deputies appeared on March 7, when Congress met. The Casa Mata rebel junta, which was committed to the convocation of a *new* congress, still remained in Puebla, its chosen base, under the presidency of Vivanco. A committee of authorities in Puebla denounced on March 12 the "nominal government in

---

[37] Archivo Histórico de Hacienda, Primer Imperio 1871, expediente 16, December 1822, and expediente 24, no. 92, ff. 165, 166, 168. Genaro García, *Documentos inéditos y muy raros para la historia de México* (Mexico City 1974), 9. Anna, *Mexican Empire of Iturbide*, 150–70. Nettie Lee Benson, "The Plan of Casa Mata," *HAHR*, 25, i (February 1945), 45–56, first raised the issues of interpretation in the Plan. Echávarri, a Spaniard, had rallied to the Plan of Iguala. A further 500 men arrived from Havana in January 1823. Frasquet, *Las caras del Águila*, 256–57.

[38] Anna, *Iturbide*, 166–78. Frasquet, *Las caras del Aguila*, 259–60.

[39] Archivo del Ayuntamiento de Puebla, *Libros de Cabildo* 92/1 (January–June 1823), ff. 133, 165, 205, Puebla 15, 20 and 24 February and 6 March 1821; ff. 168v, Puebla 27 February 1823; f. 233v, 24 March 1823; f. 314v, 17 April 1823.

Mexico City."[40] When the Casa Mata rebels declared the restored Congress illegitimate, the future of the Emperor was placed in doubt.[41]

The Emperor broke the deadlock by abdication on March 19. A week later, the Army of Casa Mata under Bravo entered the capital. Congress, with 103 deputies present, debated the issues on March 29. The abdication pointed for the first time to a republican solution. The success of the military factions that made up the Casa Mata movement initiated a long-lasting tradition in Mexico of sections of the Army claiming to represent the real interests of the people and calling for removal of the government of the day. The rebellion reflected a combination of the regionalized military command during the fighting in the 1810s with the provincial consequences of the constitutionalized politics under the Cádiz Constitution. That process left the provinces as *de facto* autonomous units, controlled by their élites, within a nominally united sovereign state without a recognized head.[42]

Congress, in its session of March 19, established a Supreme Executive Power, consisting of three generals, Pedro Celestino Negrete (a Spaniard, former Royalist, and ex-*iturbidista*) and the two former insurgent leaders, Bravo and Victoria. Michelena and Miguel Domínguez, former Corregidor of Querétaro in 1810, who had been Iturbide's Minister of Justice, represented Bravo and Victoria, absent with their forces. Alamán, Secretary of External and Internal Relations, soon became the predominant force in the government, determined to oppose regional fragmentation. This virtual triumvirate managed to maintain itself in power from March 30, 1823 until October 10, 1824. Congress, thereupon nullified the Plan of Iguala and the Treaties of Córdoba, proclaiming by ninety-four to seven votes that Iturbide's elevation to the position of emperor was the result of an act of violence and henceforth illegitimate. In the meantime, the provinces constructed their own governments. The Second Constituent Congress convened in October. The success of the Army of Casa Mata signified the end of the Constitution of 1812 in the former New Spain.[43]

---

[40] Archivo de la Catedral de Puebla, *Libros de Cabildo*, tomo 60, f. 192v, Puebla 12 March 1823: at the head of this committee were Vivanco, Echávarri, and Negrete, with the support of the Provincial Deputation, three representatives of the City Council, three parish priests, and representatives of the merchant body and distinguished citizens.

[41] Anna, *Iturbide*, 180–93. Iturbide's military commander in Mexico City was the future Mexican President, Manuel Gómez Pedraza. Frasquet, *Caras del Águila*, 283.

[42] Anna, *Iturbide*, 197–204.

[43] Anna, *Iturbide*, 204–25. Frasquet, *Caras del Águila*, 266–67, 307.

The provinces had seized the political initiative. In Guadalajara, the Provincial Deputation sent a Manifesto on March 12 to the towns of New Galicia, steeped in the regional sentiment of the Mexican western territories. The Manifesto rejected outright any claim on the part of Mexico City to exercise full dominion over the provinces. Instead, it proposed a confederation of free, sovereign states. Rejecting what it described as the dominance of the "central aristocracy" in "the new Tenochtitlán," it claimed for New Galicia a share in the exercise of sovereignty as the fulfillment of the process of Independence. The Manifesto warned that resistance to any attempt by the center to prevent this new position would be met by resistance equal to that of the Tlaxcalans who had assisted Cortés to bring down the old Tenochtitlán.[44]

The Provincial Deputation of Guadalajara sent two commissioners, Prisciliano Sánchez and Juan Cayetano Portugal, both of whom would become well-known figures in subsequent decades, to spread the message of the formation of a federal republic to those of San Luis Potosí, Zacatecas, Guanajuato, and Oaxaca. With the full support of the Military Commander, Luis Quintanar, the political authorities in Guadalajara proclaimed the "Free and Sovereign State of Xalisco" on June 16 under the protection of the Virgin of Zapopan. There would be twenty-eight districts. Five days later, it became clear that the type of state-sovereignty envisaged was absolute, depending upon no other sovereign body but offering confederation with other such states or provinces. Xalisco would provide its own constitution but, in collaboration with other states, would formulate a general constitution for the Mexican Republic, with a congress in Mexico City as the focus of union for a confederated Republic. The State of Xalisco would reserve the right to determine whether general-government laws and decrees should apply or not within its territory.[45]

In Monterrey, representatives from the provinces of Coahuila-Texas, Nuevo Santander, and Nuevo León formed in April a federation of their own as a basis for working out a future relationship with the rest of Mexico. These provinces had constituted the colonial-era *Provincias Internas del Oriente*. As in Puebla and Guadalajara, many of the principal

---

[44] Archivo Municipal de Guadalajara, paquete 55, legajo 8: Diputación provincial a los pueblos de la Nueva Galicia, Guadalajara 12 March 1823. This has been published in José María Muriá (ed.), *El Federalismo en Jalisco (1823)* (Guadalajara 1973), doc. 5, pp. 33–37.

[45] Muriá, *El Federalismo en Jalisco*, doc. 6, pp. 37–39; doc. 8, pp. 41–43; doc. 9, pp. 43–45; doc. 10, pp. 45–46; doc. 11, p. 46; doc. 13, pp. 47–49.

families in local commerce and politics were also behind the federalist movement in Oaxaca.[46]

The position championed among the élites of Puebla, Guadalajara, Monterrey, Oaxaca, and Yucatán represented a radical interpretation of federalism, which would result, if brought into effect, in a weak national executive and central power. As such, it was unacceptable to the Supreme Executive Power, particularly Alamán, and to notable opponents of radical federalism, such as Mier, Zavala, and in particular Bustamante, who denounced the process as separatism, which, however, it was not.[47] No province at that time envisaged separation from the political entity created in the colonial era with its capital in Mexico City. It was a struggle to determine the *distribution* of power within a republic. Yet, neither the nature of a specifically Mexican Republic nor of federalism was properly understood at that time.[48]

CONTRADICTORY ROADS FOR PERU

Royalist Peru finally expired in 1824–25, not as agony but anti-climax. Patriot Peru, a fluctuating territory with an indeterminate political process, saw failures on a grand scale in the period from 1820 to 1826 – the collapse of San Martín's Protectorate and the disintegration of Bolívar's Dictatorship instituted on February 10, 1824. After the nullification of the Cádiz Constitution of 1812 by San Martín's regime in Lima, the Peruvian Patriots notoriously failed to provide a viable alternative. The failure of the Guayaquil Interview with Bolívar on July 27, 1822, followed by San Martín's departure from Peru signified the end of any prospect of a monarchy and the real beginning of the republican era in Peru.

[46] Luis Jáuregui, "Nuevo León, 1823–1825. Del Plan de Casa Mata a la promulgación de la Constitución Estatal"; Jaime Olveda, "Jalisco: el proncunciamiento federalista en Guadalajara"; Alicia Tecanhuey Sandoval, "Tras las trincheras del federalismo. Intereses y fuerzas regionales en Puebla, 1823–1825," all in Josefina Zoraída Vázquez (coordinator), *El establecimiento del federalismo en México, 1821–1827* (Mexico City 2003), 189–213, 351–84, 475–503. Brian R. Hamnett, "Oaxaca: las principales familias y el federalismo de 1823," in Angeles Romero Frizzi (comp.), *Lecturas históricas de Oaxaca*, 4 vols. (Mexico City and Oaxaca 1990), vol. 2, 51–69.

[47] Carlos María de Bustamante, *Historia del Emperador D. Agustín de Iturbide hasta su muerte y sus consecuencias, y establecimiento de la República Popular Federal* (Mexico City 1846), 110–13, 160–61.

[48] Lorenzo de Zavala, *Opinión de Don Lorenzo de Zavala acerca de la actitud de las provincias y los diputados dentro del congreso: sesión del 1 de agosto de 1823*, in *Obras* (Mexico City 1969), 754. Zavala, from Yucatán, later supported the modified federal system of 1824–36.

A Constituent Congress was summoned on December 27, 1821 to convene on May 1, the following year but then delayed. It did not finally meet until September 20, 1822, the day San Martín resigned the Protectorate.

The Peruvian Constituent Congress was divided among Liberal factions and their military support. The former were mainly products of the colleges distinguished in the late Enlightenment. Future political leaders, such as José Faustino Sánchez Carrión and the Arequipa cleric, Francisco Xavier Luna Pizarro, who had been in Cádiz during the first two years of the constitutional period, emerged to prominence in these years. They and their contemporaries such as Francisco Javier Mariátegui and Francisco de Paula González Vigil, were the post-Independence heirs of the pre-crisis Peruvian Enlightenment. Constitutionalists rather than protagonists of a defunct reforming absolutism, they sought a moderate reform policy in alliance with San Martín or Bolívar during the years 1821–26. While upholding the Catholic establishment, Congress also maintained the Bourbon policy of *regalismo* with regard to Church–State relations. Congress finally closed, after four sessions, on March 10, 1825 without formulating a viable constitution.[49]

In contrast to Mexico, the absence of a strong federalist movement among the Peru élites, despite regional sentiment in the north and the south, was striking. Royalist suppression of the Cuzco Rebellion in 1815 had weakened the idea of alternative Peruvian political processes not based in Lima. Even so, the capital remained politically and militarily isolated from much of the central and southern interior over a long period between 1821 and the final Royalist defeats at Junín and Ayacucho in 1824.

Factionalism among the Lima notables seriously delayed a political solution for Patriot Peru. Personal rivalry between Riva Agüero and Torre Tagle was particularly toxic. The Patriot Army of Observation under Arenales, based in the central Valley of Jauja, criticized Congress' lack of attention to the military conflict in the interior. Its second-in-command, Santa Cruz, with the support of Gamarra, both former Royalists, intervened to impose Riva Agüero as President of Peru in the so-called Mutiny of Balconcillo on February 27, 1823. This, then, was

---

[49] AGI Lima 800, *Colección*, pp. 33–34. Basadre, *Historia de la República del Perú*, I, 82, 84–85. Puente Candamo, *San Martín y el Perú*, 79–85, 174–76. The Congress, consisting of ninety-one members, twenty-eight of whom were lawyers and twenty-six clerics, suspended the first Peruvian Constitution (November 13, 1823) on February 17, 1824 and terminated its sessions. Raúl Ferrero Rebagliati, *El liberalismo peruano. Contribución a una historia de ideas* (Lima 1958), 19–22.

the second military intervention in two years. The coup of 1823 led immediately to conflict between the new Executive and Congress. Torre Tagle opposed the Riva Agüero Presidency with the result that two regimes existed henceforth within Patriot Peru.[50]

The chaos in Lima enabled Canterac's Royalist forces (some 9000 men) to broaden their offensive in the central Andes and sweep down to Lima on June 18, 1823. The Royalists recovered Arequipa on August 8. In early September, Santa Cruz lost the initiative in Upper Peru to the Royalist commanders, La Serna, Valdés, and Olañeta, and 5700 of his men out of an original force of 7000 perished. Olañeta retook La Paz on September 24. It seemed as though San Martín's work was unravelling and that the future existence of Independent Peru hung in the balance. The total number of forces available to Royalist commanders at that time was estimated at 20,000 men. Such Royalist activity in Peru during 1822 and 1823 posed a threat to every independent Hispanic state on the South American sub-continent. This explained the arrival of Sucre and Bolívar in Peru.[51]

Sucre's imminent arrival obliged the Royalists to abandon Lima on July 17, 1823 and regroup in Huancavelica, where they still posed a threat to the Patriot position on the coast. Bolívar, invited by Sánchez Carrión and Olmedo, arrived in Lima on September 1, bringing with him the hatred of federalism acquired in Venezuela and a desire to construct a strong central and executive power in the Perus. He soon developed an intense dislike of the Lima notables, regarding them as untrustworthy and self-interested. They, for their part, became his bitter opponents. Leaving the Lima notables to their own devices, Bolívar focused his campaign on finishing off Royalist forces in the central and southern Andean zone. There he and Sucre operated in conjunction with the guerrilla bands, nominally under Arenales. Bolívar's victory over Canterac at Junín on August 6, 1824 began the final process of elimination. Yet, the Royalists still had double the size of the Patriot forces, with 5000 men under La Serna and a further 4000 men under Pedro Antonio Olañeta in Upper Peru. The later, however, had broken with La Serna in December 1823, with the result that two rival Royalist regimes existed for a time in the Perus. The unexpected collapse of La Serna's Royalists at Ayacucho on December 9 explains why Sucre's victory remains such a mystery and so enshrouded with controversy. In Spain, the Royalists

---

[50] Basadre, *República*, I, 85. Sobrevilla Perea, *Santa Cruz*, 70–71.
[51] John Miller, *Memoirs of General Miller*, 2 vols. (London 1828–29), vol. II, 57–81.

who arrived back in their original homeland found themselves regarded as traitors.[52]

Recruitment into guerrilla bands, usually from 50 to 150 men, came from the local peasant population. Royalist counter-guerrillas operated against the Patriot bands. In many instances, a war between rival armed bands displaced the superficial struggle of emancipation from the Spanish Crown. The villages suffered the burdens of recruitment, seizure of resources, and punishment by both sides. Even so, the demands of the agricultural cycle usually prevailed in the world of the rural villages. Leadership seems to have come primarily from provincial middle sectors – minor *caciques*, *principales*, lesser *gamonales*, or boss-figures – of the population rather than from below, although local bandit groups also made their contribution when it suited them. Nevertheless, the guerrilla bands represented a degree of popular mobilization. Their main zones of operation were between Huaylas, Huánuco, and Huaraz, to the north, and Cerro de Pasco, Jauja, and Huancayo, major regions of mining, commerce, and transit in the central zones rather than in the previously rebellious south. They received support from sympathetic artisans, muleteers, and clerics. Some clerics suffered at the hands of the Royalists for collaboration. Even so, the majority remained loyal to the Crown in these areas. Eventually, the guerrillas controlled large stretches of the countryside further to the south, in Junín, Ayacucho, Huancavelica, and Ancash, spreading thence into Arequipa and Ica. Both San Martín in 1821 and 1822, and Bolívar and Sucre in 1823 and 1824, strove to establish control over them. Popular recruitment may have resulted from local grievances, whether against landowners, merchants, or mine-operators, or against colonial officials, usually in league with them. In that sense, it represented something of a continuity with past grievances before the 1810s. On the other hand, the political situation in Peru during the 1810s and 1820s was strikingly different from those earlier times. This time, local bands were operating, at least in theory, in coordination with regular armies, which had won astounding victories against the colonial order and were in control of the capital city of the former viceroyalty for most of the time. Royalist forces under La Serna and Canterac (who still commanded an

---

[52] AGI Lima 762, La Serna to Minister of Grace and Justice (Madrid), no. 31, Cuzco 15 March 1824. Miller, *Memoirs*, pp. 151–62. Sobrevilla Perea, *Santa Cruz*, 74–83. Bolívar removed both Riva Agüero and Torre Tagle, leaving the future way open to southern generals like Gamarra and Santa Cruz.

army of 9000 men in the central Valley of Mantaro), took severe measures against insurgent activity, burning villages as punishment.[53]

Guerrilla chieftains, such as Marcelino Carreño and J. M. Guzmán, who operated from Huancayo in November 1823, chose their own allegiances, preferring Riva Agüero, who commanded an army of 3000 men in Trujillo, to Bolívar during their struggle for supremacy between these rival Patriot leaders. Conflicts within Patriot ranks such as these led to desertions from their bands and to defections to the Royalist side. Disdain shown by Platine or Colombian officers toward Peruvian "cholos" and "indios" hardly helped matters. Bolívar, early in 1824, put the guerrillas under the supreme command of Sucre and appointed the Englishman, General John Miller, commander of Patriot cavalry in Peru, to lead those of the Centre. Miller had little confidence in the guerrilla leaders, whom he saw as operating on their own account rather than in the interests of the general cause. At the same time, he doubted the loyalty of Indian villages that professed allegiance to the Patriot cause and distrusted the influence of pro-Royalist clergy. He regarded the Indian communities of Huanta, Huancavelica, Chincheros, and Huando as particularly unreliable, especially since Patriot forces totally only 6000 men against some 13,000 Royalists in the autumn of 1824. Given these circumstances, it was not surprising that La Serna and Valdés were able to recover Huamanga on November 16. Miller saw the key areas as Junín and Ayacucho, where the final decision in the war would be made.[54]

The position of Olañeta became crucial at this stage. Serious division within Royalist ranks ultimately enabled the Patriots, with their smaller force, to overcome the four Royalist commanders. That would mark the definitive end of Royalist Peru. However, it would not be simply a mopping-up operation but one involving the recognition of deep

[53] Dunbar Temple, *Acción patriótica*, I, doc. 329, pp. 348–49, Juan Evangelista Vivas to San Martín, Huaquis 17 August 1821, on the Royalists' village-burning in the province of Jauja. Raúl Rivera Serna, *Los guerrilleros del Centro en la emancipación peruana* (Lima 1958), 21–31, 46–48, 53–54, 127–32. On January 11, 1824, Viceroy La Serna ordered the village of Cangallo to be wiped off the map. Gustavo Vergara Arias, *Montoneros y guerrillas en la etapa de la emancipación del Perú (1820–1825)* (Lima 1973). Heraclio Bonilla, "Bolívar y las guerrillas indígenas del Perú," *Cultura: Revista del Banco Central del Ecuador*, VI, no. 16 (May-August 1983), 81–95. See also Miller, *Memoirs*, II, 121. Bolívar, *Decretos*, I, 133, Cuartel General en Huamanga 30 August 1824, exempted residents of *pueblos* burned by the Royalists in the province from all contributions for a ten-year period and instructed the Prefects to cooperate in reconstruction.

[54] Miller, *Memoirs*, II, 151–62. Rivera Serna, *Los guerrilleros del Centro*, 76, 84–87, 108–9.

political rifts concerning the future status of Upper Peru. The significance of Olañeta's separate stance lay precisely in that issue. Olañeta, whose base of support lay in Oruro, had risen through the ranks as an experienced campaigner in Upper Peru. His resentment of the arrogant newcomers from Spain, such as the other three commanders, simmered for years and finally broke to the surface with the news that Ferdinand VII had abolished the constitutional system for a second time. That provided the opportunity for the breach. Olañeta's nephew, Casimiro Olañeta, was a leading figure in the Audiencia of Charcas, close to the city's élite and consonant with the Natural Law tradition of the University of San Francisco Xavier in Chuquisaca. The two made a powerful political combination, especially when Pedro Antonio declared in January 1824 that the future of Upper Peru should be decided by local people, that is, not in Lima or Buenos Aires, and not by "foreign" generals. Much also depended upon what territories were to be included in this autonomous form of Charcas, which appeared to be still under the Spanish Monarchy. Olañeta's idea was that it should include the adjacent interior provinces of the former Viceroyalty of the River Plate, aggrieved by the predominance asserted by the port of Buenos Aires. "Greater Charcas" would thereby include Jujuy and Salta, but with the addition of Puno and the Pacific coastal district of Atacama and Tarapacá. This was intended to give the proposed government in Chuquisaca control of Lake Titicaca and access to the sea.[55]

In Spain, it even seemed as though the Peruvian Royalists might not only hold out against the republican separatists, but also defeat them through their greater number, thereby opening the way for a victorious campaign against Buenos Aires and then Colombia. French diplomats in Madrid remained pessimistic about Spanish illusions, especially since, in their view, the British government appeared anxious to recognize the independence of the Spanish American territories. Peru might seem the last hope, but this glimmer would not last long.[56]

---

[55] Marta Irurozqui, "Cuando Charcas devino en Bolivia. Algunas Reflexiones sobre el cambio político," in Frasquet and Slemian (eds.), *De la Independencias iberoamericanas a los estados nacionales*, 163–64.

[56] AAE, CP Espagne, tome 727 (April–August 1824), no. 62, ff. 29–36v., Marquis de Talaru (French Ambassador) to Viscomte de Chateaubriand (Minister of Foreign Affairs), Madrid 7 April 1824; AAE, CP: Espagne tome 729 (October-November 1824), no. 41, ff. 86, 102, Chargé d'Affaires Boislecomte to Marquis de Damas (Minister of Foreign Affairs), El Escorial 12 October 1824.

Once Sucre had finished off Olañeta during the course of 1825, the issue of the political future of the two Perus became foremost. It turned out that there were at least three views on this subject. The local notables in both Perus believed that they should be the natural rulers in two separate republics. Bolívar believed that they should either be reunited as one state on the pre-1776 model, or Upper Peru reunited with the other provinces of the former Viceroyalty of the River Plate in order to provide a bastion against Spanish reconquest and European intervention by the Counter-Revolutionary Powers. As in the case of the ill-fated Republic of Colombia (1819–30), such a view ignored late colonial developments within these territories and their growing apart. Sucre's view was that it would be impossible to resist the Upper Peruvian notables' desire for independence from both Buenos Aires and Lima. When Sucre convened a Constituent Assembly in Chuquisaca on August 6, 1825 by indirect suffrage, the majority of the forty-eight delegates were products of the University, who opted for this latter solution.[57]

Although a distinct Republic of Bolivia had not been to Bolívar's liking, he provided a centralist and authoritarian constitution, which proved largely unworkable in the actual circumstances of the country. He then wished to impose this Constitution of the Republic of Bolivia (1826) on other South American territories as his ideal solution to their common problems. It controversially provided for a life-long presidency and the right of the incumbent to select his successor. Although it also established equality before the law, civil liberties, an independent judiciary, and abolished slavery from the date of publication, the life-presidency became the bone of contention. The Indian majority of the population (80 percent), furthermore, was disqualified from political participation until 1835 on grounds of illiteracy. The Bolivian Congress upheld the Catholic establishment, despite Bolívar's opposition. Sucre was his choice for the life presidency.[58]

Bolivia's inherited social problems ensured that the Bolivarian principles would not transform the country in the desired manner, despite Sucre's enlightened rule. Economic stagnation, flight of capital, the absence of entrepreneurial spirit, entrenched privilege, and ethnic subordination continued to characterize the country. Congress reflected the perceptions of the local creole property-owners. Although Bolívar had

---

[57] Irurozqui, "Cuando Charcas devino Bolivia," 164–67.
[58] Lynch, *Bolívar*, pp. 202–5. Sucre took office on October 28, 1826 but left office in July 1828. Sobrevilla Perea, *Santa Cruz*, 84–113.

abolished Indian tribute on December 22, 1825, it was restored in June 1826, in part because of non-Indian resentment at the requirement to pay income and property tax in the form of a *contribución directa única*, abolished subsequently in December 1826. Restoration of Tribute, however, exempted Indians from payment of *alcabalas* and from military service, and, in that sense, was not unwelcomed by them. The fiscal dependence of the Bolivian state on Indian community contributions proved essential in following decades. Sucre abolished the constitutional municipalities established under the terms of the Cádiz Constitution of 1812, which implied the restoration of the traditional Andean *repúblicas de indios*. Although Bolívar had abolished the *mita*, personal service on haciendas in return for rented plots of land continued to be the norm for non-community Indians. The propertied classes, furthermore, did not intend to cooperate with the Bolivarian aim in 1825 of facilitating the emergence of a free and property-owning peasantry through the redistribution of land. Congress suspended the distribution of state land on September 20, 1827.[59]

In Cuzco, Bolívar defined for the local Andean population what the implications of the Peruvian Constitution were. It did not recognize hereditary titles and his decree of July 4, 1825 abolished the position of *cacique*. Henceforth, the local authorities would exercise the faculties enjoyed by *caciques*, since the Provincial Intendants and District Governors were the only authorities to be recognized. Bolívar explained that the basis of the Constitution was the equality of all citizens. This principle was incompatible with subjection of the Indian population by all types of authority – officials, *hacendados*, mine-operators, priests, or *caciques*, especially in cases of work without pay. He reiterated the principal of division of the communal properties among families, which would also become the means by which the Republican government compensated indigenous families dispossessed in the Royalist repression after 1814–15. Such families could expect one-third more land than the rest. The new possessors were not to sell until 1850 – and never to put their lands into mortmain.[60]

Bolívar, as Dictator, convened a new congress for Peru on May 20, 1825, which would meet in Lima on February 10, 1826. This congress

---

[59] Lynch, *Bolívar*, 205–9. Irurozqui, "Cuando Charcas devino Bolivia," 171–73.

[60] Bolívar, *Decretos*, I, 406–12, Cuzco 4 July 1825. Garrett, *Shadows of Empire*, 255: "the abolition of the *cacicazgo* and of legal nobility culminated a process that had begun forty years earlier – or rather, several processes."

adopted the Bolivian "Constitución Vitalicia," but omitted the clause abolishing slavery, since the coastal haciendas depended on slave labor. The Life-Constitution looked perilously like monarchy in republican guise. Bolívar, however, had no intention of following Iturbide down the road to monarchy. His objective was to resolve the problem of political instability through strengthening presidential power in a centralized state, while, at the same time, risking the charge of "caesarism." The Life-Presidency meant the reduction of the power of Congress in relation to the executive office. Bolívar's departure from Peru on September 2, 1826, however, made this constitution a dead-letter.[61]

In reality, the image of post-Independence Peru gleaned from legislation emanating from the capital city proved to be quite different in the provinces and localities. The Lima State was in no position to transform community peasantry into a rural proletariat dependent upon landowners. As Carlos Contreras has indicated, there had to be a prior demand from landowners for access to communal lands, and the State in Lima had to possess the capacity to enforce such a transfer. The haciendas, in any case, already held the best quality lands and had little desire in the decades after Independence to increase landholdings in the more impoverished sierra. Peasant communities rather than haciendas, furthermore, controlled resources in the Valley of Mantaro, which was the bread-basket of Lima. Their members could work, if they so chose, on hacienda lands. This area was closely integrated into the market economy, in contrast to the southern Andean zone, which in the course of the nineteenth century experienced a demonetarizing process with the collapse of the Cuzco economy. The Mantaro Valley was linked both to the coast and to the mining districts of the central Andes at Cerro de Pasco. Stable prices in the central sierra enabled the province of Jauja to absorb the burden of tribute-payment. In any case, the law of 1826 establishing the "contribución de indígenas," in a significant departure from colonial practice, made tribute-payment an individual rather than a community responsibility. It also freed the indigenous population from military service. Contreras observes a tacit understanding between these peasant families and the liberal republican system.[62]

---

[61] Basadre, *República*, I, 121–25. The Royalist commander, Rodil, held on to the port of Callao until February 19, 1826, somewhat longer than the continued Royalist hold on San Juan de Ulua opposite Veracruz. Aljovín de Losada, *Caudillos y constituciones*, 103–5.

[62] Carlos Contreras, "Estado republicano y tributo de indígenas en la Sierra Central en la post-Independencia," *RI*, vol. XLVIII, nos. 182–83 (enero-agosto 1988), 517–50:

After Bolívar's departure from Peru, the federalist idea re-emerged. Benito Lasso, Prefect of Puno, wrote at the end of 1826 to Gamarra, Prefect of Cuzco, and La Fuente, Prefect of Arequipa, proposing a meeting in the town of Lampa to complain about Lima centralism and propose a federal solution. The Arequipa newspaper, *El Federal*, explored the question of separate status for these three southern provinces. Sucre strongly opposed such tendencies, warning the Prefects on December 11 that they threatened the break-up of Peru.[63] For Peruvian republican thinkers such as Sánchez Carrión, Luna Pizarro, or Bartolomé Herrera, consideration of some form of federalism or confederation was overridden by fears of anarchy in a society of mass illiteracy and ethnic complexity. This remained the rule in the ten-year period from 1825 to 1835.[64] Peru's 1828 Constitution provided for indirect election of the president and created elected "departmental juntas" in six provinces, in order to counterbalance central power. Executive supremacy and federalized provincial administration proved to be too contradictory to sustain the constitution for any length of time. Under Gamarra's auspices, the 1834 Constitution reverted to the stronger presidency in a centralized system.[65]

The question of reuniting the two Perus remained in the air after 1826. It contributed to the project for the construction of a confederation during the later 1830s. This was to be the solution to weakness, bankruptcy, failure, and division. In the years 1824–27, the Bolivian government put forward ideas of a Grand Andean Federation, including Colombia, Peru, and Bolivia in one unit. One motive was the fear in Spanish South America of the Empire of Brazil, which had avoided political fragmentation in 1822–24. To the Lima élite, however, such an idea seemed like a project for authoritarian government under the principal Bolivian military leader, Santa Cruz. Sucre, in 1826 and 1827, suggested partition of Peru as a prerequisite for an Andean Federation. While such a policy won advocates in the press of the southern Peruvian cities welcoming the end of Lima dominance, it pointed to Bolivian predominance. Realizing the

---

see pp. 517–19, 521–22, 537–40, 547. Florencia E. Mallon, *The Defence of Community in Peru's Central Highlands. Peasant Struggle and Capitalist Transition, 1860–1940* (Princeton 1983), 54–57, also refers to "the economic strength and internal solidity of the central-highland village." Aljovín de Losada, *Caudillos y constituciones*, 206–15.

[63] Basadre, *República*, I, 110–11.

[64] See Alex Loayza and Cristóbal Aljovín de Losada, "Federalismo: Perú," in Fernández Sebastián (director), *Diccionario político y social. I*, 517–24.

[65] Aljovín de Losada, *Caudillos y constituciones*, 106–9, 152–54.

opposition in Lima, Sucre suggested a federation of Bolivia, Chile, and Buenos Aires, again to counterbalance Brazil, but when this also encountered opposition, not least in Chile, he dropped the idea. The scheme of a Peru-Bolivia Confederation was revived by Santa Cruz in 1835. A Peru-Bolivia Confederation, however, presented both Buenos Aires and Chile with the prospect of a larger and unwelcome political entity on their borders.[66] The collapse of this project in 1839 left two weak, impoverished, and divided states: the Republics of Peru and Bolivia.[67]

---

[66] Robert N. Burr, *By Reason or Force. Chile and the Balancing of Power in South America, 1830–1905* (Berkeley and Los Angeles 1967), 26–69.

[67] Loayza and Aljovín de Losada, "Peru," 520–21. Sobrevilla Perea, *Santa Cruz*, 114–204.

IO

Independence – Territories, Peoples, Nations

It is doubtful that any semblance of national consciousness existed in Ibero-America in the pre-Independence era. Even so, the new sovereign states generally established themselves formally as hypothetical nations. Regional sentiment, localism, corporate identities, inherited legal systems, patriarchal relationships, and patron–client dependencies characterized much of ordinary life in the Latin American societies of the time.[1] The eighteenth-century reforms in the Ibero-American territories had departed from several accepted traditions but they had not sought to break down the juridical structures inherited from the past. While it is true that some privileges were curtailed, metropolitan governments at the same time created new corporate forms, whether as chartered companies or state monopolies such as the Tobacco Revenue, or as *consulados*. Bourbon and Braganza administrations clipped ecclesiastical privilege, while in Spanish America, the metropolitan government created an entirely new form of the *fuero militar*, which would apply to the newly created militia companies.

THE "NATIONAL PROJECT" – A POST-INDEPENDENCE PHENOMENON

In the last decades of Iberian colonialism, a press of wider circulation and the first representative institutions did open the way for the emergence of a political culture the survival of which was in no way

---

[1] See, for instance, François-Xavier Guerra, *Le Mexique. De l'Ancien Régime à la Révolution*, 2 vols. (Paris 1985), I, 226–28, 239.

guaranteed, as the two restorations of absolutism in Spain in 1814 and 1823 demonstrated. In Ibero-America, much of the nineteenth century would be spent in developing new identities and in constructing new communities. There is little evidence that leaders of Independence movements or insurgencies, regardless of geographical location or historical epoch, held clear ideas of the type of political construction appropriate for the post-imperial age. Most were aware, however, that a national consciousness and identity did not exist in the countries they wished to emancipate from imperial rule.

In Ibero-America during the course of the period from the 1770s through the 1820s, the idea of the two Monarchies each as "One, Sole Nation" persisted. Metropolitan unitarism and restrictions, whether under absolutist or constitutionalist systems, undermined this idea. After 1808, despite demonstrations of loyalty from the Americas, the issue soon became whether American identities were, in fact, compatible with the One Nation idea. That discussion brought to the surface previously subterranean discussion of the nature of sovereignty. Similarly, it fueled radical pressures and ultimately made separatism the only feasible course for many Latin Americans, who initially had not wanted a breach with Spain or Portugal. The political Bolívar struggled with two pressing difficulties: what forms of government might correspond to existing realities? – and whether existing territorial units could become sovereign states.

Jonathan Eastwood has argued that "nationalism, when it emerged in Latin America, was a novel phenomenon in the Hispanic world." He proposes two salient characteristics of nationalism – "civic" and "collectivistic." The former implies transcendence of ethnic and regional origins and identities; the latter implies that individual identities should be regarded within the broader organism of the nation. This would represent the classic expression of nationalism as it has developed from the nineteenth century, that is, an initial liberalism soon in conflict with a national collectivism. Eastwood identifies an implicit egalitarianism in the idea of a nation, since it purports to be above specific component parts, local identities, corporate hierarchies, and class divisions. In that sense, it appears to be "modern" – as opposed to "traditional," and can be put to political use against both entrenched upper-class power and lower-class consciousness. In proposing that nationalism "appealed to individuals suffering from pronounced status-inconsistency," we find the ground shifting from sociology to social psychology. It does explain, however, the character of nationalism as surrogate religion. In Eastwood's view, "status-inconsistency has been the common denominator in the spread of the national idea across world regions ... " It could appeal, for instance, to élites, such as the Spanish American creoles, believing themselves to be disadvantaged through a decline in status brought on by actions of the metropolitan power in the course of the eighteenth century.[2] The radical press in Rio de Janeiro, pushing the political élite to go further and break with Portugal, offered a definition of what a Brazilian nation might be like. The newspaper, "Reverbero Constitucional," on January 22, 1822, said that "it is a union of peoples who obey the same law and the same system of government." The paper then went on to say that the privileged classes did not form part of this nation, since their juridical exemptions and prerogatives put them out of it. Sovereignty lay with the larger entity, although who the people were was not defined. This was not the position that prevailed, however, under the Brazilian Empire.[3]

Eastwood, for instance, sees nothing inevitable in the development of a Venezuelan nation. His examination of pamphlets issued in the 1820s did not reveal any argument that Venezuela was a natural nation. The territory's secession from the Republic of Colombia in 1830 was justified by its architects not on national but on pragmatic grounds – that it would be easier to govern as a smaller unit.[4] In fact, regionalism was the norm, that is to say that *plurality* rather than unity remained the order of the day, stimulated no end by the armed struggles of the 1810s and early 1820s. Ongoing tension between capital-city politicians and provincial élites continued through the republican era.[5]

A growing sense of *American* identity, as distinct from European, characterized the political consciousness of creole élites by the time of dynastic crisis of 1808. Whether in Brazil it was intensified or stultified by the presence of the Court and government in Rio de Janeiro from 1808 to 1821 remains an open issue. It certainly took distinct forms across continental America. Alongside this, however, customary allegiances still persisted. Such loyalties were by no means exclusive to creoles, since

[2] Jonathan Eastwood, The *Rise of Venezuelan Nationalism* (Gainesville 2006), 14–17, 153–54.

[3] Rodrigues, *Independência*, vol. 1, 318.   [4] Eastwood, *Rise of Nationalism*, 105, 150.

[5] Reuben Zahler, *Ambitious Rebels: Remaking Honor, Law, and Liberalism in Venezuela, 1780–1850* (Tucson 2013), 26–27, 37, 40–41: Andean Mérida was republican through resentment at the hegemony of Royalist Maracaibo in the coastal zone. Victor M. Uribe-Uran, "The Changing Meaning of Honor, Status and Class: The *Letrados* and Bureaucrats of New Granada in the Late Colonial and Early Post-Colonial Period," in Victor M. Uribe-Uran (ed.), *State and Society in Spanish America during the Age of Revolution* (Wilmington, DE 2001), 59–87: see pp. 67–69, 73–74, 83 note 35.

they spanned the entire social and ethnic spectrum.[6] Did "creole patriotism" signify anything more than traditionalist provincialism? Or did it represent something ethnically and geographically less constrained? As Palti points out, nationality was not the same as creole consciousness.[7] In Mexico, the first tentative move beyond it seems to have been in 1811–13, when Morelos, during the second phase of the insurgency, spoke of the "Nation." It was clear that this was neither a casual reference nor an extenuation of *criollismo*. On the contrary, Morelos' Aguacatillo declaration of November 1810 identified two actions as essential prerequisites for the construction of a Mexican nation – the implication being that one did not actually exist. These were, first, the establishment of equality of "castes," a society, that is, without the formalized racial and ethnic distinctions that had characterized the colonial legal and fiscal systems. The second prerequisite was the destruction of corporate identities, with the exception, however, of the Church. Such corporate identities did include the separate juridical status of the *repúblicas de indios*, constituted and protected by the colonial system.[8]

The vaunted "creole patriotism" of the colonial era implied no transformation of the juridical structure of society. There is no sense that non-élite sectors of the colonial population, that is, the vast majority, participated in pressures for an increased voice for the principal corporations of the realm, as expressed by the metropolitan *cabildos* from the 1770s through into the 1800s. There is similarly no sense that the protagonists envisaged any degree of popular participation. Moreover, the idea of *patria* was confused between larger territories, such as viceroyalties or captaincies-general and home provinces. In Portuguese America, for instance, the latter concept of *pátria* as the specific place of origin prevailed well into the nineteenth century. The task of territorial integration became an arduous ongoing project for all regimes thereafter.[9]

---

[6] Múnera, *El fracaso de la nación*, argues that stronger regional interests, identities, and loyalties precluded the construction of a nation out of the Viceroyalty of New Granada during the 1810s.

[7] Palti, *La nación como problema*, 133.

[8] See Michael T. Ducey, *A Nation of Villages: Riot and Rebellion in the Mexican Huasteca, 1750–1850* (Tucson 2004), and by the same author, "Liberal Theory and Peasant Practice: Land and Power in Northern Veracruz, Mexico, 1826–1900," in Robert Jackson (ed.), *Liberals, the Church and Indian Peasants: Corporate Lands and the Challenge of Reform in Nineteenth-Century Spanish America* (Albuquerque 1997), 65–94.

[9] Rodrigues, *Independência*, vol. 1, 52–60, 320.

Indigenous communities in Hispanic America had not only survived but been conserved through the colonial era, despite the general submerging of social status among the indigenous population and its classification as "indios" subject to Tribute payment. All such loyalties considerably modified any instinctive impulse toward a hypothetical national identity.[10]

Nineteenth- and twentieth-century nationalism differed from earlier national sentiment or identity through the new *sine qua non* of sovereignty of the people or of the nation. Both doctrines emerged with some insistence during the latter part of the eighteenth century. The British North-American and the French Revolutions, and early Spanish American home-rule movements in Venezuela and New Granada evolved doctrines of sovereignty of the nation or the people, often with declarations of rights designed to make graphic what this meant in practice. The early French Revolutionaries, the Cádiz constitutionalists, and Spanish American revolutionaries drew back from the democratic implications of popular sovereignty by vesting sovereignty in the nation and adopting indirect electoral systems or dividing male society into "active" and "passive" citizens, those with a vote and those without. They sought to preserve the new constitutionalist élite of well-educated gentlemen from the electoral pressures of "the mob."

This endeavor served primarily to expose the necessity at some stage of defining who "the people" were and what relation they might have to "the nation." This proved to be very much the case when electoral contests between rival factions or political parties required the mobilization of maximum support, not least through the extension of the franchise. In Latin America, redefinition of "the people" would involve widespread inclusion of hitherto marginalized ethnic groups into the political processes. Much of Latin America's nineteenth-century history would be taken up with working out the implication of such a process for the formation of the nation. The citizenship envisaged by Bolívar in his Angostura Address of 1819 would require laborious construction. In Venezuela, for example, around 80 percent of the population was illiterate in the immediate Post-Independence era. Early Venezuelan Constitutions delayed the literacy requirement for the vote, until this was finally eliminated in 1858.[11]

---

[10] Anthony Pagden, "The Effacement of Difference: Colonialism and the Origins of Nationalism," in Gyan Prakash (ed.), *After Colonialism. Imperial Histories and Postcolonial Displacements* (Princeton 1995), 129–52.

[11] Eastwood, *Rise of Nationalism*, 134. Zahler, *Ambitious Rebels*, 36, 53, 55.

The disaggregation of the Iberian Empires on the American continent did not result in the automatic formation or emergence of "nation-states." It is best to describe the states that emerged as "successor states." The collapse of Iberian power in continental America presented a range of difficult problems for each of the new sovereign units to resolve. In most cases, this took a long time and had profound repercussions lasting into the contemporary age. Javier Ocampo López describes the Independence process as unleashing a wide range of problems with no easy solutions, which included the issues of national sovereignty and continent-wide associations.[12]

One of the most problematic of the successor states was the Republic of Peru. Continued dispute surrounds the origins of a Peruvian sense of nationhood.[13] It could be argued that a national consciousness developed in Peru in response to the presence of foreign, liberating armies from Buenos Aires, Chile, or Bolivarian Colombia in the territory of the former viceroyalty during the period of struggle with resistant Royalism from 1821 to 1826. Even so, this might reflect more especially the particular hostility of the Lima élite. Since this hostility was directed against other South Americans, rather than toward Spaniards, it marked a pronounced shift away from general American sentiment in the direction of a specifically Peruvian national sentiment.[14] Yet, another perspective dates Peruvian national consciousness more than fifty years later, during the conflicts over the formation of the Peru-Bolivia Confederation in 1836–39. The coastal élite disliked the Bolivian project in part on the grounds that it resembled the Andean perspective on the nature of the Perus. Furthermore, it did not regard the indigenous population as included in the Peruvian national project.[15]

The Royalist Army and its supporters struggled to salvage what they could from the maelstrom of insurgency. Christon Archer has vividly

---

[12] Javier Ocampo López, *El proceso ideológico de la Emancipación. Las ideas de Génesis, la Independencia, Futuro e Integración en los Orígenes de Colombia* (Bogotá 1980), 41, 220–35, 387–401.

[13] Alberto Flores Galindo, "La Nación como utopía," in *Obras completas*, 4 vols. (Lima 1996), vol. IV, 371–82.

[14] Aljofín de Losada, *Caudillos y constituciones*, 238–39, identifying José de la Riva Agüero as a principal figure in this shift.

[15] This is discussed in Jesús A. Cosamalón Aguilar, "Identidades políticas locales y cambios en los primeros años de la República en el Perú," in Cristina Mazzeo de Vivó (ed.), *Las relaciones de poder en el Perú. Estado, regiones e identidades locales. Siglos XVII-XIX* (Lima 2011), 215–35: p. 216.

described this latter process as the "melt-down" of New Spain.[16] Whether the conflict between Royalists and insurgents became the "forge" of a Mexican national consciousness, or not, will continue to be debated. After Independence, the issue was whether the abolition of colonial ethnosocial categories actually implied integration into the political life in the new republics. Several of Mexico's early commentators, Mora, Zavala, Mariano Otero, Guillermo Prieto, all representing one or other branch of Liberalism, held the view that Indians could only "join" the new nation once they had forsaken their ethnic identity. Francisco Pimentel, who specifically examined this issue in 1864, concluded that

while the *naturales* remain in their present condition, Mexico cannot aspire to the level of a nation in the proper sense. A nation is a union of men who profess common beliefs, motivated by the same idea and with the same objective.

Pimentel, Prefect of Mexico City in 1865–66 during the Second Empire, regarded the juridical inheritance of the colonial *ancien régime* as an obstacle to progress, which impeded Mexico's development as a nineteenth-century nation. Liberal in social policy, he welcomed post-Independence legislation removing corporate privilege. He regarded the Laws of the Indies as a "fatal" legacy and argued that "the system of community and isolation needs to be totally eradicated." Pimentel bewailed the survival of around a hundred indigenous languages in the Republic and that Indians "do not speak Spanish except out of necessity but their own native language among themselves." Even so, he was prepared to make allowance for priests teaching them the Catholic religion in their own languages, since he saw religion as a precondition for instilling a sense of Mexican national identity.[17]

Just as the Independent Greeks laid claim to the ancient past, eighteenth-century Mexican and Peruvian thinkers appropriated the Aztec or Inca eras as their own past. Nineteenth-century Mexicans became, thereby, the latter-day "Mexica" and the President of the Republic the heir of Moctezuma and Cuauthémoc. Throughout Spanish America, from Mexico to Argentina and Chile, similar tendencies were taking place as part of the search for distinct American identities in the present founded upon the Pre-Columbian past. The objective was to stress the distinction

---

[16] Christon I. Archer, "Fighting for Small Worlds: Wars of the People during the Independence era in New Spain, 1810–1821," in McFarlane and Wiesebron (coordinadores), *Violencia social y conflict civil*, 63–92: p. 66.

[17] Francisco Pimentel, *Memoria sobre las causas que han originado la situación actual de la raza indígena de México y medios de remediarla* (Mexico City 1864), 217, 220, 222.

between Europeans and Americans by rejecting the colonial past and derivation from imperial Spain. This struggle for authenticity explained the intellectual reconstruction of the indigenous cultures, accompanied by the excavation of ruined sites and the establishment of national museums in capital cities. Appropriation of the Indian past, as the "Ancient World" of national history, and the rhetorical repudiation of the Spanish Conquest, did not lead automatically to the improvement of living standards for ordinary working Indians of the new centuries.[18]

Were these incipient national-states "imagined communities" or not? A recent historian of the formation of the Mexican state, Timothy Anna, roundly rejects the notion of an "imagined" community. He views the option for federalism as strictly pragmatic:

In Mexico, the 'national project' took the form of a federal republic. One cannot understand federalism without starting with the provinces ... And I believe that nations are not so much imagined as they are forged; that is, they are the result of the political and social processes by which institutions of government and administration are established that conform with the existing identities, institutions, and history of a territorial space. They are processes of discovery and construction from the pragmatic exercise of the human will, not born fully formed from some mystical consanguinity ... The transition to a federal republic was the real 'revolution' because the old ways gave way to the new in Mexican history ... In the light of the long continuation of colonial control in Mexico, the creation of a federal republic of sovereign states can be seen not as a dissolution but as the attempt to define a nation out of many longstanding regional identities.[19]

Despite nationalist *ex post facto* rhetoric and the nineteenth-century tendency to write "national histories" under the assumption that "nations" existed before history and were the natural goal of human experience, the Ibero-American Independence movements were not nationalist movements. Nationalist historiography developed after Independence, and in varying forms to the present day provided a new mythology. The initial objective was to justify separation from the Iberian Monarchies through an authentic legitimacy at a time when Legitimacy was the predominant creed in the Restoration Europe of 1814–30. Elías

---

[18] Rebecca A. Earle, *The Return of the Native: Indians and Myth-Making in Spanish America, 1810–1930* (Durham, NC, and London 2007), and Cecilia Méndez, "Incas si, Indios no: Notes on Peruvian Creole Nationalism and Its Contemporary Crisis," *JLAS*, 28, i (February 1996), 197–225.

[19] Timothy E. Anna, *Forging Mexico, 1821–1835* (Lincoln and London 1998), x, xii.

Palti's study of nationalism's relationship to Latin America realities points to the narrative construction of an idea of the national past during the course of the nineteenth century. The aim of the governing élites was to challenge the legitimacy of the colonial regime with a new legitimacy of their own. The prime difficulty lay in the similarity of the American-continental states to their mother countries in language, traditions, and the dominant ethnicity. Such shared traits needed to be counterbalanced by a historical narrative that stressed differences. One course lay in blackening the peninsular contribution to make it read like tyranny, discrimination, and exploitation. When the question of the right to secede from the mother country became foremost, an entirely new discourse was required.[20]

The awakening of a political nationalism in Brazil did not really occur until the aftermath of the War of the Triple Alliance (1864–70). The collapse of the monarchy in 1889 and the establishment of the federal republic in 1891 should be understood in that context. Nationalism, as it developed in Brazil, acquired four salient characteristics: rejection of the Portuguese colonial inheritance, disdain for and studied lack of interest in Spanish American states' long history of instability, belief that the African past and its continued presence contributed to Brazilian backwardness, and the idea that Europeanization would enable the country to fulfill its promise in the future. With the marginalizing of the north-east, the Afro-Brazilian contribution to the shaping of Brazilian culture became pushed into the background in favor of mythical exaltation of the Indian past, as in the novels of José de Alencar (1829–79), and encouragement of European immigration.

We should add to this the complicated relationship between the component regions and the central government. The latter saw in nationalist sentiment a powerful means of curbing regional sentiment. The "Old Republic" of 1889–1930 consciously adopted such a strategy after the restoration of civilian control in 1894. However, central-government weakness ensured that this policy would be practiced less through institutions than through personal arrangements between regional and central authorities. Under federalism, state governors became key figures in the political process. As a result, national elections, including at the presidential level, became subsumed into the balancing act among the elites.

---

[20] Elías Palti, *La nación como problema. Los historiadores y la 'cuestión nacional'* (Buenos Aires and Mexico City 2002), 131–34.

Effectively, the Army remained the only really national institution from the time of the War of the Triple Alliance.[21]

The political supremacy of the Barão do Rio Branco (1845–1912), Foreign Minister from 1902 to 1912, became a period in which the republican government promoted Brazilian national sentiment in part through clear definition of the country's territorial integrity in relation to French and Dutch Guyana, Bolivia, and Peru, and in part in terms of its position in relation to the rest of Latin America and to the United States, in particular. A dispute with Bolivia over the rubber-rich territory of Acre, which led to mobilization on both sides, was resolved in the Treaty of Petrópolis in November 1903. Competition with Argentina, which saw itself as the Spanish-speaking rival to the United States for hegemony in South America, soured relations with Brazil, also a candidate for the hegemonic position, but, at the same time, stimulated national identities. Accordingly, the Rodrigues Alves government began the reorganization of the Brazilian Army and Navy. Rio Branco, however, was more than a Brazilian nationalist: he also promoted Pan-American solidarity, a tradition virtually dormant since the days of Bolívar. The third Pan-American Conference of 1906, held in Rio de Janeiro, gave expression to this.[22]

---

[21] Ori Preuss, *Bridging the Island: Brazilians' View of Spanish America and Themselves, 1865–1912* (Madrid and Frankfurt 2011).

[22] Luis Viana Filho, *A vida do Barão do Rio Branco* (segunda edición, São Paulo, 1967). Carlos de Meira Mattos, *Brasil, Geopolítica e Destino* (Rio de Janeiro 1975), 49–50, 188–89, 204.

Final Reflections

I have long believed in the need for a re-evaluation of the events surrounding Ibero-American Independence. This book has viewed the break-up of the two Iberian Monarchies, including their European metropoles, Portugal and Spain, globally as a broad-ranging process, though with divergent patterns. I have sought to identify themes and issues running through them. My approach has been twofold. First, it has been to look at the two Monarchies, the Hispanic and Lusitanian, as a whole and often comparatively, while, at the same time, avoiding too much detail. Second, it has been to focus primarily on the problem of disaggregation, taking the periodization from roughly 1770 to 1830. In the historical literature, there has been very little attempt to link conditions within the metropoles to those in continental America, and almost none to view the Spanish and Portuguese Empires together. I have argued that the roots of the imperial crises lay not in the polarity between Americans and Europeans but in the specific condition of their respective metropoles.

Iberian rule on the American continent persisted more by negotiation than through coercion. In many respects, the Spanish and Portuguese American Empires were less absolutist systems than superstructures covering a range of conflicting and contradictory elements. They often seemed like huge marquees in a strong wind, not flying off because many interested parties were holding on to the tent pegs. The survival of the Iberian Monarchies on the American continent seemed to depend more on the holders of the pegs in the Americas than on the power and authority of the metropolitan governments. Tensions abounded, but when interests and linkages interlocked, the Monarchies in their American sectors proved to be enduring and resilient.

In practice, the colonial system within the Americas worked well in the sense that it benefitted the interests of those concerned with the survival of existing structures and practices. This was evident especially in the defining period, c. 1640- c.1770, when the colonial system matured. Informal linkages, commercial or familial, bound these structures together within the American territories and with metropolitan Spain or Portugal.

Eighteenth-century reforms in both monarchies exposed strategic weaknesses in the mobilization of resources and the extraction of revenues through the existing fiscal systems, phenomena besetting Spain and Portugal as well as their overseas dependencies. The Spanish government, while attempting to reassert royal authority through a renovated absolutism, its legitimacy reinforced by religious symbolism, refused to listen to calls from American municipalities for a greater share in political decision-making in their own territories or from ministers, such as Francisco Saavedra or colonial magistrates like Victorián de Villava for a broadening of the political base. Instead, they pursued political centralization, of which the principal exponents were José de Gálvez, Visitor General of New Spain in 1765–71 and Minister of the Indies from 1776 to 1787, and his close associate José Antonio de Areche, Visitor General of Peru from 1777 to 1782. The period of reform should be viewed, as I have tried to do, from both sides of the Atlantic at the same time.

Pombal similarly sought closer integration of Brazil with the Portuguese metropolis. The significant difference, however, was that he drew the Brazilian oligarchy into this process. In this way, he secured its collaboration. The Lisbon government, accordingly, did not face the prospect of alienating the upper classes upon which ultimately its authority depended. Pombal's objective was to enable Portugal to compete with its powerful rivals, particularly the British merchants evident in and behind the Monarchy's commercial activities.

Impressive as the changes were, they proved insufficient to stimulate a powerful enough dynamism to preserve the unity of the Monarchy. The exception was Cuba, where new networks of interest were linked to the political factions in Madrid and dedicated to the retention of ties with the metropolis. The government of Charles IV, moreover, responded to the interests of the Cuban planters by further opening access to the slave trade in the early stages of the sugar boom. The Constituent Cortes of 1810–13 continued this policy by choosing not to move toward the abolition of slavery.

Disaggregation resulted from different causes in each of the two Monarchies. In Spain, it stemmed from the metropolitan inability to mobilize sufficient resources to enable the country to continue sustaining the burden of imperial rule. This was despite the attempted renovation of institutions and commercial regulations during the course of the eighteenth century. Many such reforms were contested in both the metropolis and the Americas. One of the most significant contributory factors was the repeated failure of financial reform. The fiscal question became severe during the 1790s, although its immediate roots lay in the previous decade. The metropolitan government resorted to complex financial strategies to raise funds in wartime, as a result of the obstruction of financial reform, in the absence of a developing banking system, and the unwillingness to summon any representative body, whether traditional or new, in order to assist it. The persistence of debt did not, of its own accord, bring down the absolutist system in Spain, but inability to manage the debt. Naval defeat and political disarray at the highest level, particularly after 1805, further contributed to the collapse of the government of Charles IV and the discredited favorite, Manuel de Godoy in March 1808. The crisis of 1808 did not result from widespread revolution from below, in contrast to the events of 1789 onward in Bourbon France.

Portugal did not share the Spanish experience of the disintegration of royal government, combined with financial chaos and military defeat. On the contrary, the prestige of the Braganza dynasty remained high, and government, although continually hard-pressed in financial terms, remained coordinated under Rodrigo de Souza Coutinho, an effective, experienced, and respected senior minister. This enabled the Court, government, and higher nobility to abandon Lisbon, when the French invaded Portugal, and regroup in Rio de Janeiro, which from 1808 to 1821 became the metropolitan center of the Lusitanian Monarchy. Preserved intact, Braganza absolutism functioned in Brazil throughout the period in which Spain passed through its first constitutional period and entered its second in March 1820. Dom João, who became King João VI in 1816, had successfully assumed the Regency in the early 1790s during the mental incapacity of his mother, Maria I. In Brazil, however, opposition to the absolutist regime in Rio led to the rebellion in Pernambuco in 1817. Although put down, it proved not to be an isolated case but the forerunner of widespread opposition across the north-east and north to the political project of the south-eastern élites, leading to the outbreak of further conflict in 1821–22 and to the Confederation of the Equator in 1824 in opposition to Emperor Pedro I's abolition of the Constitution of 1822.

I have argued that the factors ultimately contributing to the break-up of the Monarchies were perceptible well before the Napoleonic intervention in the Iberian peninsula in 1807–8. Hence my choice of periodization. I stress that this intervention was not the cause of disaggregation, although it certainly made the situation worse. American perceptions of the dubious legitimacy of the peninsular regimes claiming to exercise sovereignty over the entire Monarchy from May 1808 onward stimulated existing desires for home rule. Similarly, the belief (mistaken, as it was) that metropolitan Spain had collapsed fueled the cause of separatism.

Governments in Spain and Portugal throughout this period, whether absolutist or constitutional, argued that their Monarchies constituted the Nation. Constitutionalists in Spain in 1810–14 and 1820–23 and in Portugal in 1820–23 stated that sovereignty lay in the Nation. These governments meant that the entire Monarchy was the Nation. In a similar vein, no single units of the overseas territories were viewed as constituting a nation in itself – no Mexican, Peruvian, Brazilian, Venezuelan, Chilean, or Spanish nation. Iberian constitutionalists, for their part, insisted first that all representation had to be concentrated in the metropolis and that sovereignty was indivisible. It could not be splintered into a plurality of sovereignties. For this reason, they denied the American territories (and the former realms of the peninsula) any right to their own distinct representative bodies, whether in the form of home rule or in a federalized Monarchy. This view, historians have described as unitarism. It became the bugbear of the Americans. Furthermore, refusal to concede American territories, described as equal and integral parts of the Monarchy, either equality of representation with peninsular deputies or in proportion to their population, stoked hostility to the idea of "One, Sole Nation." Refusal to grant American territories the same right of commerce with foreign states, which peninsular ports enjoyed, looked to Americans a futile attempt to preserve colonial monopolies outmoded by international trends and as a disagreeable assumption of their subordination to metropolitan interests. Last, the Spanish Cortes' denial of the exercise of political rights to mixed-bloods of African descent, a measure also advocated by some American deputies, alienated potential support in Venezuela and New Granada, where African-derived components of the population had been fighting for the Royalist cause.

Tensions, irritants, and contradictions within the Monarchies ensured that the official idea of a Hispanic or Lusitanian Nation carried little conviction in practice. Independence, however, was not inevitable; few desired or foresaw it in 1808–10. The process was not completed until

1825–30. For much of the intervening time, the preference would have been for some form of home rule within the Monarchies. The violence of Royalist counter-revolution undid much of this deeply rooted loyalism in key parts of the Spanish empires, notably Venezuela, New Granada, and New Spain.

Metropolitan Spain's collapse in 1808 left the American territories without a clear alternative form of government, while a powerful foreign army disputed control of home territory. Attempted home rule in New Spain led to a swift peninsular coup in September 1808, thereby eliminating the capital city as a potential source of political leadership. That state of affairs set New Spain apart from the initiatives that would be taken from 1809 onward across Spanish South America. In Quito, La Paz, Caracas, Buenos Aires, Santa Fe de Bogotá, and Santiago de Chile, by contrast, American-led movements, usually from the city councils, began the process of establishing home governments of their own. These movements, however, were led for the most part by products of the colonial order. They represented internal continuity by different political means. Once the overriding revolutionary objective of replacing government by viceroy, captain general, and *audiencia* had been accomplished, no further revolutionary actions were envisaged. This was intended to be government by those who had been denied the right to it under Caroline absolutism. It might, then, be described as an oligarchic or corporative seizure of power, at least in the first instance.

Three major points considerably modify previous perceptions of the Independence era. First, areas loyal to the Royalist cause during the revolutionary wars were widespread and long-lasting. Second, the revolutions did not uniformly dismantle – or even seek to weaken – existing institutions and practices deriving from the internal colonial *ancien régime*. In several states, slavery remained. In Peru and Venezuela, it lasted until 1854. In Cuba, it expanded in response to a booming sugar industry through the century until final abolition in 1886. In Peru and Bolivia, the colonial Indian tribute was restored under another name from the mid-1820s. Third, little evidence of radicalism appeared in the American movements of autonomy or separation. In many respects, few, if any of them, moved as far as the Cádiz Constitution in terms of popular representation.

Local, provincial, corporate, and ethnic identities proved stronger than any incipient national sentiment well into the nineteenth century. In Portuguese America, the concept of *pátria* as the specific place of origin prevailed over national identity. At Independence, the legacy of regional identification would prove difficult to overcome by the Brazilian Empire of 1822–89. The task of territorial integration became an arduous ongoing project for all regimes thereafter. Little in the history of Portuguese America suggested a rising tide of national sentiment in the period from 1770 to 1824. I have stressed the provincial outlook of the regional elites, evident in 1789 in the Minas Gerais conspiracy and in those of Pernambuco, the north-east, and the north in 1817 and 1821–24. Provincial mentalities predominated even in the Portuguese Cortes of 1821–23. Preliminary attempts to project the idea of a nation on to the complicated events of the day did appear from time to time in Brazil, for example in the radical press in Rio de Janeiro.

In Hispanic America, the transition from prime identity with the *patria* to overriding loyalty to the nation came about fitfully and over a long period. Nowhere – not even within states – was it uniform. If sovereignty was to be spoken of – and, once let out of the bag, it would never be put in again, then explanations were required for what was the "nation" and who were the "people." Either one of these, it was supposed, possessed it and had the incontrovertible right to exercise it. And, then, what exactly was sovereignty? Was it indivisible or could it be shared? The sovereign states would have to define which groups were to be regarded as "citizens" and which not. Disparities of wealth and ethnic differences across the American territories explained both the competition for power and resistance to it. Federalism, which provided for divided sovereignties, originated from provincial roots. It expressed regional identities and sentiment within larger territorial units in which concentration of power at the center had already become an issue before Independence. No country found federalism to be an easy system to put into lasting effect.

Élite leverage into positions of power, whether at central government or in the provinces, did not pass unchallenged from middling, educated sectors, from the powerful chieftains thrown up by the revolutionary wars, from peasant and artisan groups, Indian communities, non-community Indians or mestizos, free negroes and mulattoes. We have seen this in our discussion of the tensions and violence of the 1810s and early 1820s. There is, fortunately, a now growing historiography of such "popular movements" both during the Independence era and in the post-Independence decades. This helps to explain how the disputes preceding and during the 1810s – and not resolved then but, on the contrary, magnified – passed, changed in form, content or locality, into the post-Independence era.

Independence left many long-standing problems unresolved or even exacerbated them. At the same time, new issues arose unique to the position in which the continental American territories found themselves in the world of the 1820s and beyond. Five of these latter stood out: How representative were the new political systems to be? – how was power to be distributed within the new territorial units? – how was power to be legitimately transferred? – what was to be the balance between executive and legislative power? – what would be the juridical position of the colonial Indian communities or pueblos in Meso-America and the Andean chain? – what was to be the future of the enslaved African population of Brazil, coastal Peru, New Granada, and the Caribbean, and how would the large racially-mixed segments of the population of the (henceforth) sovereign states be socially and politically accommodated?

Incipient nations were not waiting to break loose within declining empires. On the contrary, weak successor states replaced imperial authority, inheriting pre-war problems, which civil war after 1810 exacerbated. Spain and Portugal also became two of these successor states, bound up like their American-continental counterparts in a far-reaching post-imperial crisis.

Should we view the political upheavals across the Lusitanian Monarchy from the Pernambuco uprising of 1817 onward as distinctive aspects of a singular process? If such a grouping of seemingly separate events in Brazil and Portugal were extended to the end of the Portuguese Civil War in 1834, we should have a parallel process to the events that shook the Hispanic Monarchy between 1808 and 1826, both resulting in the collapse of their European metropoles. Certainly, the dynastic civil wars in Spain (1833–40) and Portugal (1828–34) revealed the depths to which these former centers of continental-American empires had sunk in international terms. For more than a century afterwards, neither Spain nor Portugal played any significant role in European political life. They were virtually eclipsed and largely excluded from the historiography.

Bibliography

ARCHIVAL

Archives des Affaires Étrangères [AAE] (Paris)

Correspondence Politique: Espagne 720, 726, 727, 728, 729; Portugal 145, 146.

Archivo General de Indias [AGI] (Seville, Spain)

Caracas 902; Cuzco 8; Escribanía de Cámara 191ᵃ; Estado 28; Indiferente General 172, 666, 1525, 1714, 2436, 2437, 2438, 2439, 2467; Lima 603, 762, 798, 800; México 452, 638, 877, 1128, 1141, 1144, 1146, 1300, 1310, 1503, 1506, 1542, 1545, 1739, 1781, 1809, 1812, 1818, 1819, 1830, 1872, 1879, 1885, 1973, 1974, 1976, 2347, 2505, 2506, 2508, 2510, 2511, 2512, 2586, 2850, 2851, 2896, 2902, 3170; Santa Fe 668.

Archivo Histórico Nacional (Madrid)

Consejos 6086.

Archivo de Palacio [AP] (Oriente Royal Palace, Madrid)

Papeles Reservados de Fernando VII: vols. 16, 21, 22, 67.

Archivo General de la Nación [AGN] (Mexico City)

Arzobispos y Obispos 11; Consolidación 4; Historia 74; Industria y Comercio 8, 20; Operaciones de Guerra 148, 29; Tierras 1110, 1202, 1205, 1239, 1261, 1323; Tributos 34; Vínculos 180; Virreyes, primera serie, 4, 26.

Archivo Histórico de Hacienda (Mexico City)

Diputaciones foráneos, leg. 463; Primer Imperio 1871.

Archivo Histórico Municipal (Guadalajara, Mexico)

Paquete 36 [1820], no. 144; Paquete 55, legajo 8.

Archivo de Instrumentos Públicos (Guadalajara)

Protocolos 11, 17, 39.

Archivo Municipal (Morelia, Mexico)

Papeles Sueltos para los años de 1816–1817.

Archivo General de Notarías (Puebla, Mexico)

Legajos 68, 146, 170, 235.

Archivo de la Catedral (Puebla)

Libros de Cabildo, tomo 60, 82, 92/1; Tomo 113, expedientes sobre alhóndigas (1801–10); 169 (1811–16).

Archivo Histórico Municipal (Puebla)

Libros de Cabildo 80, 81, 82, 83, 92/1, 92/2, 93/1; Tomos 113, 117, 169; Papeles sueltos (1816–17).

Archivo del Registro Público (Puebla)

Libro de Censos 40, 41.

Archivo General del Poder Ejectivo del Estado de Oaxaca (Mexico)

Real Intendencia, section 1 (1792–1810), legajo 10.

Archivo Nacional de Historia del Ecuador (Quito)

Presidencia de Quito, vols. 468, 483, 484, 510–516, 531, 532, 567, 584
República de Colombia, vols. 596, 603, 607.

Biblioteca de Meléndez Pelayo (Santander, Spain)

MSS de Joaquín de la Pezuela (1761–1830); Sección de Fondos Modernos, MSS 395 (8.2.39).

Biblioteca Nacional (Rio de Janeiro, Brazil)

Manuscript Collection: Coleção Linhares 1-29-13-16; 1-19-13-22.

British Library (London, UK): Manuscripts Section

Add.Mss. 13,975, *manuscritos de Indias.*

Centro de Estudios de Historia de México (CONDUMEX, Mexico City)

Fondo XCII (1783).

National Archives (Great Britain)

Foreign Office 63 (Portugal), vols. 332, 334, 336, 340, 357; 72 (Spain), vol. 159.

PRIMARY PUBLISHED MATERIALS

Actas de la sesiones de la Legislatura Ordinaria de 1813 (1 October – 19 February 1814) (Madrid 1876).
Actas de las sesiones de la Legislativa Ordinaria de 1814 (1 March to 10 May) (Madrid 1874).
Actas de las sesiones secretas de las Cortes Generales Extraordinarias de la Nación española (Madrid 1874).
Argüelles, Agustín, *De 1820 a 1824. Reseña histórica* (Madrid 1864).

Artola, Miguel, *Memorias de tiempos de Fernando VII*, vol. 98, Biblioteca de Autores Españoles, II (Madrid 1957).

Blanco-Fombona, R. (ed.), *Últimos virreyes de Nueva Granada. Relación de mando del virrey Francisco Montalvo y noticias del virrey Sámano sobre la pérdida del reino (1813–1819)* (Madrid 1919).

Blanco White, José María, '*El Español*,' 8 tomes (London 1810–14).

Bolívar, Simón, *Address to the Venezuelan Congress at Angostura*, February 15, 1819 (Cambridge 1923 [text in Spanish]).

Bustamante, Carlos María de, *Historia del Emperador D. Agustín de Iturbide hasta su muerte y sus consecuencias, y establecimiento de la República Popular Federal* (Mexico City 1846).

Canga Argüelles, José, *Diccionario de Hacienda con aplicación a España*, 2 vols. (Madrid 1833–34).

Cartas de Jovellanos y Lord Vassall Holland sobre la Guerra de Independencia (1808–1811), 2 vols. (Madrid 1911).

Colección Documental de la Independencia peruana, 37 tomes consisting of 86 vols. (Lima 1971–76).

Constitución Política de la Monarquía Española, promulgada en Cádiz a 19 de marzo de 1812 (Barcelona 1836).

Decretos del Libertador, 3 vols. (Los Teques 1983).

Decretos del Rey Nuestro Señor D. Fernando VII, 17 vols. (Madrid 1815–33).

Documentos para la Historia del Libertador General San Martín, 19 tomes (Buenos Aires 1953–2007).

Galván Rivera, Mariano (ed.), *Colección de constituciones de los Estados Unidos Mexicanos: régimen constitucional de 1824* (Mexico City 1988 [1828]).

García, Genaro, *Documentos Históricos Mexicanos*, 7 vols. (Mexico City 1910–12).

Documentos inéditos y muy raros para la historia de México (Mexico City 1974).

Grandmaison, Charles Alexandre Geoffroy de (ed.), *Correspondance du Comte de La Forest, Ambassadeur de France en Espagne, 1808–1813*, 7 vols. (Paris 1905–13).

Hernández Silva, Cuauhtémoc and Zevallos Juan Manuel Pérez, (eds.), *Fray Melchor Talamantes. Escritos póstumos, 1808* (Mexico City 2009).

Hernández y Dávalos, Juan Eusebio, *Colección de documentos para la historia de la guerra de independencia de México de 1808 a 1821*, 6 vols. (Mexico City 1877–82).

Instrucciones que los virreyes de la Nueva España dejaron a sus sucesores, 2 vols. (Mexico City 1877 and 1882).

Memoria de Gobierno del virrey Joaquín de la Pezuela, virrey del Perú, 1816–1821 (Seville 1947).

Memorias de tiempos de Fernando VII (Madrid, Biblioteca de Autores Españoles, 1957), with Preliminary Study by Miguel Artola.

Mesonero Romanos, Ramón, *Memorias de un setentón, natural y vecino de Madrid* (Madrid 1975 [1880]).

Mier, Fray Servando Teresa de, *Historia de la Revolución de Nueva España Antiguamente Anáhuac o Verdadero orígen y causas de ella con relación de sus progresos hasta el presente año de 1813* (Paris 1990 [London 1813]), edited by Saint-Lu, André and Marie-Cécile Bénassy-Berling.

Miller, John, *Memoirs of General Miller*, 2 vols. (London 1828–29).

Miraflores, Marqués de, *Apuntes histórico-críticos* (London 1834).

Morillo, Pablo, *Mémoires du Général Morillo, Comte de Carthagène, Marquis de la Puerta, Rélatifs aux principaux évenements de ses campagnes en Amérique de 1815 à 1821* (Paris 1826).

Ortiz, Sergio Elías (compiler), *Colección de documentos para la historia de Colombia (Época de la Independencia)*, third series (Bogotá 1966), pp. 241–45.

Pezuela, Joaquín de la, *Compendio de los sucesos ocurridos en el Ejército del Perú y sus provincias (1813–1816)*, edited by Ortemberg, Pablo and Natalia Sobrevilla Perea (Santiago, Chile 2011).

Pimentel, Francisco, *Memoria sobre las causas que han originado la situación actual de la raza indígena de México y medios de remediarla* (Mexico City 1864).

Quirós, José María, *Memoria de Instituto* (Havana 1814).

Reglamento y aranceles reales para el comercio libre de España a Indias de 12 de octubre de 1778 (Sevilla 1979), edited by Torres Ramírez, Bibiano and Javier Ortiz de la Tabla, Javier.

Restrepo, José Manuel, *Historia de la revolución de la república de Colombia en la América meridional*, 4 vols. (Besançon 1858).

Revillagigedo, Viceroy Conde de, *Instrucción reservada, en Instrucciones que los virreyes de Nueva España dejaron a sus sucesores*, 2 vols. (Mexico City 1867–73).

Saavedra, Francisco de, *Los decenios. Autobiografía de un sevillano de la Ilustración*, transcription, introduction and notes by Morales Padrón, Francisco (Seville 1995).

Diario de D. Francisco de Saavedra durante la comisión que tuvo a su cargo desde 25 de junio de1780 hasta 20 del mismo mes de 1783, edited by Morales Padrón, Francisco (Seville 2004).

Sanz Cid, Carlos, *La Constitución de Bayona* (Madrid 1922).

Solórzano y Pereira, Juan de, *Política indiana* (Antwerp 1703 [original Latin version, Madrid 1647]).

Zamora y Coronado, J. M., *Biblioteca de legislación ultramarina en forma de diccionario alfabético*, 6 tomes (Madrid 1844–49).

SECONDARY SOURCES

Abad León, Felipe, *El Marqués de la Ensenada. Su vida y su obra*, 2 vols. (Madrid 1985).

Adelman, Jeremy, *Sovereignty and Revolution in the Iberian Atlantic* (Princeton 2006).

"An Age of Imperial Revolutions," *AHR*, 113 (April 2008), 319–40.

Albi de la Cuesta, Julio, *El último virrey* (Madrid 2009).

Aldana Rivera, Susana, *Poderes de una región de frontera. Comercio y familia en el norte, 1700–1830* (Lima 1999).

"Un norte diferente para la Independencia peruana," *RI*, 57, no. 209, 141–64.

Alexandre, Valentim, *Os sentidos do Império. Questão colonial na crise do Antigo Regime Português* (Oporto 1993).

Aljovín de Losada, Cristóbal, *Caudillos y constituciones. Peru: 1821–1845* (Lima 2000).

Álvarez Junco, José, *Mater Dolorosa. La idea de la España en el siglo XIX* (Madrid, tenth edition, Madrid 2007 [2001]).

Amadori, Arrigo, *Negociando la obediencia. Gestión y reforma de los virreinatos americanos en tiempos del conde-duque de Olivares (1621-1643)* (Madrid 2013).

Andrien, Kenneth J., *Crisis and Decline. The Viceroyalty of Peru in the Seventeenth Century* (Albuquerque 1985).

"The Sale of Fiscal Offices and the Decline of Royal Authority in the Viceroyalty of Peru, 1633–1700," *HAHR*, 62, i (February 1982), 49–71.

and Johnson, Lyman L., (eds.), *The Political Economy of Spanish America in the Age of Revolution, 1750–1850* (Albuquerque 1994).

Anna, Timothy E., *The Fall of the Royal Government in Peru* (Lincoln and London 1979).

Spain and the Loss of America (Lincoln and London 1983).

The Mexican Empire of Iturbide (Lincoln and London 1990).

Forging Mexico, 1821–1835 (Lincoln and London 1998).

Annino, Antonio, (compiler), *Historia de las elecciones en Iberoamérica, siglo XIX* (Mexico City 1995).

Archer, Christon I., "'La Buena Causa:' The Counterinsurgency Army of New Spain and the Ten Years' War," in Rodríguez, Jaime (ed.), *The Independence of Mexico and the Creation of the New Nation* (Los Angeles 1989), 85–108.

"Bite of the Hydra: The Rebellion of the Cura Miguel Hidalgo, 1810–1811," in Rodríguez, Jaime E., (ed.), *Patterns of Contention in Mexican History* (Wilmington, DE, 1992), 69–93.

"The Cutting Edge: The Historical Relationship between Insurgency, Counterinsurgency and Terrorism during Mexican Independence, 1810–1821," in Howard, Lawrence (ed.), *Terrorism: Roots, Impact, Responses* (Westport, CT, 1992), 29–46.

"Politicization of the Army in New Spain during the War of Independence," in Rodríguez, Jaime (ed.), *The Evolution of the Mexican Political System* (Wilmington, DE, 1993), 17–43.

"Years of Decision: Félix Calleja and the Strategy to End the Revolution of New Spain," in Archer, Christon I. (ed.), *The Birth of Modern Mexico, 1780–1824* (Wilmington, DE, 2003), 125–49.

Arcila, Farías, *Eduardo, Comercio entre Venezuela y México en los siglos XVII y XVIII* (Mexico City 1950).

Ardit, Manuel, *Revolución liberal y revuelta campesina. Un ensayo sobre la desintegración del régimen feudal en el Pais valenciano (1793–1840)* (Barcelona 1977).

Artola, Miguel, *Orígenes de la España contemporánea*, 2 vols. (Madrid 1959).

La burguesía revolucionaria (1808–1869) (Madrid 1973).

(ed.), *Las Cortes de Cádiz* (Madrid 2003).

Aymes, Jean-René, *La guerra de España contra la Revolución francesa (1793–1795)* (Alicante 1991).

L'Espagne contre Napoléon: la guerre de l'independence espagnole (1808–1814) (Paris 2003).

Barbier, Jacques, "Peninsular Finance and Colonial Trade: The Dilemma of Charles IV's Spain," *JLAS* 12, no. I (May 1980), 21–37.

Barman, Roderick J., *Brazil. The Forging of a Nation, 1798–1852* (Stanford 1988).

Barreda, Felipe A., *Manuel Pardo Ribadeneira, regente de la Real Audiencia del Cuzco* (Lima 1954).

Bartley, Russell H., *Imperial Russia and the Struggle for Latin American Independence 1808–1828*, (Austin 1978).

Basadre, Jorge, *El azar en la historia y sus límites* (Lima 1973).

Historia de la República del Perú, 11 vols., seventh edition (Lima 1983).

Bastos Pereira das Neves, Lúcia Maria, *Corundas e constitucionais. A cultura política da Independência (1820–1822)* (Rio de Janeiro 2003).

Bayly, C. A., *The Birth of the Modern World, 1780–1914* (Blackwell, Oxford 2004).

Benedict, Bradley, "El Estado en México en la época de los Habsburgo," *HM*, XVIII (julio 1973-julio 1974), 551–610.

Benson, Nettie Lee, *Mexico and the Spanish Cortes, 1810–1822. Eight Essays* (Austin 1966).

"The Plan of Casa Mata," *HAHR*, 25, i, (February 1945), 45–56.

Bernades, Denis Antônio de Mendonça, *O patriotismo constitucional: Pernambuco, 1820–1822* (São Paulo and Recife 2006).

Bernal, Antonio Miguel, *La lucha por la tierra en la crisis del antiguo régimen* (Madrid 1979).

Blanco Valdés, Roberto, *Rey, cortes y fuerza armada en los orígenes de la España liberal, 1808–1823* (Madrid 1988).

Boehrer, George C. A., "The Flight of the Brazilian Deputies from the Cortes Gerais of Lisbon, 1822," *HAHR*, 40, iv, (November 1960), 497–512.

Bonilla, Heraclio, "Bolívar y las guerrillas indígenas del Perú," *Cultura: Revista del Banco Central del Ecuador*, VI, no. 16 (May-August 1983), 81–95.

Bonney, Richard (ed.), *Economic Systems and State Finances* (Oxford 1995).

Boxer, C. R., *The Golden Age of Brazil, 1695–1750* (Berkeley and Los Angeles 1962).

Portuguese Society in the Tropics: The Municipal Councils of Goa, Macao, Bahia and Luanda, 1510–1800 (Madison 1965).

The Portuguese Seaborne Empire, 1415–1825 (London 1991 [1969]).

Brading, D. A., *Merchants and Miners in Bourbon Mexico, 1763–1810* (Cambridge 1971).

Breña, Roberto, *El primer liberalismo y los procesos de emancipación de América, 1808–1824. Una revisión historiográfica del liberalismo hispánico* (Mexico City 2006).

Brines Blasco, Juan, "Deuda y desamortización durante el Trienio Constitucional (1820–1823), *Moneda y Crédito*, 124 (March 1973), 51–67.

Brooker, Jackie, *Veracruz Merchants, 1770–1829. A Mercantile Elite in Late Bourbon and Early Independent Mexico* (Boulder, CO, 1993).

Brown, Jonathan C., *A Socioeconomic History of Argentina, (1776–1860)* (Cambridge 1979).

Brown, Matthew, and Paquette, Gabriel (eds.), *Connections after Colonialism: Europe and Latin America in the 1820s* (Tuscaloosa 2013).

Burga, Manuel, *Nacimiento de una utopia. Muerte y resurrección de los incas* (Lima 1988).

Burgin, Miron, *The Economic Aspects of Argentine Federalism, 1820–1852* (Cambridge, MA, 1946).

Burkholder, Mark A. and Chandler, D. S., *From Impotence to Authority. The Spanish Crown and the American Audiencias, 1687–1808* (Columbia, MO, and London 1977).
"Creole Apppointments and the Sale of Audiencia Positions in the Spanish Empire under the Early Bourbons, 1701–1750," *JLAS*, 4, ii (November 1972), 187–206.
Büschges, Christian, *Familia, honor y poder. La nobleza en la ciudad de Quito en la época colonial tardía (1765–1822)* (Quito 2007 [Stuttgart 1996]).
Bushnell, David, *The Santander Régime in Gran Colombia* (Newark, DE, 1954).
The Making of Modern Colombia. A Nation in Spite of Itself (Berkeley and Los Angeles 1993).
Cabral de Mello, Evaldo, *A outra Independência. O federalismo pernambucano de 1817 a 1824* (São Paulo 2004).
Cahill, David P., "Crown, Clergy, and Revolution in Bourbon Peru: The Diocese of Cuzco, 1780–1814," unpublished Ph. D. dissertation, University of Liverpool [1984].
"Una vision andina: el levantamiento de Ocongate de 1815, *Histórica*, XII, no. 2 (December 1988), 133–59.
"Repartos ilícitos y familias principales. El sur andino: 1780–1824," *RI*, XLVIII, 1 and 2, nos. 182–183 (January-August 1988), 449–73.
"Taxonomy of a Colonial 'Riot': The Arequipa Disturbances of 1780," in Fisher, John R., Kuethe, Allan J., and McFarlane, Anthony (eds.), *Reform and Insurrection in Bourbon New Granada and whose pedigree had been recognised Peru* (Baton Rouge and London 1990), 255–91.
"New Viceroyalty, New Nation, New Empire: A Transitional Imaginary for Peruvian Independence," *HAHR*, 91, no. 2 (May 2011), 203–55.
Calderón, María Teresa, and Thibaud, Clément, *La Majestad de los pueblos en la Nueva Granada y Venezuela, 1780–1832* (Bogotá 2010).
Callahan, William J., *Church, Politics, and Society in Spain, 1750–1874* (Cambridge, MA 1984).
Campbell, Leon G., *The Military and Society in Colonial Peru, 1750–1810* (Philadelphia 1978).
Cañeque, Alejandro, *The King's Living Image. The Culture and Politics of Viceregal Power in Colonial Mexico* (New York and London 2004).
Capella Martínez, Miguel, and Matilla Tascón, A., *Los Cinco Gremios Mayores de Madrid. Estudio crítico-histórico* (Madrid 1957).
Cardim, Pedro, *Cortes e cultura política no Portugal do Antigo Regime* (Lisbon 1998).

Carrera Damas, Germán, *Boves. Aspectos socioeconómicos de la Guerra de Independencia* (Caracas, third edition, Caracas 1972 [1968]).

Castañeda, Carmen (ed.), *Elite, clases sociales y rebelión en Guadalajara y Jalisco: siglos XVIII y XIX* (Guadalajara 1988).

Castro, Concepción de, *La revolución liberal y los municipios españoles (1812–1868)* (Madrid 1979).

Castro Arenas, M., "La rebelión de Juan Santos Atahualpa," *Cuadernos Americanos*, 199 (1975), 125–45.

Cespedes del Castillo, Guillermo, "Lima y Buenos Aires. Repercusiones económicas y políticas de la creación del virreinato del Plata," *AEA*, iii (1946), 669–874.

Chambers, Sarah C., *From Subjects to Citizens: Honor, Gender, and Politics in Arequipa, Peru, 1780–1854* (Pennsylvania 1999).

Chiaramonte, José Carlos, *Nación y estado en Iberoamérica: El lenguaje político en tiempos de las independencias* (Buenos Aires 2004).

"¿Provincias o estados? Los orígenes del federalismo rioplatense," in Guerra, François-Xavier (ed.), *Las revoluciones hispánicas. Independencias americanas y liberalismo español* (Madrid 1995), 167–205.

"Autonomía e independencia en el Río de la Plata, 1808–1810," *HM*, 229, vol. lviii, no. 1 (July-September 2008), 325–68.

"The Ancient Constitution after Independence (1808–1852)," *HAHR*, 90, iii (August 2010), 455–89.

Chowning, Margaret, *Wealth and Power in Provincial Mexico. Michoacán from the Late Colony to the Revolution* (Stanford 1998).

Chust, Manuel, *La cuestión nacional americana en las Cortes de Cádiz* (Valencia 1999).

(ed.), *Las Independencias iberoamericanas en su laberinto. Controversias, cuestiones, interpretaciones* (Valencia 2010).

"Las Cortes de Cádiz, la Constitución de 1812 y el autonomismo americano, 1808–1837," *Bicentenario. Revista de Historia de Chile y América*, 5, no. 1 (2006), 63–84.

Coatsworth, John H., "The Limits of Colonial Absolutism: The State in Eighteenth Century Mexico," in Spalding, Karen (ed.), *Essays in the Political, Economic and Social History of Colonial Latin America* (Newark, DE: University of Delaware Press, 1982), 25–51.

Coclet da Silva, Ana Rosa, *Inventando a Nação: Intelectuais Ilustrados e Estadistas Luso-Brasileiros na Crise do Antigo Regime Português, 1750–1822* (São Paulo 2006).

Collier, Simon, *Ideas and Politics of Chilean Independence, 1808–1833* (Cambridge 1967).

"Nationality, Nationalism, and Supranationalism in the Writings of Simón Bolívar," *HAHR*, 63, i (February 1983), 37–64.

Comellas, José Luis, *Los realistas en el Trienio Constitucional,* (Pamplona 1958).

El Trienio constitucional (Madrid 1963).

Connaughton, Brian F. *Dimensiones de la identidad patriótica. Religión, política y regiones en México. Siglo XIX* (México 2001).

Clerical Ideology in a Revolutionary Age. The Guadalajara Church and the Idea of the Mexican Nation (1788–1853) (Calgary and Boulder, CO 2003).

with Illiades, Carlos, and Pérez Toledo, Sonia (eds.), *Construcción de la legitimidad política en México* (Mexico City and Zamora 1999).

Conrad, Robert, *The Destruction of Brazilian Slavery, 1850–1888* (Berkeley, Los Angeles, London 1972).

Contreras, Carlos, "Estado republicano y tributo de indígenas en la Sierra Central en la post-Independencia," *RI,* XLVIII, nos. 182–183, (enero-agosto 1988), 517–50.

"El impuesto de la contribución personal en el Perú del siglo XIX," *Histórica,* XXIX, no. 2 (2005), 67–106.

Cornejo Bouroncle, Jorge, *Pumacahua. La revolución del Cuzco de 1814. Estudio documentado* (Cuzco 1956).

Correia de Andrade, Manuel (organizador), *Confederação do Equador* (Recife 1988).

Corts, Ramón, *L'arquebisbe Fèlix Amat (1750–1824): l'última Il. lustració espanyola* (Barcelona 1992).

Costeloe, Michael P., *Response to Revolution. Imperial Spain and the Spanish American Revolutions, 1810–1840* (Cambridge 1986).

Couturier, Edith Boorstein, *The Silver King: The Remarkable Life of the Count of Regla in Colonial Mexico* (Albuquerque 2003).

Coverdale, John F., *The Basque Phase of Spain's First Carlist War* (Princeton 1984).

Cruz, Jesús, *Gentlemen, Bourgeois, and Revolutionaries. Political Change and Cultural Persistence among the Spanish Dominant Groups, 1750–1850* (Cambridge 1996).

Cuenca Toribio, J. M., *D. Pedro de Inguanzo y Rivero (1764–1836), último primado del antiguo régimen* (Pamplona 1965).

Dealey, James Q., "The Spanish Sources of the Mexican Constitution of 1824," *The Quarterly of the Texas State Historical Association,* III, no. 3 (January 1900), 161–69.

Deans Smith, Susan, *Bureaucrats, Planters, and Workers. The Making of the Tobacco Monopoly in Bourbon Mexico* (Austin, Texas 1992).

Dedieu, Jean-Pierre, Bertrand, Michel, Enríquez, Lucretia, and Hernández, Elizabeth, "Abriendo la conciencia del reino: Cádiz y las independencias americanas," *Boletín de la Academia Chilena de la Historia,* Año LXXVIII, no. 121 (2012), 61–96.

Del Valle Pavón (coordinator), *Mercaderes, comercio y consulados de Nueva España en el siglo XVIII* (Mexico City 2003).

De la Torre Villar, Ernesto, *La Constitución de Apatzingán y los creadores del Estado mexicano* (Mexico City 1964).

Delgado, Jaime, "La misión a México de D. Juan de O'Donojú," *RI*, no. 35 (enero-marzo de 1949), 25–87.

Delgado Riba, Joseph M., *Dinámicas imperiales (1650–1796). España, América y Europa en el cambio institucional del sistema colonial español* (Barcelona 2007).

"La integración de Hispanoamérica en el mercado mundial (1797–1814)," *Boletín Americanista*, Año XXIII, no. 31 (1981), 41–52.

Dérozier, Albert, *L'histoire de la Sociedad del Anillo de Oro pendant le triennant constitutionnel, 1820–1823: la faillité du système libèral* (Paris 1965).

Manuel Josef Quintana et la naissance du libèralisme en Espagne, 2 vols. (Paris 1968–1970).

"Argüelles y la cuestión de América en las Cortes de Cádiz de 1810–1814," in Gil Novales, Alberto (ed.), *Homenaje a Noël Salomon. Ilustración española e Independencia de América* (Barcelona 1979), 159–64.

Di Meglio, Gabriel, *¡Viva el bajo pueblo! La plebe urbana de Buenos Aires y la política entre la Revolución de Mayo y el rosismo, (1810–1829)* (Buenos Aires 2007).

Dias Tavares, Luis Henrique, *A Independência do Brasil na Bahia* (Rio de Janeiro 1977).

Dickenson, John, and Roberta Delson, *Enterprise under Colonialism: A Study of Pioneer Industrialization in Brazil, 1700–1830* (Working Paper 12, Liverpool 1991).

Disney, A. R., *A History of Portugal and the Portuguese Empire*, 2 vols. (Cambridge 2009).

Dominguez, Jorge, *Insurrection or Loyalty: The Breakdown of the Spanish American Empire* (Cambridge, MA, 1980).

Ducey, Michael T., *A Nation of Villages: Riot and Rebellion in the Mexican Huasteca, 1750–1850* (Tucson 2004).

"Liberal Theory and Peasant Practice: Land and Power in Northern Veracruz, Mexico, 1826–1900," in Jackson, Robert (ed.), *Liberals, the Church and Indian Peasants: Corporate Lands and the Challenge of Reform in Nineteenth-Century Spanish America* (Albuquerque 1997), 65–94.

Durán López, Fernando, *José María Blanco White o la conciencia errante* (Seville 2005).

Durand Flores, Luis, *Independencia e integración en el plan político de Tupac Amaru* (Lima 1973).

Dym, Jordana, *From Sovereign Villages to National States. City, State and Federation in Central America, 1759–1839* (Albuquerque 2006).

Earle, Rebecca A., *Spain and the Independence of Colombia, 1810–1825* (Exeter 2000).

The Return of the Native: Indians and Myth-Making in Spanish America, 1810–1930 (Durham, NC, and London 2007).

"Popular Participation in the Wars of Independence in New Granada," in McFarlane, Anthony, and Posada-Carbó, Eduardo (eds.), *Independence and Revolution in Spanish America: Perspectives and Problems* (London 1999), 87–101.

Eastman, Scott, *Preaching Spanish Nationalism across the Hispanic Atlantic, 1759–1823* (Baton Rouge 2011).

"'America Has Escaped Our Hands:' Rethinking Empire, Identity and Independence during the Trienio Liberal in Spain, 1820–1823," *European History Quarterly*, 41, no. 3 (July 2011), 428–43.

and Sobrevilla Perea, Natalia (eds.), *The Rise of Constitutional Government in the Iberian Atlantic World. The Impact of the Cádiz Constitution of 1812* (Tuscaloosa 2015).

Eastwood, Jonathan, *The Rise of Venezuelan Nationalism* (Gainesville 2006).

Echeverría, Marcela, *Indian and Slave Royalism in the Age of Revolution: Reform, Revolution, and Royalism in the Northern Andes, 1780–1825* (Cambridge 2016).

"Popular Royalism. Empire and Politics in Southwestern New Granada, 1809–1819," *HAHR*, 91, ii (May 2011), 237–69.

Eissa-Barroso, Francisco A. "'Of Experience, Zeal, and Selflessness': Military Officers as Viceroys in Early Eighteenth-Century Spanish America," *The Americas*, 68, no. 3 (January 2012), 317–45.

Elliot, J. H., "A Europe of Composite Monarchies," *Past and Present*, 137 (1992), 48–71.

Escobar Ohmstede, Antonio, "Del gobierno indígena al Ayuntamiento constitucional en las Huastecas hidalguenses y veracruzanos, 1780–1853," *Mexican Studies/Estudios Mexicanos*, 12, no. 1 (1996), 1–26.

with Falcón, Romana, and Buve, Raymond (compilers), *Pueblos, comunidades y municipios frente a los proyectos modernizadores en América Latina* (San Luis Potosí and Amsterdam 2002).

Escorcia, José, "Haciendas y estructura agraria del valle del Cauca, 1810–1815," *Anuario Colombiano de Historia social y de la cultura*, X (1982), 119–38.

Esdaile, Charles, *The Peninsular War. A New History* (London 2002).

Fernández Albaladejo, Pablo, *La crisis del antiguo régimen en Guipúzcoa, 1766–1833. Cambio económico e historia* (Madrid 1975).

Materia de España. Cultura política e identidad en la España moderna (Madrid 2007).

Fernández Sebastián, José (director), *Diccionario político y social del mundo iberamericano. I, Iberoconceptos* (Madrid 2009).

Ferrer Muñoz, Manuel, *La Constitución de Cádiz y su aplicación en la Nueva España (Pugna entre Antiguo y Nuevo Régimen en el virreinato, 1810–1821)* (Mexico City 1993).

Ferrero Rebagliati, Raúl, *El liberalismo peruano. Contribución a una historia de ideas* (Lima 1958).

Ferry, Robert J., *The Colonial Elite of Early Caracas. Formation and Crisis, 1567–1767* (Berkeley, Los Angeles, London 1989).

Filho, Luis Viana, *O Negro na Bahia* (Rio de Janeiro 1988 [1946]).

Fisher, John R., *Government and Society in Colonial Peru. The Intendant System, 1784–1814* (London 1970).

Commercial Relations between Spain and Spanish Americas in the Era of Free Trade, 1778–1796 (Liverpool, 1985).

Flores Galindo, Alberto, *Arequipa y el sur andino: ensayo de historia regional: siglos xvii–xix* (Lima 1977).

Independencia y Revolución, 2 vols. (Lima 1987).

Obras completas, 4 vols. (Lima 1996).

Flores Ochoa, Jorge, and Valencia E., Abraham, *Rebeliones indígenas quechuas y aymaras* (Cuzco 1980).

Florescano, Enrique, *Precios del maíz y crisis agrícolas en México (1708–1810). Ensayo sobre el movimiento de los precios y sus consecuencias económicas y sociales* (Mexico City 1969).

Etnía, estado y nación. Ensayo sobre las identidades colectivas en México (Mexico City 1997).

and Gil Sánchez, Isabel, (eds.), *Descripciones económicas generales de Nueva España, 1784–1817* (Mexico City 1973).

Flory, R., and Smith, D. G., "Bahian Merchant Planters in the Seventeenth and Eighteenth Centuries," *HAHR*, 58, iv, (November 1978), 574–91.

Fontana, Josep, *La quiebra de la monarquía absoluta, 1814–1820. La crisis del antiguo régimen en España* (Barcelona 1971).

De en medio del tiempo. La segunda restauración española, 1823–1834 (Barcelona 2006).

Frasquet, Ivana, *Las caras del águila. Del liberalismo gaditano a la república federal mexicana (1820–1824)* (Castelló de la Plana 2008).

Garavaglia, Juan Carlos, *Mercado interno y economía colonial* (Mexico City 1992).

and Grosso, Juan Carlos, "La región de Puebla/Tlaxcala en la economía novohispana (1670–1821)," *HM*, XXXV (1986), 549–600.

García Monerris, Encarna, and García Monerris, Carmen, "Tiempo de liberalismo y Revolución: España en la primera mitad del siglo XIX," in Frasquet, Ivana and Slemian, Andréa (eds.), *De las Independencias iberoamericanas a los estados nacionales (1810–1850)* (Madrid and Frankfurt 2009), 263–93.

García Vera, José Antonio, *Los comerciantes trujillanos (1780–1840)* (Lima 1989).

"Aduanas, comerciantes y nación mercantil: Trujillo, 1776–1836," *RI*, XVIII, nos. 182–83, (January-August 1988), 435–47.

Garrett, David T., *Shadows of Empire. The Indian Nobility of Cusco, 1750–1825* (Cambridge 2005).

Gil Novales, Alberto, *Las sociedades patrióticas: las libertades de expresión y de reunión en el origen de los partidos políticos, 1820–1823*, 2 vols. (Madrid 1975).

Glave, Luis Miguel, *Vida, símbolos y batallas. Creación y recreación de la comunidad indígena. Cuzco, siglos XVI–XX* (Mexico City 1992).

"Antecedentes y naturaleza de la revolución del Cuzco en 1814 y el primer proceso electoral," in O'Phelan Godoy (compiler), *La Independencia en el Perú* (2001), 77–97.

"La Ilustración y el pueblo: el 'loco' Bernardino Tapia. Cambio y hegemonía cultural en los Andes al fin de la colonia. Azángaro, 1818," *Historias*, 60 (enero-abril 2005), 93–112.

"Un héroe fragmentado. El cura Muñecas y la historiografía andina," *Andes*, no. 13 (2002).

"Una perspectiva histórico-cultural de la revolución del Cuzco de 1814," *Revista de la América. Historia y Presente*, no. 1 (Spring 2003), 11–38.

"Cultura política, participación indígena y redes de comunicación en la crisis colonial. El virreinato del Perú," *HM*, 229, vol. LVIII, no. 1 (July-September 2008), 369–426.

Golte, Jürgen, *Repartos y rebeliones: Tupac Amaru y las contradicciones de la economía colonial* (Lima 1980).

Gómez Hoyos, Rafael, *La revolución granadina de 1810. Ideario de una generación y de una época (1781–1821)*, 2 vols. (Bogotá 1962).

González Sánchez, Isabel, *Haciendas y Ranchos de Tlaxcala en 1712* (Mexico City 1969).

Grafe, Regina, *Distant Tyranny. Markets, Power, and Backwardness in Spain, 1650–1800* (Princeton 2012).

Grafenstein Garcis, Johanna von, *Nueva España en el circuncaribe, 1779–1808. Revolución, competencia imperial y vínculos internacionales* (Mexico City 1997).

Greenow, Linda, *Credit and Socioeconomic Change in Colonial Mexico: Loans and Mortgages in Guadalajara, 1720–1820* (Boulder, CO 1983).

Griffiths, Nicholas, *The Cross and the Serpent. Religious Repression and Resurgence in Colonial Peru* (Norman and London 1996).

Guardino, Peter F., *Peasants, Politics and the Formation of Mexico's National State: Guerrero, 1800–1857* (Stanford 1996).

The Time of Liberty. Popular Political Culture in Oaxaca, 1750–1850 (Durham, NC and London 2005).

Guedea, Virginia, *En busca de un gobierno alterno: Los Guadalupes de México* (Mexico City 1992).

La insurgencua en el Departamento del Norte: los Llanos de Apan y la Sierra de Puebla, 1810–1816 (Mexico City 1996).

Gueniffey, Patrice, *La politique de la Terreur* (Paris 2000).

Guerra, François-Xavier, *Le Mexique. De l'Ancien régime à la Révolution*, 2 vols. (Paris 1985).

Modernidad e independencias. Ensayos sobre las revoluciones hispánicas (Mexico City, second edition, Mexico City 1993 [Madrid 1992]).

Guerra, Ramón, *La corte española del siglo XVIII* (Madrid 1991).

Gutiérrez Ardila, Daniel, *Un Nuevo Reino. Geografía política, pactismo y diplomacia durante el interregno en Nueva Granada (1808–1816)* (Bogotá 2010).

Las asambleas constituyentes de la Independencia. Actas de Cundinamarca y Antioquia (1811–1812) (Bogotá 2010).

Las vacilaciones de Cartagena. Polémicas neogranadinas en torno a la creación del Consejo de Regencia (Bogotá 2012).

Gutiérrez Ramos, Jairo, "La Constitución de Cádiz en la Provincia de Pasto, Virreinato de la Nueva Granada, 1812–1822," *RI*, 68, no. 242 (January – April 2008), 207–24.

Guzmán Pérez, Moisés, *Miguel Hidalgo y el gobierno insurgente en Valladolid* (third edition, Morelia 2011 [1996]).

"Lecturas militares. Libros, Escritos y Manuales de Guerra en la Independencia," *Relaciones*, 110, vol. xxviii (primavera 2007), 95–140.

Haber, Stephen H., *Industry and Underdevelopment. The Industrialization of Mexico, 1890–1940* (Stanford 1989).

and Klein, Herbert S., "The Economic Consequences of Brazilian Independence," in Haber, Stephen (ed.), *How Latin America Fell Behind. Essays on the Economic Histories of Brazil and Mexico, 1800–1914* (Stanford 1997), 243–59.

Halperín Donghi, Tulio, *Politics, Economics and Society in Argentina in the Revolutionary Period* (Cambridge 1975).

Reforma y disolución de los Imperios ibéricos, 1750–1850 (Madrid 1985).

Hamill, Hugh M., *The Hidalgo Revolt. Prelude to Mexican Independence* (Gainesville 1966).

Hamilton, Earl J., "Monetary Problems in Spain and the Spanish Empire, 1751–1800," *Journal of Economic History*, IV (1944), 21–48.

Hamnett, Brian R., *Politics and Trade in Southern Mexico, 1750–1821* (Cambridge 1971; Spanish edition, 1976; second Spanish edition with new Introduction, 2013, 9–59).

Revolución y contrarrevolución en México y el Perú. Liberales, realistas y separatistas, 1800–1824 (second edition, Mexico City 2011 [1978]).

"Factores regionales en la desintegración del régimen colonial en la Nueva España: el federalismo de 1823–24," in Buisson, Inge, Kahle, Günter et al. (eds.), *Problemas de la formación del Estado y de la Nación en Hisoanoamérica* (Bonn 1984), 305–17.

"Popular Insurrection and Royalist Reaction: Colombian Regions, 1810–1823," in Fisher, John R., Kuethe, Allan J., and McFarlane, Anthony (eds.), *Reform and Insurrection in Bourbon New Granada and Peru* (Baton Rouge and London 1990), 293–326.

"Oaxaca: las principales familias y el federalismo de 1823," in Romero Frizzi, Angeles (comp.), *Lecturas históricas de Oaxaca*, 4 vols. (Mexico City and Oaxaca 1990), vol. 2, 51–69.

Hampe-Martínez, Teodoro, "Recent Works on the Inquisition in Peruvian Colonial Society, 1570–1820," *LARR*, 33, ii (1996), 43–69.

Hanson, Carl A., *Economy and Society in Baroque Portugal, 1668–1703* (Minneapolis 1981).

Hébrard, Véronique, and Verdo, Geneviève (eds.), *Las Independencias hispanoamericanas. Un objeto de historia* (Madrid 2013).

Helg, Aline, *Liberty and Equality in Caribbean Colombia, 1770–1835* (Chapel Hill 2004).

"The Limits of Equality: Free Peoples of Color and Slaves during the First Independence of Cartagena, Colombia (1810–1815)," *Slavery and Abolition*, 20, no. 2, (August 1999), 1–30.

Heredia, Edmundo A., *Los vencidos. Estudio sobre los realistas en la guerra de independencia* (Córdoba [Argentina] 1997).

Hernández de Alba Lesmes, Guillermo, *Recuerdos de la reconquista. El Consejo de Purificación* (Bogotá 1935).

Hernández García, Elizabeth del Socorro, *La Elite piurana y la Independencia del Perú: la lucha por la continuidad en la naciente república (1750–1824)* (Lima and Piura 2008).

Herr, Richard, "Hacia el derrumbe del antiguo régimen: crisis fiscal y desamortización bajo Carlos IV," in *Moneda y Crédito* [Madrid], 118, (September 1971), 37–100.

and Poll, John H. R., (eds.), *Iberian Identity: Essays in the Nature of Identity in Spain and Portugal* (Berkeley 1989).

Hespanha, António Manuel, *As Vésperas do Leviathan. Instituições e Poder político. Portugal – Século XVII* (Coimbra 1994).

História de Portugal modern: político e institucional (Lisbon 1995).

Hillgarth, Jocelyn N., "Spanish Historiography and Iberian Reality," *History and Theory*, 24, no. I (1985), 23–43.

Hoberman, Louisa Schell, *Mexico's Merchant Elite, 1590–1660* (Durham and London 1991).

"Merchants in Seventeenth-Century Mexico City: A Preliminary Portrait," *HAHR*, 57, no. 3 (1977), 479–503.

Hussey, Roland D., *The Caracas Company, 1728–1784* (Cambridge, MA 1934).

Ibarra, Antonio, "Mercado global, economías coloniales y corporaciones comerciales: los Consulados de Guadalajara y Buenos Aires," *HM* LXII, no 4 (April-June 2013), no. 248, 1421–58.

and Del Valle Pavón, Guillermina, *Redes sociales e institucionales comerciales en el imperio español, siglos XVII al XIX* (Mexico City 2007).

Irurozqui Victoriano, Marta, "Soberanía y castigo en Charcas. La represión militar y judicial de las juntas de La Plata y La Paz, 1808–1810," *Revista Complutense de Historia de América*, 37 (2011), 49–72.

Jacobsen, Nils, and Puhle, Hans-Jürgen (eds.), *The Economies of Mexico and Peru during the Late Colonial Period, 1760–1810* (Berlin 1986).

Jago, Charles, "Habsburg Absolutism and the Cortes of Castile," *AHR*, no. 86 (1981), 307–26.

Jancsó, István, *Na Bahia, contra o Império. História do Ensaio de Sedição de 1798* (São Paulo and Salvador 1996).

Jáuregui, Luis, *La Real Hacienda de Nueva España. Su administración en la época de los intendentes, 1786–1821* (Mexico City 1999).

Johnson, Sherry, *The Social Transformation of Eighteenth Century Cuba* (Gainesville 2001).

Kamen, Henry, *Spain, 1469–1714. A Society of Conflict* (second edition, London 1991 [1983]).

Spain's Road to Empire. The Making of a World Power, 1492–1765 (London 2002).

Kennedy, J. N., "Bahian Elites, 1750–1822," *HAHR*, 53, iii, (August 1978), 415–39.

Kicza, John, *Colonial Entrepreneurs: Families and Business in Bourbon Mexico City* (Albuquerque 1985).

King, James F., "The Coloured Castes and American Representation in the Cortes of Cádiz," *Hispanic American Historical Review*, XXXIII, i (February 1953), 33–64.

Knight, Franklin W., "Origins of Wealth and the Sugar Revolution in Cuba, 1750–1859," *HAHR*, 57 (May 1977), 231–53.

and Liss, Peggy K., (eds.), *Atlantic Port Cities. Economy, Culture, and Society in the Atlantic World, 1650–1850* (Knoxville 1991).

Kray, Hendrik, *Race, State, and Armed Forces in Independence-Era Brazil* (Stanford 2001).

Kuethe, Allan J., *Cuba, 1753–1815. Crown, Military, and Society* (Knoxville, TN 1986).

"The Development of the Cuban Military as a Sociopolitical Élite, 1763–83," *HAHR*, 61 (November 1981), 695–704.

and Andrien, Kenneth J., *The Spanish Atlantic World in the Eighteenth Century. War and the Bourbon Reforms, 1713–1796* (Cambridge 2014).

and Inglis, G. Douglas, "Absolutism and Enlightened Reform: Charles III, the Establishment of the Alcabala, and Commercial Reorganization in Cuba," *Past and Present*, 109 (1985), 118–43.

La Parra López, Emilio, *El primer liberalismo español y la Iglesia. Las Cortes de Cádiz* (Alicante, 1985).

Ladd, Doris M., *The Mexican Nobility at Independence, 1780–1826* (Austin 1976).

The Making of a Strike: Mexican Silver Workers' Struggles in Real del Monte, 1766–1775 (Lincoln and London 1988).

Lamikiz, Xabier, *Trade and Trust in the Eighteenth-Century Atlantic World. Spanish Merchants and Their Overseas Networks* (Woodbridge 2010).

"Transatlantic Networks and Merchant Guild Rivalry in Colonial Trade with Peru, 1729–1780: A New Interpretation," *HAHR*, 91, ii (May 2011), 299–331.

Landavazo, Marco Antonio, "Para una historia social de la violencia insurgente: el odio al 'Gachupín,'" *HM*, 233, vol. LIX, no. 1 (July-September 2009), 195–255.

Larkin, Brian, *The Very Nature of God. Baroque Catholicism and Religious Reform in Bourbon Mexico City* (Albuquerque 2010).

Lasa Iraola, Ignacio, "El primer proceso de los liberales," *Hispania*, XXX, no. 113 (1970), 327–83.

Lasso, Marixa, *Myths of Harmony. Race and Republicanism during the Age of Revolution, Colombia, 1795–1831* (Pittsburg 2007).

"Race War and Nation in Caribbean Gran Colombia, Cartagena, 1810–1832," *AHR*, III, no. 2 (April 2006), 336–61.

Lehnertz, Jay F., "Juan Santos: Primitive Rebel on the Campa Frontier (1742–1752)," in *Actas y Memorias del XXIX Congreso Internacional de Americanistas*, 6 vols. (Lima 1972), vol. 4, 111–23.

Libby, Douglas Cole, "Proto-industrialisation in a Slave Society. The Case of Minas Gerais," *JLAS*, 23, i (1991), 1–35.

Liehr, Reinhard, *Stadtrat und stätische Oberschicht von Puebla am Ende der Kolonialzeit (1787–1810)* (Wiesbaden 1971).

Lieven, Dominic, "Dilemmas of Empire, 1850–1918. Power, Territory, Identity," *JCH*, 34, no. 2 (April 1999), 163–200.

Lindley, Richard B., *Haciendas and Economic Development. Guadalajara, Mexico, at Independence* (Austin 1983).

Liss, Peggy K., *Atlantic Empires: The Network of Trade and Revolution, 1712–1828* (Baltimore 1983).

Llorens, Vicente, *Liberales y Románticos. Una emigración española en Inglaterra, 1823–1834* (Madrid 1968).

Lohmann Villena, Guillermo, *El corregidor en el Perú bajo las Austrias* (Madrid 1957).

Los ministros de la Audiencia de Lima en el reinado de los Borbones, (1700–1821) (Seville 1974).

Lombardi, John V., *The Decline of Negro Slavery in Venezuela, 1820–1854* (Westport, CT 1971).

Venezuela. The Search for Order, The Dream of Progress (New York – Oxford 1982).

Lovett, Gabriel, *Napoleon and the Birth of Modern Spain*, 2 vols. (New York 1965).

Lucena Salmoral, Manuel, *La economía americana del primer cuarto del siglo XIX, vista a través de las memorias escritas por D. Vicente Basadre, Intendente de Venezuela* (Caracas 1983).

Lynch, John, *Spanish Colonial Administration, 1782–1810. The Intendant System in the Viceroyalty of the Río de la Plata* (London 1958).

The Spanish American Revolutions (second edition, New York and London 1986 [1973]).

Simón Bolívar. A Life (New Haven and London 2006).

San Martín. Argentine Soldier, American Hero (New Haven and London 2009).

MacCormack, Sabine, *Religion in the Andes. Vision and Imagination in Early Colonial Peru* (Princeton 1991).

MacLachlan, Colin M., *Spain's Empire in the New World. The Role of Ideas in Institutional and Social Change* (California 1989).

Malerba, Jurandir, *A Corte no Exílio. Civilização e poder no Brasil as vésperas da Independência (1808–1821)* (São Paulo 2004).

Manchester, Alan K., *British Pre-Eminence in Brazil: Its Rise and Decline* (Durham, NC 1933).

Marchena Fernández, Juan, *Oficiales y soldados en el ejército de America* (Seville 1983).

Marichal, Carlos, *Bankruptcy of Empire. Mexican Silver and the Wars between Spain, Britain and France, 1760–1810* (Cambridge 2007).

"Beneficios y costos fiscales del colonialismo: las remesas americanas a España, 1760–1814," *Revista de Historia Económica*, 15, iii, 475–505.

Marks, Patricia H., *Deconstructing Legitimacy. Viceroys, Merchants and the Military in Late Colonial Peru* (Pennsylvania 2007).

"Confronting a Mercantile Elite: Bourbon Reformers and the Merchants of Lima, 1765–1795," *The Americas*, 60, no. 4 (April 2004), 519–58.

Martí Gilabert, Francisco, *Carlos III y la política religiosa* (Madrid 2004).

Martínez Shaw, Carlos, *Cataluña en la carrera de Indias* (Barcelona, 1981).

Martínez Torrón, Diego, *Ideología y literatura en Alberto Lista* (Seville 1993).

Martins Filho, A. V., and Martins, R. B., "Slavery in a Non-Export Economy: Nineteenth-Century Minas Gerais Revisited," *HAHR*, 63, iii (August 1983), 537–68.

Marzahl, Peter, *Town in the Empire. Government, Politics, and Society in Seventeenth-Century Popayán* (Austin 1978).

Mattos, Carlos de Meira, *Brasil, Geopolítica e Destino* (Rio de Janeiro 1975).

Maxwell, Kenneth, *Pombal. Paradox of the Enlightenment* (Cambridge 1995).

"The Generation of the 1790s and the Idea of Luso-Brazilian Empire," in Alden, Dauril (ed.), *Colonial Roots of Modern Brazil* (Berkeley 1973), 107–44.

"Portuguese America," *The International History Review*, vol. VI, no. 4 (November 1984), 529–50.

Mazzeo de Vivó, Cristina, (ed.), *Las relaciones el poder en el Perú. Estado, regiones e identidades locales. Siglos XVII-XIX* (Lima 2011).

"El Consulado de Lima y la política comercial española frente a las coyunturas de cambio de fines del periodo colonial (1806–1821)," in Hausberger, Bernd, and Ibarra, Antonio (eds.), *Comercio y poder en América colonial. Los consulados de comerciantes, siglos xvii–xix* (Madrid and Mexico City, 2003).

McFarlane, Anthony, *Colombia before Independence: Economy, Society and Politics under Bourbon Rule* (Cambridge 1993).

War and Independence in Spanish America (New York 2014).

and Posada-Carbó, Eduardo (eds.), *Independence and Revolution in Spanish Anerica: Perspectives and Problems* (London 1999).

and Wiesebron, Marianne (coordinators), *Violencia social y conflict civil: América latina, siglo XVIII-XIX* (Ridderkerk 1998).

McKinley, P. Michael, *Pre-Revolutionary Caracas. Politics, Economy, and Society, 1777–1811* (Cambridge 1985).

McNeill, J. R., *Mosquito Empires. Ecology and War in the Greater Caribbean, 1620–1914* (Cambridge 2010).

Medina, José Toribio, *Historia del Tribunal del Santo Oficio de Cartagena*, (Santiago, Chile 1899).

Medrano, José Miguel, and Malamud Rickles, Carlos, "Las actividades de los Cinco Gremios Mayores en Perú. Apuntes preliminares," *RI*, XLVIII, nos. 182–83 (January-August 1988), 421–34.

Meissner, Jochen, *Eine Elite im Umbruch. Der Stadrat von Mexiko zwischen koloniale Ordnung und unabhängigen Staat* (Stuttgart 1993).

Méndez, Cecilia, "Incas si, Indios no: Notes on Peruvian Creole Nationalism and Its Contemporary Crisis," *JLAS*, 28, i (February 1996), 197–225.

Méndez Reyes, Salvador, *Las Élites criollas de México y Chile ante la Independencia* (Mexico City 2004).

Mendíburu, Manuel de, *Diccionario histórico-biográfico del Perú*, 15 tomes (Lima 1931–5).

Mestre Sanchis, Antonio, *Apología y crítica de España en el siglo XVIII* (Madrid 2003).

Mills, Kenneth, *Idolatry and Its Enemies: Extirpation and Colonial Andean Religion, 1640–1750* (Princeton 1997).

Monteiro, Nuno G. F., *Elites e Poder. Entre o Antigo Regime e o Liberalismo* (Lisbon 2003).

with Cardim, Pedro, and Soares da Cunha, Mafalda (orgs.), *Optima Pars. Elites Ibero-Americanas do Antigo Regime* (Lisbon 2005).

Moore, Rachel A., *Forty Miles from the Sea. Xalapa, the Public Sphere, and the Atlantic World in Nineteenth-Century Mexico* (Tucson 2011).

Morales Moreno, Humberto, and Fowler, William (coordinators), *El Conservadurismo mexicano en el siglo XIX (1810–1910)* (Puebla 1999).

Morelli, Federica, *Territorio o Nación. Reforma y disolución del espacio imperial en Ecuador 1765–1830* (Madrid 2005 [2001]).

Moreno Alonso, Manuel, *La forja del liberalismo en España. Los amigos españoles de Lord Holland, 1798–1808* (Madrid 1997). *La Junta Suprema de Sevilla* (Seville 2001).

Moreno Cebrián, Alfredo, *El Corregidor de Indios y la economía peruana del siglo XVII: los repartos forzosos de mercancías* (Madrid 1977).

Mosher, Jeffrey C., *Political Struggle, Ideology and State-Building: Pernambuco and the Construction of Brazil, 1817–1850* (Lincoln and London 2008).

Mousnier, Roland, "Les concepts d' 'ordres,' d' 'états,' de fidélité' et de 'monarchie absolue' en France de la fin du XVe siècle à la fin du XVIIIe," in *Revue Historique*, 502 (abril-juin 1972), 289–312.

Múnera, Alfonso, *El fracaso de la nación: región, clase y raza en el Caribe colombiano (1717–1810)* (Bogotá 1998).

Muriá, José María, (ed.), *El Federalismo en Jalisco (1823)* (Guadalajara 1973).

Myrup, Erik Lars, Power and Corruption in the Early Modern Portuguese World, (Baton Rouge 2015).

Navarro García, Luis, "La crísis del reformismo borbónico bajo Carlos IV," *Temas Americanos*, 13, (Sevilla 1997), 1–8.

Newitt, Malyn, and Robson, Martin, *Lord Beresford and British Intervention in Portugal, 1807–1820* (Lisbon 2004).

Nieto Vélez, Armando, *Contribución a la historia del fidelismo en el Perú (1808–1810)* (Lima 1960).

Nizza da Silva, Maria Beatriz (coordinadora), *O Império Luso-Brasileiro, 1750–1822* (Lisbon 1986).

Novinsky, Anita, *Cristãos novos na Bahia: a Inquisição* (São Paulo second edition, São Paulo 1992).

Nunes Dias, Manuel, *Fomento e Mercantilismo: A Companhia Geral do Grão Pará e Maranhão (1755–1778)*, 2 vols. (Pará 1970).

O'Phelan Godoy, Scarlett, *La Gran Rebelión en los Andes: De Túpac Amaru a Túpac Catari* (Cuzco 1995). (compiler), *La Independencia en el Perú. De los Borbones a Bolívar* (Lima 2001).

"Elementos étnicos y de poder en el movimientos tupacamarista, 1780–81," *Nova Americana*, 5 (1982), 79–101.

"Las reformas borbónicas y su impacto en la sociedad colonial del Bajo y el Alto Perú," in Jacobsen, and Puhle, *Economies of Mexico and Peru* (1986), 340–56.

"El mito de la 'Independencia concedida:' los programas políticos del siglo XVIII y temprano XIX en el Perú y Alto Perú, 1730–1814," in Flores Galindo, Alberto (compiler), *Independencia y Revolución*, 2 vols. (Lima 1987), II, 145–99.

and Saint-Geours, Yves, (compilers), *El Norte en la Historia Regional. Siglos XVIII–XIX* (Lima 1998).

and Lomné, Georges (eds.), *Abascal y la contra-independencia de América del Sur* (Lima 2013).

Ocampo López, Javier, *El proceso ideológico de la Emancipación. Las ideas de génesis, la Independencia, futuro e integración en los orígenes de Colombia* (Bogotá 1980).

Oliveira Marques, A. H. (coordinator), *Nova História de Portugal, volumen IX: Portugal e a Instauração do Liberalismo* (Lisbon 2002).

Olveda Legaspi, Jaime, *Gordiano Guzmán: un cacique del siglo XIX* (Mexico City 1980).

Documentos sobre la Insurgencia. Diócesis de Guadalajara (Guadalajara 2009).

Ortiz de la Tabla, Javier, *Comercio exterior de Veracruz, 1778–1821: crisis de dependencia* (Seville 1978).

"El obraje colonial ecuatoriano. Aproximación a su estudio," *RI*, nos. 149–50, (1977), 471–541.

Ortiz Escamilla, Juan, *Guerra y gobierno. Los pueblos y de independencia de México* (Mexico City and Seville 1997).

and Serrano Ortega, José Antonio (eds.), *Ayuntamientos y liberalismo gaditano en México* (Zamora and Xalapa 2007).

and Frasquet, Ivana (eds.), *Jaque a la Corona. La cuestión política en las Independencias iberoamericanas* (Castelló 2010).

Ossa Santa Cruz, Juan Luis, *Armies, Politics and Revolution. Chile, 1808–1826* (Liverpool 2014).

Palti, Elías, *La nación como problema. Los historiadores y la 'cuestión nacional'* (Buenos Aires and Mexico City 2002).

Paquette, Gabriel, *Enlightenment, Governance, and Reform in Spain and Its Empire, 1759–1808* (Basingstoke and New York 2008).

Imperial Portugal in the Age of Atlantic Revolutions. The Luso-Brazilian World, c. 1770–1850 (Cambridge 2013).

(ed.), *Enlightened Reforms in Southern Europe and Its Atlantic Colonies, c. 1750–1830* (Farnham and Burlington, VT 2009.)

"State-Civil Society Cooperation and Conflict in the Spanish Empire: The Intellectual and Political Activities of the Ultramarine Consulados and Economic Societies, c. 1780–1810," *JLAS*, 39 (2007), 263–98.

Parry, J. H., *Trade and Dominion. The European Overseas Empires in the Eighteenth Century* (London 1971).

Pedreira, Jorge Miguel Viana, *Estructura industrial e Mercado colonial. Portugal e Brasil (1780–1830)* (Lisbon 1994).

Peralta, Ruiz Víctor, *En defensa de la autoridad. Política y cultura bajo el gobierno del virrey Abascal, Perú, 1806–1816* (Madrid 2002).

La Independencia y la cultura política del Perú (1808–1821) (Lima 2010).

"Elecciones, constitucionalismo y revolución en el Cuzco, 1809–1815," in Malamud, Carlos (ed.), *Partidos políticos y elecciones en América Latina y la península ibérica, 1830–1930*, 2 vols. (Madrid 1995), vol. 1, 83–112.

Pérez Ledesma, Manuel, and Burdiel, Isabel (eds.), *Liberales eminentes* (Madrid 2008).

Phelan, John Leddy, *The Kingdom of Quito in the Seventeenth Century* (Madison 1967).

"Authority and Flexibility in the Spanish Imperial Bureaucracy," *Administrative Science Quarterly*, 5, no. 1, (June 1960), 47–65.

Phillips, Carla Rahn, "The Growth and Composition of Trade in the Iberian Empires, 1450–1750," in Tracy, James D. (ed.), *The Rise of Merchant Empires. Long-Distance Trade in the Early Modern World, 1350–1750* (Cambridge 1993 [1990]), 34–101.

Piel, Jean, "The Place of the Peasantry in the National Life of Peru in the Nineteenth Century," *Past and Present*, 46 (February 1970), 108–33.

Pieper, Renate, *La Real Hacienda bajo Fernando VI y Carlos III (1753–1788)* (Madrid 1992).

Pimenta, João Paulo G., *Estado e nação no fim dos impérios ibéricos no Prata (1808–1828)* (São Paulo 2002).

Brasil y las independencias de Hispanamérica (Castellón 2007).

"Resistiendo a la revolución: el Brasil en 1810," *Historia y Política*, 24 (Madrid: July-December 2010), 169–86.

Pinto Rodríguez, Jorge, "Los Cinco Gremios Mayores de Madrid y el comercio colonial del s. XVIII," *RI*, LI, núm. 192 (mayo-agosto 1991), 293–326.

Portillo, José María, *Crisis atlántica. Autonomía e independencia en la crisis de la monarquía hispana* (Madrid 2006).

Priestley, H. I., *José de Gálvez. Visitor-General of New Spain (1765–1771)* (Berkeley 1916).

Puente Candamo, José Agustín de la, *San Martín y el Perú. Planteamiento doctrinario* (Lima 1948).

Purnell, Jennie, "Citizens and Sons of the Pueblo: National and Local Identities in the Making of the Mexican Nation," *Ethnic and Racial Studies*, 25, no. 2 (2002), 213–37.

Quintas, Amaro, *A revolução de 1817* (Rio de Janeiro 1985 [1939]).

Radcliffe, Sarah, and Westwood, Sallie, *Remaking the Nation. Place, Identity and Politics in Latin America* (London 1996).

Ramírez Flores, José, *El Real Consulado de Guadalajara: notas históricas* (Guadalajara 1952).

Ramos, Demetrio, *Trigo chileno, navieros del Callao y hacendados limeños entre la crisis agrícola del siglo XVII y la comercial de la primera mitad del siglo XVIII* (Madrid 1967).

Ramos, Frances L., *Identity, Ritual and Power in Colonial Puebla* (Tucson 2012).

Reina, Leticia, *Historia de la cuestión agraria mexicana. Estado de Oaxaca*, 2 vols., vol. I, Prehispánico – 1924 (México 1988).

(coordinator), *La indianización de América, siglo XIX* (Mexico City 1997).

Reis, João José, *Rebelião escrava no Brasil. A história do levante dos malês* (São Paulo 1987 [1986]).

Restrepo, Vicente, *Estudio sobre las minas de oro y plata en Colombia* (Medellín 1979).

Rieu-Millán, Marie-Laure, "Rasgos distintivos de la representación peruana en las Cortes de Cádiz y Madrid (1810–1814)," *RI*, XLVIII (1, 2), nos. 182–83, (January–August 1988), 475–515.

Rivera Serna, Raúl, *Los guerrilleros del Centro en la emancipación peruana* (Lima 1958).

Robertson, William Spence, "Russia and the Emancipation of Spanish America, 1816–1826," *HAHR*, 21, ii (May 1941), 196–221.

"Metternich's Attitude towards Revolutions in Latin America," *HAHR*, 21, no. 4 (November 1941), 538–58.

Rodrigues, José Honório, *Independência: Revolução e contra-revolução*, 5 vols. (Rio de Janeiro 1975).

Rodríguez, Mario, *The Cádiz Experiment in Central America, 1808 to 1826* (Berkeley 1978).

Rodriguez O., Jaime E., *The Independence of Spanish America* (Cambridge 1998).

Nosotros somos ahora los verdaderos españoles, 2 vols. (Zamora and Mexico City 2009).

Röhrig Assunção, Matthias, *De Caboclos a Bem-Te-Vis. Formação do campesinato numa sociedade escravista: Maranhão, 1800–1850* (São Paulo 2015).

Rojas Ingunza, Ernesto, *El báculo y la espada. El obispo Goyeneche y la Iglesia ante la 'Iniciación de la República,' Peru 1825–1841* (Lima 2006).

Romano, Ruggiero, *Coyunturas opuestas. La crisis del siglo XVII en Europa e Hispanoamérica. Siete ensayos* (Mexico City 1995).

Ruiz Guiñazú, Ernesto, *La magistratura indiana* (Buenos Aires 1916).

Rúspoli, Enrique, *Godoy. La lealdad de un gobernante ilustrado* (Madrid 2004).

Russell-Wood, A. J. R., *A World on the Make: The Portuguese in Asia, Africa and the Americas, 1415–1808* (Manchester 1992).

"Local Government in Portuguese America," *CSSH*, 16, no. 2 (March 1974), 187–231.

"Centers and Peripheries in the Luso-Brazilian World, 1500–1808," in Daniels, Christine, and Kennedy, Michael J., (eds.), *Negotiated Empires. Center and Periphery in the Americas, 1500–1820* (New York and London 2002), 105–42.

(ed.), *From Colony to Nation. Essays on the Independence of Brazil* (Baltimore and London 1975).

Saether, Steiner, "Independence and the Redefinition of Indians around Santa Marta, Colombia, 1750–1850," *JLAS*, 37 (2005), 55–80.

Saiz Pastor, Candelaria, and Vidal Olivares, Javier, *El fin del antiguo régimen (1808–1868)* (Madrid 2001).

Sala i Vila, Núria, *Y se armó el tole tole. Tributo indígena y movimientos sociales en el virreinato del Perú, 1784–1814* (1996).

"La participación indígena en la rebelión de Angulo y Pumacahua, 1814–1816," in García Jordán, Pilar, and Izard, Miguel (coordinators), *Conquista y Resistencia en la Historia de América* (Barcelona 1992), 273–88.

Salvucci, Richard J., *Textiles and Capitalism in Mexico. An Economic History of the Obrajes, 1539–1840* (Princeton 1987).

Sánchez-Blanco, Francisco, *El absolutismo y las Luces en el reinado de Carlos III* (Madrid, 2002).

Schmidt-Nowara, Christopher, *Slavery, Freedom, and Abolition in Latin America and the Atlantic World* (Albuquerque 2011).

Schultz, Kirsten, *Tropical Versailles. Empire, Monarchy, and the Portuguese Royal Court in Rio de Janeiro, 1808–1821* (New York and London 2001).

"Royal Authority, Empire, and the Critique of Colonialism: Political Discourse in Rio de Janeiro, 1808–1821, *LBR*, 37, no. 2 (2000), 7–31.

Schwartz, Stuart B., *Sugar Plantation in the Formation of Brazilian Society, 1550–1835* (Cambridge 1985).

"Colonial Brazil: The Role of the State in Slave Social Formation," in Spalding, Karen (ed.), *Essays in the Political, Economic, and Social History of Colonial Latin America* (Newark, DE 1982), 1–23.

"The Formation of Colonial Identity in Brazil," in Canny, Nicholas, and Pagden, Anthony (eds.), *Colonial Identity in the Atlantic World, 1500–1800* (Princeton 1987), 15–50.

Sempat Assadourian, Carlos, *El sistema de la economía colonial. Mercado interno, regiones y espacio económico* (Lima 1982).

Serrano Ortega, José Antonio, *Jerarquía territorial y transición política. Guanajuato, 1790–1836* (Mexico City and Zamora 2001).

(coordinator), *El sexenio absolutista. Los últimos años insurgentes. Nueva España (1814–1820)* (Zamora, Mexico 2014).

and Jáuregui, Luis (coord.), *Hacienda y política. Las finanzas en la Primera República Federal Mexicana* (Mexico City 1998).

Serulnikov, Sergio, *Subverting Colonial Authority. Challenges to Spanish Rule in Eighteenth-Century Southern Andes* (Durham and London 2003).

Revolution in the Andes: The Age of Tupac Amaru (Durham, NC 2013 [translation, Revolución en los Andes: La Era de Tupac Amaru, Buenos Aires 2012]).

Sewell, William H., "Collective Violence and Collective Loyalties in France. Why the French Revolution made a difference," Politics and History, 18, no. 4 (December 1990), 527–52.

Shumway, Nicholas, *The Invention of Argentina* (Berkeley, Los Angeles, and London 1991).

Silva Santisteban, Fernando, *Los obrajes en el virreinato del Perú* (Lima 1964).

Silverblatt, Irene, *Modern Inquisitions. Peru and the Colonial Origins of the Civilized World* (Durham and London 2004).

Smith, Robert S., "The Puebla Consulado, 1821–1824," *RHA*, no. 21 (1946), 151–60.

and Ramírez Flores, José, *Los Consulados de comerciantes de Nueva España* (Mexico City 1976).

Soasti Toscano, Guadalupe, *El Comisionado regio, Carlos Montúfar y Larrea. Sedicioso, insurgente y rebelde* (Quito 2009).

Sobrevilla Perea, Natalia, *The Caudillo of the Andes. Andrés de Santa Cruz* (Cambridge 2012).

Souto Mantecón, Mathilde, *Mar Abierto. La política y el comercio del Consulado de Veracruz en el ocaso del sistema imperial* (Mexico City 2001).

Spalding, Karen, *De indio a campesino: cambios en la estructura social del Perú colonial* (Lima 1974).

Huarochirí. An Andean Society under Inca and Spanish Rule (Stanford 1984).

Stavig, Ward, *The World of Túpac Amaru: Conflict, Community and Identity in Colonial Peru* (Lincoln and London 1999).

"Ethnic Conflict, Moral Economy, and Population in Rural Cuzco on the Eve of the Thupa Amaru II Rebellion," *HAHR*, 68, iv (November 1988), 737–70.

Stein, Barbara H., and Stein, Stanley J., *Edge of Crisis. War and Trade in the Spanish Atlantic, 1789–1808* (Baltimore and London 2009).

Stein, Barbara H., and Stein, Stanley J., Crisis in an Atlantic Empire: Spain and New Spain, 1808–1810, (Baltimore 2014).

Stein, Stanley J., *Vassouras. A Brazilian Coffee County, 1850–1900* (New York 1970).

"Bureaucracy and Business in the Spanish Empire, 1759–1804. Failure of a Bourbon Reform in Mexico and Peru," *HAHR*, 61, i, (Feb. 1981), 2–28.

and Stein, Barbara H., *Silver, Trade, and War. Spain and America in the Making of Early Modern Europe* (Baltimore and London 2000).

Apogee of Empire: Spain and New Spain in the Age of Charles III, 1759–1789 (Baltimore and London 2003).

Stern, Steve J., (ed.), *Resistance, Rebellion, and Consciousness in the Andean Peasant World. 18th to 20th Centuries* (Madison and London 1987).

Stevens, Donald Fithian, *Origins of Instability in Early Republican Mexico* (Durham, NC, and London 1991).

Stoan, Stephen K., *Pablo Morillo and Venezuela, 1815–1820* (Columbus, OH 1974).

Storrs, Christopher, The Resilience of the Spanish Monarchy, 1665–1700, (Oxford 2006).

The Spanish Resurgence, 1713–1748, (Yale 2017).

Street, John, *Artigas and the Emancipation of Uruguay* (Cambridge 1959).

Super, John C., *La vida en Querétaro durante la colonia, 1531–1810* (Mexico City 1983).

"Querétaro Obrajes: Industry and Society in Provincial Mexico, 1600–1810," *HAHR*, 56, ii, (May 1976), 197–216.

Szeminski, Jan, *La utopia tupamarista* (Lima 1984).

Tavares, Luis Henrique Dias, *História da Bahia* (Salvador 1974).

Taylor, William B., *Magistrates of the Sacred: Priests and Parishioners in Eighteenth-Century Mexico* (Stanford 1996).

Tecanhuey Sandoval, Alicia, *La formación del consenso por la independencias. Lógica de la ruptura del juramento. Puebla, 1810–1821* (Puebla 2010).

Tejada, Luis Alonso, *Ocaso de la Inquisición en los últimos años de Fernando VII. Junta de Fe, Juntas Apostólicos, Conspiraciones Realistas* (Madrid 1969).

TePaske, John, "The Financial Disintegration of the Royal Government of Mexico during the Epoch of Independence," in Rodriguez, Jaime E. (ed.), *The Independence of Mexico and the Creation of the New Nation* (Los Angeles 1989), 63–83.

Ternavasio, Marcela, *Gobernar la Revolución: Poderes en disputa en el Río de la Plata* (Buenos Aires 2007).

Thibaud, Clément, *Repúblicas en Armas. Los ejércitos bolivarianos en la Guerra de Independencia en Colombia y Venezuela* (Bogotá and Lima 2003).

La Academia Carolina y la independencia de América. Los abogados de Chuquisaca (1776–1809) (Sucre 2010).

and Entin, Gabriel, Gómez, Alejandro, Morelli, Federica (compilers), *L'Atlantique révolutionnaire: une perspetive ibéro-américaine* (Paris 2013).

Thomson, Guy P. C., *Puebla de los Angeles. Industry and Society in a Mexican City, 1700–1850* (Boulder, San Francisco, and London 1989).

Thomson, Sinclair, *We Alone Will Rule. Native Andean Politics in the Age of Insurgency* (Madison 2002).

Thurner, Mark, *From Two Republics to One Divided: Contradictions of Postcolonial Nationmaking in Andean Peru* (Durham and London 1996).

"Historicizing 'the Post-colonial' from Nineteenth-Century Peru," *Journey of Historical Sociology*, 9, i (1996), 1–18.

Toledo Machado, Luiz, *Formação do Brasil e Unidade Nacional* (São Paulo 1980).

Torales Pacheco, María Cristina (co-ordinadora), *La Compañía de Comercio de Francisco Ignacio de Yraeta (1767–1797)*, 2 vols. (Mexico City 1985).

Torras Elías, Jaime, *Liberalismo y rebeldía campesina, 1820–1823* (Barcelona 1976).

Torre Villar, Ernesto de la, *La Constitución de Apatzingán y los creadores de Estado mexicano* (Mexico City 1964).

Torres Puga, Gabriel, *Opinión pública y censura en Nueva España. Indicios de un silencio imposible, 1767–1794* (Mexico City 2010).

Torres Ramírez, Bibiano, *Alejandro O'Reilly en las Indias* (Seville 1969).

Torres Sánchez, Rafael, "'Las prioridades de un monarca ilustrado,' o las limitaciones del estado fiscal-militar de Carlos III," *Hispania*, LXVIII, no. 229 (May-August 2008), 407–36.

Tovar Pinzón, Hermés, "Insolencia, tumulto e invasiones de los Naturales de Zacoalco (México) a fines del siglo XVIII," *Cuadernos de Historia social y económica*, 10 (1985), 1–18.

Tutino, John, *From Insurrection to Revolution in Mexico. Social Bases of Agrarian Violence, 1750–1940* (Princeton 1986).

Twinam, Ann, "Enterprise and Élites in Eighteenth-Century Medellín," *HAHR*, 59, no. 3 (August 1979), 444–75.

Uribe-Uran, Víctor (ed.), *State and Society in Spanish America during the Age of Revolution* (Wilmington, DE 2001).

Uslar Pietri, Juan, *Historia de la rebelión popular de 1814* (Paris 1954).

Valcárcel, C. Daniel, *Tupac Amaru. Precursor de la independencia* (Lima 1977).

"Fidelismo y separatismo en el Perú," *RHA*, nos. 37–38 (January-December 1954), 133–62.

Valencia Vega, Alipio, *Julián Tupaj Katari* (Buenos Aires 1950).

Valle de Siles, María Eugenia, "Tupac Katari y la rebelión de 1781," *AEA*, XXXIV (1977), 633–64.

Van Young, Eric, *Hacienda and Market in Eighteenth-Century Mexico. The Rural Economy of Guadalajara, 1675–1820* (Berkeley, Los Angeles, and London 1981).
The Other Rebellion. Violence, Ideology, and the Mexican Struggle for Independence, 1820–1821 (Stanford 2001).
Vargas Ezquerra, Juan Ignacio, *Un hombre contra un continente. José Abascal, rey de América, (1806–1816)* (Astorga 2010).
Vázquez, Josefina Zoraída (coordinator), *El establecimiento del federalismo en México, 1821–1827* (Mexico City 2003).
Vergara Arias, Gustavo, *Montoneros y guerrillas en la etapa de la emancipación del Perú (1820–1825)* (Lima 1973).
Viana Filho, Luis, *A vida do Barão do Rio Branco* (second edition, São Paulo, 1967).
Vilar de Carvalho, Gilberto, *A liderança do clero nas revoluções republicanas, 1817–1824* (Petrópolis 1979).
Viotti da Costa, Emilia, *The Brazilian Empire. Myths and Histories* (Chicago 1985).
Walker, Charles F., *Smoldering Ashes: Cuzco and the Creation of Republican Peru, 1780–1835* (Durham, NC, and London 1999).
The Tupac Amaru Rebellion (Cambridge, MA 2014).
(compiler), *Entre la retórica y la insurgencia: las ideas y los movimientos sociales en los Andes. Siglo XVIII* (Cuzco 1996).
Webster, C. K., *Britain and the Independence of Latin America, 1812–1830*, 2 vols. (London 1938).
Zahler, Reuben, *Ambitious Rebels: Remaking Honor, Law, and Liberalism in Venezuela, 1780–1850* (Tucson 2013).

Index

Printed in the USA
CPSIA information can be obtained
at www.ICGtesting.com
LVHW052206070923
757601LV00004B/97